# BUDGETING BASICS & *Beyond*

## A Complete Step-by-Step Guide for NONFINANCIAL MANAGERS

### JAE K. SHIM

### JOEL G. SIEGEL

**PRENTICE HALL**
Englewood Cliffs, New Jersey 07632

Prentice-Hall International (UK) Limited, *London*
Prentice-Hall of Australia Pty. Limited, *Sydney*
Prentice-Hall Canada, Inc., *Toronto*
Prentice-Hall Hispanoamericana, S.A., *Mexico*
Prentice-Hall of India Private Limited, *New Delhi*
Prentice-Hall of Japan, Inc., *Tokyo*
Simon & Schuster Asia Pte. Ltd., *Singapore*
Editora Prentice-Hall do Brasil, Ltda., *Rio de Janeiro*

10 9 8 7 6 5 4 3 2

**Library of Congress Cataloging-in-Publication Data**

Shim, Jae K.
    Budgeting basics and beyond : a complete step-by-step guide for
nonfinancial managers / Jae K. Shim and Joel G. Siegel.
      p.    cm.
    Includes index.
    ISBN 0-13-085572-3 — ISBN 0-13-312232-8 (pbk.)
    1. Budget in business.   I. Siegel, Joel G.   II. Title.
HG4028.B8S558   1994
658.15'4—dc20                                94-21394
                                                     CIP

ISBN 0-13-085572-3

ISBN 0-13-312232-8 (pbk.)

**PRENTICE HALL**
**Career & Personal Development**
**Englewood Cliffs, NJ 07632**

Simon & Schuster, A Paramount Communications Company

Printed in the United States of America

to

**CHUNG SHIM**
Dedicated wife

and

**ROBERTA M. SIEGEL**
Loving wife and colleague

**ARNOLD SIEGEL**
Loving brother

**DAVID HAWKINS**
Distinguished intellectual and friend

# CONTENTS

# ABOUT THE AUTHORS

JAE K. SHIM is President of the National Business Review Foundation, a consultant to several companies, and Professor of Accounting and Finance at California State University, Long Beach. He received his Ph.D. degree from the University of California at Berkeley.

Dr. Shim has 38 books to his credit and has published over 50 articles in accounting and financial journals including *Financial Management, Decision Sciences, Management Science, Long Range Planning,* and *Management Accounting.* Many of his articles have dealt with planning, forecasting, and financial modeling.

Dr. Shim received the 1982 Credit Research Foundation Award for his article on financial management.

JOEL G. SIEGEL, Ph.D., CPA, is a self-employed management consultant and Professor of Accounting and Finance at Queens College of the City University of New York.

He was previously associated with Coopers and Lybrand, CPAs and Arthur Andersen, CPAs. Dr. Siegel currently serves and has acted as a consultant to many companies including Citicorp, International Telephone and Telegraph, and United Technologies.

Dr. Siegel is the author of 42 books and approximately 200 articles on business topics including many articles in the area of budgeting. His books have been published by Prentice-Hall, McGraw-Hill, HarperCollins, John Wiley, Macmillan, Probus, International Publishing, Barron's, and the American Institute of CPAs.

His articles have appeared in many business journals including *Financial Executive, Financial Analysts Journal,* and *The CPA Journal.*

In 1972, he was the recipient of the Outstanding Educator of America Award. Dr. Siegel is listed in *Who's Where Among Writers* and *Who's Who in the World.*

Dr. Siegel is at the present time the chairperson of the National Oversight Board.

# ACKNOWLEDGMENTS

We acknowledge with great thanks Drew Dreeland, George MacNeill and Caroline Carney for their outstanding editorial advice and assistance on this manuscript. Their efforts are much appreciated and recognized. Thanks is expressed to Anique Qureshi, Ph.D., CPA, for coauthoring Chapter 6. Thanks also goes to Abraham J. Simon, Ph.D., CPA for the coauthoring of Chapter 10. Marc Levine, Ph.D., CPA, deserves credit for coauthoring Chapter 13. Chung J. Liew, Ph.D., coauthored Chapter 16. Jeffrey Brauchler coauthored Chapter 21. The authors also thank Susan Weinschenk and Paul Borgwald, research assistants at Queens College, for their coauthoring of Chapter 5. Finally, Catherine Carroll, a research assistant at Queens College, did excellent work in assisting with this book.

# PREFACE

Better budgets can boost your department and your career to higher levels of performance and success. Savvy executives use the budgeting process to take stock of their direction, refine their goals, and share their mission with their staff. Their budgeting reveals their position in the market, places untapped resources at their command, and motivates all employees to greater levels of productivity. They use their budgets to propel them towards the top of their industry. This book will show you how to get there.

*Budgeting Basics and Beyond* shows you how the budget can be your most powerful tool for strategy and communications. It points out that the budget brings into stark relief all of the factors that every manager must consider such as industry conditions, competition, degree of risk, stability of operations, capacity limitations, pricing policies, turnover rates in assets, production conditions, product line and service considerations, inventory balances and condition, trends in the market place, number of employees and their technical abilities, availability and cost of raw materials, available physical resources, technological considerations, economy, and political aspects. Then, it uncovers the role each of those factors plays in achieving your corporate goals. And, since those goals cannot be achieved single-handedly, this book suggests ways to use the budget to help each employee appreciate how they will contribute to the division's profitability.

Aside from playing a vital role in creating and achieving a sound business strategy, this book shows how budgets can increase your effectiveness every day of the week. In particular, it delivers these on-the-job budgeting tools:

- Techniques for preparing more accurate, realistic, and reliable estimates.
- Control and variance analysis devices that signal revenue, cost, and operations thresholds.
- Pricing guidelines for products and services.

- Planning and scheduling production and related costs.
- Profit planning and identifying looming problems.
- Financial models that show the relationship among all facets of the business.
- Spreadsheet applications for planning, budgeting, and control purposes.

We follow the example of each of these tools with examples of how you can use them to make a difference in your work right away. And, we use step-by-step guidelines to pinpoint what to look for, what to watch for, what to do, how to do it, and how to apply it on the job. And, through step-by-step illustration, it shows how you can put these tools to use.

We hope that you will keep *Budgeting Basics and Beyond* handy for easy, quick reference and daily use.

# Chapter 1

# INTRODUCTION

Profit planning results in the maximization of earnings. All budgets ideally contribute to keeping the cost per dollar of sales to a minimum and the gross profit of the production mixture at a maximum. The time period covered by a budget will vary depending upon the nature of the business and the level of detail desired.

A short-term budget is for one year or less. An intermediate-term budget is for two to three years. A long-term budget is for three or more years. There are more details and specifics in a short-term budget. Intermediate-term budgets examine current and proposed projects to accomplish long-term goals. Long-term budgets are broad and can be translated into short-term plans.

A short-term budget is more suitable for a business subject to rapid changes. A shorter budgeting period allows for less uncertainty and more reliable predicted amounts. In this connection, the manager may establish a few budgeting cycles throughout the year (e.g., semi-annual budgets).

Budgets assist department areas such as marketing, management, personnel, production, purchasing, quality control, research, distribution, legal, and engineering. Each manager should have his own budget priorities and know how he fits in. The manager must set his overall goals and find ways to accomplish them. Some objectives are profit and return on investment maximization, improving the sales base, cost minimization, increasing production volume, generating significant cash flow, and improving product or service quality.

Budgets should be organized, clear, and comprehensive. Budget figures should be within established limitations based on previous results, current trends, competition, economy, desired growth rate, future prospects, and equipment or labor constraints. There should be integration between budget preparation, review, and approval. The budget process should be open, unemotional, and devoid of political pressures. Information should be coordinated between departments.

Budget figures should not be too tight (which leads to worker frustration and resentment) or too loose (workers will loaf). They should be realistic, attainable, and documented.

A budget is only as accurate as the figures within it. These figures should be modified to allow for changes in sales or manufacturing volume. Budgets should provide for potential problems and the manager should solve them. The budget should accommodate the management by exception principle.

The following factors have to be considered in budgeting:

- Life cycle of products—developing, growing, maturing, and declining. In addition, new product ideas should be taken into account
- Consumer base and changing tastes
- Degree of competition
- Manpower and employee relations
- Technological trends
- Degree of business and financial risk
- Production requirements and manufacturing resources
- Inventory levels and turnover rates
- Availability and cost of raw materials
- Marketing and advertising conditions, including the market share
- Pricing of product or service
- Obsolescence of products or services
- Financing needs and availability of funds

- Corporate and industry stability, including product demand, labor relations, and government regulation
- Cyclical and seasonal aspects
- Economic and political factors

There may exist self-contained, self-justified increments of projects. Each one contains resource utilization and benefits. Where possible, the manager should assign budgetary cost and revenue responsibilities to specific individuals.

The sales manager needs to project future sales volume by product or service as well as the selling price. He will likely budget revenue by sales territory and customer. The manager then budgets related costs such as salaries, commissions, promotion and entertainment, and travel.

The production manager is responsible for the quality of the manufactured product. He may be responsible for increasing or reducing the level of production, scheduling production, supervising workers, deciding on the best production methods, maintaining quality, and identifying machinery needing repair. He must decide on a product rejection rate based on approved specifications.

The production manager estimates the future costs to manufacture the product or service and the cost per unit. He may have to budget work during the manufacturing process so that work flows smoothly. The manager must consider manufacturing cost formulas. For example, if raw material or labor costs increase, other production or packaging costs may be reduced to maintain profit margins. Product components in terms of quantity or quality may be reduced (e.g., reduction in package contents). A quality control manager evaluates the quality of production, identifies problems and their causes, recommends remedial action, and provides quality control specifications.

The purchasing manager budgets unit and dollar purchases. A breakdown by supplier may be made. A cost budget will be prepared for salaries, rent, and supplies.

The personnel manager maintains employee records, evaluates and analyzes performance, including reasons for absences, and budgets personnel needs in terms of staff size and salary levels.

The credit manager is responsible for increasing sales by extending credit limits (if justified) but at the same time minimizing uncollectible accounts. He has to balance increased sales with lower bad debts.

In preparing budgets, subjectivity should be kept to a minimum. However, some managers inflate the budgetary request so that when they receive a reduction by upper management they may have gotten what they realistically deserved in the first place.

## BUDGET PARTICIPATION

Department managers must have important input in budgeting revenues and costs because they are directly involved and knowledgeable about their departments' activities.

Budgets can be used to motivate employees to improve performance and attitudes. Workers should offer recommendations, revise budgetary figures as required, and approve or disapprove major items. Employee input is needed because they are familiar with operations.

## BUDGET PROCESS

A budget is the focal point of the whole planning and control process. The budget aids the manager in planning activities and monitoring the operating and profit performance of the responsibility center.

The manager should state goals, establish limits, set physical and human resource needs, examine requirements, provide flexibility, consider assumptions, give feedback, and take complaints into account.

The budget process should be standardized with budget forms, instructions, and procedures.

## BOTTOM-UP APPROACH TO BUDGETING

Nonfinancial managers should make use of the bottom-up approach to budgeting. It begins at the bottom or operating (departmental) level. These operating levels must be consistent with overall corporate goals. The manager's individual budget is then incorporated into the company's overall budget.

The manager's budget is reviewed, adjusted, and approved by upper management. (If the budget is passed down from upper management, which is not desirable, the manager will make recommendations and provide greater detail.)

Under this approach, sales are projected by product or other appropriate category (e.g., sales). From that, company sales are budgeted. Once sales have been forecast, cost of sales and operating expenses are projected.

The bottom-up approach is useful when unit managers are innovative. Department managers know what has to be accomplished, where opportunities present themselves, what problem areas have to be rectified, and what the resources are and how they are to be used.

Some questions asked in bottom-up budgeting are:

- What promotional and travel expenses are expected?
- How many workers are needed?
- What salary increases, if any, are projected?
- What kind of and how many raw materials and supplies are needed?

## TYPES OF BUDGETS

The manager should prepare a master budget, which consists of integrated subbudgets to summarize planned activities. The size and nature of the budget varies with departmental characteristics. Budgeted amounts may be at expected, optimistic, or pessimistic levels to allow for flexibility.

The manager may budget for sales, cost of sales, production, purchases, direct material, direct labor, overhead, general and administrative expenses, selling expenses, programs (e.g., research and development), cash flows, working capital, and capital expenditures. Once sales are projected, manufacturing costs and operating expenses must be estimated since they are often related to sales. The manager must know how these budgets interrelate with each other.

An operating budget is used for the costs of products produced or services rendered. It examines the manufacturing and operating aspects of the business.

A financial budget may be used to examine the financial condition of the division by examining assets to liabilities, cash flow, working capital, profitability, and any other statistic bearing on financial soundness.

A cash budget should be used for cash planning and control. It looks at expected cash inflow to expected cash outflow for a stated time period. The cash budget helps the manager to maintain cash balances in reasonable relationship to business needs. The cash budget assists the manager in avoiding idle cash and possible cash shortages.

The capital expenditure budget lists key long-term projects and capital (fixed assets such as plant and equipment) to be bought. The estimated cost of the project and the timing of the capital expenditures are given. The budgetary period is usually three to ten years. The capital budget typically classifies projects by objective such as developing new product lines, reducing costs, replacing obsolete or poorly functioning equipment, expanding or enhancing product lines, and meeting safety regulations.

A supplemental budget gives additional funding for items not included in the regular budget.

Incremental budgeting appraises the increase in the budget in dollars or percentage terms without considering the entire budget.

Add-on budgeting reviews previous years' budgets and adjusts them for recent data such as inflation and personnel changes. Additional funds are added to the budget to satisfy current needs. In an add-on situation, no incentive for efficiency exists but competition requires new and better ways of doing things.

A bracket budget is a contingency plan where costs are predicted at higher and lower amounts than the base figure. Sales are then predicted at those levels. If the base sales figure is not achieved, the bracket budget gives the manager a feeling for the earnings effect and a contingency plan. This budget might be suitable where there are downside risks and a sharp reduction in sales is anticipated.

A stretch budget is an optimistic one. It is typically employed for sales projected on the high side. It is rarely used for costs. However, if expense projections are made, they should be based on the standard budget sales target. Stretch figures may be informal or formal. Operating managers should not be held responsible for stretch figures.

Activity-based budgeting are expected costs for particular activities or functions.

A strategic budget integrates strategic planning and budgeting control. It is useful during uncertain and unstable periods.

A target budget is a plan that categorizes major expenditures and matches them to divisional objectives. Significant dollar expenditures require special approval.

The manager may roll a budget, which is a recurring budget for an additional period at the end of the current one. The new period is added to the remaining periods to form the new budget.

The advantages of continuous budgets are to reinforce planning, reconsider past data, and incorporate emerging developments.

Program budgets are used for products and services. Existing and new products are examined. Program budgets include engineering, research and development, maintenance, training, marketing, and public relations. Fund allocation is based on cost/benefit, risk, and expected rate of return.

## BUDGET REQUESTS

Funding for projects should be based on achieving the greatest corporate goal. The goal set must be realistic.

The manager must decide which programs to fund. He or she must explain and justify proposed budgetary amounts. To obtain approval for a capital project, the manager should submit a special authorization request containing specific information about the proposal. Upper management will typically then decide whether to fund the proposal depending upon its nature and cost.

## BUDGET PREPARATION

The budget should be comprehensible and attainable. There should be innovation and flexibility to meet unexpected occurrences. Budgeted figures may be expressed in dollars, units, hours, pounds, and employees.

In budgeting, the following have to be considered by the manager:

- Type of products and services
- Number of employees and their abilities
- Manufacturing conditions and capacity constraints
- Stability of operations
- Pricing
- Availability and cost of raw materials
- Physical and human resources

- Inventory balances and conditions
- Turnover rates in assets (e.g., receivables, equipment)
- Cyclicality
- Technological aspects, including the degree of obsolescence
- Quality control and service capability
- Market conditions
- Financing requirements
- Economic and political environment

To be effective, a budget should have the following characteristics:

- Predictive ability
- Clear channels of communication, authority, and responsibility
- Accurate and timely information
- Compatibility, comprehensiveness, and clearness of information
- Support within the organization from all affected parties

The steps to be followed in budgeting include:

1. Establishing objectives
2. Evaluating available resources
3. Negotiating between affected parties on budgetary figures
4. Coordinating and reviewing components
5. Final approval
6. Distributing the approved budget

A fixed (static) budget presents budgeted amounts at the expected capacity level. It is best used when the department's activities (e.g., sales) are stable. A deficiency with the static budget is the lack of flexibility to adjust to unexpected changes.

The fixed budget is suitable for a department whose work load does not have a direct relationship to sales, production, or other volume related to a department's operations. The work load is primarily determined by management decision instead of sales volume. Examples include administrative and marketing. Fixed budgets may be used for projects involving fixed appropriations for specific programs such as capital expenditures, advertising and promotion, and major repairs.

Table 1.1 illustrates a fixed budget.

The flexible budget allows for variability in business activity and unanticipated changes. Flexible budgets adjust budget allowances to actual activity and are useful when volumes vary within a narrow range.

Other steps involved in a flexible are:

1. Estimate the range of expected activity for the period.

2. Analyze cost behavior trends, whether fixed, variable, or mixed.

3. Separate costs by behavior, i.e., break up mixed costs into variable and fixed.

4. Determine what costs will be incurred at different levels of activity.

**Table 1.1**
**X-RAY UNIT MEDICAL SERVICE CORPORATION**
**PERFORMANCE REPORT—STATIC BUDGET MAY 1994**

|  | Master budget | Actual | Variance |
| --- | --- | --- | --- |
| Units | 2,000 | 1,200 | 800 |
| Sales revenue | $60,000 | $36,000 | $24,000* |
| Variable costs: |  |  |  |
| Film | 16,000 | 11,500 | 4,500 + |
| Other material | 4,000 | 3,000 | 1,000 + |
| Technician | 3,000 | 2,500 | 500 + |
| Other labor | 900 | 600 | 300 + |
| Other variable | 2,400 | 2,000 | 400 + |
| Total variable | 26,300 | 19,600 | 6,700 + |
| Contribution margin | 33,700 | 16,400 | 17,300* |
| Fixed costs: |  |  |  |
| Rent | 800 | 800 | 0 |
| Depreciation | 400 | 400 | 0 |
| Supervision | 2,000 | 2,000 | 0 |
| Other fixed | 3,500 | 3,300 | 200 + |
| Total fixed | 6,700 | 6,500 | 200 + |
| Operating income | 27,000 | 9,900 | 17,100* |

*Unfavorable.
+Favorable.

Tables 1.2 and 1.3 illustrate a flexible budget.

The sales budget includes sales volume and selling price. While sales are usually the target income sales, in some cases the manager may use break-even sales.

The manager should provide the prime assumptions which are the basis for the numbers. Assumptions include percentage increase in sales, inflation rate, and increase in salary and fringe benefits.

Exhibit 1.1 presents an illustrative budget showing revenue and expenses by product.

A well-prepared budget will result in less cost, more man-hours, and minimization of conflict. Fewer revisions will be required.

Do not cut a line item budget across-the-board. The amount of cuts depend on the importance of the program. Nonfinancial managers should be discouraged from spending their full budget out of fear that a shortfall will

**Table 1.2**
**X-RAY UNIT MEDICAL SERVICE CORPORATION**
**FLEXIBLE BUDGET MAY 1994**

| | Budgeted per unit | Number of x-rays per month | | | | |
|---|---|---|---|---|---|---|
| | | 1000 | 1200 | 1400 | 1800 | 2000 |
| Sales revenue | $30.00 | $30,000 | $36,000 | $42,000 | $54,000 | $60,000 |
| Variable costs: | | | | | | |
| Film | 8.00 | 8,000 | 9,600 | 11,200 | 14,400 | 16,000 |
| Other material | 2.00 | 2,000 | 2,400 | 2,800 | 3,600 | 4,000 |
| Technician | 1.50 | 1,500 | 1,800 | 2,100 | 2,700 | 3,000 |
| Other labor | 0.45 | 450 | 540 | 630 | 810 | 900 |
| Other variable | 1.20 | 1,200 | 1,440 | 1,680 | 2,160 | 2,400 |
| Total variable | 13.15 | 13,150 | 15,780 | 18,410 | 23,670 | 26,300 |
| Contribution margin | 16.85 | 16,850 | 20,220 | 23,590 | 30,330 | 33,700 |
| Fixed costs: | | | | | | |
| Rent | | 800 | 800 | 800 | 800 | 800 |
| Depreciation | | 400 | 400 | 400 | 400 | 400 |
| Supervision | | 2,000 | 2,000 | 2,000 | 2,000 | 2,000 |
| Other fixed | | 3,500 | 3,500 | 3,500 | 3,500 | 3,500 |
| Total fixed costs | | 6,700 | 6,700 | 6,700 | 6,700 | 6,700 |
| Operation income | | 10,150 | 13,520 | 16,890 | 23,630 | 27,000 |

Table 1.3
X-RAY UNIT MEDICAL SERVICE CORPORATION
PERFORMANCE REPORT—FLEXIBLE BUDGET MAY 1994

| Units | Costs incurred | Flexible budget | Variance explanation |
|---|---|---|---|
| Units | 1,200 | 1,200 | 0 |
| Sales revenue | $36,000 | $36,000 | 0 |
| Variable cost: | | | |
|     Film | 11,500 | 9,600 | 1,900* |
|     Other material | 3,000 | 2,400 | 600* |
|     Technician | 2,500 | 1,800 | 700* |
|     Other labor | 600 | 540 | 60* |
|     Other variable | 2,000 | 1,440 | 560* |
|         Total variable | 19,600 | 15,780 | 3,820* |
| Contribution margin | 16,400 | 20,220 | 3,820* |
| Fixed costs: | | | |
|     Rent | 800 | 800 | 0 |
|     Depreciation | 400 | 400 | 0 |
|     Supervision | 2,000 | 2,000 | 0 |
|     Other fixed | 3,300 | 3,500 | 200 + |
|         Total fixed costs | 6,500 | 6,700 | 200 + |
| Operation income | 9,900 | 13,520 | 3,620* |

*Unfavorable
+Favorable

bring about budget cuts next period. Instead, they should be given credit and rewards for cost savings. Further, their funding for next year should not automatically be curtailed.

## TIME PERIOD

The manager should start thinking about next year's budget several months before the beginning of the year. If a calendar year budget is used, preliminary preparations should start on October 1.

A budget may cover any time period. However, the longer the time span of a budget, the less reliable it is. A short-term budget is more reliable and shows specific plans and tactics.

Exihibit 1.1

STATEMENT OF REVENUE AND EXPENSES BY PRODUCT FOR THE YEAR ENDED 1998

|  | All Products | | X | | Y | | Z | |
|  | | Percentage of | | Percentage of | | Percentage of | | Percentage of |
| Description | Amount | Net sales | Amount | Net sales | Amount | Net sales | Amount | Net Sales |
|  | | | | | | | | |
| Gross revenue | | | | | | | | |
| Less: Sales returns and allowances | | | | | | | | |
| Net revenue | | | | | | | | |
| Less: Variable cost of sales | | | | | | | | |
| Manufacturing contribution margin | | | | | | | | |
| Direct distribution costs | | | | | | | | |
| Variable | | | | | | | | |
| Fixed | | | | | | | | |
| Semi-direct distribution | | | | | | | | |
| Variable costs | | | | | | | | |
| Contribution margin | | | | | | | | |
| Continuing costs | | | | | | | | |
| Fixed overhead | | | | | | | | |
| Other indirect costs | | | | | | | | |
| Total | | | | | | | | |
| Income before taxes | | | | | | | | |
| Less: Taxes | | | | | | | | |
| Net income | | | | | | | | |

The budget period should vary with the manager's objectives and the use of budgeting in planning. The time period depends on sales, production, manufacturing and operating methods, processing cycle, stability, risk, accuracy of input data, type of product line, seasonality, inventory turnover, financial characteristics, availability of resources (material, labor), and government regulations. The period also depends on the need for evaluation.

Most companies have a monthly and yearly reporting system. However, some companies report weekly, quarterly, and semi-annually. Over a 12-month reporting period, peaks and valleys may distort results. These cycles are referred to as seasonality and may significantly affect customer demand and supply and availability of raw materials. The cycles may result from a number of causes, such as climate.

## BUDGET REVISIONS

A budget should be monitored closely. Budget revisions may arise due to new developments, changes in overall planning, new technology, feedback, and errors. The longer and more complex a budget, the greater the likelihood that changes will be necessary.

When a budget is revised, the manager should provide detailed reasons. An example is when a costly planned capital addition is dropped due to a recessionary environment.

## ANALYSIS

Actual figures should be compared with budgeted figures and the reasons for variances ascertained, along with the responsible parties. Sales variances may be separated by sales volume and selling price. Cost variances consist of price and quantity.

The profit variance is composed of the variance in sales and costs. The manager must find ways to improve profitability, such as by considering the interrelationship between variances. For example, an unfavorable material price variance arising from higher prices due to better quality material may, in fact, result in favorable material quantity and labor quantity variances because of the higher quality. The net effect may be favorable, resulting in improved earnings.

Unfavorable variances should be corrected. For example, if the price of raw materials is much higher than expected, a cheaper supplier may be found. Any inefficiencies must be corrected.

However, it should be noted that a cost budget may have authorized variances that permit an increase in an initial budget for unfavorable variances. This may arise from unexpected salary increases, higher raw material prices, and incremental costs due to a strike situation. The manager should be able to justify the cost excess.

Exhibit 1.2 presents a typical performance report for a division.

Alternative courses of action have to be considered. A computer template may be used to facilitate what-if analysis. As one variable changes, other related variables automatically change. A budget is only as good as the estimates.

The manager should not make across-the-board cuts. He should not overstate profitability by cutting back on immediate needed expenses for long-term viability of his responsibility unit. For example, by cutting back on repairs and maintenance the machinery may break down, causing future production and manufacturing problems.

Other expenditures may be needed for profit growth such as R&D, advertising, and training. The manager should perform a post-audit project review to determine how the projects are doing and if problems exist, they should be rectified.

Exhibit 1.2
XYZ COMPANY
DIVISIONAL PERFORMANCE VALUATION
DECEMBER 31, 19XX

| Division | Net Sales Actual | Net Sales Expected | Over (Under) Plan | Net Income Actual | Net Income Expected | Over (Under) Plan |
|---|---|---|---|---|---|---|
| A | $2000 | $4000 | $(2000) | $1000 | $800 | $200 |
| B | 3000 | 5000 | (2000) | 700 | 600 | 100 |
| C | 5000 | 6000 | (1000) | 600 | 1000 | (400) |
| Total | $10,000 | $15,000 | ($5,000) | $2,300 | $2,400 | $(100) |

## CONTROL

Internal factors (e.g., labor) are more controllable by managers than external factors (e.g., inflation, competition). If controllable, corrective action should be taken. At the start of the period, the budget is a plan. At the end of the period, the budget is a control device to measure performance against expectations, so that future performance may be improved.)

The budget is a control device for revenue, costs, and operations. Budget control should exist over financial and nonfinancial (e.g., product life cycle, seasonality) activities. Control is achieved through continuous reporting of actual progress and expenditures relative to plans (budgets). Input-output relationships have to be considered.

Cost appraisal and control policies should be implemented to assure that projects are profitable.

Exhibit 1.3 presents a budget control report.

Exhibit 1.4 depicts the budget control process.

**Exhibit 1.3**
**BUDGET CONTROL REPORT**

A. BUDGET SAVINGS

    One-year savings    $
    Two-year savings    $
    Three-year savings   $
    More than three-year savings   $
    Savings explanation:

B. BUDGETARY EFFECTS

    Reduction in current year budget
      Budget account:       Budget amount:
    Explanation of budgetary adjustment (if any):

C. BUDGET PARTICIPANTS

    Name:       Management Employee Level:
             Job Responsibility:

D. MANAGEMENT INCENTIVES

E. EMPLOYEES' AWARDS

    Preparer:
    Reviewer:
    Final Approval:

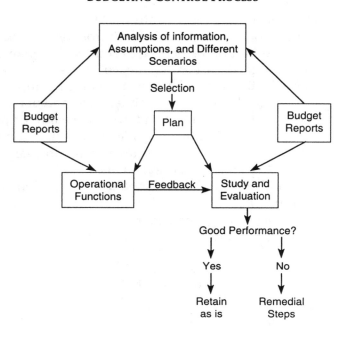

**Exhibit 1.4**
**BUDGETING CONTROL PROCESS**

## COMPUTER APPLICATIONS

A computer should be used to make quick and accurate calculations, keep track of projects instantly, and make proper comparisons.

With the use of a spreadsheet program, budgeting can be used as an effective tool to evaluate what-if scenarios. This allows the manager to find the best course of action among various alternatives through simulation. If the manager does not like the result, he may alter the contemplated decision and planning set. There is also specialized software solely devoted to budget preparation and analysis.

## MEETINGS

The manager should hold periodic budget meetings where such important topics as objectives, human and physical resources, and time schedules are discussed. There should be justification for the numbers, along with key assumptions.

## CONCLUSION

Forecasting is predicting the outcome of events. It is an important part of budgeting. Crucial areas in budgeting include coordinating, directing, and evaluating.

Budgets are typically prepared for all departments and their segments. Budgets from interrelated departments may be shown to add cohesion to the organization. For example, cooperation will be fostered when marketing, purchasing, personnel, and finance departments cooperate.

Budgets are used to allocate department resources, including machinery and staff, make employee changes, schedule manufacturing, and operate department activities. Budgets reflect the goals and objectives of each department and responsibility center.

A budget may warn of possible problems. It may avoid a crisis mandating overtime or high transportation charges to receive supplies on a rush order. Inadequate planning may result in strained labor, overloaded machinery, unavailable storage, and lack of available raw materials.

# Chapter 2

# PLANNING BY MANAGERS:

*Process, Budget Preparation, and Control*

Planning should take into account the conditions in the company, industry, and economy. It should link short-term, intermediate-term, and long-term goals. The annual budget should conform with long-term business goals.

Planning should be interrelated to improve profitability. There should be a congenial climate between budget participants.

Planning is more important in long-term management. The performance within the plan must be regularly monitored in terms of accomplishment and how long it takes. The objectives must be specific and measurable. One specific target is to increase sales by 10% or more by the end of the year. The progress toward meeting this goal must be determined.

The manager should break down general objectives into specific objectives for particular supportive areas. For example, assume the general objective is to increase market share by 20%. This objective may be broken down into the specific objectives of improving sales through better quality and/or lower price, enhancing distribution outlets, improving packaging, improving product design, and engaging in an aggressive advertising and sales promotion plan.

This chapter discusses what a plan is, including its characteristics, the planning process, budget preparation and analysis, planning the time period, strategic plans, short-term plans, profit plans, operational plans, development plans, contingency planning, budget revisions, and control and analysis.

## WHAT IS A PLAN?

A plan is a realistic, predetermined action course. It details activities to meet objectives. Plans should establish evaluative criteria and measurement standards. They should encourage creativity and flexibility. Planning must consider who has authority and responsibility for what.

Planning predetermines what should be done, how it should be carried out, and the dates it should be performed. The plan should identify the problems, reasons for them, nature of the business constraints, characteristics, categorization, and alternative ways to accomplish the objectives. Plan assumptions must be supported by documentation.

## CHARACTERISTICS OF PLAN

Planning considers the quantity and quality of new and existing products and services, phasing out of products, manufacturing conditions, and growth opportunities. Planning allocates human and physical resources to responsibility centers. Planning is usually the first manufacturing function performed. It shows departmental strategies, how resources will be used, and daily policies. There are specified objectives, performance norms, and appraisal of performance.

The plan specifies the details of meeting the strategy. It may be expressed in sequential order, including the costs and timing for each step, and deadline dates. Planning is made easy when the business is stable. It is harder to plan when there are diverse products operating in volatile markets.

Long-term plans should take into account emerging opportunities, diversification, competition, expansion, ability to adjust, and financial condition.

## PLANNING PROCESS

A plan is a detailed, structured outline to achieve long-term objectives. An objective is a quantifiable target.

Planning starts at the smallest business segment under the bottom-up approach. There should be a categorization of products, services, facilities, and markets. Performance reports should be issued monthly.

Sound communication is needed in the budget process. Department managers should make the budget goals clear to their subordinates.

The manager should compare his budget to prior years, to other departments within the company, and to comparable departments in similar companies. Areas to be further taken advantage of and problems to be rectified should be listed.

## BUDGETS

Budgets express quantitatively the yearly profit plan and show operating performance each month. A shorter budgeting period results in greater reliability. A cumulative budget may add the next month and drop the previous month. An expense item may be used partly or in full in more than one budget-comparison report. Program budgets involve the allocation of resources.

A representative department budget appears in Exhibit 2.1. An illustrative checklist for the budgeting system appears in Exhibit 2.2.

Probabilities may be used in budgeting. Of course, the total probabilities must add up to 100%.

### Example 1

The sales manager assigns the following probabilities to expected sales for the year:

| Probability | Expected Sales | Probable Sales |
|---|---|---|
| 50% | $3,000,000 | $1,500,000 |
| 30% | 2,000,000 | 600,000 |
| 20% | 4,000,000 | 800,000 |
| 100% | | $2,900,000 |

Exhibit 2.1

## XYZ COMPANY DEPARTMENT BUDGET REPORT

Department _____

Department _____

Administrator _____

| Classification | Dollar Amount | | Over or Under | | Percent Realized Current Month | Moving Average | |
|---|---|---|---|---|---|---|---|
| | Budget | Actual | Current Month | Cumulative to Date | | Current | Prior |
| Direct Labor | | | | | | | |
| 1 | | | | | | | |
| 2 | | | | | | | |
| 3 | | | | | | | |
| 4 | | | | | | | |
| 5 | | | | | | | |
| Total Direct Labor | | | | | | | |
| Indirect Labor | | | | | | | |
| Indirect Salaries | | | | | | | |
| Supervisor Salaries | | | | | | | |
| Cleaning | | | | | | | |
| Holidays and vacations | | | | | | | |
| Idle Time | | | | | | | |
| Other Salaries | | | | | | | |
| Sub-total | | | | | | | |
| Other Department Costs | | | | | | | |
| Operating Supplies | | | | | | | |
| Tools | | | | | | | |
| Telephone | | | | | | | |
| Travel | | | | | | | |
| Consultants | | | | | | | |
| Memberships | | | | | | | |
| Misc. Department Expenses | | | | | | | |
| Sub-total | | | | | | | |
| Total Department Expenses | | | | | | | |

Exhibit 2.2
A BUDGETARY CHECKLIST

| Schedule | Who Is Accountable? | Date Required | Date Received |
|---|---|---|---|
| 1. Establish overall goals. | | | |
| 2. Set division and department objectives. | | | |
| 3. Estimate | | | |
|    a. Capital resource needs. | | | |
|    b. Personnel requirements. | | | |
|    c. Sales to customers. | | | |
|    d. Financial status. | | | |
| 4. Preparation of budgets for: | | | |
|    a. Profitability | | | |
|    b. Revenue | | | |
|    c. Production | | | |
|        Direct material | | | |
|        Direct labor | | | |
|        Factory overhead | | | |
|    d. Marketing budget | | | |
|        Advertising and promotion | | | |
|        Sales personnel and administration | | | |
|        Distribution | | | |
|        Service and parts | | | |
|    e. Cash budget | | | |
|    f. Budgeted balance sheet | | | |
|    g. Capital facilities budget | | | |
|    h. Research and development budget | | | |
| 5. Prepare individual budgets and the master budget. | | | |
| 6. Review budgets and prepare required changes. | | | |
| 7. Prepare monthly performance reports. | | | |
| 8. Determine difference between budget and actual costs (revenue). | | | |
| 9. Prepare recommendations to improve future performance. | | | |

The probabilities are based on the nonfinancial manager's best judgment. The probabilities may be expressed in either quantitative (percentages) or relative terms (high or low probability of something happening).

### Example 2

If the probability of a strike is high, the manager will not enter into a purchase contract for raw materials. If the probability of a strike is low, the manager will feel safe in contracting to buy raw materials.

In preparing his or her budget, the manager may ask the following questions:

- Do I understand all the numbers in the budget and can I properly defend them to upper management? Can I document these numbers from internal and external sources?
- Does my budget satisfy my goals as well as the company's goals?
- Whom do I need input from, why, and when?
- Does my budget contain clarifying devices such as exhibits, charts, and figures?

## TIME PERIOD

Most budgets are prepared on a monthly basis, but the time frame for a budget should be as long as is useful. This time frame depends on the type of market, construction period for capital facilities, product life cycle, turn-over rates, manufacturing period, time to develop products, nature of industry, cyclicality, accuracy of financial information, time for raw material sources, and how the data are to be used.

A shorter budget period is more appropriate when there are uncertainties and unstable occurrences during the year.

## STRATEGIC PLANNING

A strategic plan is of a long-term overall nature ranging from 2 to 30 years with 5–10 years being most representative. It is a continual process and looks at where the department manager wants to be in the future. Division managers may have some input in deriving plans. The plan should specify the company and division's objectives by activity area, the degree of competition, and relative status within the industry.

The division manager uses strategic plans to examine current and prospective products and marketing. Departmental activities, priorities, and goals are considered. The division manager wants to position the division to take advantage of opportunities. Decisions involving risk may have to be made. However, the line manager is typically not involved with long-term plans.

Goals that the division manager wants to achieve include:

- Improved market share
- Employee development
- Enhanced product leadership and promotion
- Superior research
- Diversification

## SHORT-TERM PLANS

Short-term plans are usually for one year. The plans consider divisional profitability and capital expenditures. Short-term plans typically rely on internal information. They are usually structured, fixed, and determinable. The manager's short-term plan should be in conformity with the near-term and long-term goals of the business.

A short-term profit plan should exist by major area, including product, service, territory, division, department, project, activity, and function.

Long-term plans are set by upper management rather than division managers.

## PROFIT PLAN

A profit plan is the basis on which the division manager formulates an action plan for the year. Alternatives need to be appraised and the plan should be modified for changing circumstances. The profit budget may supplement the cost budget. Profit budgets may be by product, service, customer, or territory.

The profit plan may include sales volume, selling price, sales mix, unit cost, advertising, research and development, competitive factors, economic considerations, and market expectation.

Profit may be enhanced through cost reduction, raising selling prices, and improved budgeting over profit elements.

## OPERATIONAL PLAN

Operational plans look at alternative strategies. The plans should be detailed and help to evaluate performance. The operational plan includes production, selling (marketing), and administration.

The operational plan summarizes the major programs and includes the following: goals, description of program, who is responsible, resource requirements (machinery, staff), costs, deadlines at each stage, input required from other divisions, and expected results.

## DEVELOPMENT PLAN

The division or department manager should have a development plan. This plan includes research and development and attempts to develop future products, services, and markets. The division manager should find financially attractive new areas having growth potential. The manager must enumerate which capital and human resources are needed to accomplish goals. The feasibility of expanding into new areas must be considered.

## CONTINGENCY PLANNING

The manager must anticipate unexpected events and circumstances. Crisis situations must be recognized and rectified immediately. In a contingency plan, a possible result must be expected, red flags as to potential problems must be posted, and corrective action must be taken.

A contingency plan may be in the form of a flexible (bracket) budget. The plan may have to be modified to accomplish optimum results, incorporate new information, and solve uncertainties.

## BUDGET ACCURACY

The accuracy of budget preparation may be determined by comparing actual numbers to budget numbers in terms of dollars and units. Budget accuracy is higher when the two figures are closer to each other.

Ratios showing budget accuracy include:

- Sales Accuracy = Actual Sales/Budgeted Sales
- Cost Accuracy = Actual Cost/Budgeted Cost
- Profit Accuracy = Actual Profit/Budgeted Profit

### Example 3

A nonfinancial manager budgeted sales for $2,000,000 but the actual sales were $2,500,000. This favorable development might be attributed to one or more of the following reasons:

- Deficient planning, because past and current information were not properly considered when the budget was prepared.
- The intentional understatement of expected sales so the manager would look like a hero when actual sales substantially exceeded the anticipated sales.
- Higher revenue arising from better economic conditions, new product lines, improved sales promotion, or excellent salesperson performance.

A significant deviation between budget and actual amounts may indicate poor planning. Is the planning unrealistic, optimistic, or due to incompetent performance? However, the problem may be with wasteful spending or inefficient operations.

## BUDGET REVISION

A budget needs modification when it no longer represents a meaningful planning and control tool. A budget requires revision where there is a major change in process or operation, significant change in costs (e.g., labor rates), and new competition.

If forecasted sales are no longer realistic, all related budgets should be adjusted.

Budgets should be constantly revised as necessary to serve as a control device. For example, a one year budget may be revised on a quarterly basis. If departmental operations are more unstable, the budget should be revised more often by the manager.

Performance measures should be used for employees, including revenue per employee, man-hours per worker, and production volume to man-hours.

## CONTROL AND ANALYSIS

Control is crucial in the budgeting process. Where possible, costs should be reduced or at least contained at current levels. Cost reduction may lower costs by improving production methods and processes, job responsibilities, and the quality of products and services.

Value analysis relates to the procedures and specifications in producing and distributing a product or service. The purpose is to identify which elements of the process can be changed to lower costs so as to increase earnings while retaining the quality and value of the product or service. Value analysis involves the participation of many different managers including, sales managers, production managers, purchasing managers, and R&D managers.

In value analysis, the following questions may be asked:

- Are workers properly trained?
- Can manufacturing costs be reduced through redesign or buying newer machinery?
- Does idle capacity exist?
- Can manufacturing be made more productive?
- Is machinery being properly utilized?
- Is the product that is being produced of acceptable quality?

Budgeted amounts should be examined for reasonableness in relationships. For example, budgeted costs should be compared to planned production volume.

A comparison should be made between budgeted and actual figures. Current month, quarter, and year should be compared to prior month, quarter, and year. The comparison should be made over similar time periods.

The manager should compare his segment to other segments within the company and to segments in competing companies. Variations from the plan should be analyzed and controlled. For example, a change in one department's plan will probably affect another department's plan.

Performance reports tell the manager how he or she is doing. After reviewing the performance reports, the manager should communicate orally and in writing a statement of corrective steps to be implemented.

## CONCLUSION

The manager must be able to plan properly if he is to adequately perform the tasks required. To do this, he should prepare a plan consisting of detailed, sequential steps, including deadlines. A provision should be made in the budget for any unexpected contingencies. The budget time period should match the usefulness of data. The manager should be familiar with the different types of plans and budgets which he may be called upon to prepare.

# Chapter 3

# ADMINISTERING THE BUDGET:
## *Reports, Analyses, and Evaluations*

Each manager should prepare a budget on a periodic basis. The budget should include objectives, policies, guidelines, expected results, employee instructions to complete budget activities, and changes in operating conditions. Budget reports may be used to accumulate information, planning, and control.

The manager may prepare short-term reports for the division, department, or responsibility center with which he is involved. Short-term reports may be for sales, costs, profit, cash flow, and capital expenditures.

The manager should monitor the progress of the budget and identify deficient areas that need attention. A critical area should be reported on more often.

Report information must be on schedule and if the report is delayed, a short update should be provided. Budget revisions may be needed due to changed objectives, new processes, changing economic environment, and mistakes. They should include narrative explanations. Subordinates should be encouraged to participate in the budget process.

The benefits derived from departmental and divisional reports should justify their cost. This chapter discusses the budget schedule, budget reports, performance reports, special reports, and budgetary control.

## BUDGET SCHEDULE

Each budget step should be identified in the form of a calendar. A time schedule and employee assignment should be given so information is received on a timely basis. The due dates must be strictly adhered to. Review and approval dates must be communicated. Schedule dates must be realistic.

## BUDGET REPORTS

The nonfinancial manager should estimate the revenues and costs associated with his or her responsibility center. The manager should obtain input from his or her employees.

Periodic reports should be prepared to compare actual and budgeted costs. Reports may be prepared monthly (usually the case), quarterly, semi-annually, and annually. Some data may be reported daily (e.g., shipments of merchandise) while other information may be reported weekly (e.g., production, sales). A cost/benefit analysis should be undertaken to determine the timeliness in reporting.

The budget report should start with the main points and a summary. Detailed information should then be provided. The reports should be understandable, clear, and concise. Information should be updated as the situation changes.

An illustrative budget worksheet is presented in Exhibit 3.1. A budget data sheet is shown in Exhibit 3.2.

Budget reports should include the following:

- Comparing actual to budget figures with explanations for variances
- Comparisons to similar departments
- Trends over representative time periods

The reports may include the following supplementary data:

- Number of employees and man-hours
- Volume produced or service hours rendered
- Sales units

- Costs relative to sales
- Alteration in selling price
- New marketing aspects
- Changes in distribution
- Percent of capacity utilization
- Impact on revenue of new products and the dropping of products

**Exhibit 3.1**
**BUDGET WORKSHEET**

Account:
For the period:
Date:

**Month**                                        **Components**

Explanation:
Assumptions:
Analysis:

**Exhibit 3.2**
**BUDGET DATA SHEET**

Date prepared:                          Time period:
Date accepted:
Date approved:
Date revised:
Cost center identifier
Account identifier
Activity unit
Amount and reason for revision

| Items | Total | Fixed | Variable | Mixed (Semi-variable) |
|-------|-------|-------|----------|------------------------|

Total Budget

The manager may include schedules, explanations, and tables. Recommendations should be included with problem areas highlighted.

The manager may want to use statistics and graphics in budget reports to aid reader comprehension. For example, graphs are more insightful in marketing reports, such as showing sales trends in units, selling price, and total dollar sales. Graphs may better present relationships and summary comparisons. Graphs include charts and diagrams.

## PERFORMANCE REPORTS

Performance reports should be prepared. Are objectives and targets being met by subordinates? Are operations being performed efficiently and effectively?

The performance-to-budget report should include budget, actual, and variance, by department for month and year-to-date. Variances may be stated in dollars and percentage terms.

Typical reports summarizing departmental performance are presented in Exhibits 3.3 and 3.4.

**Exhibit 3.3**
**Summary of Department Performance**

| Item and Explanation | Actual | Budget | Percent of Budget |
| --- | --- | --- | --- |

Exhibit 3.4
## PERFORMANCE-TO-BUDGET REPORT

Department Identifier _____  Activity _____
Nonfinancial Manager _____  Budget _____
Actual _____
Percent of Budget _____

| Year-to-Date | | | This Period | | | | |
| --- | --- | --- | --- | --- | --- | --- | --- |
| Budget | Actual | Variance | Budget | Actual | Variance | Cause of Variance | Extra Budgetary Allowance for Variance |
| | | | | | | | |

Totals

## SPECIAL REPORTS

Special budgets may be prepared and analyzed for problems, important areas, or for negative trends requiring special attention. An example is when costs are significantly increasing even though a cost reduction plan has been enacted. Special budgets and studies may review products and services, activities and programs, territories, salesperson performance, and warehousing. The reports usually contain detailed information, exceptions found, and recommendations. Flash reports should be issued for unusual occurrences.

## BUDGETARY CONTROL

Control reports emphasize performance and areas requiring improvement. Variances between budget and actual should be determined by product, service, personnel (e.g., salespeople), and geographic area. Control requires follow-up procedures.

## CONCLUSION

The manager must effectively administer his budget so that operations run smoothly. Budget reports must be carefully prepared, considering all factors, so that reliable figures are forthcoming. These reports may consider performance evaluation by comparing actual to budget amounts. In some cases, special reports are needed for an unusual or unique situation that requires analysis and evaluation.

# Chapter 4

# BREAK-EVEN AND CONTRIBUTION MARGIN ANALYSIS:
## Profit, Cost, and Volume Changes

Break-even and contribution margin analysis, also known as cost-volume-profit (CVP) analysis, helps managers perform many useful analyses. It deals with how profit and costs change with a change in volume. More specifically, it looks at the effects on profits of changes in such factors as variable costs, fixed costs, selling prices, volume, and mix of products sold. By studying the relationships of costs, sales, and net income, management is better able to cope with many planning decisions.

Break-even analysis determines the break-even sales. Break-even point—the financial crossover point when revenues exactly match costs—does not show up in corporate earnings reports, but managers find it an extremely useful measurement in a variety of ways.

## QUESTIONS ANSWERED BY BREAK-EVEN AND CONTRIBUTION MARGIN ANALYSIS

Break-even and contribution margin analysis tries to answer the following questions:

(a) What sales volume is required to break even?
(b) What sales volume is necessary to earn a desired profit?

(c) What profit can be expected on a given sales volume?

(d) How would changes in selling price, variable costs, fixed costs, and output affect profits?

(e) How would a change in the mix of products sold affect the break-even and target income volume and profit potential?

## THE CONTRIBUTION MARGIN INCOME STATEMENT

The traditional income statement for external reporting shows the functional classification of costs, that is, manufacturing costs vs. non-manufacturing expenses (or operating expenses). An alternative format of income statement, known as the contribution margin income statement, organizes the costs by behavior rather than by function. It shows the relationship of variable costs and fixed costs a given cost item is associated with, regardless of the functions.

The contribution approach to income determination provides data that are useful for managerial planning and decision making. The statement highlights the concept of contribution margin, which is the difference between sales and variable costs. The traditional format, on the other hand, emphasizes the concept of gross margin, which is the difference between sales and cost of goods sold.

These two concepts are independent and have nothing to do with each other. Gross margin is available to cover non-manufacturing expenses, whereas contribution margin is available to cover fixed costs. A comparison is made between the traditional format and the contribution format below.

| TRADITIONAL FORMAT | | | CONTRIBUTION FORMAT | | |
|---|---|---|---|---|---|
| Sales | | $15,000 | Sales | | $15,000 |
| Less: Cost of Goods Sold | | 7,000 | Less: Variable Expenses | | |
| Gross Margin | | $8,000 | Manufacturing | $4,000 | |
| Less: Operating Expenses | | | Selling | 1,600 | |
| Selling | $2,100 | | Administrative | 500 | 6,100 |
| Administrative | 1,500 | 3,600 | Contribution Margin | | $8,900 |
| Net Income | | $4,400 | Less: Fixed Expenses | | |
| | | | Manufacturing | $3,000 | |
| | | | Selling | 500 | |
| | | | Administrative | 1,000 | 4,500 |
| | | | Net Income | | $4,400 |

## CONTRIBUTION MARGIN (CM)

For accurate break-even and contribution margin analysis, a distinction must be made between costs as being either variable or fixed. Mixed costs must be separated into their variable and fixed components (to be covered in Chapter 7).

In order to compute the break-even point and perform various break-even and contribution margin analyses, note the following important concepts.

CONTRIBUTION MARGIN (CM). The contribution margin is the excess of sales (S) over the variable costs (VC) of the product or service. It is the amount of money available to cover fixed costs (FC) and to generate profit. Symbolically, CM = S − VC.

UNIT CM. The unit CM is the excess of the unit selling price (p) over the unit variable cost (v). Symbolically, unit CM = p − v.

CM RATIO. The CM ratio is the contribution margin as a percentage of sales, i.e.,

$$\text{CM ratio} = \frac{CM}{S} = \frac{S - VC}{S} = 1 - \frac{VC}{S}$$

The CM ratio can also be computed using per-unit data as follows:

$$\text{CM ratio} = \frac{\text{Unit CM}}{P} = \frac{p - v}{p} = 1 - \frac{v}{p}$$

Note that the CM ratio is 1 minus the variable cost ratio. For example, if variable costs account for 70 percent of the price, the CM ratio is 30 percent.

### Example 1

To illustrate the various concepts of CM, consider the following data for Flip Toy Store:

|  | Total | Per Unit | Percentage |
|---|---|---|---|
| Sales (1,500 units) | $37,500 | $25 | 100% |
| Less: Variable costs | 15,000 | 10 | 40 |
| Contribution margin | $22,500 | $15 | 60% |
| Less: Fixed costs | 15,000 |  |  |
| Net income | $ 7,500 |  |  |

From the data listed above, CM, unit CM, and the CM ratio are computed as:

$$CM = S - VC = \$37{,}500 - \$15{,}000 = \$22{,}500$$
$$Unit\ CM = p - v = \$25 - \$10 = \$15$$

$$CM\ ratio = \frac{CM}{S} = \frac{\$22{,}500}{\$37{,}500} = 60\%\ or\ \frac{Unit\ CM}{p} = \frac{\$15}{\$25} = 0.6 = 60\%$$

## BREAK-EVEN ANALYSIS

The break-even point represents the level of sales revenue that equals the total of the variable and fixed costs for a given volume of output at a particular capacity use rate. For example, you might want to ask the break-even occupancy rate (or vacancy rate) for a hotel or the break-even load rate for an airliner.

Generally, the lower the break-even point, the higher the profit and the less the operating risk, other things being equal. The break-even point also provides nonfinancial managers with insights into profit planning. It can be computed using the following formulas:

$$Break\text{-}even\ point\ in\ units = \frac{Fixed\ costs}{Unit\ CM}$$

$$Break\text{-}even\ point\ in\ dollars = \frac{Fixed\ costs}{CM\ ratio}$$

### Example 2

Using the same data given in Example 1, where unit CM = $25 − $10 = $15 and CM ratio = 60%, we get:

$$Break\text{-}even\ point\ in\ units = \$15{,}000/\$15 = 1{,}000\ units$$
$$Break\text{-}even\ point\ in\ dollars = \$15{,}000/0.6 = \$25{,}000$$

Or, alternatively,

$$1{,}000\ units \times \$25 = \$25{,}000$$

## GRAPHICAL APPROACH IN A SPREADSHEET FORMAT

The graphical approach to obtaining the break-even point is based on the so-called break-even (B-E) chart as shown in Figure 1. Sales revenue, variable costs, and fixed costs are plotted on the vertical axis while volume, x, is plotted on the horizontal axis. The break-even point is the point where the total sales revenue line intersects the total cost line. The chart can also effectively report profit potentials over a wide range of activity and therefore be used as a tool for discussion and presentation.

The profit-volume (P-V) chart as shown in Figure 2, focuses directly on how profits vary with changes in volume. Profits are plotted on the vertical axis while units of output are shown on the horizontal axis. The P-V chart provides a quick condensed comparison of how alternatives on pricing, variable costs, or fixed costs may affect net income as volume changes. The P-V chart can be easily constructed from the B-E chart. Note that the slope of the chart is the unit CM.

## DETERMINATION OF TARGET INCOME VOLUME

Besides determining the break-even point, break-even and contribution margin analysis determines the sales required to attain a particular income level or target net income. The formula is:

$$\text{Target income volume} = \frac{\text{Fixed costs} + \text{Target income}}{\text{Unit CM}}$$

### Example 3

Using the same data given in Example 1, assume that Flip Toy Store wishes to attain a target income of $15,000 before tax.

Then, the target income volume would be:

$$\frac{\$15,000 + \$15,000}{\$25 - \$10} = \frac{\$30,000}{\$15} = 2,000 \text{ units}$$

Figure 4.1 shows a break-even chart.

In Figure 4.2, a profit-volume (P-V) chart is presented.

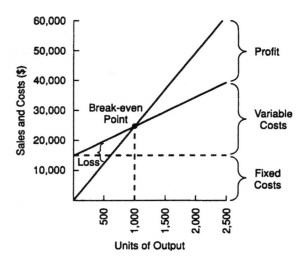

**Figure 4.1**
**BREAK-EVEN CHART**

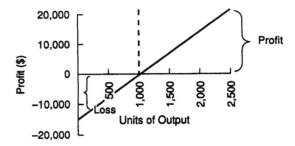

**Figure 4.2**
**PROFIT-VOLUME (P-V) CHART**

## IMPACT OF INCOME TAXES

If target income is given on an after-tax basis, the target income volume formula becomes:

$$\text{Target income volume} = \frac{\text{Fixed costs} + \left[\text{Target after-tax income}/(1-\text{tax rate})\right]}{\text{Unit CM}}$$

### Example 4

Assume in Example 1 that Flip Toy Store wants to achieve an after-tax income of $6,000. The tax rate is 40 percent. Then,

$$\text{Target income volume} = \frac{\$15,000 + [\$6,000/(1-0.4)]}{\$15}$$

$$= \frac{\$15,000 + \$10,000}{\$15} = 1,667 \text{ units}$$

## MARGIN OF SAFETY

The margin of safety is a measure of difference between the actual sales and the break-even sales. It is the amount by which sales revenue may drop before losses begin, and is expressed as a percentage of expected sales:

$$\text{Margin of safety} = \frac{\text{Break-even sales}}{\text{Expected sales}}$$

The margin of safety is used as a measure of operating risk. The larger the ratio, the safer the situation since there is less risk of reaching the break-even point.

### Example 5

Assume Flip Toy Store projects sales of $35,000 with a break-even sales level of $25,000. The projected margin of safety is

$$\frac{\$35,000 - \$25,000}{\$35,000} = 28.57\%$$

## SOME APPLICATIONS OF CONTRIBUTION MARGIN ANALYSIS AND "WHAT-IF" ANALYSIS

The concepts of contribution margin and the contribution income statement have many applications in profit planning and short-term decision making. Many "what-if" scenarios can be evaluated using them as planning tools, especially utilizing a spreadsheet program such as Lotus 1-

2-3. Some applications are illustrated in Examples 6 to 10 using the same data as in Example 1.

### Example 6

Recall from Example 1 that Flip Toy Store has a CM of 60 percent and fixed costs of $15,000 per period. Assume that the company expects sales to go up by $10,000 for the next period. How much will income increase?

Using the CM concepts, we can quickly compute the impact of a change in sales on profits. The formula for computing the impact is:

Change in net income = Dollar change in sales × CM ratio

Thus:

Increase in net income = $10,000 × 60% = $6,000

Therefore, the income will go up by $6,000, assuming there is no change in fixed costs.

If we are given a change in unit sales instead of dollars, then the formula becomes:

Change in net income = Change in unit sales × Unit CM

### Example 7

Assume that the store expects sales to go up by 400 units. How much will income increase? From Example 1, the company's unit CM is $15. Again, assuming there is no change in fixed costs, the income will increase by $6,000.

400 units × $15 = $6,000

### Example 8

What net income is expected on sales of $47,500?
The answer is the difference between the CM and the fixed costs:

| | |
|---|---|
| CM: $47,500 × 60% | $28,500 |
| Less: Fixed costs | 15,000 |
| Net income | $13,500 |

### Example 9

Flip Toy Store is considering increasing the advertising budget by $5,000, which would increase sales revenue by $8,000. Should the advertising budget be increased?

The answer is no, since the increase in the CM is less than the increased cost:

| | |
|---|---|
| Increase in CM: $8,000 × 60% | $4,800 |
| Increase in advertising | 5,000 |
| Decrease in net income | $ (200) |

## Example 10

Consider the original data. Assume again that Flip Toy Store is currently selling 1,500 units per period. In an effort to increase sales, management is considering cutting its unit price by $5 and increasing the advertising budget by $1,000.

If these two steps are taken, management feels that unit sales will go up by 60 percent. Should the two steps be taken?

The answer can be obtained by developing comparative income statements in a contribution format:

| | (A)<br>Present<br>(1,500 units) | (B)<br>Proposed<br>(2,400 units) | (B − A)<br>Difference |
|---|---|---|---|
| Sales | $37,500 (@$25) | $48,000 (@$20) | $10,500 |
| Less: Variable cost | 15,000 | 24,000 | 9,000 |
| CM | $22,500 | $24,000 | $ 1,500 |
| Less: Fixed costs | 15,000 | 16,000 | 1,000 |
| Net income | $ 7,500 | $ 8,000 | $ 500 |

The answer, therefore, is yes.

## SALES MIX ANALYSIS

Break-even and contribution margin analysis requires some additional computations and assumptions when a company produces and sells more than one product. In multi-product firms, sales mix is an important factor in calculating an overall company break-even point.

Different selling prices and different variable costs result in different unit CM and CM ratios. As a result, the break-even and contribution relationships vary with the relative proportions of the products sold, called the sales mix.

In break-even and contribution margin analysis, it is necessary to pre-determine the sales mix and then compute a weighted average unit CM. It is also necessary to assume that the sales mix does not change for a speci-fied period. The break-even formula for the company as a whole is:

$$\text{Break-even sales in dollars} = \frac{\text{Fixed costs}}{\text{CM ratio}}$$

## Example 11

Assume that Panda, Inc. is a producer of recreational equipment. It expects to produce and sell three types of sleeping bags—the Economy, the Regular, and the Backpacker. Information on the bags is given below:

|  | BUDGETED | | | |
|  | Economy | Regular | Backpacker | Total |
| --- | --- | --- | --- | --- |
| Sales | $30,000 | $60,000 | $10,000 | $100,000 |
| Sales mix | 30% | 60% | 10% | 100% |
| Less: VC | 24,000 | 40,000 | 5,000 | 69,000 |
| CM | $ 6,000 | $20,000 | $ 5,000 | $ 31,000 |
| CM ratio | 20% | 33$^1$/₃% | 50% | 31% |
| Fixed costs |  |  |  | $ 18,600 |
| Net income |  |  |  | $ 12,400 |

The CM ratio for Panda, Inc. is $31,000/$100,000 = 31$ percent. Therefore the break-even point in dollars is

$$\$18,600/0.31 = \$60,000$$

which will be split in the mix ratio of 3:6:1 to give us the following break-even points for the individual products:

Economy:    $60,000 × 30% = $18,000
Regular:     $60,000 × 60% =  36,000
Backpacker: $60,000 × 10% =   6,000
                             $60,000

One of the most important assumptions underlying break-even analy-sis in a multi-product firm is that the sales mix will not change during the planning period. But if the sales mix changes, the break-even point will also change.

## Example 12

Assume that total sales from Example 11 was achieved at $100,000 but that an actual mix came out differently from the budgeted mix (i.e., for Economy, 30% to 55%, for Regular, 60% to 40%, and for Backpacker, 10% to 5%).

|  | Economy | **ACTUAL**<br>Regular | Backpacker | Total |
|---|---|---|---|---|
| Sales | $55,000 | $40,000 | $ 5,000 | $100,000 |
| Sales mix | 55% | 40% | 5% | 100% |
| Less: VC | 44,000 | 26,667* | 2,500** | 73,167 |
| CM | $11,000 | $13,333 | $ 2,500 | $ 26,833 |
| CM ratio | 20% | 33$^1$/3% | 50% | 26.83% |
| Fixed costs |  |  |  | $ 18,600 |
| Net income |  |  |  | $ 8,233 |

*$26,667 = $40,000 × (100% − 33 1/3%) = $40,000 × 66 2/3%
**$2,500 = $5,000 × (100% − 50%) = $5,000 × 50%

*Note:* The shift in sales mix toward the less profitable line, Economy, has caused the CM ratio for the company as a whole to drop from 31 percent to 26.83 percent.

The new break-even point will be

$$\$18,600/0.2683 = \$69,325$$

The break-even dollar volume has increased from $60,000 to $69,325.

The deterioration (improvement) in the mix caused net income to go down (up). It is important to note that generally, the shift of emphasis from low-margin products to high-margin ones will increase the overall profits of the company.

## CONTRIBUTION MARGIN ANALYSIS AND NONPROFIT ORGANIZATIONS

Break-even and contribution margin analysis is not limited to profit firms. It not only calculates the break-even service level for nonprofit organizations, but helps answer a variety of "what-if" decision questions.

## Example 13

OCM, Inc., a Los Angeles county agency, has a $1,200,000 lump-sum annual budget appropriation for an agency to help rehabilitate mentally ill patients. On top of this, the agency charges each patient $600 a month for board and care. All of the appropriation and revenue must be spent. The variable costs for rehabilitation activity average $700 per patient per month. The agency's annual fixed costs are $800,000. The agency manager wishes to know how many patients can be served. Let x = number of patients to be served.

$$\text{Revenue} = \text{Total expenses}$$

$$\text{Lump sum appropriation} + \$600 \,(12)\, x = \text{Variable expenses} + \text{Fixed costs}$$
$$\$1,200,000 + \$7,200\, x = \$8,400\, x + \$800,000$$
$$(\$7,200 - \$8,400)\, x = \$800,000 - \$1,200,000$$
$$- \$1,200\, x = -\$400,000$$
$$x = \$400,000/\$1,200$$
$$x = 333 \text{ patients}$$

We will investigate the following two "what-if" scenarios:

(1) Suppose the manager of the agency is concerned that the total budget for the coming year will be cut by 10% to a new amount of $1,080,000. All other things remain unchanged. The manager wants to know how this budget cut affects the next year's service level.

$$\$1,080,000 + \$7,200\, x = \$8,400\, x + \$800,000$$
$$(\$7,200 - \$8,400)\, x = \$800,000 - \$1,080,000$$
$$- \$1,200\, x = -\$280,000$$
$$x = \$280,000/\$1,200$$
$$x = 233 \text{ patients}$$

(2) The manager does not reduce the number of patients served despite a budget cut of 10%. All other things remain unchanged. How much more does he/she have to charge his/her patients for board and care? In this case, x = board and care charge per year.

$$\$1,080,000 + 333\, x = \$8,400\, (333) + \$800,000$$
$$333x = \$2,797,200 + \$800,000 - \$1,080,000$$
$$333\, x = \$2,517,200$$
$$x = \$2,517,200/333 \text{ patients}$$
$$x = \$7,559$$

Thus, the monthly board and care charge must be increased to $630 ($7,559/12 months).

## ASSUMPTIONS UNDERLYING BREAK-EVEN CONTRIBUTION MARGIN ANALYSIS

The basic break-even and contribution margin models are subject to a number of limiting assumptions. They are:

(a) The selling price per unit is constant throughout the entire relevant range of activity.

(b) All costs are classified as fixed or variable.

(c) The variable cost per unit is constant.

(d) There is only one product or a constant sales mix.

(e) Inventories do not change significantly from period to period.

(f) Volume is the only factor affecting variable costs.

## CONCLUSION

Break-even and contribution margin analysis is useful as a frame of reference, as a vehicle for expressing overall managerial performance, and as a planning device via break-even techniques and what-if scenarios.

The following points highlight the analytical usefulness of contribution margin analysis as a tool for profit planning:

1. A change in either the selling price or the variable cost per unit alters CM or the CM ratio and thus the break-even point.

2. As sales exceed the break-even point, a higher unit CM or CM ratio will result in greater profits than a small unit CM or CM ratio.

3. The lower the break-even sales, the less risky the business and the safer the investment, other things being equal.

4. A large margin of safety means lower operating risk since a large decrease in sales can occur before losses are experienced.

5. Using the contribution income statement model and a spreadsheet program such as Lotus 1-2-3, a variety of "what-if" planning and decision scenarios can be evaluated.

6. In a multi-product firm, sales mix is often more important than overall market share. The emphasis on high-margin products tends to maximize overall profits of the firm.

We discussed how the traditional contribution analysis can be applied to the profit and nonprofit setting. Illustrations were provided. Managers can prepare the income statement in a contribution format, which organizes costs by behavior rather than by the functions of manufacturing, sales, and administration. The contribution income statement is widely used as an internal planning and decision-making tool.

# Chapter 5

# PROFIT PLANNING:
*Targeting and Reaching
Achievable Goals*

In profit planning, we must determine the strategy, which is one of several ways to reach a goal. But we must also determine the objective, which is the target that can be quantified and that is developed from analysis of the situation at present and in the future. And finally, we must see what is needed to implement the plan.

Profit planning involves setting realistic profit objectives and targets and accomplishing them. The plan must consider the organization structure, product line (e.g., up-to-date, obsolete), services rendered, selling prices, sales volume, costs (manufacturing and operating expenses), market share, territories, skill of labor force, sources of supply, economic conditions, political environment, risk, salesforce effectiveness, financial health (e.g., cash flow to fund programs), physical resources and condition, production schedules, human resources (e.g., number and quality of employees, training programs, relationship with union), distribution facilities, growth rate, technological ability, motivational aspects, and publicity.

Each part of the plan must be evaluated for reasonableness, as well as its effect on other parts of the plan. Trouble spots must be identified and corrected. Information should be in the simplest and clearest form. Profits may be increased by increasing revenue (selling price and/or sales volume) and reducing costs, eliminating duplication of work and inconsistencies).

A manager can improve profitability of his responsibility unit by:

- Operating his department with the minimum number of employees. This may include downsizing through layoffs.
- Reducing operating costs, such as using automation and robotics to replace the cost of manual labor
- Buying rather than leasing when cost beneficial
- Emphasizing previous success. For example, if growth has come from product development, then allocate more funds to R&D.
- Keeping up-to-date
- Using high-technology equipment
- Self-constructing assets when feasible
- Eliminating useless operations and paper work (e.g., reports)
- Being productive and progressive in obtaining efficiencies realizable with existing resources and capabilities
- Improving the reliability of the product and service
- Expanding into new operations and areas so every opportunity is pursued
- Improving supplier relationships, including negotiating better prices and terms. Alternative sources of supply may be bought when cost-effective.
- Screening new hires for honesty and competence
- Having adequate insurance, including business interruption and product liability

The profit plan should be in writing, consistently applied, and contain the following key elements:

- Statement of objectives
- Parameters of achieving those objectives (e.g., prohibition of reducing discretionary costs, such as research and development, in the current year just to bolster near-term profits when this will have long-term negative effects)

- Plans (operating and financial)
- Schedules
- Ways to measure and track performance
- Review procedures
- Mechanism for making needed changes

An operating plan tells how the objective is to be achieved. For example, an operating plan for a sales manager may provide for a reduction in selling expenses of 10% by improving salesperson productivity through better training, reducing the number of salespeople, and increasing the number of calls per salesperson.

The financial plan is a budget expressed in dollars that quantifies the operating plan. Lower-level managers are more involved with operational specifics (details) and carrying out plans than upper-level managers.

Planning should occur within a reasonable time frame, not rushed, considering alternatives that accomplish the long-term objectives of the manager. For example, a new product should undergo test marketing before it is introduced on a massive scale. Further, profit planning for the next year should begin as early as possible. It must be in place by January 1 of that year.

The profit plan may be for one year and multiyears. For example, in a 5-year plan, there should be profit objectives set for each of the years included in that plan. A 5-year plan should be the maximum time period because the longer the time horizon the more difficult it is to predict. Further, a 5-year period would be more practical and attainable then longer periods. The time period chosen should take into account the nature and stability of the business.

Reports should provide the manager with the right information needed to make a good decision. Once that decision has been made, control reports should show whether or not it has worked out. Further, the manager should not procrastinate once he or she has made a decision. The manager should not keep changing his or her mind because of employee reaction.

The manager must address what is crucial. For example, material costs are important to a manufacturing company but not to a financial service business. In airlines, passenger revenue per mile is crucial.

Information has to be given to the right manager and must directly relate to his operation. The type of profit plan and its components will differ among companies, depending on their unique characteristics, features, problems, conditions, and requirements. Unfortunately, profit planning has become more difficult because of competition, the high cost associated with introducing new products (e.g., research and development), more educated consumers, and government regulation.

This chapter discusses establishing and evaluating profit targets, planning objectives, role of nonfinancial managers, plan assumptions and alternatives, manager responsibilities, participation in the planning process, employee relations, coordination and communication, scheduling, handling problems, and analysis and control of the profit plan.

## GOAL CONGRUENCE

We must keep in mind goal congruence, which is top management's viewpoint agreeing with the lower level managers' viewpoint. Some of this activity could be misdirected if each manager assumes, as is human, that what is best for his responsibility center is best for the company. Therefore, the manager must consider general company goals and assumptions as a background for all planning activity.

The standard philosophy is that more is better. That is, more sales, products, fields of activity, profit, and return. Most businesses feel that ceasing to grow is beginning to die.

## PROFIT TARGETS

Profit planning sets a target profit which takes into account expected sales and costs for next year and for longer periods. The manager should track, on a regular basis, the progress in meeting the profit plan so any needed adjustments may be made in selling effort or cost containment. For example, if the yearly target is an increase in sales of 20% and in the first quarter sales have actually decreased by 2%, a problem is indicated. On the other hand, if the plan calls for a reduction in yearly costs of 10% and at the end of the second quarter costs have been trimmed by 12%, the situation is quite favorable.

A profit target can apply to the individual components of that profit. For example, a company which now derives 80% of its earnings from one product may have as its profit goal in three years to derive 40% of its profit from this product and 60% of its profit from other products. This goal may be achieved through developing new products, enhancing existing products, change in advertising and sales promotion, and R&D efforts.

## OBJECTIVES IN THE PROFIT PLAN

An objective states what is going to be done. The objective must be clear, quantifiable, compatible, practical, strong, realistic, and attainable. The objective should be in writing. Objectives changed too often become meaningless. Further, objectives must not conflict with each other.

The objective must be specific. For example, an objective of increasing sales should state by how much, where, and when. It may take the following form: "The divisional objective is to increase sales by 50,000 units of product X in territory A for 19XX." The manager should clearly communicate objectives to subordinates.

Objectives should be established in priority order. An example is a marketing department that should give primary emphasis to the existing, successful product line and secondary emphasis to unproven, high-risk new products. Another example is the R&D manager who should give first priority to basic research to improve the existing products and a lower level of priority to research on new products.

Objectives should be ranked in terms of those having the highest return. The progress toward meeting the objective should be measured at regular intervals (e.g., quarterly).

## ROLE OF NONFINANCIAL MANAGERS

The nonfinancial manager must abandon sacred cows to increase profits. For example, a less expensive raw material may be used to result in cost savings without sacrificing product quality. Another example is to lower the quality of a product to save on costs and reduce the selling price to attract more business from price-oriented customers. A company that sells only to a few prestigious accounts that are willing to pay a higher price may produce greater overall profits by lowering the quality and price to get a huge number of price sensitive accounts. Conversely, the company may keep its high-priced product as is and develop a new second product line of lower prices with a different label to attract the price conscious consumer.

The marketing manager may increase profits by increasing the selling price, increasing volume, improving quality and service, reducing the time to respond to customer complaints, concentrating on high-demand products, modifying geographic locations, having clean facilities, altering distribution outlets, introducing new products, redesigning packaging, using more attractive styling, discontinuing unprofitable products, increasing personal selling, changing the salesforce, and modifying advertising and sales promotion policy.

The marketing manager should determine how much of each sales dollar goes to meeting marketing expenses. He or she should determine the ratio of the change in marketing expenses over the year to expenses last year to indicate the degree of cost control. The manager must also keep abreast of marketing trends for products and services.

The manager should rate salespeople in terms of the net profitability brought in. A comparison should be made between the salesperson's actual sales relative to the costs to obtain those sales. Other performance measures are dollar sales quotas and the number of orders from existing and new customers.

A sales analysis should examine orders booked, orders backlogged, orders lost by out of stock or delayed shipments, ratio of orders billed to orders booked, and aging of orders. A sales effort analysis involves the number of sales calls, number of advertisements and mailings, number of new customers, market share, and sales mix.

The production manager can maximize profits by spreading manufacturing as regularly as possible over the entire year. This may add stability to manufacturing and lower costs (e.g., eliminate overtime, layoffs vs. rehiring and training). The manager may also increase profits through private labeling for other companies. This would achieve better plant and machinery utilization and spread fixed costs over more units. The manager should also maintain plant facilities, obtain givebacks from employees or not give raises, derive optimum inventory balances and reduce inventory costs, lower raw material costs, and properly schedule production.

He should use the following factory performance measures: capacity in use and units produced, percentage of rejects and rework, yield percentages for direct materials and purchased parts, and trends in costs of service, especially during new product learning curve periods.

The purchasing manager can increase profits by properly timing the purchase of raw materials, obtaining volume and cash discounts, changing suppliers to obtain lower prices (assuming reliability in delivery), and inspecting items to assure quality.

The transportation manager can boost profits by scheduling delivery routes to economize on time and by lowering mileage costs, including fuel and depreciation.

The personnel manager can improve profits by instituting an incentive plan to improve dollar revenue per employee and sales volume per worker. The ratio of annual terminations to the average number of employees can also be examined.

The research director can contribute by substituting low-cost components for high-cost ones without sacrificing quality or customer acceptance.

The engineering manager can reduce the number of diverse elements in use (e.g., 100) to standardized ones (e.g., 20), and find fewer cost combinations of inputs (e.g., materials and labor mix).

The service manager is concerned with the percentage of billable time, standard and average billing rate, average cost per hour of employee time, and overhead (or markup) rate to labor time. The manager should maintain a system that can differentiate quickly and accurately between customers based on the degree of service they require and the revenues their patronage is likely to generate.

The credit manager can reduce bad debts and the collection period without losing sales.

Because a nonfinancial manager's responsibility is to plan and control, he or she must be able to communicate effectively in order to accomplish goals. Communication may be written (formal financial reports, ratios, statistics, narrative), graphical (charts, diagrams, pictures), and oral (conferences, group meetings).

## ASSUMPTIONS

Profit plans rely on assumptions and projections. Nonfinancial mangers will have to make assumptions in order to predict the future. The assumptions must be continually updated. Any revisions require special approval.

If the assumptions are not realistic, for example, for an increase in selling price if there is a high degree of competition and/or a recession, the basis of the profit plan is in doubt. Further, an increase in selling price may result in a decline in sales volume, hurting overall profits because consumers will switch to cheaper brands (e.g., away from Philip Morris cigarettes).

## ALTERNATIVES

The financial impact of alternatives in the profit plan has to be considered. Alternative plans can allow for such possibilities as a strike. The alternative selected should be practical and result in the highest profit in conformity with the nonfinancial manager's goals. The bottom line, and not the personal tastes of the manager, is all that counts. For example, the sales manager may prefer to sell through direct mail but he or she should use the manufacturer's representatives if that is more profitable.

The sales manager should try to obtain the most profitable sales at the minimum cost. Some of the sales manager's options are:

- Modify advertising and sales promotion.
- Change the method of distribution.
- Eliminate unprofitable products.
- Develop new markets and products.
- Combine small orders to reduce transportation charges.
- Redesign truck routes to economize on fuel.
- Change the sales territory.
- Alter the selling price.
- Change credit and collection policies.
- Alter packaging and labeling.

The production manager is responsible for manufacturing sufficient quantities to meet sales needs at the lowest practical cost while maintaining quality within a desired time period.

The production manager may:

- Improve the production process and supervision of workers.
- Change the repair and maintenance policy.

- Move production elements (e.g., machinery) or entire facilities.
- Use higher technology equipment.
- Determine the best production run.
- Properly schedule work flow and employee time.
- Synchronize production and inventory levels.
- Reduce fixed costs.

The purchasing manager is responsible for buying materials and supplies at the least cost while maintaining quality. The purchasing manager should:

- Carefully inspect the quality of purchased items.
- Decrease the days that elapse between purchase and delivery.
- Decide on less expensive product substitutes.
- Obtain volume discounts from larger orders.
- Reduce inventory cost with more frequent deliveries.
- Emphasize standardized (uniform) items.
- Change unreliable suppliers

The personnel manager can:

- Expand job training.
- Improve recruitment.
- Establish merit increases based on performance.
- Select the right person for the right job.
- Self-insure to eliminate insurance premiums such as health care.

## RESPONSIBILITY

Profit planning requires that managers be held accountable for their results if they have authority over the items in question. Responsibility without authority causes the profit planning system to fail and results in manager frustration.

Planning should avoid conflicts which have a net negative profit impact on the business. An example is a sales manager who accepts short-term, low-volume sales orders even though they result in unusually high manufacturing costs for the production manager.

A solution is to make nonfinancial managers jointly responsible for an objective that affects both. Interrelated departments must as a group work to maximize company profit by considering the net advantage or disadvantage to the business. The managers should share credit or blame for these interrelated performances. In this way, managers will work toward meeting overall company objectives.

The manager must determine whether responsibility unit managers are contributing to the profit plan in the expected proportion.

## PARTICIPATION

Profit planning involves effort and input by managers in sales, production, distribution, research and development, service, engineering, finance, traffic, and general business.

Line managers are concerned with operating and executing plans. Staff managers assist others in an advisory capacity. In either case, the manager must be able to change and try new things.

Financial people should spend time with operating personnel so they familiarize themselves with operations, problems, and requirements. The manager should encourage financial personnel to discuss with him the nature and characteristics of their department's or responsibility unit's operations. In this way, the accountant or financial executive can prepare meaningful budget information and performance reports that can be used by nonfinancial managers.

The managers should insist on getting reports, schedules, and forms that are useful. Otherwise, the information may not be suitable or relevant and will be discarded.

Nonfinancial managers should communicate clearly to financial managers the type and nature of information they need. Otherwise, time and money will be wasted on useless information for managers. As a result, the managers may waste time accumulating accounting numbers themselves.

## SUBORDINATES

The manager should monitor the performance of subordinates but should give them latitude in making decisions.

Subordinates should be rewarded (e.g., salary increases, merit bonuses) on the basis of results that improve divisional profitability. The optimum pay raise is the minimum pay increase that will yield the maximum productivity increase. Managers whose decisions have hurt profitability should be called to account. They should learn from their errors. If too many errors have been made, a replacement might be appropriate.

Compensation to subordinates should be competitive with other companies in the industry. No limit should be placed on salaries or the successful employee may quit.

## COORDINATION

Profit planning is a team effort involving all managers, line and staff, to accomplish the profit goal. For example, there should be coordination between the sales manager, production supervisor, purchasing manager, receiving manager, director of engineering, and quality control supervisor, since interrelationships exist between them.

## SCHEDULING

A product introduced should be planned and scheduled in the most economical way. Workers should be available when needed. Each step should proceed logically. Profit planning involves delivering products on time by such means as reducing workers' absentee rates.

## PROBLEMS

Problems must be identified, addressed with solutions, and profit impacts considered. If the problems cannot be rectified (e.g., uncontrollable by the company) the adverse effects must also be taken into account. An example is when a manufacturer loses some retail accounts because of competitors' price cuts and an existing poor relationship between the manufacturer and the retailers because of delivery delays due to a strike.

## CONTROL, EVALUATION, AND ANALYSIS

A management information system (MIS) includes financial information that allows the manager to compare actual results with target figures. It is better to analyze variances more often, perhaps monthly. For example, quarterly variance analysis may be too late to give managers the opportunity to correct problems.

A comparison should be made over time between actual profit and budgeted profit. Related useful ratios are actual revenue to budgeted revenue and actual costs to budgeted costs.

The profit expectation of the plan should be compared to prior years' experience as an indicator of reasonableness. For example, it may not be reasonable to project a sales increase for next year of 40% when in previous years the sales increase has never exceeded 20%. There must be hard evidence (e.g., something in the current year and expected for a future year to justify it) for this dramatic increase.

The projections in the profit plan should be compared to competing companies' experiences. For example, company X will start a new program or project if it earns a rate of return of 30%. However, six competing companies have already tried this program or project and either have lost money or earned a return rate below 5%. This makes the company's projected 30% rate of return questionable unless it can be shown that special or unique reasons justify it.

Ratios may be prepared comparing projected performance to historical performance. Some useful ratios include return on investment (net income/total assets), profit margin (net income/sales), cost of sales to sales, direct material to sales, direct labor to sales, factory overhead to sales, selling expenses to sales, and general and administrative expenses to sales. However, in making ratio calculations, the data must be comparable over the years.

The manager should not overstate current year profit at the expense of sacrificing future profitability.

The manager must track the status of a project or program and make immediate decisions if an operation is not productive or profitable. Further, part of a department that no longer serves a useful purpose may be disbanded.

A comparison may be made between the unit costs of the old and the new manufacturing operation to see if the latter is successful.

After a product has been marketed, the company must continually evaluate and improve it, based on customer reaction. Feedback should occur on a timely basis so that necessary corrective steps may be taken.

In order to make valid comparisons between the company and a competitor, there must be a comparable base. For example, if one company has old and inefficient plant facilities it is not comparable to one with modern, efficient facilities.

An illustrative profit plan is presented in Exhibit 5.1.

## INTERNAL CONTROLS

Internal controls are fundamental in profit planning. Assets should be safeguarded and controlled. An individual's work should be checked by another. One person should not have control over a transaction from beginning to end. Requests and requisitions should be reviewed and approved. Before an item is paid, make certain it is appropriate.

## REAL-LIFE ILLUSTRATIONS IN PROFIT PLANNING

Staples, the office supply company, achieves the lowest net-landed cost in the entire office stationery business. But it has also come into a particular market: companies employing fewer than 50 people. To further the relationship with this market segment, Staples has created a club. Customers join at no extra cost and get at least a 5% discount on fast moving items. In order to get the discount the customers must show their cards, allowing Staples to track sales by customer and gain useful data for satisfying its market. Some store managers now have incentives based on customer satisfaction.

Some companies look at a customer's lifetime value to the company, not the value of a single transaction. Home Depot is an example of such a company.

Clerks do not spend time with customers to be nice. They do so because the company's business strategy is built around not only selling home repair and improvement items inexpensively, but around customers' needs for information and service.

Although new products win new markets, it may be better in some cases to stick with existing customer segments. It is easier to build sales

**Exhibit 5.1**
**PROFIT PLAN**

| | Jan. | Feb. | Mar. | First Quarter | Remainder of year | Total for Year |
|---|---|---|---|---|---|---|
| Sales | | | | | | |
| Units | | | | | | |
| Dollars | | | | | | |
| Less: Returns | | | | | | |
| Discounts | | | | | | |
| Net Sales | | | | | | |
| Expenses | | | | | | |
| Cost of Goods Sold | | | | | | |
| General & Administrative Expenses | | | | | | |
| Selling Expenses | | | | | | |
| Total Expenses | | | | | | |
| Operating Profit | | | | | | |

volume with customers who already know the company. When Entenmann's of New York, a loyalty leader in specialty bakery products, saw its sales leveling off, it monitored customer purchase patterns in each local market.

Through telephone surveys and focus groups, the company found that their customers were looking for fat-free and cholesterol-free items. Entenmann's determined that it was much more economical to develop new health products than to go with another group of customers. Its new product line has been highly successful. By addressing the changing needs of the core clientele and also attracting new customers.

The Olive Garden restaurant chain is another company that believes that customer loyalty plays a major role in profit planning. The chain goes against the norm of promoting successful managers to other restaurants every few years and letting assistants take over. They hire local managers whose major asset is that they are known and trusted in the community. Managers stay where they are. They get to know the customers and their long-time hires add value to the company. It is with employees that the customer builds a bond of trust and expectations and when those people leave, the bond is broken.

Another company which uses this same philosophy is State Farm, the insurance company. Its focus on customer service has resulted in faster growth than most other multiple-line insurers. But rather than being consumed by growth, its capital has mushroomed (all through internally generated surplus) to more than $18 billion, representing the largest capital base of any financial services company in North America.

State Farm began by choosing the right customers and because of this they were still able to build the capital necessary to protect their policyholders in years such as 1992, when they incurred $4.7 billion in catastrophe losses.

State Farm agents work from neighborhood offices, which allows them to build long-lasting relationships with their customers and provide personal service. For example, agents scan the local newspaper for the high school honor roll and are sure that their young customers' good grades are recognized with discounts. Commissions are structured to encourage long-term thinking. Rather than bringing in lots of new customers, the company's marketing efforts encourage existing customers to buy additional products, like home and life insurance.

State Farm's success in building customer loyalty is reflected in retention rates that exceed 90%, consistently the best performance of all the national insurers that sell through agents.

Dell Computer has focused on operational excellence to boost profits. Operational excellence is a specific strategy involving the production and delivery of products and services. The objective of this strategy is to lead its industry in price and convenience. Dell's goal is to show PC buyers that they do not have to sacrifice quality or state of the art technology in order to buy personal computers easily and inexpensively.

In the mid 1980s, while Compaq concentrated on making its PC's less expensive and faster than IBM's, Dell saw the opportunity to outdo both IBM and Compaq by focusing not on the product, but on the delivery system. Dell came onto the scene with a radically different and far more efficient operating mode.

Dell realized that Compaq's marketing strategy of selling PC's through dealers to novices could be outperformed by a model that cut dealers out of the distribution process altogether. By selling to customers directly, building to order rather than to inventory, and creating a disciplined and extremely low cost culture, Dell has been able to undercut Compaq and other PC manufacturers in price and service.

While Dell has risen to $1.7 billion in revenue in less than 10 years, Compaq has been forced to cut prices and overhead.

Morgan Bank realized that the key to more profit was better service and lower costs. They selected a strategy based on its capacity to achieve a 24-hour turnaround time and tracked performance daily.

First, they had to figure out how to reduce customer delivery time. They created an improvement plan showing week by week subgoals. This was posted next to a chart showing daily performance.

New procedures for communicating between shifts allowed management to anticipate workload peaks and reassign personnel from one shift to another. This made performance improvement an act of rational decision-making based on evidence. The plan was first introduced in the microfilm department. When this department succeeded in meeting the 24-hour turnaround goal, it was carried out in the other units and yielded significant service improvements and several million dollars of cost savings within the first year.

Global competition, changing markets, and new technologies are opening new roads to reinvent value. IKEA is one company that accomplished this. It changed from a small Swedish mail order furniture operation into the world's largest retailer of home furnishings, with a global network of 100 enormous stores. In 1992, these stores were visited by more than 96 million people, generated revenues of $4.3 billion, and had an average annual growth rate of 15% with profit margins that estimate between 8% and 10%.

IKEA's huge suburban stores sell simple high quality knock-down furniture kits that customers transport and assemble themselves. A portion of what IKEA saves on low cost components, efficient warehousing, and customer self-service it passes on to its customers in the form of lower prices—anywhere from 25% to 50% below those of competitors.

IKEA's strategy is to allow customers to take on key tasks that were traditionally done by manufacturers and retailers, such as the assembly of products and delivery to customers' homes. And for doing this it promises substantially lower prices. Part of their goal is to make themselves not just a furniture store but a family outing destination. They provide free strollers, child care, and playgrounds as well as wheelchairs for the disabled and elderly. They also have dining facilities.

IKEA's strategic intent is to have its customers understand that their role is not to consume value but to create it. It provides customers with catalogs, tape measures, pens, and notepaper to help them make choices without the need of salespeople. IKEA's goal is not to relieve customers of doing certain tasks but to mobilize them to do easily certain things they have never done before. They have set out to reinvent value and the business system that delivers value for customers and suppliers alike.

The question is, "Does IKEA offer a product or a service?" The answer is neither—and both.

This change of values can be compared to cash withdrawals from automatic teller machines (ATMs). Not long ago, it was inconceivable that a customer would replace a personal relationship with a bank teller for a computer system. But today most cash withdrawals come from ATMs.

There are many implications for profit planning. First, value for customers can be restated to mobilize customers to take advantage and create value for themselves. Second, companies do not compete with each other anymore. Rather, it is the offerings that compete for the customers' money. Third, a result of a company's strategic task is the reconfiguration of its relationships and business systems. And finally, to win at this strategy the key is to keep offerings competitive. This is why IKEA has become the world's largest furniture retailer and this strategy could be applied to many industries.

## CONCLUSION

A profit plan may be stated as target return on investment (e.g., 20% ROI), growth in earnings (e.g., 5%) or in earnings per share and percentage of sales.

Performance reporting compares actual results with expectations.

All efforts must be expended to accomplish profit goals. Problems have to be identified and addressed immediately.

The manager should rank items in terms of profit potential and growth.

## REFERENCES

Richard Normann and Rafael Ramirez, "Designing Interactive Strategy," *Harvard Business Review*, July/August 1993, pp. 65–77.

Frederick Reichheld, "Loyalty-based Management," *Harvard Business Review*, March/April 1993, pp. 64–73.

# Chapter 6

# MASTER BUDGET:
## Genesis of Forecasting and Profit Planning

A comprehensive—master—budget is a formal statement of management's expectation regarding sales, expenses, volume, and other financial transactions for the coming period. It consists basically of a pro forma income statement, pro forma balance sheet and cash budget.

At the beginning of the period, the budget is a plan or standard. At the end, it serves as a control device to help management measure its performance against the plan so that future performance may be improved.

With the aid of computer technology, budgeting can be used as an effective device for evaluation of what-if scenarios. Management can find the best course of action among various alternatives through simulation. If management does not like what it sees on the budgeted financial statements in terms of financial ratios such as liquidity, activity (turnover), leverage, profit margin, and market value ratios, it can always alter its contemplated decision and planning set.

The budget is classified broadly into two categories:

1. Operating budget
2. Financial budget

The operating budget consists of:

- Sales budget
- Production budget
- Direct materials budget
- Direct labor budget
- Factory overhead budget
- Selling and administrative expense budget
- Pro forma income statement

The financial budget consists of:

- Cash budget
- Pro forma balance sheet

The major steps in preparing the budget are:

1. Prepare a sales forecast.
2. Determine expected production volume.
3. Estimate manufacturing costs and operating expenses.
4. Determine cash flow and other financial effects.
5. Formulate projected financial statements.

Figure 6.1 presents a master budget.

To illustrate how all these budgets are put together, we will focus on a manufacturing company called the Norton Company, which produces and markets a single product. We will assume that the company develops the master budget in contribution format for the year 19B on a quarterly basis. We will highlight the variable cost-fixed cost breakdown throughout the illustration.

## THE SALES BUDGET

The sales budget is the starting point in preparing the master budget, since estimated sales volume influences nearly all other items in the master budget. The sales budget should show total sales in quantity and value. The

## Figure 6.1
## MASTER BUDGET

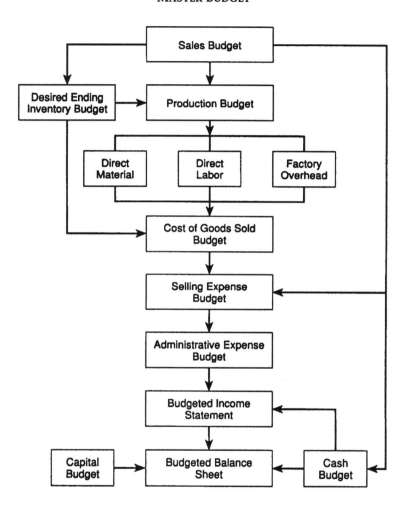

total sales can be break-even, target income, or projected sales. They may be analyzed further by product, territory, customer and seasonal pattern of expected sales.

Generally, the sales budget includes a computation of expected cash collections from credit sales, which will be used later for cash budgeting.

## Example 1

**THE NORTON COMPANY**
**Sales Budget**
**For the Year Ending December 31, 19B**

|  | Quarter | | | | |
| --- | --- | --- | --- | --- | --- |
|  | 1 | 2 | 3 | 4 | Total |
| Expected sales in units | 800 | 700 | 900 | 800 | 3,200 |
| Unit sales price | ×$80 | ×$80 | ×$80 | ×$80 | ×$80 |
| Total sales | $64,000 | $56,000 | $72,000 | $64,000 | $256,000 |

SCHEDULE OF EXPECTED CASH COLLECTIONS

|  | 1 | 2 | 3 | 4 | Total |
| --- | --- | --- | --- | --- | --- |
| Accounts receivable, 12/31/19A | 9,500* | | | | $9,500 |
| 1st quarter sales ($64,000) | 44,800† | $17,920‡ | | | 62,720 |
| 2d quarter sales ($56,000) | | 39,200 | $15,680 | | 54,880 |
| 3d quarter sales ($72,000) | | | 50,400 | $20,160 | 70,560 |
| 4th quarter sales ($64,000) | | | | 44,800 | 44,800 |
| Total cash collections | $54,300 | $57,120 | $66,080 | $64,960 | $242,460 |

*All $9,500 accounts receivable balance is assumed to be collectible in the first quarter.

†70 percent of a quarter's sales are collected in the quarter of sale.

‡28 percent of a quarter's sales are collected in the quarter following and the remaining 2 percent are uncollectible.

## THE PRODUCTION BUDGET

The production budget is a statement of the output by product and is generally expressed in units. It should take into account the sales budget, plant capacity, whether stocks are to be increased or decreased and outside purchases. The number of units expected to be manufactured to meet budgeted sales and inventory requirements is set forth in the budget. The expected volume of production is determined by subtracting the estimated inventory at the beginning of the period from the sum of the units expected to be sold and the desired inventory at the end of the period. The production budget is illustrated as follows:

### Example 2

**THE NORTON COMPANY**
**Production Budget**
**For the Year Ending December 31, 19B**

|                              |       | Quarter |       |       |         |
| ---------------------------- | ----- | ------- | ----- | ----- | ------- |
|                              | 1     | 2       | 3     | 4     | Total   |
| Planned sales (Example 1)    | 800   | 700     | 900   | 800   | 3,200   |
| Desired ending inventory*    | 70    | 90      | 80    | 100†  | 100     |
| Total needs                  | 870   | 790     | 980   | 900   | 3,300   |
| Less: Beginning inventory‡   | 80    | 70      | 90    | 80    | 80      |
| Units to be produced         | 790   | 720     | 890   | 820   | 3,220   |

*10 percent of the next quarter's sales.
†Estimated.
‡The same as the previous quarter's ending inventory.

## THE DIRECT MATERIAL BUDGET

When the level of production has been computed, a direct material budget should be constructed to show how much material will be required for production and how much material must be purchased to meet this requirement. The purchase will depend on both expected usage of materials and inventory levels. The formula for computation of the purchase is:

Purchase in units = Usage + Desired ending material inventory units
− Beginning inventory units

The direct material budget is usually accompanied by a computation of expected cash payments for materials.

## Example 3

THE NORTON COMPANY
Direct Material Budget
For the Year Ending December 31, 19B

| | Quarter | | | | |
| --- | --- | --- | --- | --- | --- |
| | *1* | *2* | *3* | *4* | *Total* |
| Units to be produced (Ex 2) | 790 | 720 | 890 | 820 | 3,220 |
| Material needs per unit (lbs) | × 3 | × 3 | × 3 | × 3 | × 3 |
| Material needs for production | 2,370 | 2,160 | 2,670 | 2,460 | 9,660 |
| Desired ending inventory of materials* | 216 | 267 | 246 | 250† | 250 |
| Total needs | 2,586 | 2,427 | 2,916 | 2,710 | 9,910 |
| Less: Beginning inventory of materials‡ | 237 | 216 | 267 | 246 | 237 |
| Materials to be purchased | 2,349 | 2,211 | 2,649 | 2,464 | 9,673 |
| Unit price | × $2 | × $2 | × $2 | × $2 | × $2 |
| Purchase cost | $4,698 | $4,422 | $5,298 | $4,928 | $19,346 |

### SCHEDULE OF EXPECTED CASH DISBURSEMENTS

| | | | | | |
| --- | --- | --- | --- | --- | --- |
| Accounts payable, 12/31/19A | $2,200 | | | | $2,200 |
| 1st quarter purchases ($4,698) | 2,349 | 2,349 ** | | | 4,698 |
| 2nd quarter purchases ($4,422) | | 2,211 | 2,211 | | 4,422 |
| 3rd quarter purchases ($5,298) | | | 2,649 | 2,649 | 5,298 |
| 4th quarter purchases ($4,928) | | | | 2,464 | 2,464 |
| Total disbursements | $4,549 | $4,560 | $4,860 | $5,113 | $19,082 |

*10 percent of the next quarter's units needed for production.
†Estimated.
‡The same as the prior quarter's ending inventory.
**50 percent of a quarter's purchases are paid for in the quarter of purchase; the remainder are paid for in the following quarter.

## THE DIRECT LABOR BUDGET

The production requirements as set forth in the production budget also provide the starting point for the preparation of the direct labor budget. To compute direct labor requirements, expected production volume for each period is multiplied by the number of direct labor hours required to produce a single unit. The direct labor hours to meet production requirements is then multiplied by the direct labor cost per hour to obtain budgeted total direct labor costs.

### Example 4

**THE NORTON COMPANY**
**Direct Labor Budget**
**For the Year Ending December 31, 19B**

| | Quarter | | | | |
| --- | --- | --- | --- | --- | --- |
| | 1 | 2 | 3 | 4 | Total |
| Units to be produced (Example 2) | 790 | 720 | 890 | 820 | 3,220 |
| Direct labor hours per unit | × 5 | × 5 | × 5 | × 5 | × 5 |
| Total hours | 3,950 | 3,600 | 4,450 | 4,100 | 16,100 |
| Direct labor cost per hour | × $5 | × $5 | × $5 | × $5 | ×$5 |
| Total direct labor cost | $19,750 | $18,000 | $22,250 | $20,500 | $80,500 |

## THE FACTORY OVERHEAD BUDGET

The factory overhead budget should provide a schedule of all manufacturing costs other than direct materials and direct labor. Using the contribution approach to budgeting requires the development of a predetermined overhead rate for the variable portion of the factory overhead. In developing the cash budget, we must remember that depreciation does not entail a cash outlay and therefore must be deducted from the total factory overhead in computing cash disbursement for factory overhead.

### Example 5

To illustrate the factory overhead budget, we will assume that
- Total factory overhead budgeted = $6,000 fixed (per quarter), plus $2 per hour of direct labor.
- Depreciation expenses are $3,250 each quarter.
- All overhead costs involving cash outlays are paid for in the quarter incurred.

**THE NORTON COMPANY**
**Factory Overhead Budget**
**For the Year Ending December 31, 19B**

|  | Quarter | | | | |
|---|---|---|---|---|---|
|  | 1 | 2 | 3 | 4 | Total |
| Budgeted direct labor hours |  |  |  |  |  |
| (Example 4) | 3,950 | 3,600 | 4,450 | 4,100 | 16,100 |
| Variable overhead rate | × $2 | × $2 | × $2 | × $2 | ×$2 |
| Variable overhead budgeted | 7,900 | 7,200 | 8,900 | 8,200 | 32,200 |
| Fixed overhead budgeted | 6,000 | 6,000 | 6,000 | 6,000 | 24,000 |
| Total budgeted overhead | 13,900 | 13,200 | 14,900 | 14,200 | 56,200 |
| Less: Depreciation | 3,250 | 3,250 | 3,250 | 3,250 | 13,000 |
| Cash disbursement for |  |  |  |  |  |
| overhead | 10,650 | 9,950 | 11,650 | 10,950 | 43,200 |

## THE ENDING INVENTORY BUDGET

The desired ending inventory budget provides us with the information required for the construction of budgeted financial statements. Specifically, it will help compute the cost of goods sold on the budgeted income statement. Secondly, it will give the dollar value of the ending materials and finished goods inventory to appear on the budgeted balance sheet.

### Example 6

**THE NORTON COMPANY**
**Ending Inventory Budget**
**For the Year Ending December 31, 19B**
*Ending Inventory*

|  | Units | Unit Cost | Total |
|---|---|---|---|
| Direct materials | 250 pounds (Example 3) | $2 | $ 500 |
| Finished goods | 100 units (Example 2) | $41* | $4,100 |

*The unit variable cost of $41 is computed as follows:

|  | Unit Cost | Units | Total |
|---|---|---|---|
| Direct materials | $2 | 3 pounds | $ 6 |
| Direct labor | 5 | 5 hours | 25 |
| Variable overhead | 2 | 5 hours | 10 |
| Total variable manufacturing cost |  |  | $41 |

## THE SELLING AND ADMINISTRATIVE EXPENSE BUDGET

The selling and administrative expense budget lists the operating expenses involved in selling the products and in managing the business. In order to complete the budgeted income statement in contribution format, variable selling and administrative expense per unit must be computed.

### Example 7

**THE NORTON COMPANY**
**Selling and Administrative Expense Budget**
**For the Year Ending December 31, 19B**

|  | Quarter | | | | |
|---|---|---|---|---|---|
|  | 1 | 2 | 3 | 4 | Total |
| Expected sales in units | 800 | 700 | 900 | 800 | 3,200 |
| Variable selling and admin. exp. per unit* | × $4 | × $4 | × $4 | × $4 | × $4 |
| Budgeted variable expense | $3,200 | $2,800 | $3,600 | $3,200 | $12,800 |
| Fixed selling and administrative expenses: | | | | | |
| Advertising | 1,100 | 1,100 | 1,100 | 1,100 | 4,400 |
| Insurance | 2,800 | | | | 2,800 |
| Office salaries | 8,500 | 8,500 | 8,500 | 8,500 | 34,000 |
| Rent | 350 | 350 | 350 | 350 | 1,400 |
| Taxes | | | 1,200 | | 1,200 |
| Total budgeted selling and administrative expenses† | $15,950 | $12,750 | $14,750 | $13,150 | $56,600 |

*Includes sales agents' commissions, shipping, and supplies.
†Paid for in the quarter incurred.

## THE CASH BUDGET

The cash budget is prepared for the purpose of cash planning and control. It presents the expected cash inflow and outflow for a designated time period. The cash budget helps management keep cash balances in reasonable relationship to its needs. It aids in avoiding unnecessary idle cash and possible cash shortages. The cash budget consists typically of four major sections:

1. The receipts section, which is the beginning cash balance, cash collections from customers, and other receipts
2. The disbursements section, which comprises all cash payments made by purpose
3. The cash surplus or deficit section, which simply shows the difference between the cash receipts section and the cash disbursements section
4. The financing section, which provides a detailed account of the borrowings and repayments expected during the budgeting period

## Example 8

To illustrate, we will make the following assumptions:
- The company desires to maintain a $5,000 minimum cash balance at the end of each quarter.
- All borrowing and repayment must be in multiples of $500 at an interest rate of 10 percent per annum. Interest is computed and paid as the principal is repaid. Borrowing takes place at the beginning of each quarter and repayment at the end of each quarter.

**THE NORTON COMPANY**
**Cash Budget**
**For the Year Ending December 31, 19B**

|  | Example | Quarter 1 | 2 | 3 | 4 | Total |
|---|---|---|---|---|---|---|
| Cash balance, beginning | Given | 10,000 | 9,401 | 5,461 | 9,106 | 10,000 |
| Add: Receipts: | | | | | | |
| Collection from customers | 1 | 54,300 | 57,120 | 66,080 | 64,960 | 242,460 |
| Total cash available | | 64,300 | 66,521 | 71,541 | 74,066 | 252,460 |
| Less: Disbursements: | | | | | | |
| Direct materials | 3 | 4,549 | 4,560 | 4,860 | 5,113 | 19,082 |
| Direct labor | 4 | 19,750 | 18,000 | 22,250 | 20,500 | 80,500 |
| Factory overhead | 5 | 10,650 | 9,950 | 11,650 | 10,950 | 43,200 |
| Selling and Admin. | 7 | 15,950 | 12,750 | 14,750 | 13,150 | 56,600 |
| Machinery purchase | Given | — | 24,300 | — | — | 24,300 |
| Income tax | Given | 4,000 | — | — | — | 4,000 |
| Total disbursements | | 54,899 | 69,560 | 53,510 | 49,713 | 227,682 |

| | Example | 1 | 2 | 3 | 4 | Total |
|---|---|---|---|---|---|---|
| | | | | *Quarter* | | |
| Cash surplus (deficit) | | 9,401 | (3,039) | 18,031 | 24,353 | 24,778 |
| Financing: | | | | | | |
| Borrowing | | — | 8,500 | — | — | 8,500 |
| Repayment | | — | — | (8,500) | — | (8,500) |
| Interest | | — | — | (425) | | (425) |
| Total financing | | — | 8,500 | (8,925) | — | (425) |
| Cash balance, ending | | 9,401 | 5,461 | 9,106 | 24,353 | 24,353 |

# THE BUDGETED INCOME STATEMENT

The budgeted income statement summarizes the various component projections of revenue and expenses for the budgeting period. However, for control purposes the budget can be divided into quarters or even months depending on the need.

## Example 9

**THE NORTON COMPANY**
**Budgeted Income Statement**
**For the Year Ending December 31, 19B**
*Example No.*

| | | | |
|---|---|---|---|
| Sales (3,200 units @ $80) | 1 | | $256,000 |
| Less: Variable expenses | | | |
| Variable cost of goods sold | | | |
| (3,200 units @ $41) | 6 | $131,200 | |
| Variable selling & admin | 7 | 12,800 | 144,000 |
| Contribution margin | | | 112,000 |
| Less: Fixed expenses | | | |
| Factory overhead | 5 | $ 24,000 | |
| Selling and Admin. | 7 | 43,800 | 67,800 |
| Net operating income | | | 44,200 |
| Less: Interest expense | 8 | | 425 |
| Net income before taxes | | | 43,775 |
| Less: Income taxes | 20% | | 8,755 |
| Net income | | | 35,020 |

## THE BUDGETED BALANCE SHEET

The budgeted balance sheet is developed by beginning with the balance sheet for the year just ended and adjusting it, using all the activities that are expected to take place during the budgeting period.

Some of the reasons why the budgeted balance sheet must be prepared are:

- It could disclose some unfavorable financial conditions that management might want to avoid.
- It serves as a final check on the mathematical accuracy of all the other schedules.
- It helps management perform a variety of ratio calculations.
- It highlights future resources and obligations.

### Example 10

To illustrate, we will use the following balance sheet for the year 19A.

**THE NORTON COMPANY**
**Balance Sheet**
**December 31, 19A**

| *Assets* | | *Liabilities and STK Equity* | |
|---|---|---|---|
| Current Assets: | | Current Liabilities: | |
| Cash | 10,000 | Accounts Payable | 2,200 |
| A/R | 9,500 | Income Tax Payable | 4,000 |
| Material Inv. | 474 | Total Cur. Liab. | 6,200 |
| Finished Gd Inv. | 3,280 | | |
| Total Cur. Assets | 23,254 | | |
| Fixed Assets: | | Stockholders' Equity: | |
| Land | 50,000 | Common Stock, No-Par | 70,000 |
| Build and Eqpt | 100,000 | Retained Earnings | 37,054 |
| Accumtd Depr | (60,000) | | |
| | 90,000 | | |
| Total Assets | 113,254 | Total Liab and Stk Eq | 113,254 |

### THE NORTON COMPANY
### Budgeted Balance Sheet
### December 31, 19B

| *Assets* | | *Liabilities and Stk Equity* | |
| --- | --- | --- | --- |
| Current Assets: | | Current Liabilities: | |
|     Cash | 24,353 (a) |     Accounts Payable | 2,464 (h) |
|     Accounts Rec | 23,040 (b) |     Income Tax Payable | 8,755 (i) |
|     Material Inv | 500 (c) |     Total Cur. Liab. | 11,219 |
|     Finished Gd Inv | 4,100 (d) | | |
| Total Cur. Assets | $51,993 | | |
| Fixed Assets: | | Stockholders' Equity: | |
|     Land | 50,000 (e) |     Common Stock, No-Par | 70,000 (j) |
|     Build and Eqpt | 124,300 (f) |     Retained Earnings | 72,074 (k) |
|     Accumtd Depr | (73,000)(g) | | |
| | 101,300 | | |
| Total Assets | 153,293 | Total Liab and Stk Eq | 153,293 |

Computations:

(a) From Example 8 (cash budget).

(b) $9,500 + $256,000 sales − $242,460 receipts = $23,040.

(c) and (d) From Example 6 (ending inventory budget).

(e) No change.

(f) $100,000 + $24,300 (from Example 8) = $124,300.

(g) $60,000 + $13,000 (from Example 5) = $73,000.

(h) $2,200 + $19,346 − $19,082 = $2,464 (all accounts payable relate to material purchases), or 50% of 4th quarter purchase = 50% ($4,928) = 2,464.

(i) From Example 9 (budgeted income statement).

(j) No change.

(k) $37,054 + $35,020 net income = $72,074.

## SOME FINANCIAL CALCULATIONS

To see what kind of financial condition the Norton Company is expected to be in for the budgeting year, a sample of financial ratio calculations are in order: (Assume 19×A after-tax net income was $15,000).

| | 19×A | 19×B |
| --- | --- | --- |
| Current ratio | | |
|     (Current assets/ | $23,254/$6,200 | $51,993/$11,219 |
|     current liabilities) | =3.75 | =4.63 |
| Return on total assets | | |
|     (Net income after taxes/ | $15,000/$113,254 | $35,020/$153,293 |
|     total assets) | =13.24% | =22.85% |

Sample calculations indicate that the Norton Company is expected to have better liquidity as measured by the current ratio. Overall performance will be improved as measured by return on total assets. This could be an indication that the contemplated plan may work out well.

## USING AN ELECTRONIC SPREADSHEET TO DEVELOP A BUDGET PLAN

Examples 1 to 10 showed a detailed procedure for formulating a master budget. In practice, a common, short cut uses computer technology. With a spreadsheet program, managers will be able to develop a master budget and evaluate various what-if scenarios.

## CONCLUSION

Forecasting is an essential element of planning and budgeting. Forecasts of future sales and their related expenses provide managers with information needed to plan other activities of the business.

This chapter has emphasized budgets. The process involves developing a sales forecast and, based on its magnitude, generating those budgets needed by a specific firm. Once developed, the budgeting system provides nonfinancial management with a means of controlling their activities and of monitoring actual performance and comparing it to budget goals.

Budgeting can be done easily with the aid of electronic spreadsheet software and there are many specialized application programs.

# Chapter 7

# COST BEHAVIOR:
## *Emphasis on Flexible Budgets*

Not all costs behave in the same way. Certain costs vary in proportion to changes in volume or activity, such as labor hours and machine hours. Other costs do not change, even though volume changes. An understanding of cost behavior is helpful to managers as follows:

1. Flexible budgeting
2. Break-even and contribution margin analysis
3. Appraisal of divisional performance
4. Short-term choice decisions

## A LOOK AT COSTS BY BEHAVIOR

Depending on how a cost will react or respond to changes in the level of activity, costs may be viewed as variable, fixed, or mixed (semi-variable). This classification is made within a specified range of activity, called the relevant range. The relevant range is the volume zone within which the behavior of variable costs, fixed costs, and selling prices can be predicted with reasonable accuracy.

VARIABLE COSTS. Variable costs vary in total with changes in volume or level of activity. Examples of variable costs include the costs of direct materials, direct labor, and sales commissions. The following factory overhead items fall into the variable cost category:

**Variable Factory Overhead**

| | |
|---|---|
| Supplies | Receiving costs |
| Fuel and power | Overtime premium |
| Spoilage and defective work | |

FIXED COSTS. Fixed costs do not change in total regardless of the volume or level of activity. Examples include advertising expense, salaries, and depreciation. The following factory overhead items fall in the fixed cost category:

**Fixed Factory Overhead**

| | |
|---|---|
| Property taxes | Rent on factory building |
| Depreciation | Indirect labor |
| Insurance | Patent amortization |

MIXED (SEMI-VARIABLE) COSTS. Mixed costs contain both a fixed element and a variable one. Salespersons' compensation including salary and commission is an example. The following factory overhead items may be considered mixed costs:

**Mixed Factory Overhead**

| | |
|---|---|
| Supervision | Maintenance and repairs |
| Inspection | Compensation insurance |
| Service department costs | Employer's payroll taxes |
| Utilities | Rental of delivery truck |
| Fringe benefits | |

Note that factory overhead, taken as a whole, would be a perfect example of mixed costs. Figure 7.1 displays how each of these three types of costs varies with changes in volume.

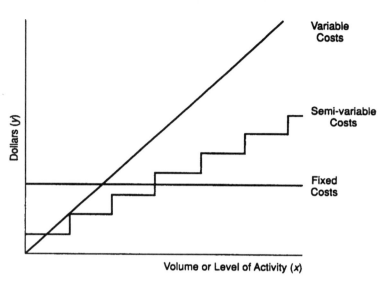

Figure 7.1
COST BEHAVIOR PATTERNS

## ANALYSIS OF MIXED (SEMI-VARIABLE) COSTS

For forecasting, planning, and budgeting, mixed costs need to be separated into their variable and fixed components. Since the mixed costs contain both fixed and variable elements, the analysis takes the following mathematical form, which is called a cost-volume formula (or flexible budget formula):

$Y = a + bX$

where $Y$ = the mixed cost to be broken up.
$X$ = any given measure of activity such as direct labor hours, machine hours, or production volume.
$a$ = the fixed cost component.
$b$ = the variable rate per unit of $X$.

Separating the mixed cost into its fixed and variable components is the same thing as estimating the parameter values a and b in the $Y = a + bX$

formula. There are several methods available to be used for this purpose, including the high-low method and regression analysis. They are discussed below.

## THE HIGH–LOW METHOD

The high–low method, as the name indicates, uses two extreme data points to determine the values of a (the fixed cost portion) and b (the variable rate) in the equation $Y = a + bX$. The extreme data points are the highest representative X-Y pair and the lowest representative X-Y pair. The activity level X, rather than the mixed cost item y, governs their selection.

The high–low method is explained, step by step, as follows:

*Step 1*:  Select the highest pair and the lowest pair

*Step 2*:  Compute the variable rate, b, using the formula:

$$\text{Variable rate} = \frac{\text{Difference in cost y}}{\text{Difference in activity x}}$$

*Step 3*:  Compute the fixed cost portion as:

Fixed cost portion = Total mixed cost − Variable cost

### Example 1

Flexible Manufacturing Company decided to relate total factory overhead costs to direct labor hours (DLH) to develop a cost function in the form of $Y = a + b X$. Twelve monthly observations are collected. They are given in Table 7.1.

The high-low method is simple and easy to use. It has the disadvantage, however, of using two extreme data points, which may not be representative of normal conditions. The method may yield unreliable estimates of a and b in our formula. In this example, the negative value for a is questionable. In such a case, it would be wise to drop them and choose two other points that are more representative of normal situations. Be sure to check the scatter diagram for this possibility.

## Table 7.1

| Month | Direct Labor Hours (X) | Factory Overhead (Y) |
|-------|------------------------|----------------------|
| January | 2510 | 82 |
| February | 2479 | 101 |
| March | 2080 | 88 |
| April | 2750 | 99 |
| May | 2330 | 93 |
| June | 2690 | 103 |
| July | 2480 | 77 |
| August | 2610 | 102 |
| September | 2910 | 122 |
| October | 2730 | 107 |
| November | 2760 | 101 |
| December | 2109 | 65 |

The high-low points selected from the monthly observations are

|  | X | Y |
|--|---|---|
| High | 122 hours | $2920 (September pair) |
| Low | 88 | 2080 (March pair) |
| Difference | 34 hours | $840 |

Thus

$$\text{Variable rate b} = \frac{\text{Difference in y}}{\text{Difference in x}} = \frac{\$840}{34 \text{ hours}} = \$24.71 \text{ per DLH}$$

The fixed cost portion is computed as

|  | High | Low |
|--|------|-----|
| Factory overhead (Y) | $2920 | $2080 |
| Variable expense ($24.71 per DLH) | ($3014) | ($2174) |
|  | ($94) | ($94) |

Therefore, the cost formula for factory overhead is

− $94 fixed plus $24.71 per DLH.

## SIMPLE REGRESSION

One popular method for estimating the cost function is regression analysis. Simple regression involves one independent variable, e.g., DLH or machine hours alone (to be discussed in detail in Chapter 16), whereas multiple regression involves two or more activity variables.

Unlike the high–low method, in an effort to estimate the variable rate and the fixed cost portion, the regression method includes all the observed data and attempts to find a line of best fit.

From the regression output (Figure 7.2), the cost–volume formula is

$Y' = 1330 + 12.58 \, X$

with $R^2 = 69.38\%$

or \$1330 fixed, plus \$12.58 per DLH

*Note:* The formula is also called the flexible budget formula, since it is used to generate budgeted (estimated) costs for various levels of activity.

**Figure 7.2**
**SIMPLE REGRESSION (OH VS. DLH)**

*Simple Regression:* $Y = b_o + b_1 X_1$

Regression Output:

| | | |
|---|---|---|
| Constant | | 1329.908 |
| Std Err of Y Est | | 150.7838 |
| R Squared | | 0.693767 |
| No. of Observations | | 12 |
| Degrees of Freedom | | 10 |
| X Coefficient(s) | 12.57958 | |
| Std Err of Coef. | 2.642924 | |
| T-value | 4.759720 | |
| $Y' = 1330 + 12.58 \, X$ with $R^2 = 69.38\%$ | | |

### Example 2

Assume 95 direct labor hours are to be expended next year. The projected factory overhead for next year would be computed as follows:

$$Y' = \$1330 + 12.58 \,(95)$$
$$= \$1330 + \$1195 = \$2525$$

## FLEXIBLE BUDGETS AND PERFORMANCE REPORTS

A flexible budget is useful in cost control. It is geared toward a range of activity rather than a single level of activity. It is dynamic rather than static. By using the cost–volume formula (or flexible budget formula), a series of budgets can be easily developed for various levels of activity.

The static (fixed) budget is geared for only one level of activity and has problems in cost control. Flexible budgeting distinguishes between fixed and variable costs, thus allowing for a budget which can be automatically adjusted (via changes in variable cost totals) to the particular level of activity actually attained. So, variances between actual costs and budgeted costs are adjusted for volume ups and downs before differences due to price and quantity factors are computed.

The primary use of the flexible budget is an accurate measurement of performance by comparing actual costs for a given output with the budgeted costs for the same level of output.

### Example 3

To illustrate the difference between the static budget and the flexible budget, assume that the Assembly Department of Suma Industries, Inc. is budgeted to produce 6,000 units during June. Assume further that the company was able to produce only 5,800 units. The budget for direct labor and variable overhead costs is as follows:

**SUMA INDUSTRIES, INC.**
**The Direct Labor and Variable Overhead Budget**
**Assembly Department**
**for the Month of June**

| | |
|---|---|
| Budgeted production | 6,000 units |
| Actual production | 5,800 units |
| Direct labor | $39,000 |
| Variable overhead costs: | |
| Indirect labor | 6,000 |
| Supplies | 900 |
| Repairs | 300 |
| | $46,200 |

If a static budget approach is used the performance report will appear as follows:

**SUMA INDUSTRIES, INC.**
**The Direct Labor and Variable Overhead Budget**
**Assembly Department**
**for the Month of June**

| | *Budget* | *Actual* | *Variance (U or F)** |
|---|---|---|---|
| Production in units | 6,000 | 5,800 | 200U |
| Direct labor | $39,000 | $38,500 | $500F |
| Variable overhead costs: | | | |
| Indirect labor | 6,000 | 5,950 | 50F |
| Supplies | 900 | 870 | 30F |
| Repairs | 300 | 295 | 5F |
| | $46,200 | $45,615 | $585F |

*A variance represents the deviation of actual cost from the standard or budgeted cost. U—unfavorable, F—favorable.

These cost variances are useless, in that they are comparing oranges with apples. The problem is that the budget costs are based on an activity level of 6,000 units, whereas the actual costs were incurred at an activity level of 5,800 units. From a control standpoint, it makes no sense to compare costs at one activity level with costs at a different activity level. Such comparisons would make a production manager look good as long as the actual production is less than the budgeted production.

Using the cost-volume formula and generating the budget based on the 5,800 actual units gives the following performance report:

**SUMA INDUSTRIES, INC.**
**Performance Report**
**Assembly Department**
**for the Month of June**

Budgeted production          6,000 units
Actual production            5,800 units

|                      | Cost-volume formula | Budget 5,800 units | Actual 5,800 units | Variance (U or F) |
|----------------------|---------------------|--------------------|--------------------|-------------------|
| Direct labor         | $6.50 per unit      | $37,700            | $38,500            | $800U             |
| Variable overhead:   |                     |                    |                    |                   |
|   Indirect labor | 1.00          | 5,800              | 5,950              | 150U              |
|   Supplies | .15                 | 870                | 870                | 0                 |
|   Repairs  | .05                 | 290                | 295                | 5U                |
|                      | $7.70               | $44,660            | $45,615            | $955U             |

Notice that all cost variances are unfavorable (U), as compared to the favorable cost variances on the performance report based on the static budget approach.

## CONCLUSION

Nonfinancial managers must investigate cost behavior for break-even and cost–volume–profit analysis, for appraisal of managerial performance, and for flexible budgeting. We have looked at three types of cost behavior—variable, fixed, and mixed. We illustrated two popular methods of separating mixed costs in their variable and fixed components: the high–low method and regression analysis. Emphasis was placed on the use of simple regression. The idea of flexible budgeting was emphasized in an attempt to correctly measure the efficiency of the cost center (e.g., assembly department).

# Chapter 8

# EVALUATING PERFORMANCE:

## *The Use of Variance Analysis*

A standard cost is a predetermined cost of manufacturing, servicing, or marketing an item during a given future period. It is based on current and projected future conditions. The norm is also dependent upon quantitative and qualitative measurements. Standards may be based on engineering studies looking at time and motion. The formulated standard must be accurate and useful for control purposes.

Standards are set at the beginning of the period. They may be in physical and dollar terms. Standards assist in the measurement of both effectiveness and efficiency. Examples are sales quotas, standard costs (e.g. material price, wage rate), and standard volume. Variances are not independent, so a favorable variance in one responsibility area may result in an unfavorable one in other segments of the business.

Variance analysis compares standard to actual performance. It could be done by division, department, program, product, territory, or any other responsibility unit. When more than one department is used in a production process, individual standards should be developed for each department in order to assign accountability to department managers. Variances may be as detailed as necessary, considering the cost-benefit relationship. Evaluation of variances may be done yearly, quarterly, monthly, daily, or hourly, depending on the importance of identifying a problem quickly. Since you do not know actual figures (e.g., hours spent) until the end of the period, variances can be determined only at this time. A material variance requires highlighting the person responsible and taking corrective action. Insignificant variances need not be looked into further unless they recur repeatedly and/or reflect potential difficulty. Generally, a variance should be investigated when the inquiry is anticipated to result in corrective action that will reduce costs by an amount exceeding the cost of the inquiry.

When the production cycle is long, variances that are computed at the time of product completion may be too late for prompt corrective action to be taken. In such a case, inspection may be undertaken at key points during the processing stage. This allows for spoilage, labor inefficiency, and other costs associated with problems to be recognized before product completion.

One measure to materiality is to divide the variance by the standard cost. A variance of less than 5% may be deemed immaterial. A 10% variation may be more acceptable to a company using tight standards compared to a 5% variation to a company employing loose standards. In some cases, materiality is looked at in terms of dollar amount or volume level. For example, you may set a policy looking into any variance that exceeds $10,000 or 20,000 units, whichever is less. Guidelines for materiality also depend upon the nature of the particular element as it affects performance and decision making. For example, where the item is critical to the future functioning of the business (e.g., critical part, promotion, repairs), limits for materiality should be such that reporting is encouraged. Further, statistical techniques can be used to ascertain the significance of cost and revenue variances.

There should be an acceptable range of tolerance established for managers (e.g., percent). Even if a variance never exceeds a minimum allowable percentage or minimum dollar amount, the manager may want to bring it to upper management's attention if the variance is consistently close to the prescribed limit each year. This may indicate the standard is out-of-date and proper adjustment to current levels is mandated to improve overall profit planning. It could also indicate lax cost control requiring a check by the operations.

Because of the critical nature of costs, such as advertising and maintenance, materiality guidelines are more stringent.

Often, the reasons for the variance are out-of-date standards or a poor budgetary process and not actual performance.

By questioning the variances and trying to find answers, the manager can make the operation more efficient and less costly. It must be understood, however, that quality should be maintained.

If a variance is out of the manager's control, follow-up action by him is not possible. For example, utility rates are not controllable internally.

Standards may change at different operational volume levels. Further, standards should be periodically appraised and when they no longer realistically reflect conditions they should be modified. Standards may not be realistic any longer because of internal events (e.g., product design) or external conditions such as management and competitive changes. For instance, standards should be revised when prices, material specifications, product designs, labor rates, labor efficiency, and production methods change to such a degree that present standards no longer provide a useful measure of performance. Changes in the methods or channels of distribution, or basic organizational or functional changes, would require changes in selling and administrative activities.

Significant favorable variances should also be investigated and should be further taken advantage of. Those responsible for good performance should be rewarded.

Regression analysis may provide reliable association between costs and revenue.

Variances are interrelated and hence the net effect has to be examined. For example, a favorable price variance may arise when lower quality materials are bought at a cheaper price but the quantity variance will be unfavorable because of more production time to manufacture the goods due to poor material quality.

In the case of automated manufacturing facilities, standard cost information can be integrated with the computer that directs operations. Variances can then be identified and reported by the computer system and necessary adjustments made as the operation proceeds.

In appraising variances, consideration should be given to information that may have been, for whatever reason, omitted from the reports. Have there been changes in the production processes which have not been reflected in the reports? Have new product lines increased set-up times that necessitate changes in the standards?

## USEFULNESS OF VARIANCE ANALYSIS

Standards and variance analyses resulting from them are essential in financial analysis and decision making.

### ADVANTAGES OF STANDARDS AND VARIANCES

- Aid in inventory costing
- Assist in decision-making
- Sell price formulation based on what costs should be
- Aid in coordinating by having all departments focus on common goals
- Set and evaluate divisional objectives
- Allow cost control and performance evaluation by comparing actual to budgeted figures. The objective of cost control is to produce an item at the lowest possible cost according to predetermined quality standards
- Highlight problem areas through the "management by exception" principle
- Pinpoint responsibility for undesirable performance so that corrective action may be taken. Variances in product activity (cost, quality, quantity) are typically the production manager's responsibility. Variances in sales orders and market share are often the responsibility of the marketing manager. Variances in prices and methods of deliveries are the responsibility of purchasing personnel. Variances in profit usually relate to overall operations. Variances in return on investment relate to asset utilization.
- Act in motivating employees to accomplish predetermined goals
- Facilitate communication within the organization, such as between top management and supervisors
- Assist in planning by forecasting needs (e.g., cash requirements)
- Establish bid prices on contracts

Standard costing is not without some drawbacks, such as the possible biases in deriving standards and the dysfunctional effects of establishing improper norms and standards.

When a variance has multiple causes, each cause should be cited.

## STANDARD SETTING

Standards may be set by engineers, production managers, purchasing managers, and personnel administrators. Depending on the nature of the cost item, computerized models can be used to corroborate what the standard costs should be. Standards may be established through test runs or mathematical and technological analysis.

Standards are based on the particular situation being appraised. Some examples follow:

| Situation | Standard |
|---|---|
| Cost reduction | Tight |
| Pricing policy | Realistic |
| High-quality goods | Perfection |

Capacity may be expressed in units, weight, size, dollars, selling price, and direct labor hours. It may be expressed in different time periods (e.g., weekly, monthly, yearly).

### TYPES OF STANDARDS

- *Basic.* These are not changed from period to period and are used in the same way as an index number. They form the basis to which later period performance is compared. What is unrealistic about it is that no consideration is given to a change in the environment.

- *Maximum efficiency.* These are perfect standards assuming ideal, optimal conditions, allowing for no losses of any kind, even those considered unavoidable. They will always result in unfavorable variances. Realistically, certain inefficiencies will occur, such as materials will not always arrive at work stations on time and tools will break. Ideal standards can not be used in forecasting and planning because they do not provide for normal inefficiencies.

- *Currently attainable (practical).* These refer to the volume of output possible if a facility operated continuously, but after allowing for normal and unavoidable losses such as vacations, holidays, and repairs. Currently attainable standards are based on efficient activity. They are possible but difficult to achieve. Considered are normal occurrences such as anticipated machinery failure and normal materials shortage. Practical standards should be set high enough to motivate employees and low enough to permit normal interruptions. Besides pointing to abnormal deviations in costs, practical standards may be used in forecasting cash flows and in planning inventory. Attainable standards are typically used in practice.

- *Expected.* These are expected figures based on foreseeable operating conditions and costs. They come very close to actual figures.

Standards should be set at a realistic level. Those affected by the standards should participate in formalizing them so there will be internalization of goals. When reasonable standards exist employees typically become cost conscious and try to accomplish the best results at the least cost. If standards are too tight, they will discourage employee performance. If they are too loose, they will result in inefficient operations. If employees receive bonuses for exceeding normal standards, the standards may be even more effective as motivation tools.

A standard is not an absolute and precise figure. Realistically, a standard constitutes a range of possible acceptable results. Thus, variances can and do occur within a normal upper-lower limit. In determining tolerance limits, relative magnitudes are more important than absolute values. For instance, if the standard cost for an activity is $100,000, a plus or minus range of $4,000 may be tolerable.

Variance analysis is usually complicated by the problem of computing the number of equivalent units of production.

Variances may be controllable, partly controllable, or uncontrollable. It is not always easy to assign responsibility, even in the case of controllable variances. The extent to which a variance is controllable depends on the nature of the standard, the cost involved, and the particular factors causing the variance.

## PLANNING VARIANCE

The planning variance arises when expected industry or other environmental factors do not materialize. For example, at the beginning of the period, the sales projection may be based on reviewing supply and demand. However, because of actual conditions in the industry, the actual sales may be much less. This sales unit variance may then be deemed a planning error and not a performance problem. Industry sales are typically considered beyond manager control.

## SALES VARIANCES

Sales standards may be established to control and measure the effectiveness of the marketing operations as well as for other relevant purposes, such as stimulating sales, reallocating sales, resources, and providing incentive awards. The usual standard set for a salesperson, branch, or territory is a sales quota. While the sales quota is typically expressed in dollars, it may also be expressed in volume. Other types of standards that may be set to evaluate sales efforts are number of calls, order size, gross profit obtained, new customers obtained, and number of regular customers retained.

Sales variances are computed to gauge the performance of the marketing function.

### Example 1

Western Corporation's budgeted sales for 19X1 were

| | |
|---|---|
| Product A 10,000 units at $6.00 per unit | $60,000 |
| Product B 30,000 units at $8.00 per unit | 240,000 |
| Expected sales revenue | $300,000 |

Actual sales for the year were

| | |
|---|---|
| Product A 8,000 units at $6.20 per unit | $ 49,600 |
| Product B 33,000 units at $7.70 per unit | 254,100 |
| Actual sales revenue | $303,700 |

There is a favorable sales variance of $3,700, consisting of the sales price variance and the sales volume variance.

The sales price variance equals
(Actual Selling Price versus Budgeted Selling Price) ×
Actual Units Sold

| | |
|---|---|
| Product A ($6.20 versus $6.00 × 8,000) | $1,600 Favorable |
| Product B ($7.70 versus $8.00 × 33,000) | 9,900 Unfavorable |
| Sales price variance | $8,300 Unfavorable |

The sales volume variance equals
(Actual Quantity versus Budgeted Quantity) × Budgeted Selling Price

| | |
|---|---|
| Product A (8,000 versus 10,000 × $6.00) | $12,000 Unfavorable |
| Product B (33,000 versus 30,000 × $8.00) | 24,000 Favorable |
| Sales volume variance | $12,000 Favorable |

The sales price variance indicates if the product is being sold at a discount or premium. Sales price variances may be due to uncontrollable market conditions or managerial decisions.

The analysis of sales volume includes consideration of budgets, standards, sales plans, industry comparisons, and manufacturing costs. Note that high sales volume does not automatically mean high profits. There may be high costs associated with the products.

An unfavorable sales volume variance may arise from poor marketing or price cuts by competing companies. If the unfavorable volume variance is coupled with a favorable price variance, the marketing manager may have lost sales by raising prices.

The sales volume variance reflects the effect on the total budgeted contribution margin that is caused by changes in the total number of units sold. The variance can be caused by unpredictable product demand, lack of product demand, or from poor sales forecasting.

An unfavorable total sales variance may signal a problem with the marketing manager because he has control over sales, advertising, and often pricing. Another possible cause of the unfavorable sales situation may be a lack of quality control, substitution of poorer quality components due to deficient purchasing, or deficient product design emanating from poor engineering.

The sales variances (price and volume) are prepared only for the product sales report and the sales district report.

The marketing manager is responsible for sales variances and must explain any deviations to upper management.

An electronic worksheet can be used to compute sales variances (refer to the July, 1985 issue of LOTUS, pp. 46–48).

## COST VARIANCES

When a product is made or a service is performed, you have to determine these three measures:

- Actual cost equals actual price times actual quantity, where actual quantity equals actual quantity per unit of work times actual units of work produced
- Standard cost equals standard price times standard quantity, where

standard quantity equals standard quantity per unit of work times actual units of work produced

- Total (control) variance equals actual cost less standard cost
    Total (control) variance has the following elements:
- Price (rate, cost) variance:
    (Standard Price versus Actual Price) × Actual Quantity
- Quantity (usage, efficiency) variance:
    (Standard Quantity versus Actual Quantity) × Standard Price
        These are computed for both material and labor

A variance is unfavorable when actual cost is higher than standard cost.

## MATERIAL VARIANCES

Quantity and delivery standards have to be established before a standard price per unit can be determined. Material price standards are set by the purchasing manager because he has knowledge of price data and market conditions. The manager should increase the initial standard price per unit to a standard weighted-average price per unit to incorporate expected price increases for the period. The standard price should reflect the total cost of buying the material, which includes the basic price less discounts plus freight, receiving, and handling. The standard price must coincide with the specific quality material. In setting the material price standard, the price should be in accord with the firm's inventory policies regarding the most economical order size and/or frequency of ordering. It is further assumed that buying, shipping, and warehousing will occur on favorable terms. Special bargain prices are ignored unless they are readily available. The material price standard should include normal or unavoidable spoilage allocations.

You can use the material price variance to evaluate the activity of the purchasing department and to see the impact of raw material cost changes on profitability. A material price variance may be isolated at the time of purchase or usage.

The material quantity variance is the responsibility of the production supervisor. Material quantity standards should include not only the raw materials but also purchased parts, cartons, and packing materials which are visible in, or can be directly related to, the product. Material quantity standards are usually determined from material specifications prepared by engineers, based on product design and production flow. The standard quantity should be based on the most economical size and quality of product. It should be increased to take into account normal waste, rejections, and spoilage. The standard should consider prior experience for the same or similar operation. Test runs may be made under controlled conditions. Material standards may be aided by analyzing previous experiences using descriptive statistics and/or test runs under controlled conditions. Physical standards for materials are based on determination of kind and quality specifications, quantity specifications, and assembly specifications.

When many different types of raw materials are needed for a product, the types and standard quantities of each raw material is itemized on the *standard bill of materials*.

### Example 2

The standard cost of one unit of output (product or service) was $15: three pieces at $5 per piece. During the period, 8,000 units were made. Actual cost was $14 per unit; two pieces at $7 per piece.

*Total Material Variance*

| | |
|---|---:|
| Standard quantity times standard price (24,000 × $5) | $120,000 |
| Actual quantity times actual price (16,000 × $7) | 112,000 |
| | $ 8,000 F |

*Material Price Variance*

| | |
|---|---:|
| (Standard price versus actual price) times actual quantity ($5 versus $7 × 16,000) | $ 32,000 U |

*Material Quantity Variance*

| | |
|---|---:|
| (Standard quantity versus actual quantity) times standard price (24,000 versus 16,000 × $5) | $ 40,000 F |

When the amount of material purchased is different from the amount issued to production, a price variance is determined at the time of purchase. When material is issued, a quantity (usage) variance is determined. In this case, the variances are determined as follows:

*Material Price Variance*

(Actual price versus standard price) times actual quantity bought

*Material Quantity Variance*

(Actual quantity issued versus standard quantity issued) times standard price

## Example 3

Material purchased was 20,000 pounds. Material issued to production was 15,000 pounds. Material budgeted per unit is one pound. Budgeted price is $2.50 per pound while actual price is $3.00 per pound. Production was 10,000 units.

*Material Price Variance*

| | |
|---|---:|
| (Actual price versus standard price) times quantity purchased | |
| ($3.00 versus $2.50) × 20,000 | $10,000 U |

*Material Quantity Variance*

| | |
|---|---:|
| (Actual quantity issued versus standard quantity) × standard price | |
| (15,000 versus 10,000) × $2.50 | $12,500 U |

You cannot control material price variances when higher prices are due to inflation or shortage situations, or when rush orders are required by the customer, who will bear the ultimate cost increase.

If the material price variance is favorable, one would expect higher quality material being acquired. Thus, a favorable usage variance should be forthcoming. If it is not, there is an inconsistency. A favorable material price variance may occur from other causes, such as when actual price is less than expected because of excess supply of the raw material.

The controllable portion of a price variance should be segregated from the uncontrollable in management reports. Exhibit 8.1 presents a Daily Material Price Variance Report.

Exhibit 8.1

DETAILS OF MATERIAL PRICE VARIANCE

Date _____ _____ Prepared by _____ _____ Approved by _____

| Voucher No. | Item No. | Item Name | Vendor No. | Quantity Purchased | Standard Cost | | Actual Cost | | Variance | | Percent from Standard | Explanation |
|---|---|---|---|---|---|---|---|---|---|---|---|---|
| | | | | | Per Unit | Total | Per Unit | Total | Per Unit | Total | | |
| | | | | | | | | | | | | |

Generally, the material quantity variance is the responsibility of the production manager. However, the purchasing manager will be responsible for inferior goods to economize on cost.

The reason and responsible party for an unfavorable material variance follows:

**Reason**

Overstated price paid, failure to take discounts, improper specifications, insufficient quantities, use of a lower grade material purchased to economize on price, uneconomical size of purchase orders, failure to obtain an adequate supply of a needed variety, purchase at an irregular time, or sudden and unexpected purchase required.

**Responsible Party**

Purchasing Manager

Poor mix of materials, poorly trained workers, improperly adjusted machines, substitution of nonstandard materials, poor production scheduling, poor product design or production technique, lack of proper tools or machines, carelessness in not returning excess materials to storeroom, or unexpected volume changes

Production Manager

Failure to detect defective goods
Inefficient labor, poor supervision, or waste on the production line

Receiving Manager
Foreman

Inaccurate standard price
Excessive transportation charges or too small a quantity purchased

Budgeting
Traffic management

Insufficient quantity bought because of a lack of funds

Financial

To correct an unfavorable material price variance, you can increase selling price, substitute cheaper materials, change a production method or specification, or engage in a cost-reduction program.

An unfavorable price variance does not automatically mean the purchasing manager is not performing well. It may point to a need for new pricing, product, or buying decisions. For these purposes, price variances may be broken down by product, vendor class, or other appropriate distinction. When several types of raw materials are used, it might be better to break down the price variance by major category of material used (e.g., steel, paint).

*Tip*: You should examine the variability in raw material costs. Look at price instability in trade publications. Emphasize vertical integration to reduce the price and supply risk of raw materials.

To aid in identifying material usage variances, if additional material is required to complete the job, additional materials requisitions could be issued in a different color with a distinctive code number to show that the quantity of material is above standard. This approach brings attention to the excessive usage of materials while production is in process and allows for the early control of a developing problem. When material usage is recorded by flow meters, such as in chemical operations, usage variances can be identified on materials usage forms in a similar manner as excess labor hours identified on labor time tickets.

Purchasing managers should have the option to acquire cheaper raw materials or to combine available resources so that overall corporate costs are minimized. For instance, slightly inferior raw materials (i.e., lower grade of metals) may intentionally be purchased at a bargain price. The material price variance may thus be quite favorable. However, such raw material component may cause above average defective finished items and/or excessive productive labor hours, resulting in an unfavorable efficiency variance. The production manager may have permission to engage in this trade-off if it results in a significant net reduction in total manufacturing costs.

A standard cost system should not be rigid in the sense that an unfavorable variance is regarded as always being bad. The production manager should look to see if overall objectives have been accomplished. Since many interdependencies exist, one should look at the entire picture rather than at just the fact that a given variance is unfavorable.

When computing material price variances, it may be good to eliminate increasing costs due to inflation, which are not controllable by nonfinancial managers.

*Illustration of How Inflationary Cost Increases May Be Isolated from the Material Price Variance*

Assume the following data for Charles Company for 19X1:

| | |
|---|---|
| Standard price of material per foot | $3.00 |
| Actual price of material per foot | 3.80 |
| Actual material used | 10,000 ft. |

The inflation rate for the year is 16%

The direct material price variance can be broken down into the inflation aspect and the controllable element.

*Price variance due to inflation*

(Standard price versus Inflation adjusted price) × actual quantity
$3.00 versus $3.48 × 10,000 ft                                          $4,800

*Controllable price variance*

(Inflation adjusted price versus actual price) × actual quantity
$3.48 versus $3.80 × 10,000 ft                                          $3,200

*Proof—Material Price Variance*

(Standard price versus actual price) × actual quantity
$3.00 versus $3.80 × 10,000 ft                                          $8,000

It is important to have prompt reporting. Production managers should immediately be informed of variances so problems are identified and corrections made at the production level.

Exhibit 8.2 presents a daily material usage report. Exhibit 8.3 presents a monthly material variance report.

**Exhibit 8.2**
**DAILY MATERIAL USAGE REPORT**

**Cost Center**          **Unit**
**Material Type**        **Date**

|      |          | *Daily*             |             | *Month*  |                     | *Year*   |                     |
|------|----------|---------------------|-------------|----------|---------------------|----------|---------------------|
| Date | Variance | Variance Percent    | Explanation | Variance | Variance Percent    | Variance | Variance Percent    |
|      |          |                     |             |          |                     |          |                     |

**Exhibit 8.3**
**MONTHLY MATERIAL VARIANCE REPORT**

|            | Month    |         | Year to Date |         |
|------------|----------|---------|--------------|---------|
| Department | Variance | Percent | Variance     | Percent |
|            |          |         |              |         |

## LABOR VARIANCES

Standard labor rates may be computed, based on the current rates adjusted for future changes in such variables as:

- Union contracts
- Changes in operating conditions
- Changes in the mix of skilled versus unskilled labor
- The average experience of workers

The wage system affects the standard cost rates. The basic rates are (1) day or hourly, (2) straight piece rate, and (3) multiple piece rates or bonus systems. Wage incentive systems can be tied to a standard cost system once standards have been formulated.

While direct labor quantities may be obtained from engineering estimates, line supervisors can corroborate the estimates by observing and timing employees.

When salary rates are set by union contract, the labor rate variance will usually be minimal. For planning purposes, the rate standard should be the average rate expected to prevail during the planning period. **Note:** Labor rates for the same operation may vary due to seniority or union agreement.

Labor time standards should include only the elements controllable by the worker or work center. If the major purpose of a cost system is control, there should be a tight labor time standard. If costing or pricing is the major purpose of the cost system, looser labor standards are needed. Labor efficiency standards are typically estimated by engineers on the basis of an analysis of the production operation. The standard time may include allowances for normal breaks, personal needs, and machine downtime.

Labor variances are determined in a manner similar to that in which material variances are determined. Labor variances are isolated when labor is used for production.

### Example 4

The standard cost of labor is four hours times $9 per hour, or $36 per unit. During the period, 7,000 units were produced. The actual cost is six hours times $8 per hour, or $48 per unit.

*Total Labor Variance*

| | |
|---|---|
| Standard quantity times standard price (28,000 × $9) | $252,000 |
| Actual quantity times actual price (42,000 × $8) | 336,000 |
| | $ 84,000 U |

*Labor Price Variance*

| | |
|---|---|
| (Standard price versus actual price) times actual quantity | |
| ($9 versus $8 × 42,000) | $ 42,000 F |

*Labor Quantity Variance*

| | |
|---|---|
| (Standard quantity versus actual quantity) × standard price | |
| (28,000 versus 42,000 × $9) | $126,000 U |

Possible causes of *unfavorable* labor variances are:

- For a labor price (rate) variance:
- Increase in wages
- Poor scheduling of production, resulting in overtime work
- Use of workers commanding higher hourly rates than expected

For a labor efficiency variance:

- Poor supervision
- Use of unskilled workers paid lower rates or the wrong mixture of labor for a given job
- Use of poor quality machinery
- Improperly trained workers
- Poor quality of materials, requiring more labor time in processing
- Machine breakdowns
- Employee unrest
- Production delays due to power failure

Possible reasons for a labor price variance and the one responsible follow.

| *Reason* | *Responsible Party* |
|---|---|
| Use of overpaid or excessive number of workers | Production manager or union contract |
| Poor job descriptions or excessive wages | Personnel |
| Overtime and poor scheduling of production | Production Planning |

In the case of a shortage of skilled workers, it may be impossible to avoid an unfavorable labor price variance.

Price variances due to external factors are beyond the nonfinancial manager's control (e.g., a new minimum wage established by the government).

The cause and responsible party for an unfavorable labor efficiency variance follows:

| Cause | Responsible Entity |
|---|---|
| Poor quality workers or poor training | Personnel or Training |
| Inadequate supervision, inefficient flow of materials, wrong mixture of labor for a given job, inferior tools or idle time from production delays | Foreman |
| Employee unrest | Personnel or Foreman |
| Improper functioning of equipment | Maintenance |
| Insufficient material supply or poor quality | Purchasing |

To control against an unfavorable labor efficiency variance due to inadequate materials or sales orders, a daily direct labor report should be prepared.

An unfavorable labor efficiency variance may indicate that better machinery is needed, plant layout should be revised, improved operating methods are needed, and better employee training and development are required.

**Exhibit 8.4**
**DAILY LABOR MIX REPORT**

| Department Skill level | Actual Hours | Actual Hours in Standard Proportions | Output Variance |
|---|---|---|---|
| I | | | |
| II | | | |
| III | | | |

**Exhibit 8.5**
**LABOR PERFORMANCE REPORT**

**Department**

| | *Day* | | | *Date* | |
|---|---|---|---|---|---|
| Machine Operator | Achieved in Percent | Explanation | Month to Date in Percent | Year to Date in Percent |
| | | | | |

If a permanent change occurs in the amount of labor required or the labor wage rate for the various types of employee help, the production manager may wish to switch to more capital assets than labor.

Variances interrelate. A favorable labor efficiency variance coupled with an unfavorable labor rate variance may mean that higher skilled labor was employed than was necessary. However, the production manager would be justified in doing this if a rush order arose in which the selling price was going to be upwardly adjusted.

Exhibit 8.4 presents a daily labor mix report. Exhibit 8.5 presents a labor performance report. Looking at this report aids in evaluating labor effectiveness and coming up with a revision in labor policies. A graph of weekly labor efficiency is presented in Figure 8.1.

**Figure 8.1**
**LABOR EFFICIENCEY BY WEEK**

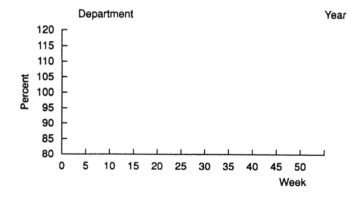

## OVERHEAD VARIANCES

Management is concerned with the tradeoff between fixed and variable costs. As the output level increases, the capital intensive business will be more efficient. The cost associated with a wrong decision is the variance between the total costs of operating the given plant and the total costs of operating the most efficient one based on the actual output level.

Overhead variances may be determined by department and by cost center. Fixed and variable overhead variances should be analyzed independently. In many firms, variances are expressed in both dollars and physical measures.

### VARIABLE OVERHEAD VARIANCES

The two variances associated with variable overhead are price (spending) and efficiency.

*Variable Overhead Price (Spending) Variance*

Actual variable overhead versus budget adjusted to actual hours (actual hours × standard variable overhead rate)

*Variable Overhead Efficiency Variance*

Budget adjusted to actual hours versus budget adjusted to standard hours (standard hours × standard variable overhead rate)

Variable overhead variance information is helpful in arriving at the output level and output mix decisions. The production manager is usually responsible for any variable overhead variance that might occur. It also assists in appraising decisions regarding variable inputs.

### Example 5

The standard hours are three hours per unit. The standard variable overhead rate is $12 per hour. Actual variable overhead is $13,000. There are 2,500 actual hours. Production is 1,000 units. The variable overhead variances are:

*Variable Overhead Price Variance*

| | |
|---|---|
| Actual variable overhead | $13,000 |
| Budget adjusted to actual hours (2,500 × $4) | 10,000 |
| Price Variance | $ 3,000 U |

*Variable Overhead Efficiency Variance*

| | |
|---|---|
| Budget adjusted to actual hours | $10,000 |
| Budget adjusted to standard hours (3,000 × $4) | 12,000 |
| Efficiency Variance | $ 2,000 F |

## FIXED OVERHEAD VARIANCES

Fixed overhead may be analyzed in terms of the budget (flexible-budget, spending) variance and volume (production volume) variances. The volume variance may be further broken down into the efficiency and pure volume variances.

*Fixed Overhead Budget Variance*

Actual fixed overhead versus budgeted fixed overhead (denominator or budget hours × standard fixed overhead rate).

**Note:** Budgeted fixed overhead may also be referred to as lump-sum amount.

*Fixed Overhead Volume Variance*

Budgeted fixed overhead versus standard overhead (standard hours × standard fixed overhead rate)

The breakdown of the volume variance follows:

*Fixed Overhead Efficiency Variance*

(Actual hours versus standard hours) × standard fixed overhead rate

*Fixed Overhead Pure Volume Variance*

(Actual hours versus budgeted hours) × standard fixed overhead rate

Fixed overhead variance data provide information about decision-making astuteness when buying some combination of fixed plant size variable production inputs. However, variances for fixed overhead are of questionable usefulness for control purposes, since these variances are usually beyond the control of the production manager.

The volume variance is a measure of the cost of deviating from denominator (budgeted) volume used to set the fixed overhead rate. When actual volume is less than budgeted volume, the volume variance will be unfavorable. In the opposite case, the volume variance is favorable because it is considered as a benefit of better than anticipated utilization of facilities.

## Example 6

Standard hours are two hours per unit. Standard fixed overhead rate is $20 per hour. Actual hours per unit are two. Total production is 9,500 units. Actual hours are 20,200. Actual fixed overhead is $420,000. The denominator activity is 10,000 units. The fixed overhead variances are:

*Fixed Overhead Budget Variance*

| | |
|---|---|
| Actual fixed overhead | $420,000 |
| Budgeted fixed overhead (10,000 × 2 = 20,000 × $20) | 400,000 |
| Budget Variance | $ 20,000 U |

*Volume Variance*

| | |
|---|---|
| Budgeted fixed overhead | $400,000 |
| Standard fixed overhead (9,500 × 2 = 19,000 × $20) | 380,000 |
| Volume Variance | $ 20,000 U |

The production volume variance of $20,000 is now broken down into the efficiency and pure volume variances.

*Fixed Overhead Efficiency Variance*

(Actual hours versus standard hours)
× standard fixed overhead rate
(20,200 versus 19,000) × $20      $ 24,000 U

*Fixed Overhead Pure Volume Variance*

(Actual hours versus budget hours)
× standard fixed overhead rate
(20,200 versus 20,000) × $20      $ 4,000 F

## VARIANCES FOR TOTAL OVERHEAD

One way, two-way, and three-way analysis may be used for total overhead.

*One-Way Method*

The total (control, net) variance is:

*Total Overhead Variance*

---

Actual overhead
Standard overhead (standard hours × standard overhead rate)

*Two-Way Method*

Under the two-variance method, the overhead variance comprises the controllable (budget, flexible budget, spending) and volume (capacity, idle capacity, activity, denominator) variances.

*Controllable Variance*

---

Actual overhead
Budget adjusted to standard hours
    Fixed overhead (denominator hours × standard fixed overhead rate)
    Variable overhead (standard hours × standard variable overhead rate)

*Volume (Production) Variance*

---

Standard overhead
Budget adjusted to standard hours

The controllable (budget) variance may indicate changes in the amount charged for overhead services or in the correlation between overhead items and the variable used to measure output. If such changes are permanent, output levels may have to be revised.

Managers use the overhead budget variance as a basis for determining the extent to which the cost centers were within their budgeted cost levels. Such variances are useful in formulating decisions regarding cost center operations.

The controllable variance is the responsibility of the foreman, since he influences actual overhead incurred. An unfavorable variance may be due to price increases, a lack of control over costs, and to waste.

The volume variance is the responsibility of production managers, since they are involved with plant utilization.

**Note:** A consistently unfavorable volume variance may be due to having purchased the incorrect size plant. An unfavorable volume variance may arise from controllable factors such as poor scheduling, lack of orders, shortages or defectiveness in raw materials, inadequate tooling, lack of employees, machine breakdowns, long operating times, and incompetent workers. Uncontrollable factors for the overhead volume variance are decrease in customer demand, excess plant capacity, and calendar fluctuations (e.g., differences in number of working days in a month).

Overhead capacity variances can bring to a production manager's attention the existence of slack resources. Idle capacity may imply long run operating planning deficiencies.

The volume of activity is often determined outside the factory, based on customer orders. If this is the case, volume variances may not be controllable by the department head or even by the plant manager. They should still be reported to plant managers to help in explaining the total overhead variance to higher management.

Responsibility for the factory overhead volume variance rests with those responsible for generating volume. In some cases, marketing managers, rather than manufacturing managers, bear this responsibility.

### Possible Reasons for a Recurring Unfavorable Overhead Volume Variance

- Buying the wrong size plant
- Improper scheduling
- Insufficient orders
- Shortages in material
- Machinery failure
- Long operating time
- Inadequately trained workers

When idle capacity exists, this may indicate long-term operating planning problems.

A deficiency of controllable overhead variance analysis is the failure to segregate the responsibility for increased costs due to inflation from those due to inefficient spending. This deficiency can be corrected through a revised method of overhead analysis, taking into account inflation [see A. Adelberg and R. Polimeni, "The Analysis of Factory Overhead Variances (Under Conditions of General and Specific Price-Level Changes)," *Cost and Management*, December 1987, pp. 28–31].

**Note:** A favorable variance may be causing an unfavorable one. For example, lower maintenance expenditures for equipment may lower the overhead budget variance, but lead to machinery breakdowns and cause an unfavorable volume variance.

*Three-Way Method*

The three-variance method involves further analysis of the two-variance method. The three-way approach consists of the spending, efficiency, and volume variances. **Note:** The volume variance is identical under the three-way and two-way approaches. The controllable variance under the two-way method is broken down into the spending and efficiency variances under the three-way method.

*Spending Variance*

Actual overhead
Budget adjusted to actual hours
    Fixed overhead (denominator hours × standard fixed overhead rate)
    Variable overhead (Actual hours × standard variable overhead rate)

*Efficiency Variance*

Budget adjusted to actual hours
Budget adjusted to standard hours

*Volume (Production) Variance*

Budget adjusted to standard hours
Standard overhead

The efficiency variance is the production manager's responsibility and arises from inefficiencies or efficiencies in the production process. The variance is unfavorable when actual hours exceed standard hours charged to production. Inefficiencies may arise from such factors as unskilled labor, modification of operations, deficient machinery, and inferior quality materials.

Spending and efficiency variances are the responsibility of the department supervisor. The volume variance is attributable to executive management since the decision as to the degree of plant utilization rests with them. Idle capacity may be due to the lack of a proper balance between production facilities and sales. It may also arise from a favorable selling price that recovers fixed overhead at an exceptionally low production level.

## Example 7

The standards for total overhead are:

Variable overhead      2 hrs. @ $ 6 = $12 per unit
Fixed overhead          2 hrs. @ $20 = $40 per unit
The actual figures are:
Production 9,500 units
Denominator activity 10,000 units
Variable overhead $115,000
Fixed overhead $420,000
Actual hours 20,200

Part 1: *One-Way Analysis*

*Control Variance*

| | |
|---|---:|
| Actual overhead ($115,000 + $420,000) | $535,000 |
| Standard overhead (9,500 × 2 = 19,000 × $26) | 494,000 |
| Control Variance | $ 41,000 U |

Part 2: *Two-Way Analysis*

*Controllable Variance*

| | | |
|---|---:|---:|
| Actual overhead | | $535,000 |
| Budget adjusted to standard hours | | |
| Fixed overhead (10,000 × 2 = 20,000 × $20) | $400,000 | |
| Variable overhead (19,000 × $6) | 114,000 | |
| | | 514,000 |
| Controllable Variance | | $ 21,000 U |

*Volume (Production) Variance*

| | |
|---|---:|
| Budget adjusted to standard hours | $514,000 |
| Standard overhead | 494,000 |
| Volume Variance | $ 20,000 U |

OR

| | |
|---|---:|
| Budgeted hours | 20,000 |
| Standard hours | 19,000 |
| Difference in hours | 1,000 |
| × Fixed overhead rate | × $20 |
| Volume Variance | $ 20,000 U |

Part 3: *Three-Way Analysis*

Spending Variance

| | | |
|---|---:|---:|
| Actual overhead | | $535,000 |
| Budget adjusted to actual hours | | |
| Fixed overhead (10,000 × 2 = 20,000 × $20) | $400,000 | |
| Variable overhead (20,200 × $6) | 121,200 | |
| | | 521,200 |
| Spending Variance | | $ 13,800 U |

*Efficiency Variance*

| | |
|---|---:|
| Budget adjusted to actual hours | $521,200 |
| Budget adjusted to standard hours | 514,000 |
| Efficiency Variance | $ 7,200 U |

OR

| | |
|---|---:|
| Actual hours | 20,200 |
| Standard hours | 19,000 |
| Difference in hours | 1,200 |
| × Standard variable overhead rate | × $6 |
| Efficiency Variance | $ 7,200 U |

*Volume Variance*

| | |
|---|---:|
| Budget adjusted to standard hours | $514,000 |
| Standard overhead | 494,000 |
| Volume Variance | $ 20,000 U |

A comprehensive illustration showing *all* the variances for material, labor, and overhead follows in Example 8:

## Example 8

The following standards are given:

|  |  | Per Unit |
|---|---|---:|
| Direct Material | 5 lbs. @ $ 4 per lb. | $ 20 |
| Direct Labor | 3 hrs. @ $12 per hr. | 36 |
| Variable overhead | 3 hrs. @ $7 per hr. | 21 |
| Fixed overhead | 3 hrs. @ $20 per hr. | 60 |
|  |  | $137 |

Actual data follow:

Production 9,800 units
Denominator (budget) activity 11,000 units
Purchases 50,000 lbs. @ $150,000
Direct material used 44,000 lbs.
Direct labor 22,000 hrs. @ $220,000
Variable overhead $125,000
Fixed overhead $450,000

Part 1: *Material*

*Material Price Variance*

(Actual price versus standard price) × actual quantity bought
($3 versus $4) × 50,000                                          $ 50,000 F

*Material Quantity Variance*

(Actual quantity issued versus standard quantity) × standard price
(44,000 versus 49,000) × $4                                      $ 20,000 F

Part 2: *Labor*

*Control Variance*

| Standard quantity × standard price (29,400 × $12) | $352,800 |
|---|---:|
| Actual quantity × actual price (22,000 × $10) | 220,000 |
| Control Variance | $132,800 F |

*Labor Price Variance*

(Actual price versus standard price) × actual quantity
($10 versus $12) × 22,000                                        $ 44,000 F

*Labor Quantity Variance*

(Actual quantity versus standard quantity) × standard price
(22,000 versus 29,400*) × $12                                    $ 88,800 F
*9,800 × 3 = 29,400

Part 3: *Variable Overhead*

*Variable Overhead Price Variance*

| | |
|---|---|
| Actual variable overhead | $125,000 |
| Budget adjusted to actual hours (22,000 × $7) | 154,000 |
| Price Variance | $ 29,000 F |

*Variable Overhead Efficiency Variance*

| | |
|---|---|
| Budget adjusted to actual hours | $154,000 |
| Budget adjusted to standard hours (9,800 × 3 = 29,400 × $7) | 205,800 |
| Efficiency Variance | $ 51,800 F |

Part 4: *Fixed Overhead*

*Fixed Overhead Budget Variance*

| | |
|---|---|
| Actual fixed overhead | $450,000 |
| Budgeted fixed overhead (11,000 × 3 = 33,000 × $20) | 660,000 |
| Budget Variance | $210,000 F |

*Fixed Overhead Volume Variance*

| | |
|---|---|
| Budgeted fixed overhead | $660,000 |
| Standard overhead (9,800 × 3 = 29,400 × $20) | 588,000 |
| Volume Variance | $ 72,000 U |

The fixed overhead volume variance is broken down into the fixed overhead efficiency variance and fixed overhead pure volume variance.

*Fixed Overhead Efficiency Variance*

(Actual hours versus standard hours) × standard fixed overhead rate
(22,000 versus 29,400) × $20                                    $148,000 F

*Fixed Overhead Pure Volume Variance*

(Actual hours versus budgeted hours) × standard fixed overhead rate
(22,000 versus 33,000) × $20                                    $220,000 U

Part 5: *One-Way Analysis*

*Total Overhead Variance*

| | |
|---|---:|
| Actual overhead | $575,000 |
| Standard overhead (29,400 × $27) | 793,800 |
| Total Overhead Variance | $218,800 F |

Part 6: *Two-Way Analysis*

*Controllable Variance*

| | | |
|---|---:|---:|
| Actual overhead | | $575,000 |
| Budget adjusted to standard hours | | |
|     Fixed overhead (11,000 × 3 = 33,000 × $20) | $660,000 | |
|     Variable overhead (9,800 × 3 = 29,400 × $7) | 205,800 | 865,800 |
| Controllable Variance | | $290,800 F |

*Volume Variance*

| | |
|---|---:|
| Budget adjusted to standard hours | $865,800 |
| Standard overhead | 793,800 |
| Volume Variance | 72,000 U |

Part 7: *Three-Way Analysis*

*Spending Variance*

| | | |
|---|---:|---:|
| Actual overhead | | $575,000 |
| Budget adjusted to actual hours | | |
|     Fixed overhead (11,000 × 3 = 33,000 × $20) | $660,000 | |
| Variable overhead (22,000 × $7) | 154,000 | 814,000 |
| Spending Variance | | $239,000 F |

*Efficiency Variance*

| | |
|---|---:|
| Budget adjusted to actual hours | $814,000 |
| Budget adjusted to standard hours | 865,800 |
| Efficiency Variance | $ 51,800 F |

*Volume Variance*

| | |
|---|---:|
| Budget adjusted to standard hours | $865,800 |
| Standard overhead | 793,800 |
| Volume Variance | $ 72,000 U |

## INTERRELATIONSHIP OF VARIANCES

With regard to variance analysis for all production costs (direct material, direct labor, and overhead), it is important to note that each variance does *not* represent a separate and distinct problem to be handled in isolation. All variances in one way or another are interdependent. For example, the labor rate variance may be favorable because lower paid workers are being used. This could lead to: (1) an unfavorable material usage variance because of a higher incidence of waste, (2) an unfavorable labor efficiency variance because it takes longer hours to make the equivalent number of products, (3) an unfavorable overhead efficiency variance because the substandard work causes more hours to be spent for a specified output, and (4) an unfavorable overhead volume variance arising from abnormally high machine breakdowns because of less skilled operators.

A tradeoff between variances may be a manager's objective. For example, a material price variance may be favorable because of a bargain purchase opportunity or because of a combination of available resources designed to save overall costs. However, the raw material acquired may be somewhat inferior in quality to that which is usually purchased. In processing, use of this material may lead to greater waste or more labor hours in producing a finished item that will satisfy product quality guidelines. The goal here may be to minimize total production costs through the tradeoff of a favorable price variance and an unfavorable quantity variance. The net effect of the variances, in this case, is what counts.

## MIX AND YIELD VARIANCES FOR MATERIAL AND LABOR

*Mix* refers to the relative proportion of various ingredients of input factors such as materials and labor. *Yield* is a measure of productivity.

### MATERIAL AND LABOR MIX VARIANCES

The material mix variance indicates the impact on material costs of the deviation from the standard mix. The labor mix variance measures the impact of changes in the labor mix on labor costs.

### Formulas

$$
\begin{array}{l}
\text{Material} \\
\text{Mix} \\
\text{Variance}
\end{array}
=
\left(
\begin{array}{ll}
\text{Actual Units} & \text{Actual Units} \\
\text{Used at} & -\ \text{Used at} \\
\text{Standard Mix} & \text{Actual Mix}
\end{array}
\right)
\begin{array}{l}
\text{Standard} \\
\times\ \text{Unit} \\
\text{Price}
\end{array}
$$

$$
\begin{array}{l}
\text{Labor} \\
\text{Mix} \\
\text{Variance}
\end{array}
=
\left(
\begin{array}{ll}
\text{Actual Hrs.} & \text{Actual Hrs.} \\
\text{Used at} & -\ \text{Used at} \\
\text{Standard Mix} & \text{Actual Mix}
\end{array}
\right)
\begin{array}{l}
\text{Standard} \\
\times\ \text{Hourly} \\
\text{Rate}
\end{array}
$$

## MIX AND YIELD VARIANCES

The material quantity variance is divided into a material mix variance and a material yield variance. The material mix variance measures the impact of the deviation from the standard mix on material costs, while the material yield variance reflects the impact on material costs of the deviation from the standard input material allowed for actual production. We compute the material mix variance by holding the total input units constant at their actual amount.

We compute the material yield variance by holding the mix constant at the standard amount. The computations for labor mix and yield variances are the same as those for materials. If there is no mix, the yield variance is the same as the quantity (or usage) variance.

### Formulas

$$
\begin{array}{l}
\text{Material} \\
\text{Yield} \\
\text{Variance}
\end{array}
=
\left(
\begin{array}{ll}
\text{Actual Units} & \text{Actual Units} \\
\text{Used at} & -\ \text{Output at} \\
\text{Standard Mix} & \text{Standard Mix}
\end{array}
\right)
\begin{array}{l}
\text{Standard} \\
\times\ \text{Unit} \\
\text{Price}
\end{array}
$$

$$
\begin{array}{l}
\text{Labor} \\
\text{Yield} \\
\text{Variance}
\end{array}
=
\left(
\begin{array}{ll}
\text{Actual Hrs.} & \text{Actual Output} \\
\text{Used at} & -\ \text{Hrs. at} \\
\text{Standard Mix} & \text{Standard Mix}
\end{array}
\right)
\begin{array}{l}
\text{Standard} \\
\times\ \text{Hourly} \\
\text{Rate}
\end{array}
$$

## PROBABLE CAUSES OF UNFAVORABLE MIX VARIANCES

(a) When capacity restraints force substitution
(b) Poor production scheduling
(c) Lack of certain types of labor
(d) Certain materials are in short supply

## PROBABLE CAUSES OF UNFAVORABLE YIELD VARIANCES

(a) The use of low quality materials and/or labor
(b) The existence of faulty equipment
(c) The use of improper production methods
(d) An improper or costly mix of materials and/or labor

### Example 9 (Mix Variances)

J Company produces a compound composed of Materials Alpha and Beta which is marketed in 20 lb. bags. Material Alpha can be substituted for Material Beta. Standard cost and mix data have been determined as follows:

|  | Unit Price | Standard Unit | Standard Mix Proportions |
|---|---|---|---|
| Material Alpha | $3 | 5 lbs. | 25% |
| Material Beta | 4 | 15 | 75 |
|  |  | 20 lbs. | 100% |

Processing each 20 lbs. of material requires 10 hrs. of labor. The company employs two types of labor, skilled and unskilled, working on two processes, assembly and finishing. The following standard labor cost has been set for a 20 lb. bag.

|  | Standard Hrs. | Standard Wage Rate | Total | Standard Mix Proportions |
|---|---|---|---|---|
| Unskilled | 4 hrs. | $2 | $ 8 | 40% |
| Skilled | 6 | 3 | 18 | 60 |
|  | 10 | 2.60 | 26 | 100% |

At standard cost, labor averages $2.60 per unit. During the month of December, 100 20-lb. bags were produced with the following labor costs:

|  | Actual Hrs. | Actual Rate | Actual Wages |
|---|---|---|---|
| Unskilled | 380 hrs. | $2.50 | $ 950 |
| Skilled | 600 | 3.25 | 1,950 |
|  | 980 |  | $2,900 |

Material records show:

| | Beginning Inventory | Purchase | Ending Inventory |
|---|---|---|---|
| Material Alpha | 100 lbs. | 800 @ $3.10 | 200 lbs. |
| Material Beta | 225 | 1,350 @ $3.90 | 175 |

We now want to determine the following variances from standard costs.

(a) Material purchase price
(b) Material mix
(c) Material quantity
(d) Labor rate
(e) Labor mix
(f) Labor efficiency

We will show how to compute these variances in a tabular form as follows:

(a) *Material Purchase Price Variance*

| | Material Price per Unit | | | Actual Quantity Purchased | Variance ($) |
|---|---|---|---|---|---|
| | Standard | Actual | Difference | | |
| Material Alpha | $3 | $3.10 | $.10 U | 800 lbs. | $ 80 U |
| Material Beta | 4 | 3.90 | .10 F | 1,350 | 135 F |
| | | | | | $ 55 F |

(b) *Material Mix Variance*

| | Units Which Should Have Been Used at Standard Mix* | Actual Units at Actual Mix** | Diff. | Standard Unit Price | Variance ($) |
|---|---|---|---|---|---|
| Material Alpha | 525 lbs. | 700 lbs. | 175 U | $3 | $525 U |
| Material Beta | 1,575 | 1,400 | 175 F | 4 | 700 F |
| | 2,100 | 2,100 | | | $175 F |

The material mix variance measures the impact on material costs of the deviation from the standard mix. Therefore, it is computed holding the total quantity used constant at its actual amount and allowing the material mix to vary between actual and standard. As shown above, due to a favorable change in mix, we ended up with a favorable material mix variance of $175.

---

*This is the standard mix proportions of 25% and 75% applied to the actual material units used of 2,100 lbs.

**Actual units used = Beginning inventory + purchases − Ending inventory.

Therefore,

Material Alpha: 700 lbs. = 100 + 800 − 200

Material Beta: 1,400 lbs. = 225 + 1,350 − 175

(c) *Material Quantity Variance*

| | Units Which Should Have Been Used at Standard Mix | Standard Units at Standard Mix | Diff. | Standard Unit Price | Variance ($) |
|---|---|---|---|---|---|
| Material Alpha | 525 lbs. | 500 lbs. | 25 U | $3 | $75 U |
| Material Beta | 1,575 | 1,500 | 75 U | 4 | 300 U |
| | 2,100 | 2,000 | | | $375 U |

The total material variance is the sum of the three variances:

| | |
|---|---|
| Purchase price variance | $ 55 F |
| Mix variance | 175 F |
| Quantity variance | 375 U |
| | $145 U |

The increase of $145 in material costs was due solely to an unfavorable quantity variance of 100 pounds of material Alpha and Beta. The unfavorable quantity variance, however, was compensated largely by favorable mix and price variances.

J Company must look for ways to cut down waste and spoilage.

The labor cost increase of $300 ($2,900—$2,600) is attributable to three causes:

1. An increase of $.50 per hour in the rate paid to skilled labor and $.25 per hour in the rate paid to unskilled labor

2. An unfavorable mix of skilled and unskilled labor

3. A favorable labor efficiency variance of 20 hours

Three labor variances are computed below.

(d) *Labor Rate Variance*

| | Labor Rate per Hr. | | | Actual Hrs. | Variance |
| | Standard | Actual | Diff. | Used | ($) |
|---|---|---|---|---|---|
| Unskilled | $2 | $2.50 | $.50 U | 380 hrs. | $190 U |
| Skilled | 3 | 3.25 | .25 U | 600 | 150 U |
| | | | | | $340 U |

(e) *Labor Mix Variance*

| | Actual Hrs. at Standard Mix | Actual Hrs. at Actual Mix | Diff. | Standard Rate | Variance ($) |
|---|---|---|---|---|---|
| Unskilled | 392 hrs. | 380 hrs. | 12 F | $2 | $24 F |
| Skilled | 588 | 600 | 12 U | 3 | 36 U |
| | 980 | 980 | | | $12 U |

*This is the standard proportions of 40% and 60% applied to the actual total labor hrs. used of 980.

(f) *Labor Efficiency Variance*

| | Actual Hrs. at Standard Mix | Standard Hrs. at Standard Mix | Diff. | Standard Rate | Variance ($) |
|---|---|---|---|---|---|
| Unskilled | 392 hrs. | 400 hrs. | 8 F | $2 | $16 F |
| Skilled | 588 | 600 | 12 F | 3 | 36 F |
| | 980 | 1,000 | | | $52 F |

The total labor variance is the sum of these three variances:

| | |
|---|---|
| Rate variance | $340 U |
| Mix variance | 12 U |
| Efficiency variance | 52 F |
| | $300 U |

which is proved to be:

*Total Labor Variance*

|  | Actual Hrs. Used | Actual Rate | Total Actual Cost | Standard Hrs. Allowed | Standard Rate | Total Standard Cost | Variance ($) |
|---|---|---|---|---|---|---|---|
| Unskilled | 380 hrs. | $2.50 | $ 950 | 400 | $2 | $ 800 | $150 U |
| Skilled | 600 | 3.25 | 1,950 | 600 | 3 | 1,800 | 150 U |
|  |  |  | $2,900 |  |  | $2,600 | $300 U |

The unfavorable labor variance, as evidenced by the cost increase of $300, may be due to:

1. Overtime necessary because of poor production scheduling resulting in a higher average labor cost per hour, and or
2. Unnecessary use of more expensive skilled labor.

J. Company should put more effort into better production scheduling.

### Example 10 (Yield Variances)

The Giffen Manufacturing Company uses a standard cost system for its production of a chemical product. This chemical is produced by mixing three major raw materials, A, B, and C. The company has the following standards.

```
 36 lbs. of Material A    @ $1.00  =  $36.00
 48 lbs. of Material B    @  2.00  =   96.00
 36 lbs. of Material C    @  1.75  =   63.00
120 lbs. of standard mix  @ $1.625 = $195.00
```

The company should produce 100 lbs. of finished product at a standard cost of $1.625 per lb. ($195.00/120 lbs.)

To convert 120 pounds of materials into 100 pounds of finished chemical requires 400 DLH at $3.50 per DLH, or $14.00 per pound. During the month of December, the company produced 4,250 pounds of output with direct labor of 15,250 hrs. @ $3.50.

|  | Materials Purchased During the month | Materials used During the month |
|---|---|---|
| Material A | 1,200 @ $1.10 | 1,160 lbs. |
| Material B | 1,800 @ 1.95 | 1,820 |
| Material C | 1,500 @ 1.80 | 1,480 |

The material *price variance is isolated at the time of purchase.* We want to compute the material purchase price, quantity, mix, and yield variances. We will show the computations of variances in a tabular form as follows:

(a) *Material Variances*

*Material Purchase Price Variance*

|  | Material Price per unit | | | Actual Quantity Purchased | Variance ($) |
|---|---|---|---|---|---|
|  | Standard | Actual | Diff. |  |  |
| Material A | $1.00 | $1.10 | $.10 U | 1,200 lbs. | $120 U |
| Material B | 2.00 | 1.95 | .05 F | 1,800 | 90 F |
| Material C | 1.75 | 1.80 | .05 U | 1,500 | 75 U |
|  |  |  |  |  | $105 U |

The material quantity variance computed below results from changes in the mix of materials as well as from changes in the total quantity of materials. The standard input allowed for actual production consists of 1,275 pounds of Material A, 1,700 pounds of Material B and 1,275 pounds of Material C, a total of 4,250 pounds. The actual input consisted of 1,160 pounds of Material A, 1,820 pounds of Material B and 1,480 pounds of Material C, a total of 4,460 pounds. To separate these two changes, the material quantity variance is subdivided into a material mix variance and a material yield variance, as shown below.

*Material Quantity Variance*

|  | Actual Units Used at Actual Mix | "Should have been" inputs based upon actual output | Diff. | Standard Unit Price | Variance ($) |
|---|---|---|---|---|---|
| Material A | 1,160 lbs. | 1,275 lbs. | 115 F | $1.00 | $115 F |
| Material B | 1,820 | 1,700 | 120 U | 2.00 | 240 U |
| Material C | 1,480 | 1,275 | 205 U | 1.75 | 358.75 U |
|  | 4,460 | 4,250 |  |  | $483.75 U |

The computation of the material mix variance and the material yield variance for the Giffen Manufacturing Company is given below.

*Material Mix Variance*

| | "Should have been" individual inputs based upon total actual throughput* | Actual Units Used at Actual Mix | Diff. | Standard Unit Price | Variance ($) |
|---|---|---|---|---|---|
| Material A | 1,338 lbs. | 1,160 lbs. | 178 F | $1.00 | $178  F |
| Material B | 1,784 | 1,820 | 36 U | 2.00 | 72  U |
| Material C | 1,338 | 1,480 | 142 U | 1.75 | 248.5 U |
| | 4,460 | 4,460 | | | $412.5 U |

*Material Yield Variance*

| | Expected Input Units at Standard Mix | "Should have been" inputs based upon actual output* | Diff. | Standard Unit Price | Variance ($) |
|---|---|---|---|---|---|
| Material A | 1,338 lbs. | 1,275 lbs. | 63 U | $1.00 | $ 63 U |
| Material B | 1,784 | 1,700 | 84 U | 2.00 | 168 U |
| Material C | 1,338 | 1,275 | 63 U | 1.75 | 110.25 U |
| | 4,460 | 4,250 | | | $341.25 U** |

*This is the standard mix proportion of 30%, 40%, and 30% applied to the actual throughput of 4,460 pounds or *output* of 4,250 pounds.

**The material yield variance of $341.25 U can be computed alternatively as follows.

*Actual input quantity at standard prices*

Material A 1,338 lbs. @  $1.00 = $1,338
Material B 1,784 lbs. @   2.00 =  3,568
Material C 1,338 lbs. @   1.75 =  2,341.5        $7,274.50

*Actual output quantity at standard price*

       4,250 lbs. @    1.625        $6,906.25

Hence, $7,247.5 − $6,906.25 = $341.25 U

The material mix and material yield variances are unfavorable, indicating that a shift was made to a more expensive (at standard) input mix and that an excessive quantity of material was used. Poor production scheduling requiring an unnecessarily excessive use of input materials and an undesirable mix of Materials A, B, and C was responsible for this result.

To remedy the situation, the company must ensure that:

(a) The material mix is adhered to in terms of the least cost combination without affecting product quality.

(b) The proper production methods are being implemented.

(c) Inefficiencies, waste, and spoilage are within the standard allowance.

(d) Quality materials, consistent with established standards, are being used.

Employees seldom complete their operations according to standard times. Two factors should be brought out in computing their variances if the analysis and computation will be used to fix responsibility:

1. The change in labor cost resulting from the efficiency of the workers, measured by a labor efficiency variance. (In finding the change, allowed hours are determined through the material input.)

2. The change in labor cost due to a difference in the yield, measured by a labor yield variance. (In computing the change, actual output is converted to allowed input hours.)

For the Giffen Manufacturing Company, more efficient workers resulted in a savings of 383.33 hours (15,250 hrs. − 14,866.67 hrs.). Priced at the standard rate per hour, this produced an unfavorable labor efficiency variance of $1,341.66 as shown below:

*Labor Efficiency Variance*

| | |
|---|---|
| Actual hrs. at standard rate | $53,375 |
| Actual hrs. at expected output | |
| (4,460 hrs. × 400/120 = 14,866.67 hrs @ $3.5) | 52,033.34 |
| | $ 1,341.66 U |

With a standard yield of 83 1/3% (=100/120), 4,250 pounds of finished material should have required 17,000 hours of direct labor (4,250 lbs. × 400 DLH/100). Comparing the hours allowed for the actual input, 14,866.67 hours with the hours allowed for actual output, 17,000 hours, we find a favorable labor yield variance of $7,466.66, as shown below.

*Labor Yield Variance*

| | |
|---|---|
| Actual hrs. at expected output | $52,033.34 |
| Actual output (4,250 lbs. × 400/100 = | |
| 17,000 hrs. @ $3.5 or 4,250 lbs. @ $14.00) | 59,500 |
| | $ 7,466.66 F |

The labor efficiency variance can be combined with the yield variance to give us the *traditional* labor efficiency variance, which turns out to be favorable as follows.

| | |
|---|---|
| Labor efficiency variance | $ 1,341.66 U |
| Labor yield variance | 7,466.66 F |
| | $ 6,125　F |

This division is necessary when there is a difference between the actual yield and standard yield, if responsibility is to be fixed. The production manager cannot be credited with a favorable efficiency variance of $6,125. Note, however, that a favorable yield variance, which is a factor most likely outside the control of the producing department, more than offsets the *unfavorable* labor efficiency variance of $1,341.66 for which the producing department should have been responsible.

## PROFIT VARIANCE ANALYSIS

Gross profit analysis is determining the causes for the change in gross profit. Any variances that have an impact upon gross profit are reported so corrective steps may be taken.

### CAUSES OF PROFIT VARIANCE:

- Changes in unit sales price and cost
- Changes in the volume of products sold
- Changes in sales mix

Analysis of the changes furnishes data needed to bring actual operations in line with budgeted expectations. Comparisons should be made between budgeted and actual operations for the current year or between actual operations for the previous year and those for the current year.

Changes in gross profit may be looked at in terms of the entire company or by product line.

In an effort to improve profitability, the change in character of sales or mix of sales is just as important as the increase in total volume. For example, if the total volume in the budget is constant, but a larger proportion of high-margin products is sold than was budgeted, then higher profits will result. For instance, in the furniture business, there is an increasing trend toward more expensive and durable pieces carrying a higher margin per unit, although volume may not be all that great. Computations and analysis of sales mix variances are a very important part of profit analysis. It provides an additional insight into (a) what caused the increase or decrease in profit over the previous year and (b) why the actual profit differed from the original expectation.

Gross profit (or contribution margin) is usually the joint responsibility of sales managers and production managers. The sales manager is responsible for the sales revenue component and the production manager is accountable for the cost-of-goods-sold component. However, it is the task of top management to ensure that the target profit is met. The sales manager must hold fast to prices, volume and mix. The production manager must control the costs of materials, labor and factory overhead, and quantities. The purchasing manager must purchase materials at budgeted prices. The personnel manager must employ the right people at the right wage rates. The internal audit manager must ensure that the budgetary figures for sales and costs are being adhered to by all departments which are, directly or indirectly, involved in contributing to making profit.

The computation of the production mix variance is very similar to that of the sales mix variance. While the sales mix variance is part of profit analysis, the production mix variance for materials and labor is an important part of cost variance analysis. We must realize, however, that the analysis of standard cost variances should be understood as part of what is broadly known as profit analysis. In industries where each cost element is substituted for each other and production is at or near full capacity, how we combine different types of materials and different classes of labor will affect the extent to which the costs are controlled and gross profit maximized. The production volume variance must be further analyzed to separate the effect on costs of a change in mix of the production inputs such as materials and labor.

The yield variances for materials, labor, and overhead are useful in controlling material consumption. In some cases, the newly found mix is accompanied by either a favorable or unfavorable yield of the finished product. Usually, the favorable mix variance may be offset by an unfavorable yield variance, or vice versa. It is the responsibility of the laboratory or the engineering manager to make sure that no apparent advantage created by one type of variance is canceled out by another.

Taken as a whole, the analysis of profit involves careful evaluation of sales variances and cost variances. Especially, the effect of changes in mix, volume, and yield on profits must be separated and analyzed. The analysis of these variances provide managers with added dimensions of responsibility since it provides additional insight into what caused the increase or decrease in profits or why the actual profit deviated from the target profit. Analyzing the change in gross profit via an effective responsibility system based on the control of costs and sales variances is a step toward maximization of profits.

We now discuss the computation of the profit variances.

Profit Variance Analysis for a Single Product:

(a) Sales price variance
= (Actual price − Budget or standard price) × Actual sales
(b) Cost price variance
= (Actual cost − Budget or standard cost) × Actual sales
(c) Sales volume variance
= (Actual sales − Budget or standard sales) × Budget or standard price
(d) Cost volume variance
= (Actual sales − Budget or standard sales) × Budget or standard
cost per unit

Profit Variance Analysis for Multiple Products:

The total volume variance in a single product situation is comprised of (a) sales mix variance and (b) sales quantity variance.

(a) Sales mix variance

$$= \left( \begin{array}{c} \text{Actual sales at budget} \\ \text{or standard mix} \end{array} - \begin{array}{c} \text{Budget or standard sales} \\ \text{at budget or standard mix} \end{array} \right) \times \begin{array}{c} \text{Budget or} \\ \text{standard CM} \\ \text{(or GM) per unit} \end{array}$$

CM = contribution margin and GM = gross margin.

(b) Sales quantity variance

$$= \begin{pmatrix} \text{Actual sales at budgeted} \\ \text{or standard mix} \end{pmatrix} - \begin{pmatrix} \text{Actual sales at budgeted} \\ \text{or standard mix} \end{pmatrix} \times \begin{array}{l} \text{Budgeted or} \\ \text{standard CM} \\ \text{(or GM) per unit} \end{array}$$

(c) Total volume variance
= Sales mix variance + sales quantity variance

$$\text{or} = \begin{pmatrix} \text{Actual sales} \\ \text{at actual mix} \end{pmatrix} - \begin{pmatrix} \text{Budgeted or standard sales} \\ \text{at budgeted or standard mix} \end{pmatrix} \times \begin{array}{l} \text{Budgeted or} \\ \text{standard CM} \\ \text{(or GM) per unit} \end{array}$$

The sales price variance and the cost price variance are calculated the same way as for a single product.

Frequently, a contribution margin approach is superior to the gross profit approach. That is because gross profit has as a deduction for fixed costs which may be beyond the control of the nonfinancial manager. A simple example follows:

| | Budget (00) omitted | | Actual (00) omitted | | Variance | |
|---|---|---|---|---|---|---|
| | Unit A | Unit B | Unit A | Unit B | Unit A | Unit B |
| Sales Price | $10 | $5 | $11 | $6 | $1 F | $1 U |
| Units | 10 | 8 | 10 | 8 | -0- | -0- |
| Variable Manufacturing Costs | $ 4 | $3 | $ 6 | $4 | $2 U | $1 U |
| Fixed Manufacturing Costs | $ 3 | $1 | $ 4 | $2 | $1 U | $1 U |
| Manufacturing Contribution Margin per Unit | $ 6 | $2 | $ 5 | $2 | $1 U | $-0- |
| Gross Profit per Unit | $ 3 | $1 | $ 1 | $0 | $2 U | $1 U |

Using the above data, an unfavorable manufacturing contribution margin variance of $10 for Unit A and $0 for Unit B is more meaningful than the

$20 and $8 unfavorable gross profit variance, if local managers had no control over fixed costs.

### Example 11 (Profit Variance Analysis)

The Lake Tahoe Ski Store sells two ski models, Model X and Model Y. For the years 19X1 and 19X2, the store realized a gross profit of $246,640 and only $211,650, respectively. The owner of the store was astounded, since the total sales volume in dollars and in units was higher for 19X2 than for 19X1, yet the gross profit actually declined. Given below are the store's unaudited operating results for 19X1 and 19X2. No fixed costs were included in the cost of goods sold per unit.

| | Model X | | | | Model Y | | | |
|---|---|---|---|---|---|---|---|---|
| Year | Selling Price | Cost of Goods Sold per Unit | Sales (in units) | Sales Revenue | Selling Price | Cost of Goods Sold per Unit | Sales (in units) | Sales Revenue |
| 1 | $150 | $110 | 2,800 | $420,000 | $172 | $121 | 2,640 | $454,080 |
| 2 | 160 | 125 | 2,650 | 424,000 | 176 | 135 | 2,900 | 510,400 |

We explain why the gross profit declined by $34,990. We include a detailed variance analysis of price changes and changes in volume for sales and cost. Also, we subdivide the total volume variance into changes in price and changes in quantity.

Sales price and sales volume variances measure the impact on the firm's CM (or GM) of changes in the unit selling price and sales volume. In computing these variances, all costs are held constant in order to stress changes in price and volume. Cost price and cost volume variances are computed in the same manner, holding price and volume constant. All these variances for the Lake Tahoe Ski Store are computed below.

*Sales Price Variance*

> Actual Sales for 19X2:
>> Model X 2,650 × $160 = $424,000
>> Model Y 2,900 ×   176 = 510,400                    $934,400

Actual 19X2 sales at 19X1 prices:

Model X 2,650 × $150 = $397,500
Model Y 2,900 ×  172 =  498,800                  896,300
                                                  $ 38,100 F

*Sales Volume Variance*

Actual 19X2 sales at 19X1 prices:                  $896,300

Actual 19X1 sales (at 19X1 prices):

Model X 2,800 × $150 = $420,000
Model Y 2,640 ×  172 =  454,080                   874,080
                                                  $ 22,220 F

*Cost Price Variance*

Actual cost of goods sold for 19X2:

Model X 2,650 × $125 = $331,250
Model Y 2,900 ×  135 =  391,500                   $722,750

Actual 19X2 sales at 19X1 costs:

Model X 2,650 × $110 = $291,500
Model Y 2,900 ×  121 =  350,900                   642,400
                                                  $ 80,350 U

*Cost Volume Variance*

Actual 19X2 sales at 19X1 costs:                  $642,400

Actual 19X1 sales (at 19X1 costs):

Model X 2,800 × $110 = $308,000
Model Y 2,640 ×  121 =  319,440                   627,440
                                                  $ 14,960 U

Total volume variance = sales volume variance − cost volume variance
= $22,250 F − $14,960 U = $7,260 F

The total volume variance is computed as the sum of a sales mix variance and a sales quantity variance as follows:

*Sales Mix Variance*

| | 19X2 Actual Sales at 19X1 Mix* | 19X2 Actual Sales at 19X2 Mix | Diff. | 19X1 Gross Profit per Unit | Variance ($) |
|---|---|---|---|---|---|
| Model X | 2,857 | 2,650 | 207 U | $40 | $ 8,280 U |
| Model Y | 2,693 | 2,900 | 207 F | 51 | 10,557 F |
| | 5,550 | 5,550 | | | $ 2,277 F |

*This is the 19X1 mix (used as standard or budget) proportions of 51.47% (or 1,800/5,440 = 51.47%) and 48.53% (or 2,640/5,440 = 48.53%) applied to the actual 19X2 sales figure of 5,550 units.

*Sales Quantity Variance*

| | 19X2 Actual Sales at 19X1 Mix* | 19X1 Actual Sales at 19X1 Mix | Diff. | 19X1 Gross Profit per Unit | Variance ($) |
|---|---|---|---|---|---|
| Model X | 2,857 | 2,800 | 57 F | $40 | $2,280 F |
| Model Y | 2,693 | 2,640 | 53 F | 51 | 2,703 F |
| | 5,550 | 5,440 | | | $4,983 F |

A favorable total volume variance is due to a favorable shift in the sales mix (that is, from Model X to Model Y) and also to a favorable increase in sales volume (by 110 units) which is shown as follows.

| | |
|---|---|
| Sales mix variance | $2,277 F |
| Sales quantity variance | 4,983 F |
| | $7,260 F |

However, there remains the decrease in gross profit. The decrease in gross profit of $34,990 can be explained as follows.

| | Gains | Losses |
|---|---|---|
| Gain due to increased sales price | $38,100 F | |
| Loss due to increased cost | | 80,350 U |
| Gain due to increase in units sold | 4,983 F | |
| Gain due to shift in sales mix | 2,277 F | |
| | $45,360 F | $80,350 U |

Hence, net decrease in gross profit = $80,350 − $45,360 =     $34,990 U

Despite the increase in sales price and volume and the favorable shift in sales mix, the Lake Tahoe Ski Store ended up losing $34,990, compared to 19X1. The major reason for this comparative loss was the tremendous increase in cost of goods sold, as indicated by an unfavorable cost price variance of $80,350. The costs for both Model X and Model Y went up quite significantly over 19X1. The Store has to take a close look at the cost picture. Even though only variable costs were included in cost of goods sold per unit, both variable and fixed costs should be analyzed in an effort to cut down on controllable costs. In doing that, it is essential that responsibility be clearly fixed to given individuals. In a retail business like the Lake Tahoe Ski Store, operating expenses such as advertising and payroll of store employees must also be closely scrutinized.

### Example 12 (Sales Mix and Quantity Variances)

Shim and Siegel, Inc., sells two products, C and D. Product C has a budgeted unit CM (contribution margin) of $3 and Product D has a budgeted unit CM of $6. The budget for a recent month called for sales of 3,000 units of C and 9,000 units of D, for a total of 12,000 units. Actual sales totaled 12,200 units, 4,700 of C, and 7,500 of D. We compute the sales volume variance and break this variance down into the sales quantity variance and sales mix variance.

Shim and Siegel's sales volume variance is computed below. As we can see, while total unit sales increased by 200 units, the shift in sales mix resulted in a $3,900 unfavorable sales volume variance.

*Sales Volume Variance*

|  | Actual Sales at Actual Mix | Standard Sales at Budget Mix | Difference | Budgeted CM per Unit | Variance ($) |
|---|---|---|---|---|---|
| Product C | 4,700 | 3,000 | 1,700 F | $3 | $5,100 F |
| Product D | 7,500 | 9,000 | 1,500 U | 6 | 9,000 U |
|  | 12,200 | 12,000 |  |  | $3,900 U |

In multiproduct firms, the sales volume variance is further divided into a sales quantity variance and a sales mix variance. The computations of these variances are shown below.

*Sales Quantity Variance*

| | Actual Sales at Budgeted Mix | Standard Sales at Budgeted Mix | Difference | Standard CM per Unit | Variance ($) |
|---|---|---|---|---|---|
| Product C | 3,050 | 3,000 | 50 F | $3 | $150 F |
| Product D | 9,150 | 9,000 | 150 F | 6 | 900 F |
| | 12,200 | 12,000 | | | $1,050 F |

*Sales Mix Variance*

| | Actual Sales at Budgeted Mix | Actual Sales at Actual Mix | Difference | Standard CM per Unit | Variance ($) |
|---|---|---|---|---|---|
| Product C | 3,050 | 4,700 | 1,650 F | $3 | $4,950 F |
| Product D | 9,150 | 7,500 | 1,650 U | 6 | 9,900 U |
| | 12,200 | 12,200 | | | $4,950 U |

The sales quantity variance reflects the impact on the CM or GM (gross margin) of deviations from the standard sales volume, whereas the sales mix variance measures the impact on the CM of deviations from the budgeted mix. In the case of Shim and Siegel, Inc., the sales quantity variance came out to be favorable, i.e., $1,050 F and the sales mix variance came out to be unfavorable, i.e., $4,950 U. These variances indicate that while there was favorable increase in sales volume by 200 units, it was obtained by an unfavorable shift in the sales mix, that is, a shift from Product D, with a high margin, to product C, with a low margin.

Note that the sales volume variance of $3,900 U is the algebraic sum of the following two variances.

| | |
|---|---|
| Sales quantity variance | $1,050 F |
| Sales mix variance | 4,950 U |
| | $3,900 U |

In conclusion, the product emphasis on high margin sales is often a key to success for multiproduct firms. Increasing sales volume is one side of the story, selling the more profitable products is another.

In view of the fact that Shim and Siegel, Inc. experienced an unfavorable sales volume variance of $3,900 due to an unfavorable (or less profitable) mix in the sales volume, the company is advised to put more emphasis on increasing the sale of Product D.

In doing that the company might wish to:

(a) Increase the advertising budget for succeeding periods to boost Product D sales.

(b) Set up a bonus plan in such a way that the commission is based on quantities sold rather than higher rates for higher margin item such as Product D or revise the bonus plan to consider the sale of Product D.

(c) Offer a more lenient credit term for Product D to encourage its sale.

(d) Reduce the price of Product D enough to maintain the present profitable mix while increasing the sale of product. This strategy must take into account the price elasticity of demand for Product D.

## NONMANUFACTURING ACTIVITIES

When nonmanufacturing activities repeat and result in a homogeneous product, standards may be used. The manner of estimating and employing standards can be similar to that applicable with a manufactured product. For instance, standards may be used for office personnel involved in processing sales orders and a standard unit expense for processing a sales order may be derived. The variance between the actual cost of processing a sales order with the standard cost can be appraised by sales managers and corrective steps taken. The number of payroll checks prepared should be a reliable measure of the activity of the payroll department. The number of invoices or vouchers prepared apply to billing and accounts payable. In these two cases, a standard cost per unit could be based on the variable expenses involved.

Variance analysis is used in non-production-oriented companies such as service businesses. Since we are not dealing with a product, a measure of volume other than units is necessary, for example, time spent. The measure of revenue is fee income.

The cost variances are still the same as in a manufacturing concern, namely budgeted costs versus actual costs. We also can derive the gross margin or contribution margin variance as the difference between that budgeted and that actually obtained. The profitability measures are expressed as a percent of sales rather than as dollars per unit. The relationship between costs and sales is often highlighted.

Service firms typically have numerous variances expressed in physical, rather than dollar, measures. Examples of physical measures are number of customers serviced and turnover rate in customers.

## AN ILLUSTRATIVE VARIANCE ANALYSIS REPORT FOR A SERVICE BUSINESS

For a service business, cost variances may be reported in special reports. For example, the variance in time and cost spent for processing payments to creditors may be analyzed. An illustrative format follows.

|  | Variance in Time | Variance in Cost |
|---|---|---|
| *Function* | | |
| Processing purchase orders | | |
| Processing receiving reports | | |
| Processing vendors' invoices | | |
| Preparing checks | | |
| Filing paid vouchers and supporting documents | | |

Variances for these functions are useful only for large companies where the volume of activity allows for the arrangement and analysis of such repetitive tasks.

## VARIANCES TO EVALUATE MARKETING EFFORT

Prior to setting a marketing standard in a given trade territory, you should examine prior, current, and forecasted conditions for the company itself and that given geographical area. Standards will vary, depending upon geographical location. In formulating standard costs for the transportation function, minimum cost traffic routes should be selected on the basis of the given distribution pattern.

Standards for advertising cost in particular territories will vary depending upon the types of advertising media needed, which are in turn based on the type of customers the advertising is intended to reach, as well as the nature of the competition.

Some direct selling costs can be standardized, such as product presentations for which a standard time per sales call can be established. Direct selling expenses should be related to distance traveled and frequency of calls made. If sales commissions are based on sales generated, standards can be based on a percentage of net sales.

Time and motion studies are usually a better way of establishing standards than prior performance, since the past may include inefficiencies.

Cost variances for the selling function may pertain to the territory, product, or personnel.

## VARIANCES IN SELLING EXPENSES

The control of selling expenses is not as significant for a company manufacturing a standard line of products with a limited number of established customers as for a manufacturer of custom products in a very competitive market. For the latter, significant advertising and salesmen costs are mandated. The variance in selling costs is equal to the actual cost versus the flexible budgeted cost.

Assume actual cost is $88,000 and the flexible budget is:

$40,000 + (5% × sales revenue) + ($.03 per unit shipped)

If sales revenue is $500,000 and 100,000 units are shipped, the flexible budgeted cost is:

$40,000 + (5% × $500,000) + ($.03 × 100,000 units) = $68,000

The variance is unfavorable by $20,000. Perhaps advertising and travel should be further investigated. These costs are highly discretionary in that they may easily be altered by marketing managers.

Further refinement of the selling expense variance is possible. Each element of selling expense (i.e., advertising, travel, commissions, shipping costs) could be looked at in terms of the difference between budgeted cost and actual cost.

## SALES PERSONNEL PERFORMANCE

Actual sales may not be the best measure of sales personnel performance. It does not take into account differing territory potentials. Also, a high volume salesperson may have to absorb high selling cost, making the profit generated by him low. Profit is what counts, not sales.

The evaluation of sales personnel based on the trend in their sales generated over the years shows signs of improvement. However, not considered here are customer's market demand, potential markets, product mix, and cost incurrence.

Travel expense standards are often formulated on the basis of distance traveled and the frequency of customer calls. Standards for salesperson automobile expense may be in terms of cost per mile traveled and cost per day. Entertainment and gift expenditures can be based on the amount, size, and potential for customers. The standard might relate to cost per customer or cost per dollar of net sales. Selling expense standards are frowned upon by sales managers because they may create ill will among sales personnel. The standards also do not take into account sales volume or product mix.

Profitability per salesperson may be a good measurement yardstick. Sales, less variable product costs, less selling expenses, per salesperson will give us the relevant profitability. Not considered here, however, are territory expectations or territory demand.

Standard costing procedures and performance measures should be used to control sales personnel costs and compute earnings generated by salesperson category. Further, revenue, cost, and profit by type of sales solicitation (i.e., personal visit, telephone call, mail) should be determined.

A break-even analysis for individual salesmen may also be performed.

Sales commissions should be higher for higher profit merchandise. Any quotas established should be based on a desired sales mix.

Consideration of fixed versus variable costs for a function is critical in marketing cost control and in deciding whether to add or drop sales regions and product lines.

Fixed marketing costs include administrative salaries, wages of warehousing and shipping personnel, rent, and insurance. Variable marketing costs are comprised of processing, storing, and shipping goods, which tend to fluctuate with sales volume. Also of a variable nature are sales personnel salaries and commissions as well as travel and entertainment.

It is difficult to project marketing costs because they may materially change as market conditions are altered. An example is a modification in the channels of distribution. Also, customer brand loyalty is difficult to predict. The point here is that it is more difficult to forecast and analyze marketing costs than manufacturing costs. Thus, standards established in this area are quite tentative and very difficult to manage.

## ILLUSTRATIVE MARKETING PERFORMANCE REPORT

An illustrative format for a marketing performance report designed for the marketing manager follows.

|  | Budget | Percent | Actual | Percent | Variance |
|---|---|---|---|---|---|
| Sales |  |  |  |  |  |
| Less: Standard variable cost of sales |  |  |  |  |  |
| Manufacturing margin |  |  |  |  |  |
| Less: Variable distribution costs |  |  |  |  |  |
| Contribution margin |  |  |  |  |  |
| Less: Regional fixed charges |  |  |  |  |  |
| Controllable regional contribution margin |  |  |  |  |  |
| Less: Marketing fixed charges (i.e., central marketing administration costs, national advertising) |  |  |  |  |  |
| Marketing contribution margin |  |  |  |  |  |

An illustrative format for a marketing performance report designed for the regional sales manager is presented below.

|  | Budget | Percent | Actual | Percent | Variance |
|---|---|---|---|---|---|
| Sales |  |  |  |  |  |
| Less: Standard variable cost of sales |  |  |  |  |  |
| Manufacturing margin |  |  |  |  |  |
| Less: Variable distribution costs (i.e., sales personnel commissions, freight out) |  |  |  |  |  |
| Contribution margin |  |  |  |  |  |
| Less: Regional fixed charges (i.e., salesmen salaries, travel and entertainment, local advertising) |  |  |  |  |  |
| Controllable regional contribution margin |  |  |  |  |  |

The marketing manager should be responsible for standard variable cost of sales, distribution costs (i.e., packing, freight out, marketing administration) and sales. Standard variable cost of sales is used to avoid having the marketing area absorb manufacturing efficiencies and inefficiencies. An illustrative format follows.

Sales

Less: Standard variable cost of sales
Less: Distribution costs
Profitability

The profit figure constitutes the marketing efforts contribution to fixed manufacturing costs and administration costs.

## HOW TO ANALYZE SALESPERSON VARIANCES

You should appraise sales force effectiveness within a territory, including time spent and expenses incurred.

### Example 13

Sales data for your company follow.

| | |
|---|---:|
| Standard cost | $240,000 |
| Standard salesperson days | 2,000 |
| Standard rate per salesperson day | $    120 |
| Actual cost | $238,000 |
| Actual salesperson days | 1,700 |
| Actual rate per salesperson day | $    140 |

*Total Cost Variance*

| | |
|---|---:|
| Actual cost | $238,000 |
| Standard cost | 240,000 |
| | $   2,000 F |

The control variance is broken down into salesperson days and salesperson costs.

*Variance in Salesperson Days*

Actual days versus standard days times standard rate per day
(1,700 versus 2,000 × $120)                                          $ 36,000 F

The variance is favorable because the territory was handled in fewer days than expected.

*Variance in Salesperson Costs*

Actual rate versus standard rate times actual days
($140 versus $120 × 1,700)                                          $ 34,000 F

An unfavorable variance results because the actual rate per day is greater than the expected rate per day.

## Example 14

A salesperson called on 55 customers and sold each an average of $2,800 worth of merchandise. The standard number of calls is 50, and the standard sales is $2,400. Variance analysis looking at calls and sales follows.

*Total Variance*

| | |
|---|---:|
| Actual calls × actual sale 55 × $2,800 | $154,000 |
| Standard calls × standard sale 50 × $2,400 | 120,000 |
| | 34,000 |

The elements of the $34,000 variance are

*Variance in Calls*

| | |
|---|---:|
| Actual calls versus standard calls × standard sale (55 versus 50 × $2,400) | $ 12,000 |

*Variance in Sales*

| | |
|---|---:|
| Actual sale versus standard sale × standard calls ($2,800 versus $2,400 × 50) | $ 20,000 |

*Joint Variance*

| | |
|---|---:|
| (Actual calls versus standard calls) × (Actual sale versus standard sale) (55 versus 50) × ($2,800 versus $2,400) | $ 2,000 |

Additional performance measures of sales force effectiveness include meeting sales quotas, number of orders from existing and new customers, profitability per order, and the relationship between salesperson costs and revenue obtained.

The trend in the ratios of selling expense to sales, selling expense to sales volume, and selling expense to net income should be computed. Are selling expenses realistic in light of revenue generated? Are selling expenses beyond limitations, pointing to possible mismanagement and violation of controls?

## Variances in Warehousing Costs

In warehousing, standards for direct labor may be in terms of cost per item handled, cost per pound handled, cost per order filled, and cost per shipment.

Variances in warehousing costs can be calculated by looking at the cost per unit to store the merchandise and the number of orders anticipated.

### Example 15

The following information applies to a product:

| | |
|---|---:|
| Standard cost | $12,100 |
| Standard orders | 5,500 |
| Standard unit cost | $ 2.20 |
| Actual cost | $14,030 |
| Actual orders | 6,100 |
| Actual unit cost | $ 2.30 |

*Total Warehousing Cost Variance*

| | |
|---|---:|
| Actual cost | $14,030 |
| Standard cost | 12,100 |
| | $ 1,930 U |

The total variance is segregated into the variance in orders and variance in cost.

*Variance in Orders*

Actual orders versus standard orders × standard unit cost
6,100 versus 5,500 × $2.20                                  $ 1,320 U

*Variance in Cost*

Actual cost per unit versus standard cost per unit × actual orders
$2.30 versus $2.20 × 6,100                                  $ 610 U

# VARIANCES IN ADMINISTRATIVE EXPENSES

As business expands, there is a tendency for administrative expenses to increase proportionately and get out of line. However, central general and administrative expenses typically are of a fixed cost nature and hence there is less need to monitor these types of costs. Here, comparison of budgeted to actual costs can be made quarterly or even yearly. These comparisons should be done by department or unit of responsibility. Suggested standards for administrative expenses appear below.

| Administrative Function | Unit of Standard Measurement |
| --- | --- |
| Handling orders | Number of orders handled |
| Billing | Number of invoices |
| Check writing | Number of checks written |
| Clerical | Number of items handled |
| Customer statements | Number of statements |
| Order writing | Number of orders |
| Personnel | Number of employees hired |
| Payroll | Number of employees |

Selling and administrative variances for nonoperating items are the responsibility of top management and staff. Such items include taxes and insurance. Performance reports may be prepared for the administrative function, such as the salaries of top executives and general department service costs such as data processing. Performance measures may also be of a non-monetary nature, such as the number of files processed, the number of phone calls taken, and the number of invoices written. Variances between the dollar and non-dollar factors can be determined and analyzed.

## CAPITAL EXPENDITURES

Variance reports are useful in controlling capital expenditures by looking at the actual versus budgeted costs as well as actual versus budgeted times for proposals at each stage of activity. Such reports enable managers to take corrective cost-saving action such as changing the construction schedule. The director of the project is held accountable for the construction cost and time budget. Component elements within the project should also be analyzed. We can also compare the expected payback period and actual payback period. This assists in measuring operational results and budgeting efficiency. Also, estimated cash flows of the project can be compared with actual cash flows.

## VARIANCE ANALYSIS REPORTS

Performance reports may be prepared that examine the difference between budgeted and actual figures for:

(1) production in terms of cost, quantity, and quality

(2) sales

(3) profit

(4) return on investment

(5) turnover of assets

(6) income per sales dollar

(7) market share

(8) growth rate

Variance reports raise questions rather than answering them. For example, is sales volume down because of deficiencies in sales effort or the manufacturer's inability to produce?

Variance analysis reports may be expressed not only in dollars, but also in percentages, ratios, graphs, and narrative.

Performance reports are designed to motivate nonfinancial managers and employees to change their activities and plans when variances exist. They should be terse and concentrate on potential difficulties and opportunities. A section for comments should be provided so that explanations may be given for variances.

The timeliness of performance reports and detail supplied depends upon the manager the report is addressed to and the nature of the costs being measured. A production manager may need daily information on the manufacturing operations, the plant manager may need only weekly data, and the vice-president of manufacturing may be satisfied with monthly performance figures for each plant. As we become more distant from the actual operation, the time interval for performance evaluation lengthens. Also, as we go up the ladder, performance reports contain data in increasingly summarized form.

Since performance reports depend upon the organizational structure, they should be designed based on the company's organization chart. Reports designed for a senior vice president might deal with the entire business operation of the firm and the earnings derived from it. The manufacturing manager would look at the efficiency of the production activity. The marketing manager would evaluate the selling and distribution function. A plant head would be concerned with the output and earnings generated from his plant. A department head within the plant would be concerned with the output and earnings generated from his area as well as with cost control.

Performance reports should contain analytical information. To obtain it we should evaluate source data such as work orders, material requisitions, and labor cards. Reasons for inefficiency and excessive costs should be noted, such as those due to equipment malfunction and low quality raw materials.

For labor, the productivity measurement ratio of volume output per direct labor hour should be computed. Further, the output of the individual or machine should be compared to the normal output established at the beginning of the reporting period. Operating efficiency can thus be measured. A labor efficiency ratio can also be computed, which is the variation between actual hours incurred and standard hours.

With regard to the evaluation of the divisional manager, fixed costs are generally not controllable by him, but variable costs are. There are instances however, where variable costs are controllable by those above the division manager's level. An example is fringe benefits. These items should be evaluated independently since the division manager has no responsibility for them. The opposite may also be true, that is, the department manager may have control over certain fixed expenses such as lease costs. In such cases he should similarly be assigned responsibility, although a successor not involved in the lease negotiation may not be assigned responsibility.

## APPRAISAL OF MARKETING DEPARTMENT

Revenue, cost, and profitability information should be provided by product line, customer, industry segment, geographic area, channel of distribution, type of marketing effort, and average order size. New product evaluations should also be undertaken, balancing risk with profitability. Analysis of competition in terms of strengths and weaknesses should be made. Sales force effectiveness measures should also be employed for income generated by salesmen, call frequency, sales incentives, sales personnel costs and dollar value of orders generated per hours spent. Promotional effectiveness measures should be employed for revenue, marketing costs, and profits before, during, and after promotional efforts, including a discussion of competitive reactions. Advertising effectiveness measures, such as sales generated based on dollar expenditure per media and media measures (i.e., audience share) are also useful. Reports discussing product warranty complaints and disposition should also be provided.

Marketing costs may be broken down into selling, promotion, credit evaluation, accounting, and administration (i.e., product development, market research). Another element is physical distribution—inventory management, order processing, packaging, warehousing, shipping outbound transportation, field warehousing, and customer services.

Control of marketing cost is initiated when such costs are assigned to functional groups such as geographic area, product line, and industry segment. Budgeted costs and rates should be provided and comparisons made between standard costs and actual costs at the end of the reporting period.

## CONCLUSION

Variance analysis is essential for the appraisal of all aspects of the business, including manufacturing, marketing, and service. Variances should be investigated if the benefits outweigh the costs of analyzing and correcting the source of the variance. Variance analysis reports should be in dollars and percentages.

Variance analysis identifies trouble spots, highlights opportunities, encourages decision making, and fosters coordination between responsibility units.

Significant unfavorable variances must be examined to ascertain whether they are controllable or uncontrollable by nonfinancial managers because they relate solely to external factors. When controllable, immediate corrective action must be undertaken to handle the problem. The manager should provide his recommendations. If a variance is favorable, an examination should be made of the reasons so that corporate policy may include the positive aspects found. Further, the responsible entity for a favorable variance should be recognized and rewarded.

Different degrees of significance of variances may be present, including:

- The variance is within tolerable and normal range and thus no remedial steps are necessary.

- The variance is intolerable and thus either performance must be improved or new standards formulated in light of the current environment.

- The decision model was inappropriate, considering the goal to be achieved, and thus a more relevant model should be developed.

Reports on operating performance should show where performance varies from standard, the trend of performance, and the reasons for the variances, including the manager's explanation.

Reporting systems differ among companies regarding the frequency and timeliness of reports, details presented, arrangement of data, employee distribution, and size of variances necessitating follow-up. Variances can be evaluated by divisions, subdivisions, departments, and cost centers.

If responsibility for a variance is joint, corrective action should also be joint. If correction of an unfavorable variance involves a conflict with a corporate policy, the policy should be re-evaluated and perhaps changed. If the policy is not changed, the variance should be considered uncontrollable.

Even if a variance is below a cut-off percent or dollar figure, the manager may still want to investigate it if the variance is consistently unfavorable, because it may reveal a problem (e.g., poor supervision, wasteful practice). The cumulative impact of a repeated small unfavorable variance may be just as damaging as an occasional one.

# Chapter 9

# MANUFACTURING COSTS:
## *Sales Forecasts and Realistic Budgets*

In a manufacturing firm, costs are divided into two major categories, by the functional activities with which they are associated. These are manufacturing costs and nonmanufacturing costs, also called operating expenses.

Manufacturing costs are subdivided into direct materials, direct labor, and factory overhead. Direct materials are all materials that become an integral part of the finished product. Examples are the steel used to make an automobile and the wood to make furniture. Glues, nails, and other minor items are called indirect materials (or supplies) and are classified as part of factory overhead, which is explained below.

Direct labor is the labor directly involved in making the product. Examples of direct labor costs are the wages of workers on an assembly line and the wages of machine tool operators in a machine shop. Indirect labor, such as wages of supervisory personnel and janitors, is classified as part of factory overhead.

Factory overhead includes all costs of manufacturing except direct materials and direct labor. Examples include depreciation, rent, taxes, insurance, fringe benefits, payroll taxes, and cost of idle time. Factory overhead is also called manufacturing overhead, indirect manufacturing expenses, and factory burden.

In order to budget for manufacturing costs, a production budget needs to be established, which in turn requires a sales budget. Figure 9.1 illustrates this relationship.

## ILLUSTRATION

To illustrate how all manufacturing cost budgets are put together, consider a manufacturing company called the Worth Company, which produces and markets a single product.

### THE SALES BUDGET

The sales budget is the starting point in preparing the manufacturing budget, since estimated sales volume influences nearly all other items appearing throughout the master budget. The sales budget should show total sales in quantity and value. The expected total sales can be break-even, target income, or sales. The budget may be analyzed further by product, territory, customer and seasonal pattern of expected sales.

**Figure 9.1**

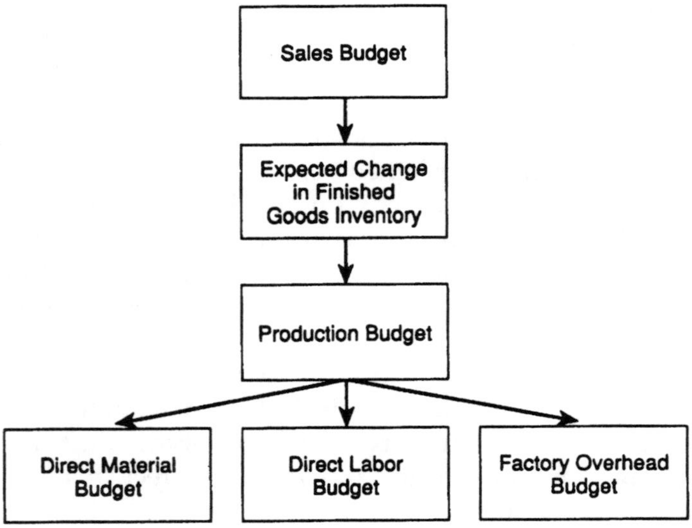

## Example 1

THE WORTH COMPANY
Sales Budget
For the Year Ending December 31, 19B

|  | *Quarter* | | | | |
|---|---|---|---|---|---|
|  | *1* | *2* | *3* | *4* | *Total* |
| Expected sales in units | 800 | 700 | 900 | 800 | 3,200 |
| Unit sales price | ×$80 | ×$80 | ×$80 | ×$80 | ×$80 |
| Total sales | $64,000 | $56,000 | $72,000 | $64,000 | $256,000 |

## THE PRODUCTION BUDGET

The production budget is a statement of the output by product and is generally expressed in units. It should take into account the sales budget, plant capacity, whether stocks are to be increased or decreased, and outside purchases. The number of units expected to be manufactured to meet budgeted sales and inventory requirements is set forth in the production budget.

The expected volume of production is determined by subtracting the estimated inventory at the beginning of the period from the sum of the units expected to be sold and the desired inventory at the end of the period. The production budget is illustrated as follows:

## Example 2

THE WORTH COMPANY
Production Budget
For the Year Ending December 31, 19B

|  | *Quarter* | | | | |
|---|---|---|---|---|---|
|  | *1* | *2* | *3* | *4* | *Total* |
| Planned sales (Example 1) | 800 | 700 | 900 | 800 | 3,200 |
| Desired ending inventory* | 70 | 90 | 80 | 100† | 100 |
| Total needs | 870 | 790 | 980 | 900 | 3,300 |
| Less: Beginning inventory‡ | 80 | 70 | 90 | 80 | 80 |
| Units to be produced | 790 | 720 | 890 | 820 | 3,220 |

*10 percent of the next quarter's sales.
†Estimated.
‡The same as the previous quarter's ending inventory.

## THE DIRECT MATERIAL BUDGET

When the level of production has been computed, a direct material budget should be constructed to show how much material will be required for production and how much material must be purchased to meet this production requirement. The purchase will depend on both expected usage of materials and inventory levels. The formula for computation of the purchase is:

$$\text{Purchase in units} = \text{Usage} + \text{Desired ending material inventory units} - \text{Beginning inventory units}$$

### Example 3

**THE WORTH COMPANY**
**Direct Material Budget**
**For the Year Ending December 31, 19B**

|  | Quarter | | | | |
|---|---|---|---|---|---|
|  | 1 | 2 | 3 | 4 | Total |
| Units to be produced (Ex 2) | 790 | 720 | 890 | 820 | 3,220 |
| Material needs per unit (lbs) | × 3 | × 3 | × 3 | × 3 | × 3 |
| Material needs for production | 2,370 | 2,160 | 2,670 | 2,460 | 9,660 |
| Desired ending inventory of materials | 216 | 267 | 246 | 250 | 250 |
| Total needs | 2,586 | 2,427 | 2,916 | 2,710 | 9,910 |
| Less: Beginning inventory of materials | 237 | 216 | 267 | 246 | 237 |
| Materials to be purchased | 2,349 | 2,211 | 2,649 | 2,464 | 9,673 |
| Unit price | × $2 | × $2 | × $2 | × $2 | × $2 |
| Purchase cost | $4,698 | $4,422 | $5,298 | $4,928 | $19,346 |

## THE DIRECT LABOR BUDGET

The production requirements as set forth in the production budget also provide the starting point for the preparation of the direct labor budget. To compute direct labor requirements, expected production volume for each period is multiplied by the number of direct labor hours required to produce a single unit. The direct labor hours to meet production requirements is then multiplied by the (standard) direct labor cost per hour to obtain budgeted total direct labor costs.

## Example 4

THE WORTH COMPANY
Direct Labor Budget
For the Year Ending December 31, 19B

| | Quarter | | | | |
|---|---|---|---|---|---|
| | 1 | 2 | 3 | 4 | Total |
| Units to be produced (Example 2) | 790 | 720 | 890 | 820 | 3,220 |
| Direct labor hours per unit | × 5 | × 5 | × 5 | × 5 | × 5 |
| Total hours | 3,950 | 3,600 | 4,450 | 4,100 | 16,100 |
| Direct labor cost per hour | × $5 | × $5 | × $5 | × $5 | × $5 |
| Total direct labor cost | $19,750 | $18,000 | $22,250 | $20,500 | $80,500 |

## THE FACTORY OVERHEAD BUDGET

The factory overhead budget should provide a schedule of all manufacturing costs other than direct materials and direct labor. Using the contribution approach to budgeting requires the development of a predetermined overhead rate for the variable portion of the factory overhead.

## Example 5

To illustrate the factory overhead budget, we will assume that the cost–volume (or flexible budget) formula is:

Total factory overhead budgeted = $6,000 fixed (per quarter), plus $2 per hour of direct labor.

THE WORTH COMPANY
Factory Overhead Budget
For the Year Ending December 31, 19B

| | Quarter | | | | |
|---|---|---|---|---|---|
| | 1 | 2 | 3 | 4 | Total |
| Budgeted direct labor hours (Example 4) | 3,950 | 3,600 | 4,450 | 4,100 | 16,100 |
| Variable overhead rate | × $2 | × $2 | × $2 | × $2 | × $2 |
| Variable overhead budgeted | 7,900 | 7,200 | 8,900 | 8,200 | 32,200 |
| Fixed overhead budgeted | 6,000 | 6,000 | 6,000 | 6,000 | 24,000 |
| Total budgeted overhead | 13,900 | 13,200 | 14,900 | 14,200 | 56,200 |

# PLANNING AND CONTROL OF MATERIAL PURCHASES AND USAGE

After determining the number of units to be produced, the company prepares the materials requirement budget and the materials purchase budget. Purchase of materials depends on production requirements and inventories. The direct materials budget involves a balancing of raw material needed for production, the raw material inventory balances, and the purchase of raw materials. The budget may provide for allowances for waste and spoilage.

This section discusses the procedures for developing material budgets in more detail.

# MATERIALS BUDGETS

The materials and inventory budgets in a typical manufacturing firm involve a determination of:

1. The quantities and cost of raw materials to be used.
2. The quantities and value of materials to be carried in the inventory. The inventory balance depends on how long it takes to receive raw materials from suppliers after the order is placed.
3. The quantities and cost of materials to be purchased. The amount to purchase considers expected production and raw material levels. The units of raw material needed equals the raw material usage multiplied by the units of production. In budgeting purchases, consideration should be given to expected price changes, interest cost to finance inventory, volume and cash discounts, desired delivery date, warehousing availability and cost, and obsolescence risk.
4. The quantity and value of finished goods to be carried in the inventory.

There are basically two methods of developing the inventory budget of raw materials:

1. Budget each important item separately, based upon the production budget.

2. Budget materials as a whole or classes of materials based upon selected production factors.

Practically all companies must use both methods to some extent.

## BUDGETING INDIVIDUAL ITEMS OF MATERIAL

The following steps should be taken in budgeting the major individual items of materials:

1. Determine the physical units of material required for each item of goods which is to be produced during the budget period.
2. Accumulate these into total physical units of each material item required for the production plan.
3. Determine for each item of material the quantity which should be on hand periodically to provide for the production budget, with a reasonable degree of safety.
4. Deduct material inventories, which it is expected will be hand at the beginning of the budget period, to ascertain the total quantities to be purchased. The formula for computation of the purchase is:

$$\text{Purchase in units} = \text{Usage} + \text{Desired ending material inventory units} \\ - \text{Beginning inventory units}$$

5. Develop a purchase policy which will insure that quantities will be on hand at the time they are needed. The purchase policy must consider such factors as economic order quantities (EOQ), economy of transportation, quantity discounts, and possible depletion of inventory.
6. Translate the inventory and purchase requirements into dollars by applying the expected prices of materials to budgeted quantities. *Note:* The dollar amount of purchases is one of the major cash disbursement items in the cash budget.

## BUDGET BASED ON PRODUCTION FACTORS

For those items of materials which cannot be budgeted individually, the budget must be based on production factors such as total budgeted labor hours, productive hours, standard allowed hours, cost of materials consumed, or cost of goods manufactured.

### Example 6

Assume that cost of materials consumed (other than basic materials which are budgeted individually) is budgeted at $2,000,000 and that past experience demonstrates that these materials and supplies should be held to a rate of 4 times per year. Then, an average inventory of $500,000 should be budgeted. This would mean that individual items of material could be held in stock about 90 days (360 days/4).

## MATERIALS PURCHASE BUDGET ILLUSTRATED

The following example illustrates a typical method of budgeting the quantities and cost of raw materials to be purchased. Assume that there are three classes of materials: X, Y, and Z.

(1) Class X—Materials for which a definite quantity and monthly distribution is established in advance. Figure 9.2 presents standard unit information by month.
(2) Class Y—Material items for which definite quantities are established for the entire budget period but for which no definite monthly distribution program is established. Figure 9.3 presents unit information for items.

**Figure 9.2**

|  | Item A | | | Item B | | |  |
|---|---|---|---|---|---|---|---|
|  | Units | Standard Unit Cost | Amount | Units | Standard Unit Cost | Amount | Total |
| July | 300 | $1.10 | $330 | 650 | $2.00 | $1,300 | $1,630 |
| August | 200 | 1.00 | 200 | 700 | 2.00 | 1400 | 1600 |
| September | 500 | 1.00 | 500 | 400 | 2.10 | 840 | 1340 |
| October | 250 | 1.00 | 250 | 250 | 2.25 | 563 | 813 |
| November | 300 | 1.00 | 300 | 350 | 2.25 | 788 | 1088 |
| December | 400 | 1.00 | 400 | 250 | 2.25 | 563 | 963 |
| Total | 1950 | | $1,980 | 2600 | | $5,453 | $7,433 |

**Figure 9.3**

|  | Total Units Required to Be Purchased | Estimated Price per Unit | Total cost |
|---|---|---|---|
| Item H | 2,500 | 0.25 | 625 |
| I | 3,400 | 0.34 | 1156 |
| J | 4,500 | 0.23 | 1035 |
| K | 2,700 | 0.45 | 1215 |
| Total | 13,100 |  | $4,031 |

Here the distribution to months of the total cost of $4,031 must be made on the basis of past experience of budgeted production factors such as machine hours. The following figures may be assumed, based on past experience. Figure 9.4 presents percentage distribution information.

(3) Class Z—Miscellaneous material items which are grouped together and budgeted only in terms of total dollar purchases for the total budget period. The distribution to months is again made on the basis of past experience or production factors. The following figures may be assumed, based on budgeted machine hours (cost of Class Z materials is assumed to be $5 per hour):

**Figure 9.4**

| | Percentage Distribution Based on Past Experience | Material Items | | | | |
|---|---|---|---|---|---|---|
| | | H | I | J | K | Total |
| July | 30% | $188 | $347 | $311 | $365 | $1,209 |
| August | 20% | $125 | $231 | $207 | $243 | $ 806 |
| September | 10% | $ 63 | $116 | $104 | $122 | $ 403 |
| October | 20% | $125 | $231 | $207 | $243 | $ 806 |
| November | 10% | $ 63 | $116 | $104 | $122 | $ 403 |
| December | 10% | $ 63 | $116 | $104 | $122 | $ 403 |
| Total | 100.00% | $625 | $1,156 | $1,035 | $1,215 | $4,031 |

**Figure 9.5**

|           | Budgeted Productive Hours | Distribution to Months |
|-----------|---------------------------|------------------------|
| July      | 150                       | $  750                 |
| August    | 240                       | $1,200                 |
| September | 175                       | $  875                 |
| October   | 80                        | $  400                 |
| November  | 95                        | $  475                 |
| December  | 100                       | $  500                 |
| Total     | 840                       | $4,200                 |

Figure 9.5 presents budgeted productive hours.
Note that total purchases required for Class Z materials amount to $4,200.

The total purchase budget may then be summarized as in Figure 9.6 which presents information by material class.

The estimated days material is to be held may be computed. Assume direct material used is budgeted at $500,000 with an expected turnover rate of 4 times. Thus, the average inventory is budgeted at $125,000. Material will be stored about 90 days (360/4). Material price and usage variances are discussed in Chapter 8. An illustrative budget is presented in Example 7.

**Figure 9.6**

|           | Class X Materials | Class Y Materials | Class Z Materials | Total     |
|-----------|-------------------|-------------------|-------------------|-----------|
| July      | $1,630            | $1,209            | $750              | $ 3,589   |
| August    | 1,600             | 806               | 1200              | 3606      |
| September | 1,340             | 403               | 875               | 2618      |
| October   | 813               | 806               | 400               | 2019      |
| November  | 1,088             | 403               | 475               | 1966      |
| December  | 963               | 403               | 500               | 1866      |
| Total     | $7,433            | $4,031            | $4,200            | $15,664   |

## Example 7

**XYZ Company**
**Purchases Budget**
**For the Year Ended December 31, 19X1**

| Type of Raw Material | Production | + | Ending Inventory | − | Beginning Inventory | Budgeted Price | Budgeted Purchases |
|---|---|---|---|---|---|---|---|
| A | 200,000 etc. | | 40,000 | | 20,000 | $1.50 | $330,000 |

## PLANNING AND CONTROL OF DIRECT LABOR

Direct labor is paid either by piecework, in which the factory labor is paid so much per piece or by day work, in which the labor is paid a stipulated hourly rate regardless of the job he is assigned.

Planning and control of direct labor has two primary objectives:

(1) To obtain the maximum output from each of the employees

(2) To ensure that product costs reflect proper labor charges.

Planning and budgeting direct labor costs is considered straightforward for two reasons. First, direct labor operations are normally of a type for which an engineered standard can be properly set.

Standard implies the amount of time it should take an average operator to perform a function under a normal operating condition. Standards are set by such means as average actual time over the years, laboratory experiment, random sampling, or a motion and time study.

Second, since almost all direct labor can be identified with a specific product or job, there is relatively little difficulty in determining where and how much direct labor costs should be charged.

The control function is equally clear. When actual results are reported, they are compared with the plan or target and quickly reveal when plans went astray.

## PLANNING AND CONTROL OF FACTORY OVERHEAD

Planning and control of overhead items have two major goals:

(1) To minimize overhead costs wherever they occur

(2) To make certain that overhead is allocated, in the most accurate manner, to the various jobs and products being manufactured.

For flexible budgeting purposes, it is important to distinguish between variable and fixed overhead expenses. Some are mixed costs that need to be divided, using such methods as the high-low method and regression analysis.

For example, the following cost-volume (flexible budget) formulas can be developed for various overhead items:

| Factory overhead costs | Formula |
|---|---|
| Electricity | $50 + $10 DLH |
| Maintenance | $100 + $15 DLH |
| Supervisors' salaries | $5,000 per month |
| Indirect materials | $8 per DLH |
| Factory depreciation | $7,000 per month |

## CONCLUSION

This chapter has emphasized manufacturing budgets. The process involves developing a sales forecast and, based on its magnitude, generating production and manufacturing expense budgets needed by a specific firm. Once developed, the budgeting system provides management with a means of controlling its activities and of monitoring actual performance and comparing it to budget goals.

A comprehensive profit planning and control program involves budgeting the materials and parts used in the production process. The budget process involving manufacturing expenses includes the material usage and purchase budgets, direct labor budgets, and factory overhead budgets.

# Chapter 10

## MARKETING:

*Budgeting for Sales, Advertising, and Distribution*

Before presenting the budgeting aspects for a marketing department, it would be informative to review Figure 10.1, which shows the usual organization of a sales division.

A marketing manager needs a promotion and advertising plan, selling expense plan, and marketing plan. Coordination should exist between the sales plan and the marketing plan. Sales promotion expenses should be budgeted by product, activity, media, territory, and salesperson. Authorization may be needed for unusual marketing expenditures.

Direct costs are directly traceable to a nonfinancial manager's segment, while indirect costs are general charges that are allocable in some way to each segment. The unit cost of an operation equals total expenditures divided by units of measure.

The manager should consider cost per order received, cost per order filled, cost per item handled, cost per customer account, transportation cost (e.g., auto, plane, train) per month, and cost per mile by category.

The number of salesperson calls and sales per call should be budgeted and then compared to actual calls and sales per call. Variances should be analyzed.

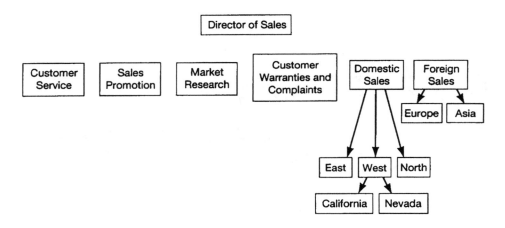

**Figure 10.1**
STRUCTURE OF A SALES DIVISION

The manager should determine if a large percentage of products, orders, or customers generate a small portion of sales. Marketing expenses typically increase in proportion to the amount of customer orders and products, not sales dollars. A change in sales mix can have a significant affect upon profitability.

The sales manager may attempt to protect profits by increasing selling prices when costs are increasing or sales volume is decreasing. However, there are circumstances in which selling prices may not be increased because it is either impractical or prohibited. Examples are government price controls, high degree of competition (e.g., airlines), and poor economic conditions.

This chapter discusses budget preparation and analysis and control over marketing costs, including selling expenses, advertising and sales promotion, distribution costs, packaging, and travel and entertainment.

## MARKETING BUDGETS

The marketing budget depends on the type of product or service, competition, market share, type of customer, costs to obtain and maintain an account, territory, anticipated sales calls, distribution channel, order size and frequency, and promotion efforts. Industry standards may be referred to when preparing marketing budgets.

Budgets aid in planning sales efforts. Sales may be budgeted by product, service, customer, territory, and salesperson. Budgets should consist of sales volume and sales dollars by salesperson broken down by territory.

A lump-sum appropriation may be made, consisting of a maximum amount of expenditure. Controllable and noncontrollable expenses should be identified.

A budget may be based on the following:

| Type of Expenditure | Budgeting Basis |
|---|---|
| Automobile | Mileage |
| Lodging, food, and telephone | Daily allowance |
| Other | Special authorization |

A typical budget for a marketing division is shown in Exhibit 10.1.

## SELLING EXPENSES

Selling expenses are those that are required to make a sale (sales commissions, salesperson salaries, advertising, and sales promotion) and to distribute the merchandise to the customer (order processing, handling, storage, and delivery charges). The manager should appraise the efficiency and effectiveness of getting and filling orders.

Sales may be appraised by customer, product, service, salesperson, sales method, territory, and distribution outlet. Selling effort is subject to diminishing returns because, after a certain point, additional sales volume from selling efforts do not justify the additional cost and time. Further, the sales manager should set sales personnel requirements by number and grade.

The manager is responsible for the selling expense budget. The variable-fixed breakdown is highly recommended. Many selling expenses may be budgeted based on a percentage of sales, including salesperson commissions and salaries, sales promotion, distribution (including freight out), travel, entertainment, warranties, and training. However, some selling expenses may be constant or initially set by the sales manager, such as rent and advertising. A fixed appropriation of selling expenses may be irreducible because a minimum amount is needed to function.

## Exhibit 10.1
## MARKETING DIVISION BUDGET

| Department | Type of Budget | Current Year Quarter | | | | Total | Prior Year | Increase (Decrease) |
|---|---|---|---|---|---|---|---|---|
| | | 1 | 2 | 3 | 4 | | | |
| ADVERTISING AND PROMOTION PROJECT | | | | | | | | |
| Illinois | | | | | | | | |
| New Jersey | | | | | | | | |
| Florida | | | | | | | | |
| DIRECT SELLING ADMINISTRATIVE | | | | | | | | |
| West | | | | | | | | |
| East | | | | | | | | |
| North | | | | | | | | |
| South | | | | | | | | |
| Total | | | | | | | | |
| STORAGE AND WAREHOUSING STANDARD | | | | | | | | |
| New York | | | | | | | | |
| California | | | | | | | | |
| Pennsylvania | | | | | | | | |
| Michigan | | | | | | | | |
| ADMINISTRATIVE | | | | | | | | |
| General and Administrative | | | | | | | | |
| Market Research Project | | | | | | | | |
| Customer Relations Administrative | | | | | | | | |
| Branch Office Administrative | | | | | | | | |
| TOTAL | | | | | | | | |

Selling expenses may be budgeted, reported, and analyzed by department, division, product, service, class of customer, territory, time period (e.g., monthly), transaction, distribution outlet, sales method, and source of sale. There should be a monthly breakdown of the target selling expenses in the budget for control and monitoring purposes.

There should be a budget provision for increased training costs, if additional salespeople are to be hired.

Standardized activities are repetitive and subject to quantitative measurement. Examples are field selling expenses and storage handling charges. Costs should be segregated by function. The field selling expense may be based on a per diem standard allowance. For example, auto expense may be at a standard mileage rate, telephone may be at a monthly allowance, and entertainment may be at a per diem rate.

Figure 10.2 graphs the ratio of selling expenses to net sales over a representative time period.

Exhibit 10.2 presents an illustrative field selling expense budget.

Exhibit 10.3 shows a typical monthly performance report for selling expenses broken down by responsibility.

If, in the monthly analysis, a selling expense item is heading over budget for the year, the nonfinancial manager notes this in the performance report, after discussing it with the responsible party. There are three options:

**Figure 10.2**
**SELLING EXPENSES TO SALES**

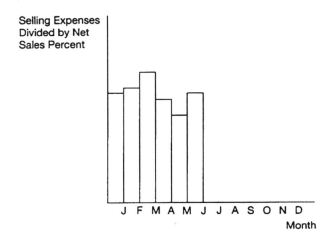

**Exhibit 10.2**
**BUDGETED FIELD SELLING EXPENSES**
**June 1995**

**Salesperson Name and Number** _____
**Sales Territory** _____

| Description | June 1995 | | | Cumulative | | | |
| | Allowance | Actual | Budget | Over (Under) Budget | Actual | Budget | Over (Under) Budget | |
| | | | | | | | Amount | Percent |
|---|---|---|---|---|---|---|---|---|
| Days traveled | | | | | | | | |
| Field Selling Expenses | | | | | | | | |
|   Food $20 per diem | | | | | | | | |
|   Lodging $100 per diem | | | | | | | | |
|   Telephone $15 per diem | | | | | | | | |
|   Valet $6 per diem | | | | | | | | |
| Travel | | | | | | | | |
|   Airplane | | | | | | | | |
|   Railroad | | | | | | | | |
|   Auto $.30 per mile | | | | | | | | |
| Conventions | | | | | | | | |
| Promotion and Entertainment | | | | | | | | |
|   $50 per diem | | | | | | | | |
|   Other $10 per diem | | | | | | | | |
| Total Expenses | | | | | | | | |
| Selling Ratios: | | | | | | | | |
|   Cost per travel day | | | | | | | | |
|   Cost per telephone call | | | | | | | | |
|   Sales generated per call | | | | | | | | |
| **Comments:** | | | | | | | | |

Exhibit 10.3
MONTHLY PERFORMANCE REPORT SALES MANAGER X

| For Month | | | | Year-to-Date | | |
|---|---|---|---|---|---|---|
| Actual | Budget | Variance | | Actual | Budget | Variance |
| | | | | | | |

1. To request a revision of the target budget.
2. To request an allocation from a contingency fund, if any.
3. To take action to keep the expense on target.

An illustrative budget report for a sales manager is shown in Exhibit 10.4.

A typical sales engineering project budget report appears in Exhibit 10.5.

Exhibit 10.4
GENERAL SALES MANAGER BUDGET REPORT

| | Current Month | | Cumulative | |
|---|---|---|---|---|
| | Actual | Over (Under) Budget | Actual | Over (Under) Budget |
| Number of salespeople | | | | |
| Costs | | | | |
| Rent | | | | |
| Insurance | | | | |
| Travel | | | | |
| Promotion and entertainment | | | | |
| Depreciation | | | | |
| Salaries | | | | |
| Fringe benefits | | | | |
| Dues | | | | |
| Supplies | | | | |
| Total Expenses | | | | |
| Percentage of net sales | | | | |

**Exhibit 10.5**

**SALES ENGINEERING PROJECT BUDGET REPORT**

| Project Number | Project Name | Hours | Actual Costs by Type | Budgeted Costs by Type | Variance | Estimated Costs to Complete | Commitments |
|---|---|---|---|---|---|---|---|
| | | | | | | | |

## ADVERTISING AND SALES PROMOTION

Advertising may be local, regional, national, or international.

The manager must determine how much, when, where and how advertising should be used to obtain the optimum benefit. Advertising depends on product leadership, degree of competition, market economy, and financial condition. It has to be coordinated with sales and production. Responsibility for advertising may be assigned to specific individuals, where appropriate.

The major considerations in budgeting, analyzing, and controlling advertising are cost, type and number of audience, advertising frequency, consistency in meeting product, price, and distribution, and demographics.

The highest percentage of a marketing budget is usually reserved for advertising. The advertising budget helps the marketing manager plan how much and where to spend. The advertising budget depends on territories, customers, products, services, activities, programs, and media. Advertising should be sufficient to accomplish objectives such as growth rate. After the advertising budget has been determined, funds have to be assigned to specific items. The advertising budget may be broken down into departmental budgets, total budget, calendar periods, media, and sales areas.

The marketing manager should set up a contingency fund so there is flexibility in the advertising budget. The fund can cover special circumstances, such as the introduction of a new product, specials available in local media, or sudden actions by competitors.

The objectives of advertising are to make potential customers aware of the products or services and how to use them, improve market share, develop new markets, stimulate new products, project a favorable image and brand loyalty, counteract bad publicity, foster a negative image for competitors or counteract competition, promote sales, increase selling price, reduce selling costs, and counteract contemplated government regulation.

There are various kinds of advertising, including:

- Promotions of a particular brand
- Mass advertising to a large population cross section
- Class of customer
- Message about the company in general, rather than about a specific product or service

The types of advertising media include directories (phone, etc.), print (newspapers, magazines, trade publications), direct mail, outdoor, broadcasts (television, radio), door-to-door solicitation, specialty items, and movies.

Sales promotion, which is directly related to advertising, is needed for future sales. It may include special programs, store fixtures, and trade shows.

The sales manager will have to justify his advertising budget to upper management. He will have to state objectives, how to accomplish them, and the cost of each component of the program. The factors to be considered in the advertising budget include profit per product, estimated advertising expense per unit, and projected additional sales volume resulting from incremental advertising expenditures.

There are various ways to determine how much should be spent on advertising and sales promotion. These include arbitrary appropriation, such as that based on prior years' advertising, all available funds, competitive parity, percentage of sales or profit, unit sales (fixed sum per unit suitable for uniform or a few products such as specialty goods), return on investment, objective-task method, and a lump sum (suitable for established products with a predictable track record and stable environment).

Advertising for necessities should be expanded in recessionary years while advertising for luxuries should be emphasized in strong economic periods. Advertising may reduce direct selling costs.

Let us now discuss the following three popular methods:

## 1. PERCENTAGE OF SALES OR PROFIT

With this widely used approach, advertising will be consistent with the budgeted or prior years' revenue (e.g., 5 years' average sales). Advertising may also be based on a percent of prior years' net profit or gross margin.

(Units × Price) × Percentage Allocated
or
Profit × Percentage

## 2. UNIT SALES METHOD

Under this approach, a fixed sum is established for each unit of product to be sold, based on experience and trade knowledge of how much advertising is required to sell each unit. The budget is basically based on units sold instead of dollar sales. For example, if \$2 is allocated for each unit of product and there are 20,000 expected units, \$40,000 would be allocated to advertising.

### 3. OBJECTIVE-TASK METHOD

This method relates the advertising appropriation, under typical conditions and in the long run, to sales volume, so that earnings and revenue are not drained.

Exhibits 10.6 and 10.7 show typical advertising budgets.

There should be a comparison between successive budgeted advertising cost and anticipated incremental profit by program.

Exhibit 10.8 shows the impact of successive advertising outlays on earnings.

Measures of advertising include:

- Trend in advertising cost to sales
- Advertising cost per unit sold
- Advertising cost per sales dollars
- Advertising cost per customer
- Advertising cost per transaction
- Advertising cost by product, media, and territory

**Exhibit 10.6**
**ADVERTISING AND PROMOTION EXPENSE BUDGET**

|  | Amount |
|---|---|
| Radio advertisements | |
| Television advertisements | |
| Newspaper advertisements | |
| Magazine advertisements | |
| Shopper advertisements | |
| Telephone advertisements and directories | |
| Catalogues | |
| Personal demonstrations | |
| Direct mail | |
| Door-to-door solicitation | |
| Samples | |
| Exhibits | |
| Total advertising and promotion expenses | |

**Exhibit 10.7**
**ADVERTISING BUDGET**

| Classification | Project Budget | Actual Expenditures | Commitment | Total | Estimated Cost to Complete | Balance Available |
|---|---|---|---|---|---|---|

**Exhibit 10.8**
**IMPACT OF INCREASED ADVERTISING ON PROFITS**

| (1) Additional Advertising Expenditures | (2) Additional Sales Volume | (3) Additional Profit per Unit | (4) = (1) ÷ (2) Incremental Advertising Cost per Unit | (5) = (3) − (4) Unit Incremental Profit | (6) = (2) × (5) Profit |
|---|---|---|---|---|---|
| $10,000 | 10,000 | $1.50 | $1 | $.50 | $5,000 |
| 10,000 | 15,000 | 1.40 | .67 | .73 | 10,950 |

The advertising plan should be reviewed periodically to assure that the right products are being emphasized. For example, the sales manager would not want to promote obsolete, unsuccessful, or hazardous products.

The marketing manager can evaluate the effectiveness of advertising by reviewing sales and profits before, during, and after promotion. The nonfinancial manager can monitor which customers are buying through coupons and reply cards. An analysis of competitors' activities should be made as they affect the company. Further, cost information for advertising programs can furnish data to make decisions on future media channels.

The marketing manager should appraise the effectiveness of a particular medium, such as by examining the cost per thousand (CPT). CPT is defined as the cost of advertising per thousand individuals reached by the media.

$$\text{Cost per Thousand} = \frac{\text{Cost of Dollars}}{\text{Circulation in Thousands}} \times 1{,}000$$

After the marketing manager has selected an appropriate media to use, the following questions should be answered. How essential is creativity? Is there a way to buy space and time that will stretch the advertising budget? How should the product or service be positioned?

Creativity involves getting attention with color, print size, layout, and contrast. Space and time are essential if the marketing manager wants to reach the target audience. For example, what days and hours do your customers watch television? If you sell sports equipment, then Saturday and Sunday are the best times.

The marketing manager should properly position advertising toward those consumers most likely to buy the product. He should also segment the market by demographics such as social class, age, gender, education, and income.

Advertising standards should be established to control costs. They may be based on cost per sales dollar, cost per sales transaction, cost per account, cost per unit of space, and cost per request for information.

Variances between budget and actual costs should be examined as a control measure. Exhibit 10.9 presents a variance analysis report for advertising and sales promotion.

Exhibit 10.10 presents a typical budget comparing sales by brand for the current month and cumulatively. Variances between budget and actual figures are expressed in dollars and percentage.

Exhibit 10.11 shows an analysis of product revenue.

Exhibit 10.9

## BUDGET AND ACTUAL ADVERTISING AND SALES PROMOTION

| Media Classification | Budget | Actual | Committed Funds | Total | Estimated Cost to Complete | Total Cost | Balance Available |
|---|---|---|---|---|---|---|---|
| Radio | $700 | $500 | $100 | $600 | $50 | $650 | $50 |
| Television | 630 | 400 | 150 | 550 | 60 | 610 | 20 |
| Magazines | 860 | 600 | 150 | 750 | 70 | 820 | 40 |
| Newspapers | 1,000 | 800 | 100 | 900 | 30 | 930 | 70 |
| Displays | 500 | 400 | 50 | 450 | 40 | 490 | 10 |
| Catalogs | 600 | 500 | 50 | 550 | 50 | 600 | 0 |
| Direct Mail | 400 | 300 | 60 | 360 | 20 | 380 | 20 |
| Total | $4,690 | $3,500 | $660 | $4,160 | $320 | $4,480 | $210 |

Exhibit 10.10

## SALES BY BRAND

| Brand | Month | | Variance | | Cumulative | | | |
|---|---|---|---|---|---|---|---|---|
| | Budget | Actual | Dollar | Percent | Budget | Actual | Dollar | Percent |
| Brand X—Green | | | | | | | | |
| Brand X—Yellow | | | | | | | | |
| Brand X—Blue | | | | | | | | |
| Total Brand X | | | | | | | | |
| Brand Y—Red | | | | | | | | |
| Brand Y—Orange | | | | | | | | |
| Total Brand Y | | | | | | | | |
| Brand Z—Small | | | | | | | | |
| Brand Z—Regular | | | | | | | | |
| Brand Z—Large | | | | | | | | |
| Brand Z—Extra Large | | | | | | | | |
| Other Brands | | | | | | | | |
| All Brands | | | | | | | | |

**Exhibit 10.11**
**ANALYSIS OF PRODUCT REVENUE**
**SOUTHERN TERROTORY**
**JUNE 1-30, 19X1**

| Week | Product W | | Product X | | Product Y | | Product Z | | Total |
|---|---|---|---|---|---|---|---|---|---|
| | Units | Dollars | Units | Dollars | Units | Dollars | Units | Dollars | Dollars |
| June 1–7 | | | | | | | | | |
| June 8–14 | | | | | | | | | |
| June 15–21 | | | | | | | | | |
| June 22–30 | | | | | | | | | |
| Total Actual | | | | | | | | | |
| Total Budget | | | | | | | | | |
| Variance | | | | | | | | | |
| Units | | | | | | | | | |
| Dollars | | | | | | | | | |

In comparing advertising costs to those of competing companies, reference may be made to *Advertising Age*.

## DISTRIBUTION COSTS

Distribution costs are costs to sell or market products in different territories. They are the costs for activities after goods are produced and until they are received by customers.

Marketing managers are responsible for budgeting and controlling distribution costs, which include packaging, advertising, transportation, credit and collection, warehousing and storage, salesperson salaries and commissions, promotion, and market research. A comparison should be made of the trend in distribution costs to total costs. There should be coordination of distribution policies in the overall marketing plan, including sales promotion, advertising, direct selling, warehousing, storage, and transportation.

Distribution factors and selling effort should be combined in such a way as to maximize sales and profits.

There is an interrelationship between the distribution cost budget and the manufacturing and financial budgets, as well as to the sales budget. Costs should be budgeted in total and for each activity. Distribution costs and efforts should be increased in those areas providing the most profitability.

For each territory, budgeted distribution costs depend on sales effort needed per dollar of cost, potential customers, buying power, population density, size of geographic area, and competition.

The manager must decide how much to pay for each type of distribution and the timing and classification of distribution expenditures.

The distribution budget aids in coordinating distribution policies and in deriving the best combination of distribution resources, including sales volume, selling prices, and selling effort. Distribution costs should be budgeted by function or activity, territory, salesperson, program or project, product, call, and type of selling effort. They should be budgeted in absolute dollars and as a percentage of net sales. The budget promotes cost control.

A typical distribution cost budget appears in Exhibit 10.12.

Exhibit 10.13 presents an illustrative project budget.

**Exhibit 10.12**
**DISTRIBUTION COST BUDGET**

| | | |
|---|---|---|
| Direct selling | | $300,000 |
| Transportation costs | | |
| Truck | $50,000 | |
| Rail | 60,000 | |
| Air | 130,000 | 240,000 |
| Storage | | 40,000 |
| Market research | | 20,000 |
| Other | | 10,000 |
| Total distribution costs | | $610,000 |

Distribution efforts should be based on market potential. Distribution costs may be reduced by modifying geographic areas to reduce selling cost and obtain more coverage, changing customer mix, altering distribution channels, modifying product mix, reassigning salespeople, and changing the method of sale. Costs for planning and control should be identified by responsibility, type of expenditure, order size, activity, program, territory, segment, distribution channel, and method of sale.

There should be a comparison of budget to actual distribution costs. Variances should be determined and analyzed. Further, distribution costs should be compared to those in competing companies.

## ANALYSIS AND EVALUATION OF DISTRIBUTION COSTS

Distribution cost analysis has as its objective obtaining the optimum distribution policy. Costs should be appraised by activity or function to promote planning and control. Cost analysis may be made by product or service, segment (department, store, branch), territory (state, city, district, county), customer type, order size, distribution channel (manufacturer, wholesaler, retailer, direct to customer), sales terms (cash, installment), salesperson, method of delivery (store delivery, over-the-counter), and method of sale (mail order, company store, salesperson, house solicitation).

There should be a comparison of each individual distribution cost to sales, such as transportation to sales. A higher ratio is unfavorable because a larger distribution expense is required for each sales dollar. Higher ratios mean less productivity. When distribution efforts are recurring and routine, it is useful to compare actual to budgeted costs for variance determination.

Exhibit 10.13
PROJECT BUDGET REPORT

| Number | Name | Hours | Salaries | Other Expenses | Total | Commitments | Estimated Cost to Complete | Total Cost | Project Budget | Under or Over Budget |
|--------|------|-------|----------|----------------|-------|-------------|----------------------------|------------|----------------|----------------------|
|        |      |       |          |                |       |             |                            |            |                |                      |

The variances are then investigated as to cause and appropriate action taken, if needed. In addition, a comparison should be made between the distribution costs in the company to those of competing companies. The differences should be analyzed.

## CONTROL OVER DISTRIBUTION COSTS

Distribution cost control involves functional responsibility and cost objectives. Costs should be assigned by responsibility center. Distribution costs by territory may be controlled by reorganizing the territory so that effort is more in line with benefits (e.g., selling expenses may be reduced with better coverage), eliminating unprofitable territories, changing the method of sale, reassigning salespeople, altering distribution channels, modifying advertising policy by territory, changing warehouse facilities, and identifying neglected customers who may buy.

## PACKAGING

Product development may take into account packaging changes and new kinds of packaging. Repackaging may be designed to save costs. The sales manager must decide on product size and form.

## TRAVEL AND ENTERTAINMENT

The budget for travel and entertainment is prepared by the sales manager after obtaining input from salespeople. The manager should evaluate entertainment expenses. Are they proportionate to the revenue obtained by salesperson, customer, and territory?

## BUDGET MEETINGS

At budget meetings, the manager should present a reasonable basis for his budget expectations. He should give an impression of being prepared, knowledgeable, and in control. A possible inconsistency in his presentation may raise doubts. For example, a manager may propose a slight budget increase in revenue because of a recession but at the same time request substantially higher expenditures because of inflation.

The manager does not want to give upper management the impression he is rushing through the budget or has not given it sufficient preparation.

## CONCLUSION

The marketing manager must prepare budgets for marketing costs so proper planning may occur. These costs include selling, advertising, and distribution. It is better to budget expenses based on a percentage of budgeted sales rather than on prior years' sales. What held in the past may not hold in the current year.

A thorough analysis and evaluation of marketing costs should be made to determine if they are excessive, such as by comparing each major expense category to sales. Problem areas must be identified and rectified. In this connection, the marketing manager should assign specific responsibilities to subordinates, such as salespeople, by territory or customer.

If sales are increasing due to higher sales prices but sales volume is about the same, only a few marketing expenses will increase. The work volume to process orders and the delivery costs will be about the same. However, advertising and promotion costs will increase to overcome sales resistance to the higher prices.

When sales volume increases, most marketing expenses increase, but they may not increase in proportion to sales volume. If the increased sales volume is from larger orders only and from existing customers, the collection, credit, and delivery costs will not increase in proportion to sales.

# Chapter 11

# RESEARCH AND DEVELOPMENT:
## Budgets for a Long-term Plan

Research and development (R&D) is needed to develop new products and services or to significantly improve existing ones in order to remain competitive and grow. R&D includes:

1) Conceptual formulation and design, as well as testing, in search for or evaluation of possible product or process alternatives

2) Modification of the formulation or design of a product or process

3) Design, construction, and testing of preproduction prototypes and models

4) Design of tools and dies involving new technology.

There should be planning and control over such R&D areas as how much to spend, what to spend it on, and how to assure that the funds are being spent properly. R&D should be accumulated by type of expenditure, by division, by department, and by responsibility center within a department. The budget for technical departments is the sum of the total budget for all R&D activities and supporting engineering services. The nonfinancial manager must constantly appraise R&D progress, success rate, problems, risks, staff, and facilities. R&D should primarily be based on long-run goals, competition, judgment, and financial capabilities.

R&D should be consistent with the goals of the division or department. Therefore, R&D should be higher for high-technology divisions. A division with older technology typically spends less on R&D and more on engineering to sustain current products and processes.

Preferably, R&D should be directed toward the future rather than to maintain current products. Its objectives should be based on a division's program. Resources may be spent for research and exploration, development, and sustainment.

R&D activities should be undertaken when the return obtained from such research justifies the costs incurred and risks assumed. In addition, R&D is worthwhile if the new product can be introduced before it is already obsolete or out of favor.

This chapter discusses the types of R&D costs, planning, establishing the proper funding level, preparation of R&D budgets, modifications to the budget, analysis and evaluation of R&D status, cost controls, risks associated with R&D efforts, and coordination of R&D policies within the company.

## R&D COSTS

There are direct and indirect costs associated with R&D projects:

- Personnel costs, including those of independent consultants. In general, personnel costs range between 50–75% of R&D costs.
- Depreciation on R&D laboratory and equipment.
- Supplies and materials
- Subscriptions to journals and magazines
- Rentals
- Travel
- Professional membership fees and attendance at technical conferences
- Property taxes

- Outside contractor fees
- Cost of intangibles purchased from others

## R&D PLANNING

In R&D, individual projects have to be planned, appraised, and controlled. Any project limitations have to be noted. The following should be considered:

- Progress of research efforts
- New and better products developed over the last 10 years
- The percentage of new products to total sales
- Average time required to proceed from the initial research stage (e.g., laboratory) to commercial production
- Cost/benefit of research
- Relationship between research and sales. Comparison should be made to success of competition in research (e.g., industry norms).

Figure 11.1 depicts the product life cycle.

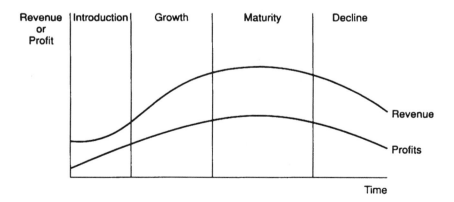

**Figure 11.1**
PRODUCT LIFE CYCLE

## FUNDING LEVEL

The manager must decide how much to fund research and which specific activities should be funded. The amount funded depends on how much support is needed to succeed, project priorities, number of programs desired, growth rate, size and capability of research staff, competition, trade and industry statistics, state of the economy, and political concerns.

The manager should set a minimum-maximum range for R&D funding and decide what circumstances would change this range.

Revised R&D calculations should be made when researchers request additional funding or time. The manager should determine if the request has merit or is a waste of additional resources. Then, he must decide whether to support the project modification or drop the product. The manager should set a high priority to fund developmental projects and these projects should be ranked after taking into account capital investment, expected costs, and anticipated earnings, including forecasted royalty receipts.

## R&D BUDGET

The R&D budget is based on an annual amount that the manager has decided to commit to develop new and improved products. The amount depends on the anticipated benefits based on previous efforts and success, desired growth rate, size of the division, risk and uncertainties, diversification, competition, market share, consumer tastes, financial resources, physical facilities, availability of raw materials, productivity, safety, reliability, price profitability, efficiency, productivity, employee number and capability, time constraints, product life cycle, stability of research program, obsolescence, and technological aspects.

A budget provision is needed so engineering keeps current products from becoming out-of-date.

The R&D budget may be based on the following:

- Estimated cost of specific projects
- A percentage of expected sales
- A percentage of current year and/or prior year sales
- A percentage of profit
- A percentage of operating income

- A percentage of investment in capital assets
- A percentage of cash flow
- R&D per unit
- R&D cost per hour equal to total R&D project costs divided by chargeable hours
- Product life cycle

The R&D budget should take into account the expected return on sales, return on investment (ROI), payback period, discounted payback period, net present value, and internal rate of return. A comparison should be made between the estimated ROI of a research project and its actual ROI. Variances should be computed and analyzed, with corrective action taken when warranted.

R&D costs should be allocated by responsibility center and then to each project or program within that segment, including support services.

In preparing the budget, there should be a reconciliation of budget costs of research efforts with the total estimated cost of maintaining R&D facilities and operations.

Program budgeting is research-related or applies to technical jobs applicable to programs. It typically follows a study of work performed.

If a proposal involving R&D cannot be scheduled, no budget should be prepared for the entire project. Instead, there should be a step-by-step budget allocating a specific amount for research work. Once the first step is completed, a budget allotment may be made for the second step.

A typical format for an R&D division budget is shown in Example 1.

**Example 1**
**R&D DIVISION BUDGET**
**For the Year Ended December 31, 19XX**

| | Quarter | | | | |
|---|---|---|---|---|---|
| | 1 | 2 | 3 | 4 | Total |

Costs

Controllable

    Salaries
    Professional dues

| | Quarter | | | | Total |
|---|---|---|---|---|---|
| | 1 | 2 | 3 | 4 | |

Heat, light, and power
Supplies
Cleaning
    Total

Noncontrollable

    Insurance
    Depreciation
    Taxes
        Total

Total R&D Costs

Examples 2 and 3 present typical R&D budgets.

### Example 2
### R& D BUDGET

Materials and Supplies

    Laboratory
    Equipment
    Repairs
        Total Materials and Supplies

Salaries

    Administrative
    Nonadministrative
    Technical staff
        Total Salaries

Other Direct Costs

    Membership Dues
    Depreciation
    Insurance
    Utilities
    Taxes
    Travel and Entertainment
        Total Other Direct Costs

Total Research and Development

**Example 3**
**R&D Budget**

| PROJECT | New Staff Required | Total Man-hours | Cost |
|---|---|---|---|

Research

    Electronic 5
    Laser 3
    Hydro 1
    Completed Projects
        Total Research

Development

    Tubes
    Gauges
    Testers
    Modes
        Total Development

Total Project Budgets

Administrative

    Patent
    Research
    Library
    General
        Total Administrative

Grand Total

Example 4 presents a budget report.

**Example 4**
**Budget Report**

Name of Department:
Name of Manager:
Period:
Date:

| Project | Current Month | | | Cumulative for Year | | |
|---|---|---|---|---|---|---|
| | Actual | Budget | Variance | Actual | Budget | Variance |
| | | | | | | |

Example 5 shows an illustrative R&D cost budget.

**Example 5**
**R&D EXPENSE BUDGET**

| Cost | Category | Actual | Latest | Estimate | Budget | Variance |
| --- | --- | --- | --- | --- | --- | --- |
| | | | | | | |

Examples 6 and 7 present illustrative project budgets.

**Example 6**
**R&D BUDGET**

| Project | Budget Man-hours | Actual Man-hours | Variance | Budgeted Cost | Actual Cost | Variance |
| --- | --- | --- | --- | --- | --- | --- |
| | | | | | | |

**Example 7**
**R&D BUDGET**

| Project | Project Number | Man-hours | Costs | Commitments | Estimated Cost and Hours to Complete | Budget Variance |
| --- | --- | --- | --- | --- | --- | --- |
| | | | | | | |

Example 8 shows a proposed R&D budget.

**Example 8**
**PROPOSED R&D BUDGET**

| Budget | Employees | Man-hours | Period Cost | Cumulative Cost |
| --- | --- | --- | --- | --- |
| | | | | |

## ANALYSIS AND EVALUATION

R&D analysis involves looking at past, current, and future projects. Each R&D project should be thoroughly analyzed in terms of marketing, production, and distribution. There should be a priority ranking so that the best R&D projects are undertaken, given the limitations of manpower, facilities, and financial resources.

R&D may be related to sales, profits, production, number of employees, labor hours, number of segments, entering new markets, expansion of product lines or services, and diversification attempts. The manager must determine whether the research staff has the technical ability and resources to undertake the project successfully.

The manager should evaluate where R&D funds are being used, how successful the R&D undertakings are by category and type, where additional funding should be placed because of potential opportunities, and where less funding should be made because of unsuccessful and problem programs.

He should evaluate R&D on a recurring, periodic basis, such as quarterly or semi-annually. Projects having greater uncertainty or risk may be evaluated more frequently, such as monthly. The manager should prepare a project screening report evaluating proposed R&D in terms of marketing, production, technical, safety, legal and financial aspects. There should be progress points to appraise and track R&D efforts.

Performance standards for research should be used and compared to actual performance. These standards include number of patents received, cost per patent, cost per operation, cost per hour, number of tests and formulas, number of requisitions, and research hours by activity. There should be a comparison between the actual costs incurred by program or activity to the funds budgeted for each R&D program or activity.

The manager should keep track of:

- R&D to net sales
- R&D by product
- Expected rates of return
- Estimated project costs
- Salaries to manhours

- Average R&D projects per period
- Research commitments

R&D employees (engineers, scientists) should be required to keep time sheets of hours spent by project, because a high percentage of R&D cost is labor.

Research programming examines research fields to be investigated and the depth of such coverage.

There should be periodic R&D status reports presenting objectives, potential, priority classification, technical achievements, amount of expenditures, and schedule of conformance.

Exhibits 11.1, 11.2, and 11.3 present R&D status reports.

## CONTROL OVER R&D

R&D is project-oriented and costs are accumulated by project. Due to the long duration of a project, adequate project control must exist to accumulate all costs from startup to the finished product. Further, R&D projects cannot be managed by quantity, volume-driven factors, or money that has been or has not been spent. For example, 75% of the money may have already been spent on the project, but that does not mean the project is 75% complete.

R&D expenditures should be in conformity with budget limitations. There should be project controls. Control reports are required by commitment and expenditure. In the control phase, there should be a comparison between the technical and financial aspects of projects. Projects should be continually appraised to determine which ones should be expanded, dropped, modified, or deferred.

A significant degree of cost control should be placed over high-risk R&D projects.

## R&D RISK

The risk must be analyzed and if there has been a high failure rate in R&D, proposed projects will have to be examined very closely. Have R&D projects in past years been completed at budget dollar amounts and within expected time periods? What has caused cost overruns and time delays? Do problems still exist or have they been rectified?

Exhibit 11.1
PROJECT STATUS REPORT

| Project | Project Identifier | Month | | | Cumulative to Date | | Purchase Commitments | Estimated Cost to Complete | | Total Cost | Project Budget | Cost (over) or under |
|---|---|---|---|---|---|---|---|---|---|---|---|---|
| | | Man-hours | Salaries | Other Expense  Total | Man-hours | Amount | | Man-hours | Amount | | | |
| PRODUCT IMPROVEMENTS | | | | | | | | | | | | |
| Project A | | | | | | | | | | | | |
| Project B | | | | | | | | | | | | |
| Project C | | | | | | | | | | | | |
| Project D | | | | | | | | | | | | |
| Total | | | | | | | | | | | | |
| NEW PRODUCT RESEARCH | | | | | | | | | | | | |
| Project X | | | | | | | | | | | | |
| Project Y | | | | | | | | | | | | |
| Project Z | | | | | | | | | | | | |
| Total | | | | | | | | | | | | |
| SALES REVENUE | | | | | | | | | | | | |
| Project P | | | | | | | | | | | | |
| Project Q | | | | | | | | | | | | |
| Total | | | | | | | | | | | | |
| FUNDAMENTAL RESEARCH | | | | | | | | | | | | |
| Project L | | | | | | | | | | | | |
| Project M | | | | | | | | | | | | |
| Total | | | | | | | | | | | | |
| Total R&D | | | | | | | | | | | | |

**Exhibit 11.2**
**R&D PROJECT STATUS REPORT**

| Project Number | Month | | Cumulative to Date | | | Cost | |
|---|---|---|---|---|---|---|---|
| | Man-hours | Expenditures | Man-hours | Expenditures | Commitments | Budget | Overrun |
| | | | | | | | |

**Exhibit 11.3**
**PROJECT STATUS REPORT**

Project Name:
Account Number:
Date Started:
Estimated Completion Date:
Priority Code:
Total Estimated Cost:
Review Date:
Budget:
Actual:
Status:
Progress and Accomplishments:
Recommendation and Comments:

R&D risk must be appraised by product and market. There is a greater risk when a manager goes from established products and markets to new products and markets. The longer the period between R&D activity and cash flows from the project, the greater the risk.

## COORDINATION

A research project may involve coordination between several departments and their managers, who must provide input and assistance to each other. They must know how to interact, what rules to follow, and how the research will benefit their particular responsibility areas and products.

## CONCLUSION

Research is defined as the testing in search for a product, while development means translating that research into a design for the new product.

R&D may be classified as new products, enhancements to current products, projects requested by salespeople and marketing, projects requested by the factory, and fundamental projects having no immediate commercial use.

The manager should continually appraise R&D programs. If a specific R&D project has excessive costs and delays, the feasibility of that project may be questionable.

The manager must decide on where to direct R&D efforts and how much to spend. The best alternative project must be selected and the progress on the project closely monitored.

# Chapter 12

# GENERAL AND ADMINISTRATIVE COSTS:
## Budgets for Maximum Productivity

The nonfinancial manager may identify general and administrative expenses by a particular function, activity, product line, service, segment, unit or other responsibility center. Managers may be assigned responsibility for administrative costs.

Administrative departments include general administration, personnel, legal, insurance, and computer services. Examples of administrative expenses are executive and office salaries, office rent, office expenses, legal expenses, and dues.

This chapter discusses the budget process, analysis and evaluation of costs, cost control, and employee considerations.

## BUDGET PROCESS

The manager may budget general and administrative expenses based on specific plans and programs. Because most administrative expenses are fixed, an analysis of the historical record will typically provide a sound basis to budget them. The variable-fixed breakdown is highly recommended.

The budgeting of administrative expenses is difficult to plan and control. One approach is to establish acceptable ranges of costs as percentages of revenue to achieve target earnings. Another is to review administrative costs and determine how much should be allocated to each area by using historical data.

It is worthwhile to break general and administrative expenses into discretionary and nondiscretionary costs. Discretionary costs, such as bonuses, are those that are not essential to satisfy short-term business goals. These costs are usually targets for cutting when costs need to be reduced.

The manager may budget rent simply by using the monthly rent figure. This figure should include an adjustment for cost of living increases, property taxes, and rent escalation clauses.

In budgeting salaries, multiply the number of employees by their monthly salaries. There should be included a provision for salary increases, sick leave time, vacation, holidays, and fringe benefits.

In budgeting taxes and licenses, use an historical percentage rate. Research city, state, and federal sources for potential increases. Divide by twelve months and apply it to each month of the budget. Payroll taxes can be approximated by taking a percentage between 10 and 15 percent of the gross payroll cost as the monthly budget.

In budgeting travel costs, determine what trips will be taken, where they will be taken, and who will be going. If only modest trips can be taken, divide the total annual dollars by twelve to determine the monthly

**Exhibit 12.1**
**DEPARTMENT BUDGET**

Department name and number:

Department manager:

Period:

| Item | Budgeted Cost | Actual Cost | Variance | Percent of Variance to Budget |
| --- | --- | --- | --- | --- |

budget. If extensive traveling is involved, calculate each month separately by the actual expected trips for that month.

A departmental budget for general and administrative expenses appears in Exhibit 12.1.

## ANALYSIS AND EVALUATION

Budgeted expenses should be documented as to how the amounts are derived and the source of information. Costs should be evaluated by type. They should be compared to sales over the years and to competing companies. If cost increases are substantially disproportionate to sales or production, the reasons must be found and, if necessary, corrective action taken. Costs may also be related to direct labor hours, operating income, and number of transactions.

Many administrative costs are not subject to specific measurement, standardization, or prediction. The manager should consider how many employees answer to him, what their job responsibilities are, and what objectives are to be met.

A manager in the engineering area should segregate his budget into suitable categories, such as product enhancement, operating difficulties, and cost reduction. The deadline dates for each major work stage should be stated.

## COST CONTROL

Cost controls must exist and there should be a balance between costs and sales. Maximum percentages by which certain costs cannot exceed sales may be set (e.g., 15% of sales). Costs may be reduced by eliminating duplicate or unnecessary activities.

## EMPLOYEES

Specific individuals should be assigned responsibility and control of general and administrative expenses. Further, there should be a balance in workload among employees. Employee bonuses and incentives should be based on earnings.

## CONCLUSION

Productivity must always be maintained in the administrative area, so the manager should exercise tight supervision. The general and administrative expense budget should be carefully prepared and analyzed, taking into account past history and the current environment.

# Chapter 13

# CAPITAL EXPENDITURES:
## Assets to Be Bought, Sold, and Discarded

Capital expenditures should be consistent with the long-term plan of the company. They may be for generating earnings by providing additional revenue or reducing costs, such as when the purchase of more efficient equipment and machinery results in lower maintenance expenditures. They should generate an adequate return and therefore a desired ROI should be set. Capital expenditures include replacing machinery to economize on costs, expanding production to increase volume, marketing of a new product, improving the quality of products or services, and manufacturing under proposed contracts. Capital expenditures should take into account current and needed facilities. Commitments must also be considered.

The capital expenditure budget reveals how much is required to invest in capital assets to meet the nonfinancial manager's objectives, so that his division or department can properly function. The budget breaks down the capital assets by major category, how much funding is needed, when that funding is required, the location of the assets, and pertinent reasons and comments.

The timing, nature, and adequacy of capital expenditures have a long-term impact on the manager's responsibility center.

Capital expenditures may be incurred because of growth, increased sales, increased production, changes in production methods, change in style, cost reduction, efficiency and effectiveness, productivity, improvement in product quality, new business, normal replacement, preventive maintenance, and counteracting competition.

The capital expenditure budget depends on such factors as future potential, return on investment, sales, profitability, productivity and efficiency, capacity utilization, payback period (how many years it takes to get the initial investment back), timing of needed capital expenditures, risk, technological obsolescence, diversification, safety concerns, financial position including cash flow, tax benefit and other government incentives, market share, new product development, maintenance and repair requirements, problem areas, replacement options, nature of industry, economic conditions, political factors, and laws and regulations (e.g., pollution requirements, restrictive uses on assets).

There are uncertain benefits for capital expenditures because of the significant cash outlay and long time period involved. In fact, if for some reason a capital expenditure fails, a significant loss is likely.

The manager should prepare the capital expenditure budget needed for his responsibility unit after consulting with engineering and technical staff. A capital asset cannot be bought unless it has been included in the capital budget.

Capital assets include equipment, furniture, machinery, storage facilities, distribution facilities, and computers.

The manager should only approve capital expenditures after detailed study and justification and, after that, continual monitoring and control are recommended. He should set up a priority listing of capital projects based on earnings or strategic importance. The planning should take into account the peculiar characteristics and nature of the industry and company.

Duplication in capital expenditures results in inefficiency and excessive costs. Control is in the form of comparing budgeted expenditures to actual expenditures. The trend in the ratio of insurance expense to the carrying value of the capital assets, and the insured value relative to replacement cost, will indicate the adequacy of insurance protection.

The timing of capital expenditures depends on available alternatives, start-up time, and funds. The manager must identify capital expenditures that are not essential, can be delayed for a reasonable time, or are urgently needed.

Some capital expenditures result in profit reductions, such as outlays that are required by law, improve R&D, and enhance employee morale. Some capital expenditures are required by government, such as for employee safety and to conform to building codes.

This chapter discusses the budget process, authorization of capital budgets, capital budget forms and reports (including special reports), budget revisions, analysis and evaluation of capital expenditures, and controls.

## THE BUDGET PROCESS

For budgeting, capital expenditures may be classified as normal or special. Normal expenditures are routine, less costly, and made to maintain current operations. Each project typically does not involve a large cash outlay. The normal capital expenditure should meet the needs of the manager's division or department. An example is a minor replacement of machinery.

Special capital expenditures are unusual, costly, and made for a specific purpose, such as the purchase of a new machine to manufacture a product for a special job of a one-time nature.

Major capital projects are typically planned and proposed by operating managers and must be approved by upper management. The manager must properly budget and package the capital expenditure. These expenditures must be classified by category, class, need, consequence, and feasibility. Capital expenditures may be required or optional. In the case of minor capital expenditures, the division and department managers may have the authority to approve them on their own.

The four steps in the capital expenditure budgetary process are approving the project, approving the estimate, authorizing the project, and follow-up. The capital expenditure proposal should contain a description, starting date, completion date, source information, and advantages and disadvantages of the proposal.

Some capital expenditures are minor and not subject to detailed planning. Examples are low-cost machinery and minor renovations. These minor expenditures may be lumped together with a blanket appropriation.

Capital expenditure policy should take into account the following:

- Desired rate of return
- Cost impact

- Age of existing assets
- Expected capacity of the item
- Asset life
- Growth potential
- Employee availability
- Competition
- Stage of the business cycle
- Legal liability exposure
- Regulatory requirements

The manager should set a priority ranking for capital expenditures in terms of operating necessities and nonnecessities. The following dates should be noted:

- Dates manpower will be available
- Marketing schedules for products to be produced
- Delivery dates when items are needed

A current capital budget usually covers 3–5 years in annual segments of planned capital expenditures.

## AUTHORIZATION OF CAPITAL BUDGET

If capital expenditures exceed authorized limits, special approval by top management is required. A project not meeting expectations or that is no longer appropriate, given current circumstances, may be cancelled. It is better to cancel a project if the cost/benefit relationship indicates that the project is no longer viable. If a project is a succession of individual projects, a partial authorization may be made.

Exhibit 13.1 is an illustrative capital budget request schedule form.

An authorization form should be filled out for approved capital expenditures. The reason and purpose of the expenditure should be given. Exhibits 13.2 and 13.3 are illustrative authorization forms.

The amount authorized should be periodically compared to actual costs incurred. In addition, commitments must be recorded and monitored because the total appropriated amount may ultimately be exceeded. The estimated cost to complete should also be noted along with any expected overruns or underruns.

**Exhibit 13.1**
**ABC COMPANY**
**ANNUAL CAPITAL BUDGET REQUEST 19X6**

| Description | Appropriations | | Total Commited | | Expected Capital Expenditures | | |
| --- | --- | --- | --- | --- | --- | --- | --- |
| | 19X5 Previous Year | 19X6 This Year | ROI | Amount | 19X5 19X6 | 19X7 | 19X8 and later   Total |
| **Absolutely Required** | | | | | | | |
| Air Pollution | | | | | | | |
| Conveyor | | | | | | | |
| Grinder | | | | | | | |
| Crusher | | | | | | | |
| **Need to Maintain** | | | | | | | |
| Competitive Position | | | | | | | |
| Quality Control Facility | | | | | | | |
| Color Retention | | | | | | | |
| **Replacements** | | | | | | | |
| **Growth and Expansion** | | | | | | | |
| DEF Recovery System | | | | | | | |
| LMN Plant | | | | | | | |
| **Minimal but Recommended** | | | | | | | |
| Lift Trucks | | | | | | | |
| Landscaping | | | | | | | |
| Roofing | | | | | | | |
| **Contingency Funding** | | | | | | | |
| **Total** | | | | | | | |

**Exhibit 13.2**
**CAPITAL EXPENDITURE AUTHORIZATION**

Division Name:
Division Number:
Location:
Date:
Reason for Authorization:
Estimated Total Cost:
Item Requested:
Description:
Estimated Cost Breakdown:
Comments and Recommendations:

| | Approved | Rejected | Date | Reason |
|---|---|---|---|---|

Requested by:
Approved by:

## CAPITAL BUDGET FORMS

Request forms should be completed and approved for capital expenditures. A commitment record contains the purchase orders issued. There is an appropriation form for capital expenditures. The form provides information on the benefits to be obtained from the proposed project and the expected cost savings. The authorization sets forth the type and scope of the project. Exhibit 13.4 is a typical annual capital budget request form.

Exhibit 13.5 is an illustrative preliminary budget request form.

An appropriation request form is filled out by the manager of the responsibility unit in detail, providing justification to support the capital proposal. The manager must thoroughly appraise the proposed capital project.

A proposal form for capital expenditures may include title of project, project objectives, description of project, proposed budget, analysis and evaluation, supporting documentation and calculations, justification, and time estimates.

Exhibits 13.6, 13.7, and 13.8 present typical appropriation request forms.

A capital budget form summarizes proposed capital projects for the period by responsibility center. Exhibit 13.9 presents an illustrative capital budget form.

### Exhibit 13.3
### CAPITAL EXPENDITURE AUTHORIZATION

Division:
Plant:
Date:

The capital expenditure is needed because of: (Check appropriate item)

___ New product
___ Normal replacement
___ Modification in production process
___ Cost reduction
___ Increased sales volume
___ New quality control standards
___ Style change

　　　Description and justification

Estimated Cost

　　Material
　　Labor
　　Overhead
　　Contingency
　　　　Total Cost

Expected Return on Investment

　　Payback Period
　　Life
　　Construction Period
　　Disposal Value

Manager's Comments and Recommendations:

Requested by:
Approved by:

### Exhibit 13.4
### ANNUAL CAPITAL BUDGET REQUEST FORM

Description　Appropriations　Capital　Expenditures　Future Commitments

**Exhibit 13.5**
**PRELIMINARY BUDGET REQUEST INFORMATION**

Division Name:
Division Number:
Department Name:
Department Number:
Date:
Responsible Individuals:
Project Classification:
Original Request or Supplementary Request:
Funds Requested:
Proposal Description:
Time Schedule:

> Beginning Date:
> Expected Ending Date:

Expected Benefits:
Priority Level:
Expected Return
Approvals

**Exhibit 13.6**
**APPROPRIATION REQUEST FORM**

Division:
Department:
Responsibility Unit:
Project Description:
Project Location:
Expected Expenditures

> Initial Request Amount
> Amount Approved to Date
> Future Request
> Total Project Cost

Return on Investment
Payback Period:
Net Present Value:
Internal Rate of Return:
Background Information:
Recommendations:
Classifications:
Nature of Capital Project Proposal:

## Exhibit 13.7
### PRELIMINARY BUDGET REQUEST INFORMATION

Date:
Division Name:                     Department Name:
Division Number:                   Department Number:

Type of Capital Expenditure

New
Expansion
Replacement
Cost Reduction
Other (Description)

Request

Initial
Supplementary

Priority Classification

Proposal Description

Identification of Capital Expenditure

Expected Rate of Return

Expected Cash Flows (net)

Time Schedule

Approvals

Department Manager:                     Date:
Division Manager:                        Date:
Vice-President:                          Date:

Comments

## Exhibit 13.8
### CAPITAL EXPENDITURES REQUEST FORM

Responsibility Unit Name:
Responsibility Unit Number:
Time Period:

| Description | Quantity | Justification | Budgeted | Cost | Date of Purchase |
| --- | --- | --- | --- | --- | --- |

Prepared by:                     Date:
Approved by:                     Date:

**Exhibit 13.9**
**CAPITAL BUDGET FORM**

| Department | Item | Description | Item Number | Status | Total Expenditure | Expected Rate of Return | Priority | Classification |
|---|---|---|---|---|---|---|---|---|
| | | | | | | | | |

## CAPITAL BUDGET

The capital asset budget includes beginning balance, additions, deletions, depreciation, construction in progress, and ending balance. The budget format should include category, class, project title, project number, project life, capital costs, and return on investment. The budget should contain a provision for explanatory comments.

Extraordinary repairs are usually included in the capital expenditure budget but ordinary repairs are included in the expense budget.

The production budget may require capital additions.

Exhibits 13.10–13.16 present illustrative capital budgets.

**Exhibit 13.10**
**CAPITAL EXPENDITURES BUDGET**
**FOR THE YEAR ENDED DECEMBER 31, 19XX**

| | |
|---|---|
| Machinery | $1,500,000 |
| Equipment | 800,000 |
| Furniture and Fixtures | 200,000 |
| Total | $2,500,000 |

**Exhibit 13.11**
**CAPITAL EXPENDITURES BUDGET**

| Item | To Maintain Current Operations | To Expand | Total |
|---|---|---|---|
| A | $300,000 | $200,000 | $500,000 |
| C | 100,000 | 50,000 | 150,000 |
| Equipment | 150,000 | 100,000 | 250,000 |
| Total | $550,000 | $350,000 | $900,000 |

**Exhibit 13.12**
**PRELIMINARY CAPITAL BUDGET**

| Item Number | Work Order Number | Appropriation Number | Description of Job by Department | Unit Projected Total Cost Classified by Date of Expenditure | | | | | Estimated Expenditures 1995–1997 Classified by Accounting Disposition | | | Expense | |
|---|---|---|---|---|---|---|---|---|---|---|---|---|---|
| | | | | Before 1995 | 1995 | 1996 | 1997 | After 1997 | Additional Facilities | Replacements | Rehabilitation | Repairs | Other |

**Exhibit 13.13**
**CAPITAL EXPENDITURE BUDGET**

| Project | Budgeted Amount | Amount Authorized | Unexpended Balance | Actual Expenditures | Amount Subject to Authorization | Amount Spent |
|---|---|---|---|---|---|---|

**Exhibit 13.14**
**CAPITAL EXPENDITURE BUDGET**

Amount to be Expended by Quarter

| | 1 | 2 | 3 | 4 | Total | In Later Periods |
|---|---|---|---|---|---|---|
| Approved Projects: | | | | | | |
| Proposed New Projects: | | | | | | |
| Proposed Replacements: | | | | | | |

**Exhibit 13.15**
**CAPITAL ASSET BUDGET**
**DIVISION X**

| Type of Project | Carryforward Amount | Commitments | | Expenditures | | | Carryforward to Future Years |
|---|---|---|---|---|---|---|---|
| | | New Commitments | Total Amount Available | On Previous Years' Commitments | Current Year Authorization | Total for Year | |
| Capital Expenditures | | | | | | | |
| Capital Leases | | | | | | | |

**Exhibit 13.16**
**BUDGET FOR CAPITAL ASSETS**

| Classification | Amount at Beginning of Year | Additions | Subtractions | Depreciation | Amount at End of Year |
|---|---|---|---|---|---|

**Exhibit 13.17**
**CAPITAL EXPENDITURES IN-PROCESS REPORT**

| Item Number | Description | Approval Amount | Initial Expected Project Completion Date | Incurred to Date | Balance for Completion | Total | Expected Variation | Favorable or Unfavorable | Expected Completion Date | Comments |
|---|---|---|---|---|---|---|---|---|---|---|

## CAPITAL EXPENDITURE REPORTS

The capital expenditure report should contain information of the authorized amount, actual costs, commited funds, unencumbered balance, estimated cost to complete, and cost overrun (underrun).

Exhibit 13.17 presents a capital expenditures process report.

Exhibits 13.18 and 13.19 present typical reports showing the comparison of budgeted expenditures to actual expenditures.

Exhibit 13.20 presents a capital expenditure status report. This report should be periodically prepared by the manager to keep track of a project so that analysis and control may be facilitated.

A progress report should be prepared to determine if all is going as

Exhibit 13.18
YEAR-TO-DATE COMPARISONS OF BUDGET TO ACTUAL CAPITAL
EXPENDITURES

| Type | Budgeted Projects | Projects Not Budgeted | Total | Amount Budgeted | Actual Expenditures | Over (Under) Budget |
|------|------|------|------|------|------|------|
| | | | | | | |

Exhibit 13.19
CAPITAL EXPENDITURESPERFORMANCE REPORT
ESTIMATED VS. ACTUAL

Department Name:
Department Number:
Authorization Number:
Description:
Today's Date:
Date Activity Began:

| Item | Authorized Amount | Cumulative Actual Amount | Variance | Percent | Reason |
|------|------|------|------|------|------|
| A | $100,000 | $103,000 | $3,000 | 3% | Delay because of strike |
| B | 80,000 | 81,000 | 1,000 | 1.25 | Higher prices for component parts |

etc.

**Exhibit 13.20**
**CAPITAL EXPENDITURES PERFORMANCE REPORT INFORMATION**

COST INFORMATION

Budgeted Amount
Cumulative Actual Expenditures
Committed Amounts
Unexpended Amount
Expected Cost to Complete
Variance Between Budget and Actual Amounts

DATES

Date Began
Expected Completion Date
Days Delayed
Reason for Delay

EXTENT OF COMPLETION

Percent of time completed to date
Percent of cost completed to date

EXPLANATORY COMMENTS

Quality
Unusual Occurrences and Reasons

planned and what corrective action is needed, if any. A detailed evaluation of capital expenditures may not be possible when a sudden, unexpected, or important development occurs. An example is a machine breakdown resulting in a production delay on the assembly line.

A capital expenditures progress report monitors each project's progress and indicates any overruns or underruns. Exhibits 13.21–13.26 present representative reports.

## BUDGET REVISIONS

Capital budgets should be revised when errors are found or circumstances change. Revisions would be required for changes in cost estimates, unexpected developments in the economy, design changes, technological devel-

**Exhibit 13.21**
**CAPITAL EXPENDITURES PROGRESS REPORT**

| Item Number | Description | Amount Approved | Expected Completion Date | Cumulative Expenditures to Date | Amount Needed for Completion | Total Actual Expenditures | Budgeted Expenditures | Variance | Comments |
|---|---|---|---|---|---|---|---|---|---|
| | | | | | | | | | |

**Exhibit 13.22**
**ABC MANUFACTURING COMPANY**

| Department and Cost | Authorized Amount | Cumulative Expenditures to Date | Purchase Commitments | Total Expenditures and Commitments | Balance Remaining |
|---|---|---|---|---|---|
| **RESEARCH** | | | | | |
| Salaries | $60,000 | $50,000 | $4,000 | $54,000 | $6,000 |
| Supplies | 80,000 | 70,000 | 7,000 | 77,000 | 3,000 |
| Power | etc. | | | | |
| Total | | | | | |
| **DEVELOPMENT** | | | | | |
| Salaries | | | | | |
| Traveling | | | | | |
| Other | | | | | |
| Total | | | | | |
| **PATENT** | | | | | |
| Legal Fees | | | | | |
| Application Fees | | | | | |
| Total | | | | | |
| **ADMINISTRATIVE** | | | | | |
| Salaries | | | | | |
| Depreciation | | | | | |
| Total | | | | | |

## Exhibit 13.23
## CAPITAL EXPENDITURE PROJECTS

| Project Number | Description | Actual Expenditures | | Commitments and Expenditures to Date | Estimated Cost to Complete | Current Estimated Total Cost | Appropriated Amount | Over/Under Appropriation |
|---|---|---|---|---|---|---|---|---|
| | | Current Month | Cumulative | | | | | |
| | | | | | | | | |

## Exhibit 13.24
## CAPITAL EXPENDITURE PROJECT STATUS REPORT

Division:
Location:
Category:
Project Title:
Project Number:
Project Appropriation and Investment:
Capital Expenditure Items:
ROI:
Payback Period:
Discounted Payback Period:
Net Present Value

| Total Actual Amount Approved | Actual Amount Spent to Date | Initial Budgeted Amount | Revised Budgeted Amount | Variance | Reason |
|---|---|---|---|---|---|
| | | | | | |

Comments and Recommendation:
Preparer
Reviewer

**Exhibit 13.25**
**CAPITAL EXPENDITURE APPROPRIATION STATUS REPORT**

| Number | Category | Description | Order Number | Amount Appropriated | Completion Date | Estimate | Commitments | Actual Expenditures | Variance |
|--------|----------|-------------|--------------|---------------------|-----------------|----------|-------------|---------------------|----------|
|        |          |             |              |                     |                 |          |             |                     |          |

**Exhibit 13.26**
**STATUS OF CAPITAL EXPENDITURES APPROPRIATED**

| Appropriation Number | Description | Work Order Number | Appropriation | Completion Date | Initial Estimate | Outstanding Commitments | Cumulative Actual Expenditures | Estimated Cost to Complete | Total Cost | Over/Under Initial Estimate |
|----------------------|-------------|-------------------|---------------|-----------------|------------------|-------------------------|--------------------------------|----------------------------|------------|------------------------------|
|                      |             |                   |               |                 |                  |                         |                                |                            |            |                              |

opments, action by competitors, change in divisional or departmental objectives, and casualty losses.

## SPECIAL PROJECTS

Special capital expenditures involve nonroutine, large cash outlays for major specific projects. An example is the purchase of new machinery to meet customer demand. Optional projects include equipment replacement, capital expansion, modified techniques, and new ventures. Capital expenditures should be consistent with the manager's desired return on investment.

## ANALYSIS OF CAPITAL PROJECTS

The manager should compare the expected profit to actual profit for each capital project. There should be an evaluation of the difference between budgeted and actual capital expenditures, along with justification.

Some questions to be answered by managers include: Are specialized equipment and machinery required? If capacity is expanded, what impact will it have on warehouse space?

## CONTROL OVER CAPITAL EXPENDITURES

The manager should control individual projects from beginning to end. Capital expenditure outlays should be documented by supplier. Contractor price quotations should be reviewed for reasonableness. Competitive comparisons should be made. Contractors may be changed when cost savings arise, quality problems exist, or delivery dates are not being met.

## CONCLUSION

The capital expenditure budget lists capital assets to be purchased, sold, or discarded. Capital expenditures may be made to replace obsolete machinery or to expand and improve operations, such as expenditures for new product lines. The manager should carefully evaluate alternative capital proposals. Further, retirement of capital assets without adequate replacement may have negative long-term effects.

# Chapter 14

# FORECASTING AND PLANNING:
## *Reducing Risk in Decision-making*

Management in both private and public organizations typically operates under conditions of uncertainty or risk. Probably the most important function of business is forecasting, which is a starting point for planning and budgeting. The objective of forecasting is to reduce risk in decision-making.

In business, forecasts form the basis for planning capacity, production and inventory, manpower, sales and market share, finances and budgeting, research and development, and top management's strategy.

Sales forecasts are especially crucial aspects of many financial management activities, including budgets, profit planning, capital expenditure analysis, and acquisition and merger analysis.

Figure 14.1 illustrates how sales forecasts relate to various managerial functions of business.

## WHO USES FORECASTS?

Forecasts are needed for marketing, production, purchasing, manpower, and financial planning. Further, top management needs forecasts for plan-

225

**Figure 14.1**
SALES FORECAST AND MANAGERIAL FUNCTIONS

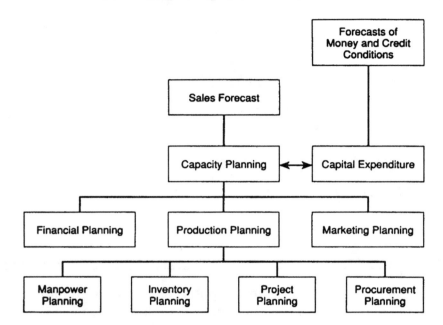

ning and implementing long-term strategic objectives and planning for capital expenditures. More specifically, marketing managers use sales forecasts to determine optimal sales force allocations, set sales goals, and plan promotions and advertising. Market share, prices, and trends in new product development are also required.

Production planners need forecasts in order to:

- Schedule production activities
- Order materials
- Establish inventory levels
- Plan shipments

Other areas that need forecasts include material requirements (purchasing and procurement), labor scheduling, equipment purchases, maintenance requirements, and plant capacity planning.

As shown in Figure 14.1, as soon as the company makes sure that it has enough capacity, the production plan is developed. If the company does not have enough capacity, it will require planning and budgeting decisions for capital spending for capacity expansion.

On this basis, the manager must estimate the future cash inflow and outflow. He must plan cash and borrowing needs for the company's future operations. Forecasts of cash flows and the rates of expenses and revenues are needed to maintain corporate liquidity and operating efficiency. In planning for capital investments, predictions about future economic activity are required so that returns or cash inflows accruing from the investment may be estimated.

Forecasts are needed for money and credit conditions and interest rates so that the cash needs of the firm may be met at the lowest possible cost. Forecasts must also be made for interest rates, to support the acquisition of new capital, the collection of accounts receivable to help in planning working capital needs, and capital equipment expenditure rates to help balance the flow of funds in the organization.

Sound predictions of foreign exchange rates are increasingly important to managers of multinational companies (MNCs).

Long-term forecasts are needed for the planning of changes in the company's capital structure. Decisions on issuing stock or debt to maintain the desired financial structure require forecasts of money and credit conditions.

The personnel department requires a number of forecasts in planning for human resources. Workers must be hired, trained, and provided with benefits that are competitive with those available in the firm's labor market. Also, trends that affect such variables as labor turnover, retirement age, absenteeism, and tardiness need to be forecast for planning and decision making.

Managers of nonprofit institutions and public administrators must also make forecasts for budgeting purposes.

Hospital administrators forecast the health care needs of the community. In order to do this efficiently, a projection has to be made of:

- The growth in absolute size of population
- The changes in the number of people in various age groupings
- The varying medical needs these different age groups will have

Universities forecast student enrollments, cost of operations, and, in many cases, the funds to be provided by tuition and by government appropriations.

The service sector, which today accounts for two-thirds of the U.S. gross domestic product (GDP), including banks, insurance companies, restaurants, and cruise ships, needs various projections for its operational and long-term strategic planning.

Take a bank, for example. The bank has to forecast:

- Demands of various loans and deposits
- Money and credit conditions so that it can determine the cost of money it lends

## FORECASTING METHODS

There is a wide range of forecasting techniques from which the company may choose. There are basically two approaches to forecasting, qualitative and quantitative. They are as follows:

1. Qualitative approach—forecasts based on judgement and opinion.

- Executive opinions
- Delphi technique
- Sales force polling
- Consumer surveys

2. Quantitative approach
   a) Forecasts based on historical data

   - Naive methods
   - Moving averages
   - Exponential smoothing
   - Trend analysis
   - Decomposition of time series

   b) Associative (Causal) forecasts

   - Simple regression

- Multiple regression
- Econometric modeling

Figure 14.2 summarizes the forecasting methods. The list presented in the Figure is neither comprehensive nor exhaustive. Sophisticated time series methods such as Box-Jenkins are reserved for an advanced forecasting text.

Quantitative models work superbly as long as little or no systematic change in the environment takes place. When patterns or relationships do change, by themselves, the objective models are of little use. It is here where the qualitative approach, based on human judgment, is indispensable. Because judgmental forecasting also bases forecasts on observation of existing trends, they too are subject to a number of shortcomings. The advantage, however, is that they can identify systematic change more quickly and interpret better the effect of such change on the future.

Figure 14.2
FORECASTING METHODS

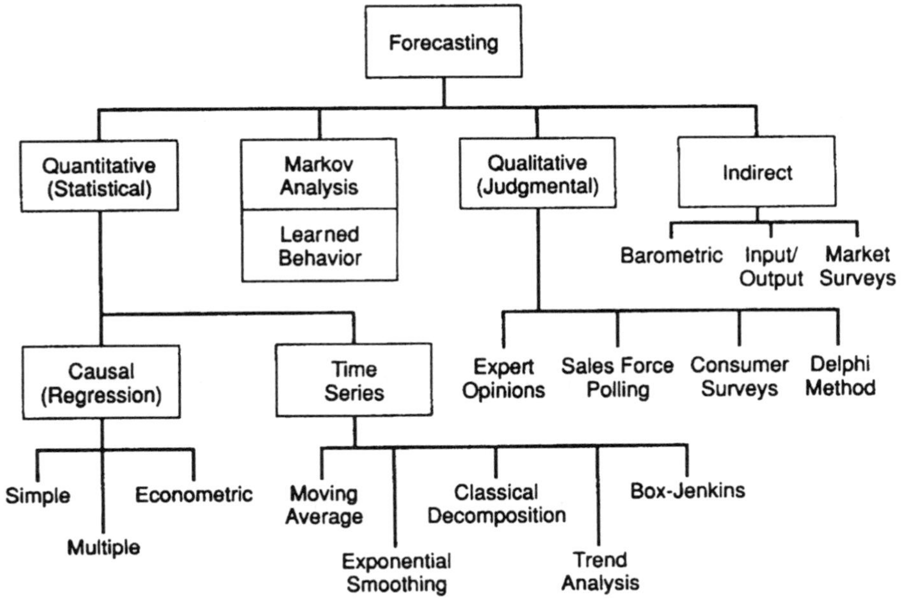

We will discuss the qualitative method in this chapter, while several quantitative methods, along with their illustrations, will be taken up in the subsequent two chapters.

## SELECTION OF FORECASTING METHOD

The choice of a forecasting technique is significantly influenced by the stage of the product life cycle and sometimes by the firm or industry for which a decision is being made.

In the beginning of the product life cycle, relatively small expenditures are made for research and market investigation. During the first phase of product introduction, these expenditures start to increase. In the rapid growth stage, considerable amounts of money are involved in the decisions, so a high level of accuracy is desirable. After the product has entered the maturity stage, the decisions are more routine, involving marketing and manufacturing. These are important considerations when determining the appropriate sales forecast technique.

After evaluating the particular stages of the product, and firm and industry life cycles, a further probe is necessary. Instead of selecting a forecasting technique by using whatever seems applicable, decision makers should determine what is appropriate. Some of the techniques are quite simple and rather inexpensive to develop and use. Others are extremely complex, require significant amounts of time to develop, and may be quite expensive. Some are best suited for short-term projections, others for intermediate- or long-term forecasts.

What technique or techniques to select depends on the following criteria:

1. What is the cost associated with developing the forecasting model, compared with potential gains resulting from its use? The choice is one of benefit–cost trade-off.
2. How complicated are the relationships that are being forecasted?
3. Is it for short-run or long-run purposes?
4. How much accuracy is desired?
5. Is there a minimum tolerance level of errors?
6. How much data are available? Techniques vary in the amount of data they require.

## THE QUALITATIVE APPROACH

The qualitative (or judgmental) approach can be useful in formulating short-term forecasts and can also supplement the projections based on the use of any of the quantitative methods.

Four of the better known qualitative forecasting methods are Executive Opinions, the Delphi Method, Sales Force Polling, and Consumer Surveys.

### EXECUTIVE OPINIONS

The subjective views of executives or experts from sales, production, finance, purchasing, and administration are averaged to generate a forecast about future sales. Usually, this method is used in conjunction with some quantitative method, such as trend extrapolation. The management team modifies the resulting forecast, based on their expectations.

The advantage of this approach is that the forecasting is done quickly and easily, without need of elaborate statistics. Also, the jury of executive opinions may be the only feasible means of forecasting in the absence of adequate data.

The disadvantage, however, is that of "group think." This is a set of problems inherent to those who meet as a group. Foremost among these are high cohesiveness, strong leadership, and insulation of the group. With high cohesiveness, the group becomes increasingly conforming through group pressure which helps stifle dissension and critical thought. Strong leadership fosters group pressure for unanimous opinion. Insulation of the group tends to separate the group from outside opinions, if given.

### THE DELPHI METHOD

This is a group technique in which a panel of experts are individually questioned about their perceptions of future events. The experts do not meet as a group, in order to reduce the possibility that consensus is reached because of dominant personality factors. Instead, the forecasts and accompanying arguments are summarized by an outside party and returned to the experts along with further questions. This continues until a consensus is reached.

This type of method is useful and quite effective for long-range forecasting. The technique is done by questionnaire format and eliminates the disadvantages of group think. There is no committee or debate. The experts are not influenced by peer pressure to forecast a certain way, as the answer is not intended to be reached by consensus or unanimity.

Low reliability is cited as the main disadvantage of the Delphi Method, as well as lack of consensus from the returns.

### SALES-FORCE POLLING

Some companies use as a forecast source sales people who have continual contacts with customers. They believe that the sales force who is closest to the ultimate customers may have significant insights regarding the state of the future market. Forecasts based on sales-force polling may be averaged to develop a future forecast. Or they may be used to modify other quantitative and/or qualitative forecasts that have been generated internally in the company.

The advantages of this forecast are:

(1) It is simple to use and understand

(2) It uses the specialized knowledge of those closest to the action

(3) It can place responsibility for attaining the forecast in the hands of those who most affect the actual results

(4) The information can be easily broken down by territory, product, customer, or salesperson

The disadvantages include salespeople's being overly optimistic or pessimistic regarding their predictions and inaccuracies due to broader economic events that are largely beyond their control.

### CONSUMER SURVEYS

Some companies conduct their own market surveys regarding specific consumer purchases. Surveys may consist of telephone contacts, personal interviews, or questionnaires as a means of obtaining data. Extensive statistical analysis is usually applied to survey results in order to test hypotheses regarding consumer behavior.

## COMMON FEATURES AND ASSUMPTIONS INHERENT IN FORECASTING

As pointed out, forecasting techniques are quite different from each other. But there are certain features and assumptions that underlie the business of forecasting. They are:

1. Forecasting techniques generally assume that the same underlying causal relationship that existed in the past will continue to prevail in the future. In other words, most of our techniques are based on historical data.

2. Forecasts are rarely perfect. Therefore, for planning purposes, allowances should be made for inaccuracies. For example, the company should always maintain a safety stock in anticipation of a sudden depletion of inventory.

3. Forecast accuracy decreases as the time period covered by the forecast (that is, the time horizon) increases. Generally speaking, a long-term forecast tends to be more inaccurate than a short-term forecast because of the greater uncertainty.

4. Forecasts for groups of items tend to be more accurate than forecasts for individual items, since forecasting errors among items in a group tend to cancel each other out. For example, industry forecasting is more accurate than individual firm forecasting.

## STEPS IN THE FORECASTING PROCESS

There are six basic steps in the forecasting process. They are:

1. Determine the what and why of the forecast and what will be needed. This will indicate the level of detail required in the forecast (for example, forecast by region, by product), the amount of resources (for example, computer hardware and software, manpower) that can be justified, and the level of accuracy desired.

2. Establish a time horizon, short-term or long-term. More specifically, project for the next year or next 5 years.

3. Select a forecasting technique. Refer to the criteria discussed before.

4. Gather the data and develop a forecast.

5. Identify any assumptions that had to be made in preparing the forecast and using it.

6. Monitor the forecast to see if it is performing in a manner desired. Develop an evaluation system for this purpose. If not, go back to step 1.

## CONCLUSION

Managers use forecasts for budgeting purposes. A forecast aids in determining volume of production, inventory needs, labor hours required, cash requirements, and financing needs. There are a variety of forecasting methods available. However, consideration has to be given to cost, preparation time, accuracy, and time period. The assumptions on which a particular forecast method is based must be clearly understood by the manager to obtain maximum benefit.

# Chapter 15

# MOVING AVERAGES AND SMOOTHING TECHNIQUES:
## *Quantitative Forecasting*

This chapter discusses several quantitative forecasting methods. The discussion includes naive models, moving averages, and exponential smoothing. Trend analysis and regressions are covered in future chapters. Qualitative methods were described in Chapter 14.

## NAIVE MODELS

Naive forecasting models are based exclusively on historical observation of sales or other variables, such as earnings and cash flows. They do not attempt to explain the underlying causal relationships which produce the variable being forecast.

Naive models may be classified into two groups. One group consists of simple projection models. These models require inputs of data from recent observations, but no statistical analysis is performed. The second group is made up of models which, while naive, are complex enough to require a computer. Traditional methods such as classical decomposition, moving average, and exponential smoothing models are some examples.

The advantage is that it is inexpensive to develop, store data, and operate. The disadvantage is that it does not consider any possible causal relationships that underly the forecasted variable.

A simple example of a naive model type:

1) Use the actual sales of the current period as the forecast for the next period. Let us use the symbol $Y'_{t+1}$ as the forecast value and the symbol $Y_t$ as the actual value. Then,

$$Y'_{t+1} = Y_t$$

2) If you consider trends, then

$$Y'_{t+1} = Y_t + (Y_t - Y_{t-1})$$

This model adds the latest observed absolute period-to-period change to the most recent observed level of the variable.

3) If you want to incorporate the rate of change rather than the absolute amount, then

$$Y'_{t+1} = Y_t \frac{Y_t}{Y_{t-1}}$$

## Example 1

Consider the following sales data:

| Month | 19X1 Monthly Sales of Product |
|-------|-------------------------------|
| 1     | $3,050                        |
| 2     | 2,980                         |
| 3     | 3,670                         |
| 4     | 2,910                         |
| 5     | 3,340                         |
| 6     | 4,060                         |
| 7     | 4,750                         |
| 8     | 5,510                         |
| 9     | 5,280                         |
| 10    | 5,504                         |
| 11    | 5,810                         |
| 12    | 6,100                         |

We will develop forecasts for January 19X2 based on the aforementioned three models:

1. $Y'_{t+1} = Y_t = \$6{,}100$

2. $Y'_{t+1} = Y_t + (Y_t - Y_{t-1}) = \$6{,}100 + (\$5{,}810 - \$5{,}504)$
$$= \$6{,}100 + \$306 = \$6{,}406$$

3.
$$Y'_{t+1} = Y_t \frac{Y_t}{Y_{t-1}}$$

$$= \$6{,}100 \times \frac{\$6{,}100}{\$5{,}810} = \$6{,}100\,(1.05)$$

$$= \$6{,}405$$

The naive models can be applied, with little need of a computer, to develop forecasts for sales, earnings, and cash flows. They must be compared with more sophisticated models, such as the regression method, for forecasting efficiency.

## SMOOTHING TECHNIQUES

Smoothing techniques are a higher form of naive models. The two typical forms are moving averages and exponential smoothing. Moving averages are the simpler of the two.

### MOVING AVERAGES

Moving averages are averages that are updated as new information is received. With the moving average, a manager simply employs the most recent observations to calculate an average, which is used as the forecast for the next period.

#### Example 2

Assume that the marketing manager has the following sales data.

| Date | Actual Sales ($Y_t$) |
|------|----------------------|
| Jan. 1 | 46 |
| 2 | 54 |
| 3 | 53 |
| 4 | 46 |
| 5 | 58 |
| 6 | 49 |
| 7 | 54 |

In order to predict the sales for the seventh and eighth days of January, the manager has to pick the number of observations for averaging purposes. Let us consider two cases. One is a six-day moving average and the other is a three-day average.

*Case 1*

$$Y_7' = \frac{46 + 54 + 53 + 46 + 58 + 49}{6} = 51$$

$$Y_8' = \frac{54 + 53 + 46 + 58 + 49 + 54}{6} = 52.3$$

where $Y'$ = predicted

*Case 2*

$$Y_7' = \frac{46 + 58 + 49}{3} = 51$$

$$Y_8' = \frac{58 + 49 + 54}{3} = 53.6$$

| Date | Actual Sales | Predicted Sales ($Y'_t$) Case 1 | Case 2 |
|------|--------------|--------|--------|
| Jan. 1 | 46 | | |
| 2 | 54 | | |
| 3 | 53 | | |
| 4 | 46 | | |
| 5 | 58 | | 51 |
| 6 | 49 | | 53.6 |
| 7 | 54 | 51 | |
| 8 | | 52.3 | |

In terms of weights given to observations, in Case 1, the old data received a weight of 5/6 and the current observation got a weight of 1/6. In Case 2, the old data received a weight of only 2/3 while the current observation received a weight of 1/3.

Thus, the marketing manager's choice of the number of periods to use in a moving average is a measure of the relative importance attached to old versus current data.

### ADVANTAGES AND DISADVANTAGES

The moving average is simple to use and easy to understand. However, there are two shortcomings:

- It requires you to retain a great deal of data and carry it along with you from forecast period to forecast period.
- All data in the sample are weighted equally. If more recent data are more valid than older data, why not give it greater weight?

The forecasting method known as exponential smoothing gets around these disadvantages.

### EXPONENTIAL SMOOTHING

Exponential smoothing is a popular technique for short-run forecasting by managers. It uses a weighted average of past data as the basis for a forecast. The procedure gives heaviest weight to more recent information and smaller weight to observations in the more distant past. The reason is that the future is more dependent upon the recent past than on the distant past.

The method is known to be effective when there is randomness and no seasonal fluctuations in the data. One disadvantage of the method, however, is that it does not include industrial or economic factors such as market conditions, prices, or the effects of competitors' actions.

### THE MODEL

The formula for exponential smoothing is:

$$Y'_{t+1} = \alpha Y_t + (1 - \alpha) Y'_t$$

or in words,

$$Y'_{new} = \alpha\, Y_{old} + (1 - \alpha)\, Y'_{old}$$

where $Y'_{new}$ = Exponentially smoothed average to be used as the forecast.
$Y_{old}$ = Most recent actual data.
$Y'_{old}$ = Most recent smoothed forecast.
$\alpha$ = Smoothing constant.

The higher the $\alpha$, the higher the weight given to the more recent information.

### Example 3

The following data on sales are given below.

| Time period (t) | Actual sales (1000) (Y) |
|:---:|:---:|
| 1 | $60.0 |
| 2 | 64.0 |
| 3 | 58.0 |
| 4 | 66.0 |
| 5 | 70.0 |
| 6 | 60.0 |
| 7 | 70.0 |
| 8 | 74.0 |
| 9 | 62.0 |
| 10 | 74.0 |
| 11 | 68.0 |
| 12 | 66.0 |
| 13 | 60.0 |
| 14 | 66.0 |
| 15 | 62.0 |

To initialize the exponential smoothing process, we must have the initial forecast. The first smoothed forecast to be used can be

1. First actual observations.
2. An average of the actual data for a few periods

For illustrative purposes, let us use a six-period average as the initial forecast $Y'_7$ with a smoothing constant of $\alpha = 0.40$.

$$Then\ Y'_7 = (Y_1 + Y_2 + Y_3 + Y_4 + Y_5 + Y_6)/6$$
$$= (60 + 64 + 58 + 66 + 70 + 60)/6 = 63$$

Note that $Y_7 = 70$. Then $Y'_8$ is computed as follows:

$$Y'_8 = \alpha\ Y_7 + (1 - \alpha)\ Y'_7$$
$$= (0.40)\ (70) + (0.60)\ (63)$$
$$= 28.0 + 37.80 = 65.80$$

Similarly.

$$Y'_9 = \alpha\ Y_8 + (1 - \alpha)\ Y'_8$$
$$= (0.40)\ (74) + (0.60)\ (65.80)$$
$$= 29.60 + 39.48 = 69.08$$

and

$$Y'_{10} = \alpha Y_9 + (1 - \alpha)\ Y'_9$$
$$= (0.40)\ (62) + (0.60)\ (69.08)$$
$$= 24.80 + 41.45 = 66.25$$

By using the same procedure, the values of $Y'_{11}$, $Y'_{12}$, $Y'_{13}$, $Y'_{14}$, and $Y'_{15}$ can be calculated.

Due to the negative and positive differences between actual sales and predicted sales, the forecaster can use a higher or lower smoothing constant $\alpha$, in order to adjust his prediction as quickly as possible to large fluctuations in the data series.

For example, if the forecast is slow in reacting to increased sales, (that is to say, if the difference is negative), he might want to try a higher value. For practical purposes, the optimal $\alpha$ may be picked by minimizing what is known as the mean squared error (MSE).

$$MSE = \Sigma(Y_t - Y'_t)^2 / (n - i)$$

where $i =$ the number of observations used to determine the initial forecast (in our example, $i = 6$).

The following table shows a comparison between the actual sales and predicted sales by the exponential smoothing method.

## COMPARISON OF ACTUAL SALES AND PREDICTED SALES

| Time period (t) | Actual sales (Yt) | Predicted sales (Y't) | Difference (Yt − Y't) | Difference$^2$ (Yt − Y't)$^2$ |
|---|---|---|---|---|
| 1 | $60.0 | | | |
| 2 | 64.0 | | | |
| 3 | 58.0 | | | |
| 4 | 66.0 | | | |
| 5 | 70.0 | | | |
| 6 | 60.0 | | | |
| 7 | 70.0 | 63.00 | 7.00 | 49.00 |
| 8 | 74.0 | 65.80 | 8.20 | 67.24 |
| 9 | 62.0 | 69.08 | −7.08 | 50.13 |
| 10 | 74.0 | 66.25 | 7.75 | 60.06 |
| 11 | 68.0 | 69.35 | −1.35 | 1.82 |
| 12 | 66.0 | 68.81 | −2.81 | 7.90 |
| 13 | 60.0 | 67.69 | −7.69 | 59.14 |
| 14 | 66.0 | 64.61 | 1.39 | 1.93 |
| 15 | 62.0 | 65.17 | −3.17 | 10.05 |
| | | | | 307.27 |

In our example,

$$MSE = 307.27/(15 − 6) = 307.27/9 = 34.14$$

The idea is to select the $\alpha$ that minimizes MSE, which is the average sum of the variations between the historical sales data and the forecast values for the corresponding periods.

### THE COMPUTER AND EXPONENTIAL SMOOTHING

As a nonfinancial manager, you will be confronted with complex problems requiring large sample data. You will also need to try different values of $\alpha$ for exponential smoothing. Virtually all forecasting software has an exponential smoothing routine. Figure 15.1 is a sample output from a computer program for exponential smoothing.

Notice that the best $\alpha$ for this particular example is .9, because it gives the least MSE.

Figure 15.1

```
        PLEASE ENTER THE NUMBER OF OBSERVATIONS.

?10
        ENTER YOUR DATA NOW.
        THE DATA SHOULD BE SEPARATED BY COMMAS.

?117,120,132,141,140,156,169,171,174,182
        ENTER THE NUMBER OF PERIODS OVER WHICH
YOU COMPUTE THE AVERAGE TO BE USED AS THE FIRST
FORECAST VALUE.

?1
        **********EXPONENTIAL SMOOTHING PROGRAM -SINGLE SMOOTHING****
******
                        JAE K. SHIM




                    ACTUAL          ESTIMATED
            PERIOD  VALUE           VALUE           ERROR
            1       117.00            .00
            2       120.00          117.00

THE VALUE OF THE EXPONENTIAL SMOOTHER IS .1
            3       132.00          117.30          14.70
            4       141.00          118.77          22.23
            5       140.00          120.99          19.01
            6       156.00          122.89          33.11
            7       169.00          126.20          42.80
            8       171.00          130.48          40.52
            9       174.00          134.54          39.46
            10      182.00          138.48          43.52
        THE TOTAL ABSOLUTE ERROR IN ESTIMATE IS   255.34
        THE MEAN SQUARED ERROR IS  1136.48

THE VALUE OF THE EXPONENTIAL SMOOTHER IS .2
            3       132.00          117.60          14.40
            4       141.00          120.48          20.52
            5       140.00          124.58          15.42
            6       156.00          127.67          28.33
            7       169.00          133.33          35.67
            8       171.00          140.47          30.53
            9       174.00          146.57          27.43
            10      182.00          152.06          29.94
        THE TOTAL ABSOLUTE ERROR IN ESTIMATE IS   202.24
        THE MEAN SQUARED ERROR IS   690.23

THE VALUE OF THE EXPONENTIAL SMOOTHER IS .3
            3       132.00          117.90          14.10
            4       141.00          122.13          18.87
            5       140.00          127.79          12.21
            6       156.00          131.45          24.55
            7       169.00          138.82          30.18
            8       171.00          147.87          23.13
            9       174.00          154.81          19.19
            10      182.00          160.57          21.43
        THE TOTAL ABSOLUTE ERROR IN ESTIMATE IS   163.66
```

Figure 15.1  *Continued*

```
THE VALUE OF THE EXPONENTIAL SMOOTHER IS .4
     3            132.00            118.20              13.80
     4            141.00            123.72              17.28
     5            140.00            130.63               9.37
     6            156.00            134.38              21.62
     7            169.00            143.03              25.97
     8            171.00            153.42              17.58
     9            174.00            160.45              13.55
    10            182.00            165.87              16.13
   THE TOTAL ABSOLUTE ERROR IN ESTIMATE IS    135.31
   THE MEAN SQUARED ERROR IS    308.97

THE VALUE OF THE EXPONENTIAL SMOOTHER IS .5
     3            132.00            118.50              13.50
     4            141.00            125.25              15.75
     5            140.00            133.12               6.88
     6            156.00            136.56              19.44
     7            169.00            146.28              22.72
     8            171.00            157.64              13.36
     9            174.00            164.32               9.68
    10            182.00            169.16              12.84
   THE TOTAL ABSOLUTE ERROR IN ESTIMATE IS    114.16
   THE MEAN SQUARED ERROR IS    226.07

THE VALUE OF THE EXPONENTIAL SMOOTHER IS .6
     3            132.00            118.80              13.20
     4            141.00            126.72              14.28
     5            140.00            135.29               4.71
     6            156.00            138.12              17.88
     7            169.00            148.85              20.15
     8            171.00            160.94              10.06
     9            174.00            166.98               7.02
    10            182.00            171.19              10.81
   THE TOTAL ABSOLUTE ERROR IN ESTIMATE IS    98.13
   THE MEAN SQUARED ERROR IS    174.23

THE VALUE OF THE EXPONENTIAL SMOOTHER IS .7
     3            132.00            119.10              12.90
     4            141.00            128.13              12.87
     5            140.00            137.14               2.86
     6            156.00            139.14              16.86
     7            169.00            150.94              18.06
     8            171.00            163.58               7.42
     9            174.00            168.77               5.23
    10            182.00            172.43               9.57
   THE TOTAL ABSOLUTE ERROR IN ESTIMATE IS    85.76
   THE MEAN SQUARED ERROR IS    140.55

THE VALUE OF THE EXPONENTIAL SMOOTHER IS .8
     3            132.00            119.40              12.60
     4            141.00            129.48              11.52
     5            140.00            138.70               1.30
     6            156.00            139.74              16.26
     7            169.00            152.75              16.25
     8            171.00            165.75               5.25
     9            174.00            169.95               4.05
    10            182.00            173.19               8.81
   THE TOTAL ABSOLUTE ERROR IN ESTIMATE IS    76.05
   THE MEAN SQUARED ERROR IS    117.91

THE VALUE OF THE EXPONENTIAL SMOOTHER IS .9
     3            132.00            119.70              12.30
     4            141.00            133.77              10.23
     5            ???.??            ???.??              ??.??
```

**Figure 15.1** *Continued*

```
        6            156.00          140.00              16.00
        7            169.00          154.40              14.60
        8            171.00          167.54               3.46
        9            174.00          170.65               3.35
       10            182.00          173.67               8.33
THE  TOTAL  ABSOLUTE  ERROR  IN  ESTIMATE  IS      68.30
THE  MEAN  SQUARED  ERROR  IS      102.23
            SUMMARY  RESULTS
```

```
THE  EXPONENTIAL  SMOOTHER   .1    WITH  A  MEAN  SQUARED  ERROR  OF     1136.48
THE  EXPONENTIAL  SMOOTHER   .2    WITH  A  MEAN  SQUARED  ERROR  OF      690.23
THE  EXPONENTIAL  SMOOTHER   .3    WITH  A  MEAN  SQUARED  ERROR  OF      447.49
THE  EXPONENTIAL  SMOOTHER   .4    WITH  A  MEAN  SQUARED  ERROR  OF      308.97
THE  EXPONENTIAL  SMOOTHER   .5    WITH  A  MEAN  SQUARED  ERROR  OF      226.07
THE  EXPONENTIAL  SMOOTHER   .6    WITH  A  MEAN  SQUARED  ERROR  OF      174.23
THE  EXPONENTIAL  SMOOTHER   .7    WITH  A  MEAN  SQUARED  ERROR  OF      140.55
THE  EXPONENTIAL  SMOOTHER   .8    WITH  A  MEAN  SQUARED  ERROR  OF      117.91
THE  EXPONENTIAL  SMOOTHER   .9    WITH  A  MEAN  SQUARED  ERROR  OF      102.23
```

## CONCLUSION

Various quantitative forecasting methods exist. Naive techniques are based solely on previous experience. Smoothing approaches include moving averages and exponential smoothing. Moving averages and exponential smoothing employ a weighted average of past data as the means of deriving the forecast.

# Chapter 16

# REGRESSION ANALYSIS:
## *Popular Sales Forecast System*

Regression analysis is a statistical procedure for estimating mathematically the average relationship between the dependent variable and the independent variable(s). Simple regression involves one independent variable, price or advertising in a demand function, whereas multiple regression involves two or more variables, such as price and advertising together. In this chapter, we will discuss simple (linear) regression (i.e., $Y = a + bX$) to illustrate the least-squares method. Multiple regression is reserved for a forecasting text.

## THE LEAST-SQUARES METHOD

The least-squares method is widely used in regression analysis for estimating the parameter values in a regression equation. The regression method includes all the observed data and attempts to find a line of best fit. To find this line, a technique called the least-squares method is used. Figure 16.1 shows the regression relationship.

To explain the least-squares method, we define the error as the difference between the observed value and the estimated one and denote it with u.

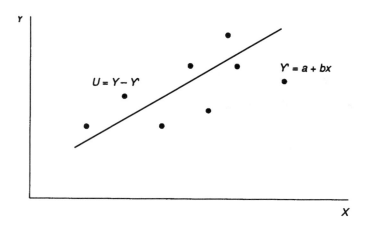

**Figure 16.1**
Y AND Y'

Symbolically, u = Y − Y'
where Y = observed value of the dependent variable
Y' = estimated value based on Y' = a + bX

The least-squares criterion requires that the line of best fit be such that the sum of the squares of the errors (or the vertical distance in Figure 16.1 from the observed data points to the line) is a minimum, i.e.,

Minimum: $\Sigma u^2 = \Sigma(Y - a - bX)^2$

Using differential calculus we obtain the following equations, called normal equations:

$$\Sigma Y = na + b\Sigma X$$
$$\Sigma XY = a\Sigma X + b\Sigma X^2$$

Solving the equations for b and a yields

$$b = \frac{n\Sigma XY - (\Sigma X)(\Sigma Y)}{n\Sigma X^2 - (\Sigma X)^2}$$

$$a = \overline{Y} - b\overline{X}$$

where $\overline{Y} = \Sigma X/n$ and $\overline{X} = \Sigma X/n$

## Example 1

To illustrate the computations of b and a, we will refer to the data in Table 16.1. All the sums required are computed and shown below.

**Table 16.1**

| Advertising X (000) | Sales Y (000) | XY | $X^2$ | $Y^2$ |
|---|---|---|---|---|
| $ 9 | $ 15 | 135 | 81 | 225 |
| 19 | 20 | 380 | 361 | 400 |
| 11 | 14 | 154 | 121 | 196 |
| 14 | 16 | 224 | 196 | 256 |
| 23 | 25 | 575 | 529 | 625 |
| 12 | 20 | 240 | 144 | 400 |
| 12 | 20 | 240 | 144 | 400 |
| 22 | 23 | 506 | 484 | 529 |
| 7 | 14 | 98 | 49 | 196 |
| 13 | 22 | 286 | 169 | 484 |
| 15 | 18 | 270 | 225 | 324 |
| 17 | 18 | 306 | 289 | 324 |
| $174 | $225 | 3,414 | 2,792 | 4,359 |

From the table above:

$$\Sigma X = 174;\ \Sigma Y = 225;\ \Sigma XY = 3,414;\ \Sigma X^2 = 2,792;\ \Sigma Y^2 = 4,359$$
$$\overline{X} = \Sigma X/n = 174/12 = 14.5;\ \overline{Y} = \Sigma Y/n = 225/12 = 18.75.$$

Substituting these values into the formula for b first:

$$b = \frac{n\Sigma XY - (\Sigma X)(\Sigma Y)}{n\Sigma X^2 - (\Sigma X)^2} = \frac{(12)(3,414) - (174)(255)}{(12)(2,792) = (174)^2} = \frac{1,818}{3,228} = 0.5632$$

$$a = \overline{Y} - b\overline{X} = 18.75 - (0.5632)(14.5) = 18.75 - 8.1664 = 10.5836$$

Thus, Y' = 10.5836 + 0.5632 X

## Example 2

Assume that the advertising of $10 is to be expended for next year. The projected sales for the year would be computed as follows:

$$Y' = 10.5836 + 0.5632\ X$$
$$= 10.5836 + 0.5632\ (10)$$
$$= \$16.2156$$

Note that $\Sigma Y^2$ is not used here but rather is computed for r-squared ($R^2$).

## USE OF LOTUS® 1-2-3 FOR REGRESSION

Spreadsheet programs such as *Lotus*® *1-2-3* have a regression routine which you can use without difficulty. Actually, you do not compute the parameter values a and b manually. Figure 16.2 shows, step by step, how to use the Lotus® regression command.

At this juncture of our discussion, we only note from the output

$$a = 10.58364$$
$$b = 0.563197$$

That is, $Y' = 10.58364 + 0.563197\ X$

Other statistics shown on the printout are discussed later in the chapter.

## A WORD OF CAUTION

Before attempting a least-squares regression approach, it is extremely important to plot the observed data on a diagram, called the scattergraph (See Figure 16.3). The reason is that you might want to make sure that a linear (straight-line) relationship existed between Y and X in the past sample.

If, for any reason, there was a nonlinear relationship detected in the sample, the linear relationship we assumed—Y = a + bX—would not give us a good fit.

In order to obtain a good fit and achieve a high degree of accuracy, you should be familiar with statistics relating to regression such as r-squared ($R^2$) and t-value, which are discussed later.

**Figure 16.2**
USING LOTUS® 1-2-3 REGRESSION COMMAND

Step 1. Enter the data on X and Y as shown below:

| (X) Adv. (000) | (Y) Sales (000) |
|:---:|:---:|
| 9 | 15 |
| 19 | 20 |
| 11 | 14 |
| 14 | 16 |
| 23 | 25 |
| 12 | 20 |
| 12 | 20 |
| 22 | 23 |
| 7 | 14 |
| 13 | 22 |
| 15 | 18 |
| 17 | 18 |

Step 2. Press "Data Regression"
Step 3. Define X and Y range
Step 4. Define output range
Step 5. Hit Go

This will produce the following regression output:

Regression Output

| | |
|---|---|
| Constant | 10.58364 (a = 10.58364) |
| Std Err of Y Est | 2.343622 |
| R Squared | 0.608373 |
| No. of Observations | 12 |
| Degrees of Freedom | 10 |
| X Coefficient(s) | 0.563197 (b = 0.563197) |
| Std Err of Coef. | 0.142893 |

The result shows:

$$Y' = 10.58364 + 0.563197$$

**Figure 16.3**
**SCATTER DIAGRAM**

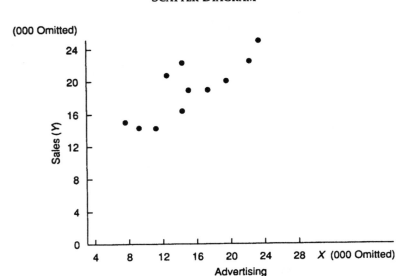

## REGRESSION STATISTICS

Regression analysis is a statistical method. Therefore, it uses a variety of statistics to tell about the accuracy and reliability of the regression results. They include:

1. Correlation coefficient (r) and coefficient of determination ($R^2$)
2. Standard error of the estimate ($S_e$) and prediction confidence interval
3. Standard error of the regression coefficient ($S_b$) and t-statistic

Each of these statistics is explained below.

*1. Correlation coefficient (r) and coefficient of determination ($R^2$)*

The correlation coefficient r measures the degree of correlation between Y and X. The range of values it takes on is between $-1$ and $+1$. More widely used, however, is the coefficient of determination, designated $R^2$ (read as R-squared). Simply put, $R^2$ tells us how good the estimated regression equation is. In other words, it is a measure of "goodness of fit" in the regression. Therefore, the higher the $R^2$, the more confidence we have in our estimated equation.

More specifically, the coefficient of determination represents the proportion of the total variation in Y that is explained by the regression equation. It has the range of values between 0 and 1.

### Example 3

The statement "Sales is a function of advertising expenditure with $R^2$ = 70 percent," can be interpreted as "70 percent of the total variation of sales is explained by the regression equation or the change in advertising and the remaining 30 percent is accounted for by something other than advertising, such as price and income."

The coefficient of determination is computed as

$$R^2 = 1 - \frac{\Sigma(Y - Y')^2}{\Sigma(Y - \overline{Y})^2}$$

In a simple regression situation, however, there is a short-cut method available:

$$R^2 = \frac{[n\Sigma XY - (\Sigma X)(\Sigma Y)]^2}{[n\Sigma X^2 - (\Sigma X)^2][n\Sigma Y^2 - (\Sigma Y)^2]}$$

Comparing this formula with the one for b, we see that the only additional information we need to compute $R^2$ is $\Sigma Y^2$.

### Example 4

To illustrate the computations of various regression statistics, we will refer to the data in Table 1.

Using the shortcut method for $R^2$,

$$R^2 = \frac{(1.818)^2}{(3,228)[(12)(4.359) - (225)^2]} = \frac{3.305,124}{(3,228)(52,308 - 50,625)}$$

$$= \frac{3.305,124}{(3,228)(1,683)} = \frac{3.305,124}{5,432,724} = 0.6084 = 60.84\%$$

This means that about 60.84 percent of the total variation in sales is explained by advertising and the remaining 39.16 percent is still unexplained. A relatively low $R^2$ indicates that there is a lot of room for improvement in our estimated forecasting formula ($Y' = \$10.5836 + \$0.5632X$). Price or a combination of advertising and price might improve $R^2$.

*2. Standard Error of the Estimate ($S_e$) and Prediction Confidence Interval*

The standard error of the estimate, designated Se, is defined as the standard deviation of the regression. It is computed as:

$$S_e = \sqrt{\frac{\Sigma(Y - Y')^2}{n - 2}} = \sqrt{\frac{\Sigma Y^2 - a\Sigma Y - b\Sigma XY}{n - 2}}$$

This statistic can be used to gain some idea of the accuracy of our predictions.

### Example 5

Going back to our example data, $S_e$ is calculated as:

$$S_e = \sqrt{\frac{4{,}359 - (10.5836)(225) - (0.5632)(3.414)}{12 - 2}}$$

$$= \sqrt{\frac{54.9252}{10}} = 2.3436$$

Suppose you wish to make a prediction regarding an individual Y value—such as a prediction about the sales when an advertising expense = \$10. Usually, we would like to have some objective measure of the confidence we can place in our prediction and one such measure is a *confidence (or prediction) interval* constructed for Y.

A confidence interval for a predicted Y, *given a value for* X, can be constructed in the following manner.

$$Y' \pm t\, S_e \sqrt{1 + \frac{1}{n} + \frac{(X_p - \overline{X})^2}{\Sigma X^2 - \frac{(\Sigma x)^2}{n}}}$$

where Y' = the predicted value of Y given a value for X;
   $X_p$ = the value of an independent variable used as the basis for prediction;

*Note:* The critical value for the level of significance employed is t. For example, for a significance level of 0.025 (which is equivalent to a 95% confidence level in a two-tailed test), the critical value of t for 10 degrees of freedom is 2.228 (See Table 5 in Appendix II). As can be seen, the confidence interval is the linear distance bounded by limits on either side of the prediction.

## Example 6

If you want to have a 95 percent confidence interval of your prediction, the range for the prediction, given an advertising expense of $10 would be between $10,595.10 and $21,836.10, as determined as follows (Note that from Example 2, Y' = $16.2156): The confidence interval is therefore established as follows:

$$\$16.2156 \pm (2.228)(2.3436)\sqrt{1+\frac{1}{12}+\frac{(10-14.5)^2}{2792-(174)^2/12}}$$

$$= \$16.2156 \pm (2.228)\,(2.3436)\,(1.0764)$$
$$= \$16.2156 \pm 5.6205$$

which means the range for the prediction, given an advertising expense of $10 would be between $10.5951 and $21.8361. Note that $10.5951 = $16.2156 − 5.6205 and $21.8361 = $16.2156 + 5.6205.

*3. Standard Error of the Regression Coefficient ($S_b$) And t-Statistic*

The standard error of the regression coefficient, designated $S_b$, and the t-statistic are closely related. $S_b$ is calculated as:

$$S_b = \frac{S_e}{\sqrt{\Sigma(X-\overline{X})^2}}$$

or in short-cut form

$$S_b = \frac{S_e}{\sqrt{\Sigma(X - \overline{X})^2}}$$

$S_b$ gives an estimate of the range where the true coefficient will actually fall.

A definition of t-statistics (or t-value) is that it is a measure of the statistical significance of an independent variable X in explaining the dependent variable Y. It is determined by dividing the estimated regression coefficient b by its standard error $S_b$. It is then compared with the table t-value (See Table 5 in Appendix II).

Thus, the t-statistic measures how many standard errors the coefficient is away from zero. Rule of thumb: Any t-value greater than +2 or less than −2 is acceptable. The higher the t-value, the greater the confidence we have in the coefficient as a predictor. Low t-values are indications of low reliability of the predictive power of that coefficient.

### Example 7

The $S_b$ for our example is:

$$S_b = \frac{2.3436}{\sqrt{2,792 - (14.5)(174)}}$$

$$= \frac{2.3436}{\sqrt{2,792 - 2,523}} = \frac{2.3436}{\sqrt{269}} = .143$$

Thus, t-statistic $= \dfrac{b}{S_b} = \dfrac{.5632}{.143} = 3.94$

Since, t = 3.94 > 2, we conclude that the b coefficient is statistically significant. As was indicated previously, the table's critical value (cut-off value) for 10 degrees of freedom is 2.228 (from Table 5 in Appendix II).

*Note:*

(1) The t-statistic is more relevant to multiple regressions which have more than one b's.

(2) $R^2$ tells you how good the forest (overall fit) is while t-statistic tells you how good an individual tree (an independent variable) is.

*Note:* In summary, the table t value, based on a degree of freedom and a level of significance, is used:

**Figure 16.4**
LOTUS® 1-2-3 REGRESSION RESULT

| | | |
|---|---|---|
| Constant | 10.58364 | |
| Std Err of Y Est | 2.343622 | $(S_e)$ |
| R Squared | 0.608373 | $(R^2)$ |
| No. of Observations | 12 | |
| Degree of Freedom | 10 | |
| | | |
| X Coefficient(s) | 0.563197 | |
| Std Err of Coef. | 0.142893 | $(S_b)$ |
| t-value | 0.394138 | (Calculated Independently) |

The result shows:

$$Y' = 10.58364 + 0.563197 \, X$$

with:

    (1) R-squared ($R^2$ = .608373 = 60.84%)
    (2) Standard Error of the Estimate ($S_e$ = 2.343622)
    (3) Standard Error of the Coefficient ($S_b$ = 0.142893)
    (4) t-value = 3.94

All of the above are the same as the ones manually obtained.

(1) To set the prediction range—upper and lower limits—for the predicted value of the dependent variable.

(2) To set the confidence range for regression coefficients.

(3) As a cutoff value for the t-test.

Figure 16.4 shows a Lotus® 1-2-3 output that contains the statistics we discussed so far.

## CONCLUSION

Regression analysis is the examination of the effect of a change in independent variables on the dependent variable. It is a popularly used method to forecast sales. This chapter discussed a well-known estimation technique, called the least-squares method.

To illustrate the method, we assumed a simple regression, which involves one independent variable in the form of $Y = a + bX$. In an attempt to obtain a good fit, we discussed various regression statistics. These statistics tell you how good and reliable your estimated equation is and help you set the confidence interval for your prediction.

Most importantly, we discussed how to utilize spreadsheet programs such as Lotus® 1-2-3 to perform regressions, step by step. The program calculates not only the regression equation, but also all the regression statistics discussed in this chapter.

# Chapter 17

# FORECASTING CASH FLOW:
## *Two Pragmatic Methods*

A forecast of cash collections and potential writeoffs of accounts receivable is essential in cash budgeting and in judging the appropriateness of current credit and discount policies. The critical step in making such a forecast is estimating the cash collection and bad debt percentages to be applied to sales or accounts receivable balances. This chapter discusses two pragmatic methods of estimating cash collection rates (or payment proportions) and illustrates how these rates are used for cash budgeting purposes.

The first approach involves a simple average. The second, empirically tested and improved by the author, offers a more pragmatic method of estimating collection and bad debt percentages by relating credit sales and collection data. This method employs regression analysis. By using these approaches, a manager should be able to

- Estimate future cash collections from customers
- Establish an allowance for bad debts
- Provide a valuable insight into better methods of managing accounts receivable

## ACCOUNT ANALYSIS

The most straightforward way to estimate collection percentages is to compute the percentages of collections realized from past months. Once the experience has been analyzed, the results can be adjusted for trends and applied to the credit sales portrayed in the sales forecast. An example illustrates the technique.

### Example 1

Assume that an analysis of collection experience for August sales revealed the following collection data:

| Description | % of Total Credit Sales |
|---|---|
| Collected in August | 2.3 |
| September | 80.2 |
| October | 9.9 |
| November | 5.1 |
| December | .5 |
| Cash discounts | 1.0 |
| Bad debt losses | 1.0 |
| Total | 100.0 |

If next year's sales in August could be expected to fall into the same pattern, then application of the percentages to estimated August credit sales would determine the probable monthly distribution of collections. The same analysis applied to each month of the year would result in a reasonably reliable basis for collection forecasting. The worksheet (August column) for cash collections might look as follows:

### Description

| Month of Sale | % Total | Sales Net | August Collection |
|---|---|---|---|
| April | .5 | $168,000 | $ 840 |
| May | 4.2 | 192,000 | 8,064 |
| June | 8.9 | 311,100 | 27,688 |
| July | 82.1 | 325,600 | 267,318 |
| August | 2.3 | 340,000 | 7,820 |
| Total Collections | | | $311,730 |

| Month of Sale | %<br>Total | Sales<br>Net | August<br>Collection |
|---|---|---|---|
| Cash Discounts (July)................1.0 | | 325,600 | (3,256) |
| Losses...............................1.0 | | 340,000 | (3,400) |
| Total.................................................................................... | | | $305,074 |

## REGRESSION APPROACH

A more scientific approach to estimating cash collection percentages (or payment proportions) is to utilize regression analysis. We know that there is typically a time lag between the point of a credit sale and realization of cash. More specifically, the lagged effect of credit sales and cash inflows is distributed over a number of periods, as follows:

$$C_t = b_1 S_{t-1} + b_2 S_{t-2} + ..b_i S_{t-i}$$

where $C_t$ = cash collection in month t
  $S_t$ = credit sales made in period t
  $b_1, b_2, ... b_i$ = collection percentages (the same as $P'_i$, and
  $i$ = number of periods lagged

By using the regression method discussed in Chapter 16, we will be able to estimate these collection rates. We can utilize Data Regression of *Lotus® 1-2-3* or special regression packages such as *SAS, Minitab* and *Systat*.

It should be noted that the cash collection percentages, $(b_1, b_2, ..b_i)$ may not add up to 100 percent because of the possibility of bad debts. Once we estimate these percentages by using the regression method, we should be able to compute the bad debt percentage with no difficulty.

Table 1 shows the regression results using actual monthly data on credit sales and cash inflows for a real company. Equation I can be written as follows:

$$C_t = 60.6\% \ (S_{t-1}) + 24.3\%(S_{t-2}) + 8.8\%(S_{t-3})$$

This result indicates that the receivables generated by the credit sales are collected at the following rates: first month after sale, 60.6 percent; second

Table 1
REGRESSION RESULTS FOR CASH COLLECTION ($C_t$)

| Independent Variables | Equation I | Equation II |
|---|---|---|
| $S_{t-1}$ | 0.606[a] | 0.596[a] |
|  | (0.062)[b] | (0.097) |
| $S_{t-2}$ | 0.243[a] | 0.142 |
|  | (0.085) | (0.120) |
| $S_{t-3}$ | 0.088 | 0.043 |
|  | (0.157) | (0.191) |
| $S_{t-4}$ |  | 0.136 |
|  |  | (0.800) |
| $R^2$ | 0.754 | 0.753 |
| Standard Error of the estimate ($S_e$) | 11.63 | 16.05 |
| Number of monthly observations | 21 | 20 |
| Bad debt percentages | 0.063 | 0.083 |

[a]Statistically significant at the 5% significance level.

[b]This figure in the parentheses is the standard error of the e estimate for the coefficient ($S_b$).

month after sale, 24.3 percent; and third month after sale, 8.8 percent. The bad debt percentage is computed as 6.3 percent (100 − 93.7%).

It is important to note, however, that these collection and bad debt percentages are probabilistic variables, that is, variables whose values cannot be known with precision. However, the standard error of the regression coefficient and the t-value permit us to assess the probability that the true percentage is between specified limits. The confidence interval takes the following form:

$b \pm t S_b$

where $S_b$ = standard error of the coefficient.

## Example 2

To illustrate, assuming t = 2 as rule of thumb at the 95 percent confidence level, the true collection percentage from the prior month's sales will be

$$60.6\% \pm 2(6.2\%) = 60.6\% \pm 12.4\%$$

Turning to the estimation of cash collections and allowance for doubtful accounts, the following values are used for illustrative purposes:

$S_{t-1}$ = \$77.6, $S_{t-2}$ = \$58.5, $S_{t-3}$ = \$76.4, and forecast average monthly net credit sales = \$75.2

Then, (a) the forecast cash collection for period t would be

$C_t$ = 60.6% (77.6) + 19.3% (58.5) + 8.8% (76.4) = \$65.04

If the manager wants to be 95 percent confident about this forecast value, then the interval would be set as follows:

$C_t \pm t S_e$
where $S_e$ = standard error of the estimate.

To illustrate, using t = 2 as a rule of thumb at the 95 percent confidence level, the true value for cash collections in period t will be

\$65.04 $\pm$ 2(11.63) = \$65.04 $\pm$ 23.26

(b) the estimated allowance for uncollectable uncollectible accounts for period t will be

6.3% (\$75.2) = \$4.74

By using the limits discussed so far, managers can develop flexible (or probabilistic) cash budgets, where the lower and upper limits can be interpreted as pessimistic and optimistic outcomes. They can also simulate a cash budget in an attempt to determine both the expected change in cash collections for each period and the variation in this value.

In preparing a conventional cash inflow budget, the manager considers the various sources of cash, including cash on account, sale of assets, and incurrence of debt. Cash collections from customers are emphasized, since that is the greatest problem in this type of budget.

## Example 3

The following data are given for Erich Stores:

|              | September Acutal | October Actual | November Estimated | December Estimated |
|--------------|------------------|----------------|--------------------|--------------------|
| Cash sales   | $ 7,000          | $ 6,000        | $ 8,000            | $ 6,000            |
| Credit sales | 50,000           | 48,000         | 62,000             | 80,000             |
| Total sales  | $57,000          | $54,000        | $70,000            | $86,000            |

Past experience indicates net collections normally occur in the following pattern:

- No collections are made in the month of sale
- 80% of the sales of any month are collected in the following month
- 19% of sales are collected in the second following month
- 1% of sales are uncollectible

We can project total cash receipts for November and December as follows:

|                         | November | December |
|-------------------------|----------|----------|
| Cash receipts           |          |          |
| Cash sales              | $8,000   | $6,000   |
| Cash collections        |          |          |
| September sales         |          |          |
| 50,000 (19%)            | 9,500    |          |
| October sales           |          |          |
| 48,000 (80%)            | 38,400   |          |
| 48,000 (19%)            |          | 9,120    |
| November sales          |          |          |
| 62,000 (80%)            |          | 49,600   |
| Total cash receipts     | $55,900  | $64,720  |

## Example 4

*Cash Collections and Discount Policy*

The manager of John Loyde Co. plans for the company to have a cash balance of $91,000 on March 1. Sales during March are estimated at $900,000.

February sales amounted to $600,000 and January sales amounted to $500,000. Cash payments for March have been budgeted at $580,000. Cash collections have been estimated as follows:

- 60% of the sales for the month are to be collected during the month
- 30% of the sales for the preceding month are to be collected during the month
- 8% of the sales for the second preceding month are to be collected during the month

The manager plans to accelerate collections by allowing a two percent discount for prompt payment. With the discount policy, he expects to collect 70 percent of the current sales and will permit the discount reduction on these collections. Sales of the preceding month will be collected to the extent of 15 percent with no discount allowed, and 10 percent of the sales of the second preceding month will be collected with no discount allowed.

This pattern of collection can be expected in subsequent months. During the transitional month of March, collections may run somewhat higher. However, the manager prefers to estimate collections on the basis of the new pattern so that the estimates will be somewhat conservative.

(1) Estimate cash collections for March and the cash balance at March 31 under the present policy.

(2) Estimate cash collections for March and the cash balance at March 31 according to the new policy of allowing discounts.

(3) Is the discount policy desirable?

(1) and (2)

|  | Under the Present Policy | Under the Discount Policy |
|---|---|---|
| Balance, March 1 | $91,000 | $91,000 |
| Collections |  |  |
| From March sales | 540,000 ($900,000 × 60%) | 617,400[a] |
| From February sales | 180,000 ($600,000 × 30%) | 90,000 ($600,000 × 15%) |
| From January sales | 40,000 ($500,000 × 8%) | 50,000 ($500,000 × 10%) |

| | Under the Present Policy | Under the Discount Policy |
|---|---|---|
| Total cash available | $851,000 | $848,400 |
| Less disbursements | 580,000 | 580,000 |
| Balance, March 31 | $271,000 | $268,400 |

a$900,000 × 70% × 98% = $617,400

(3) (No, because under the discount policy, the March 31 cash balance will be smaller as indicated above ($268,400 as compared to $271,000 under the present policy).

### Example 5

The following is a sample printout of a cash budget generated from *Up Your Cash Flow*. (See Figure 17.1).

## IS CASH FLOW SOFTWARE AVAILABLE?

Computer software allows for day-to-day cash management, forecasting and budgeting cash flows, determining cash balances, planning and analyzing cash flows, finding cash shortages, investing cash surpluses, accounting for cash transactions, automating accounts receivable and payable, and dial-up banking.

Computerization improves availability, accuracy, timeliness, and monitoring of cash information at minimal cost. Daily cash information aids in planning how to use cash balances. It enables the integration of different kinds of related cash information, such as collections on customer accounts and cash balances, and the effect of cash payments on cash balances.

Spreadsheet program software such as *Lotus® 1-2-3*, *Microsoft's Excel*, and *Quattro Pro* can assist you in developing cash budgets and answering a variety of what-if questions. For example, you can see the effect on cash flow from different scenarios (e.g., the purchase and sale of different product lines).

There are computer software packages specially designed for cash budgeting and management. Three popular ones are briefly described below.

## 1. UP YOUR CASH FLOW

This program contains automatically prepared spreadsheets for profit/loss forecasts, cash flow budgets, projected balance sheet, payroll analysis, term loan amortization schedule, sales/cost of sales by product, ratio analysis, and graphs. It is a menu-driven system and you can customize it to your forecasting needs. The system requirements are:

PC compatibles, DOS version 2.0 or later
512K RAM

It is available from:

Granville Publications Software
10960 Wilshire Blvd., Suite 826
Los Angeles, CA 90024
(800) 873-7789

## 2. CASH FLOW ANALYSIS

This software provides projections of cash inflow and cash outflow. You input data into eight categories: sales, cost of sales, general and administrative expense, long-term debt, other cash receipts, inventory build-up/reduction, capital expenditures (acquisition of long-term assets such as store furniture), and income tax. The program allows changes in assumptions and scenarios and provides a complete array of reports. The system requirements are:

PC compatibles, DOS version 2.0 or later
512K RAM

It is available from:

Superior Software
16055 Ventura Blvd., Suite 725
Encino, CA 91436
(800) 421-3264
(818) 990-1135

## 3. QUICKEN

This is a fast, easy to use, inexpensive program that can be useful to your small business. It helps manage cash flow. You record bills as post-

# Figure 17.1
## Your Company, Inc. Cash Collection on the Year

| | Jan. | Feb. | Mar. | Apr. | May | Jun. | Jul. | Aug. | Sep. | Oct. | Nov. | Dec. | Total |
|---|---|---|---|---|---|---|---|---|---|---|---|---|---|
| Sales | 129,030 | 129,030 | 129,030 | 129,030 | 192,610 | 192,610 | 162,690 | 129,030 | 192,610 | 129,030 | 162,690 | 192,610 | 870,000 |
| Previous Months December Previous Years | 20,000 | 10,000 | | | | | | | | | | | 30,000 |
| Collection Current Year | | | | | | | | | | | | | |
| Jan. 129,030 × 45;40;15 | 58,063 | 51,612 | 19,355 | | | | | | | | | | 129,030 |
| Feb. 129,030 × 45;40;15 | | 58,063 | 51,612 | 19,355 | | | | | | | | | 129,030 |
| Mar. 129,030 × 45;40;15 | | | 58,063 | 51,612 | 19,355 | | | | | | | | 129,030 |
| Apr. 129,030 × 45;40;15 | | | | 58,063 | 51,612 | 19,355 | | | | | | | 129,030 |
| May 192,610 × 45;40;15 | | | | | 86,675 | 77,044 | 28,891 | | | | | | 192,610 |
| Jun. 192,610 × 45;40;15 | | | | | | 86,675 | 77,044 | 28,891 | | | | | 192,610 |

| | | | | | | | | | | | | | Total |
|---|---|---|---|---|---|---|---|---|---|---|---|---|---|
| Jul. 162,690 × 45;40;15 | | | | | | | 73,210 | 65,076 | 24,404 | | | | 162,690 |
| Aug. 129,030 × 45;40;15 | | | | | | | | 58,063 | 51,612 | 19,355 | | | 129,030 |
| Sep. 192,610 × 45;40;15 | | | | | | | | | 86,675 | 77,044 | 28,891 | | 192,610 |
| Oct. 129,610 × 45;40;15 | | | | | | | | | | 58,063 | 51,612 | 19,355 | 129,030 |
| Nov. 162,690 × 45;40;15 | | | | | | | | | | | 73,210 | 65,076 | 138,286 |
| Dec. 192,610 × 45;40;15 | | | | | | | | | | | | 86,674 | 86,674 |
| Total Collections | 78,063 | 119,675 | 129,030 | 129,030 | 157,642 | 183,074 | 179,145 | 152,030 | 162,691 | 154,462 | 153,713 | 171,105 | 1,769,660 |

The assumption used for cash collection is that:
45% of the months sales are collected in the month the sale is made.
40% of the sale is collected in the 1st month following the sale
15% is collected in the 2nd month following the sale in otherwords 45;40;15

dated transactions when they arrive and the program's *Billminder* feature automatically reminds you when bills are due. You can then print checks for due bills with a few keystrokes. Similarly, you can record invoices and track aged receivables. Together, these features help you to maximize cash on hand. The system requirements are:

> PC compatibles, DOS version 2.0 or later
> At least 320K \RAM.

It is available from:

> Intuit, Inc.
> P.O. Box 3014
> Menlo Park, CA 94026
> (800) 624-8742

## CONCLUSION

Two methods of estimating the expected collectible and uncollectible patterns of customer accounts were presented. The regression approach is relatively inexpensive to use because all it requires is data on cash collections and credit sales. Furthermore, credit sales values are all predetermined. Since previous months' credit sales are used to forecast cash collections, there is no need to forecast credit sales. The model allows you to make all kinds of statistical inferences about the cash collection percentages and forecast values.

The chapter also illustrated how collection rates are used for cash budgeting purposes.

# Chapter *18*

# FINANCIAL MODELING:
## *Tools for Budgeting and Profit Planning*

Many companies are increasingly using financial modeling to develop their budgets. In this chapter, we discuss:

- What is a financial model?
- What are some typical uses of financial models?
- What are the types of financial modeling?
- How widespread is the use of financial modeling in practice?
- How do we go about building a financial model?

We will describe the use of spreadsheets and financial modeling languages for financial modeling in the next chapter.

## A FINANCIAL MODEL

A financial model, narrowly called a budgeting model, is a system of mathematical equations, logic and data which describes the relationships among financial and operating variables. A financial model can be viewed as a subset of broadly defined corporate planning models or a stand-alone functional system that attempts to answer a certain financial planning problem.

A financial model is one in which:

(1) One or more financial variables appears (expenses, revenues, investment, cash flow, taxes, and earnings)

(2) The model user can manipulate (set and alter) the value of one or more financial variables

(3) The purpose of the model is to influence strategic decisions by revealing to the decision-maker the implications of alternative values of these financial variables

Figure 18.1 shows a flowchart of a simplified financial planning model.

Financial models fall into two types: simulation, better known as "what-if" models, and optimization models. "What-if" models attempt to simulate the effects of alternative management policies and assumptions about the firm's external environment. They are basically a tool for management's laboratory.

Optimization models are ones in which the goal is to maximize or minimize an objective such as present value of profit or cost. Experiments are being made on multiobjective techniques, such as goal programming.

Models can be deterministic or probabilistic. Deterministic models do not include any random or probabilistic variables, whereas probabilistic models incorporate random numbers and/or one or more probability distributions for variables such as sales and costs.

Financial models can be solved and manipulated computationally to derive from them the current and projected future implications and consequences. Due to technological advances in computers (such as spreadsheets, financial modeling languages, graphics, data base management systems, and networking), more companies are using modeling.

## BUDGETING AND FINANCIAL MODELING

Basically, a financial model is used to build a comprehensive budget (that is, projected financial statements, such as the income statement, balance sheet, and cash flow statement). Such a model can be called a budgeting model, since we are essentially developing a master budget with such a

**Figure 18.1**
FLOW CHART OF A SIMPLIFIED FINANCIAL PLANNING MODEL

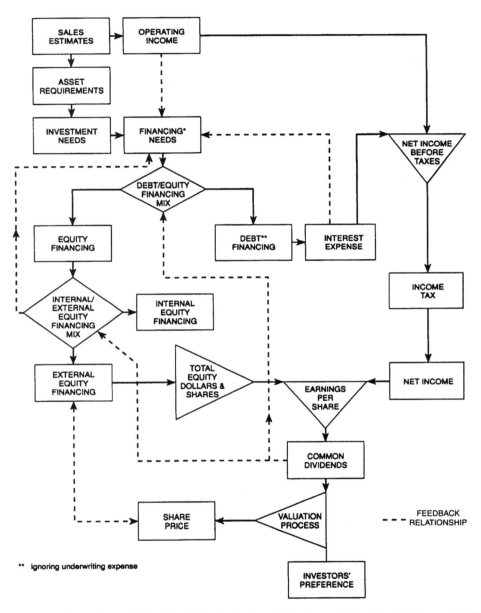

*Source: Naylor, Thomas (ed.), Simulation in Business Planning and Decision Making, p. 91, The Society for Computer Simulation, La Jolla, CA 1981.*

model. Applications and uses of the model, however, go beyond developing a budget. They include:

- Financial forecasting and analysis
- Capital expenditure analysis
- Tax planning
- Exchange rate analysis
- Analysis for mergers and acquisitions
- Labor contract negotiations
- Capacity planning
- Cost–volume–profit analysis
- New venture analysis
- Lease/purchase evaluation
- Appraisal of performance by segments
- Market analysis
- New product analysis
- Development of long-term strategy
- Planning financial requirements
- Risk analysis
- Cash flow analysis
- Cost and price projections

## USE OF FINANCIAL MODELING IN PRACTICE

The use of financial modeling, especially a computer-based financial modeling system, is rapidly growing. The simple reason is the growing need for improved and quicker support as a management decision support system (DSS) and wide and easy availability of computer hardware and software.

Some of the functions currently served by financial models, as described by the users, are:

- Projecting financial results under any given set of assumptions, evaluating the financial impact of various assumptions and alternative strategies, and preparing long range forecasts.

- Computing income, cash flow, and ratios for five years by months, as well as energy sales, revenue, power generation requirements, operating and manufacturing expenses, manual or automatic financing, and rate structure analysis.
- Providing answers and insights into financial "what-if" questions and providing scheduling information, such as production planning.
- Forecasting the balance sheet and income statement with emphasis on alternatives for the investment securities portfolio.
- Projecting operating results and various financing needs, such as plant and property levels and financing requirements.
- Computing manufacturing profit, any desired processing sequence through the manufacturing facilities, and simulating effect on profits of inventory policies.
- Generating profitability reports of various responsibility centers.
- Projecting financial implications of capital investment programs.
- Showing the effect of various volume and activity levels on budget and cash flow.
- Forecasting corporate sales, costs, and income by division and by month.
- Providing sales revenue for budget, a basis for evaluating actual sales department performance, and other statistical comparisons.
- Determining pro forma cash flow for alternative development plans for real estate projects.
- Analyzing the impact of an acquisition on company earnings.
- Determining economic attractiveness of new ventures, i.e., products, facilities, and acquisitions.
- Evaluating alternatives of leasing or buying computer equipment.
- Determining corporate taxes as a function of changes in price.
- Evaluating investments in additional capacity at each major refinery.
- Generating income statements, cash flow, present value, and discounted rate of return for potential mining ventures, based on production and sales forecasts.

Supported by the expanded capabilities provided by models, many companies are increasingly successful in including long-term strategic considerations in their business plans, thus enabling them to investigate the possible impact of their current decisions on the long-term welfare of the organization.

## DEVELOPING FINANCIAL MODELS

Development of financial models essentially involves definition of variables, input parameter values, and model specification. As far as model specification goes, we will concentrate only on the simulation-type model specification in this section.

Generally speaking, the model consists of three important ingredients:

- Variables
- Input parameter values
- Definitional and/or functional relationships

### DEFINITION OF VARIABLES

Fundamental to the specification of a financial model is the definition of the variables to be included. Basically, the three types of variables are policy variables $(Z)$, external variables $(X)$, and performance variables $(Y)$.

Policy variables (often called control variables) are those over which management can exert some degree of control. Examples of financial variables are cash management, working capital, debt management, depreciation, tax, merger-acquisition decisions, the rate and direction of the firm's capital investment programs, the extent of its equity and external debt financing and the financial leverage represented thereby, and the size of its cash balances and liquid asset position.

Policy variables are denoted by the symbol $Z$ in Figure 18.2.

External variables are the environmental variables that are external to the company and which influence the firm's decisions from outside. Generally speaking, the firm is embedded in an industry environment. This environment, in turn, is influenced by overall general business conditions.

General business conditions exert influences upon particular industries in several ways. Total volume of demand, product prices, labor costs, material costs, money rates, and general expectations are among the industry variables affected by the general business conditions.

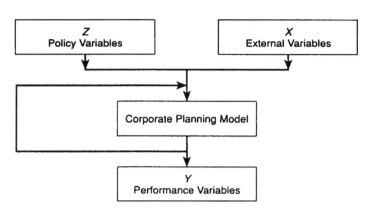

**Figure 18.2**
FLOWCHART OF VARIABLES IN A CORPORATE MODEL

The symbol X represents the external variables in Figure 18.2.

Performance variables, which measure the firm's economic and financial performance are usually produced internally. We use the symbol Y in the diagram. The Y's are often called output variables. The output variables of a financial model would be the line items of the balance sheet, cash budget, income statement, or statement of cash flows.

How the output variables of the firm are defined will depend on the goals and objectives of management. They basically indicate how management measures the performance of the organization or some segments of it. Management is likely to be concerned with the firm's level of earnings, growth in earnings, projected earnings, growth in sales, and cash flow.

Frequently, when we attempt to set up a financial model, we face risk or uncertainty associated with particular projections. In a case such as this, we treat some of these variables, such as sales, as random variables with given probability distributions. The inclusion of random variables in the model transforms it from a deterministic model to a risk analysis model. However, the use of the risk analysis model in practice is rare because of the difficulty involved in modeling and computation.

## INPUT PARAMETER VALUES

The model includes various input parameter values. For example, in order to generate the balance sheet, the model needs to input beginning balances of various asset, liability, and equity accounts. These input and parameter values are supplied by management. The ratio between accounts receivable and financial decision variables, such as the maximum desired debt–equity ratio, would be good examples of parameters.

## MODEL SPECIFICATION

Once we define various variables and input parameters for our financial model, we must then specify a set of mathematical and logical relationships linking the input variables to the performance variables. The relationships usually involve either definitional equations or behavioral equations.

Definitional equations take the form of accounting identities. Behavioral equations involve theories or hypotheses about the behavior of certain economic and financial events. They must be tested and validated before they are incorporated into the financial model.

### Definitional Equations

Definitional equations are exactly what the term implies—mathematical or accounting definitions. For example:

> Assets = Liabilities + Equity
> Net Income = Revenues − Expenses

These definitional equations are fundamental definitions in accounting for the balance sheet and income statement, respectively.

Another example is:

$$CASH = CASH(-1) + CC + OCR + DEBT - CD - LP$$

This equation is a typical cash equation in a financial model. It states that ending cash balance (CASH) is equal to the beginning cash balance (CASH(−1)) plus cash collections from customers (CC) plus other cash receipts (OCR) plus borrowings (DEBT) minus cash disbursements (CD) minus loan payments (LP).

Another example is:

$$INV = INV(-1) + MAT + DL + MO - CGS$$

This equation states that ending inventory (INV) is equal to the beginning inventory (INV(−1)) plus cost of materials used (MAT) plus cost of direct labor (DL) plus manufacturing overhead (MO) minus the cost of goods sold (CGS).

### Behavioral Equations

Behavioral equations describe the behavior of the firm regarding the specific activities that are subject to testing and validation. The classical demand function in economics is:

$$Q = f(P) \text{ or more specifically } Q = a - bP$$

It simply says that the quantity demanded is negatively related to the price. That is to say, the higher the price, the lower the demand. However, the firm's sales are more realistically described as follows:

$$SALES = f(P, ADV., I, GNP, Pc, etc.) \text{ or}$$

assuming linear relationship among these variables, we can specify the model as:

$$SALES = a + bP + cADV + dI + eGNP + fPc$$

which says that the sales are affected by such factors as price (P), advertising expenditures (ADV), consumer income (I), gross national product (GNP), and prices of competitive goods (Pc).

With the data on SALES, P, ADV, I, GNP, and Pc, we will be able to estimate parameter values a, b, c, d, e, and f, using linear regression. We can test the statistical significance of each of the parameter estimates and evaluate the overall explanatory power of the model, measured by the t-statistic and r-squared, respectively.

This way we will be able to identify the most influential factors that affect the sales of a particular product. With the best model chosen, management can simulate the effects on sales of alternative pricing and advertising strategies. We can also experiment with alternative assumptions regarding the external economic factors such as GNP, consumer income, and prices of competitive goods.

## Model Structure

A majority of financial models that have been in use are recursive and/or simultaneous models. Recursive models are the ones in which each equation can be solved one at a time by substituting the solution values of the preceding equations into the right hand side of each equation.

An example of a recursive model is:

```
(1) SALES    = A - B*PRICE + C*ADV
(2) REVENUE = SALES*PRICE
(3) CGS      =.70*REVENUE
(4) GM       = SALES - CGS
(5) OE       = $10,000 +.2*SALES
(6) EBT      = GM - OE
(7) TAX      =.46*EBT
(8) EAT      = EBT - TAX
```

In this example, the selling price (PRICE) and advertising expenses (ADV) are given. A, B and C are parameters to be estimated and

```
SALES    = sales volume in units
REVENUE = sales revenue
CGS      = cost of goods sold
GM       = gross margin
OE       = operating expenses
EBT      = earnings before taxes
TAX      = income taxes
EAT      = earnings after taxes
```

Simultaneous models are frequently found in econometric models which require a higher level of computational methods, such as matrix inversion. An example of a simultaneous model is:

```
(1) INT   =.10*DEBT
(2) EARN = REVENUE - CGS - OE - INT - TAX - DIV
(3) DEBT  = DEBT(-1) + BOW
(4) CASH  = CASH(-1) + CC + BOW + EARN - CD - LP
(5) BOW   = MBAL - CASH
```

Note that earnings (EARN) in equation (2) is defined as sales revenue minus CGS, OE, interest expense (INT), TAX, and dividend payment (DIV). But INT is a percentage interest rate on total debt in equation (1). Total debt in equation (3) is equal to the previous period's debt (DEBT(−1)) plus new borrowings (BOW). New debt is the difference between a minimum cash balance (MBAL) minus cash. Finally, the ending cash balance in equation (5) is defined as the sum of the beginning balance (CASH(−1)), cash collection, new borrowings and earnings minus cash disbursements and loan payments of the existing debt (LP).

Even though the model presented here is a simple variety, it is still simultaneous in nature, which requires the use of a method capable of solving simultaneous equations. Very few of the financial modeling languages have the capability to solve this kind of system.

### Decision Rules

The financial model may, in addition to definitional equations and behavioral equations, include basic decision rules specified in a very general form. The decision rules are not written in the form of conventional equations. They are described algebraically using conditional operators, consisting of statements of the type: "IF...THEN...ELSE."

For example, suppose that we wish to express the following decision rule: "If X is greater than 0, then Y is set equal to X multiplied by 5. Otherwise, Y is set equal to 0." Then we can express the rule as follows:

Y = IF X GT 0 THEN X*5 ELSE 0

Suppose the company wishes to develop a financing decision problem based upon alternative sales scenarios. To determine an optimal financing alternative, managers might want to incorporate some decision rules into the model for a what-if or sensitivity analysis.

Some examples of these decision rules are as follows:

- The amount of dividends paid are determined on the basis of targeted earnings available to common stockholders and a maximum dividend payout ratio specified by management.
- After calculating the external funds needed to meet changes in assets as a result of increased sales, dividends, and maturing debt, the

amount of long-term debt to be floated is selected on the basis of a prespecified leverage ratio.

- The amount of equity financing to be raised is chosen on the basis of funds needed which are not financed by new long-term debt, but is constrained by the responsibility to meet minimum dividend payments.

In the model we have just described, simultaneity is quite evident. A sales figure is used to generate earnings and this in turn leads to, among other items, the level of long-term debt required. Yet the level of debt affects the interest expense incurred within the current period and, therefore, earnings.

Furthermore, as earnings are affected, so are the price at which new shares are issued, the number of shares to be sold, and earnings per share. Earnings per share then feed back into the stock price calculation.

### Lagged Model Structure

Lagged model structure is common in financial modeling. Virtually all balance sheet equations or identities are of this type. For example:

$$\text{Capital} = \text{capital}(-1) + \text{net income} + \text{contributions} - \text{cash dividends}$$

More interestingly,

$$CC = a*SALES + b*SALES(-1) + c*SALES(-2)$$
where CC = cash collections from customers
    a = percent received in the month of sale.
    b = percent received in the month following sale.
    c = percent received in the second month following sale.

This indicates that the realization of cash lags behind credit sales. Figure 18.3 illustrates a sample financial (budgeting) model.

## CONCLUSION

Budgeting and financial models comprise a functional branch of a general corporate planning model. They are essentially used to generate pro forma

**Figure 18.3**
**COMPREHENSIVE FINANCIAL MODEL**

A comprehensive corporate financial model is illustrated

*A Corporate Financial Model*

## Balance Sheet Equations

$$\text{Cash}_t = \text{Cash}_{t-1} + \text{Cash receipts}_t - \text{Cash disbursements}_t$$

$$\text{Accounts receivable}_t = (1-a)\,\text{Sales} + (1-b-a)\,\text{Sales}_{t-1}$$
$$+ (1-c-b-a)\,\text{Sales}_{t-2}$$

$$\text{Inventory}_t = \text{Inventory}_{t-1} + \text{Inventory purchase}_t$$

$$- \text{Variable cost per unit} \left( \frac{\text{Sales}_t}{\text{Selling price per unit}} \right)$$

$$\text{Plant} = \text{Initial value}$$

$$\text{Accounts payable}_t = (m)\,\text{Variable selling/administrative expenses}_{t-1}$$
$$+ (n)\text{Variable selling/administrative expenses}_t$$
$$+ \text{Inventory purchase}_t + \text{Fixed expenses}_t$$

$$\text{Bank loan}_t = \text{Bank loan}_{t-1} + \text{Loan}_t - \text{Loan repayment}_t$$

$$\text{Common stock} = \text{Initial value}$$

$$\text{Retained earnings}_t = \text{Retained earnings}_{t-1} + \text{Net income}_t$$

## Income Statement and Cash Flow Equations

$$\text{Cash receipts}_t = (a)\,\text{Sales}_t + (b)\,\text{Sales}_{t-1} + (c)\,\text{Sales}_{t-2} + \text{Loan}_t$$

$$\text{Cash disbursements}_t = \text{Accounts payable}_{t-1} + \text{Interest}_t$$
$$+ \text{Loan repayments}_t$$

$$\text{Inventory purchase}_t\,[\geq 0] = \text{Variable cost per unit}$$
$$\left( \frac{\text{Sales}_t + \text{Sales}_{t-1} + \text{Sales}_{t-2} + \text{Sales}_{t-3}}{\text{Selling price per unit}} \right) - \text{Inventory}_{t-1}$$
$$\text{Interest}_t = (i)\,\text{Bank loan}_t$$

$$\text{Variable cost of sales}_t = \text{Sales}_t \left( \frac{\text{Variable cost per unit}}{\text{Selling price per unit}} \right)$$

$$\text{Variable selling,}$$
$$\text{administrative expenses}_t = (x)\,\text{Sales}_t$$

$$\text{Net income before taxes}_t = \text{Sales}_t - \text{Interest}_t + \text{Variable cost of sales}_t$$
$$+ \text{Variable selling/administrative expenses}_t$$
$$- \text{Fixed expenses}_t - \text{Depreciation}_t$$

**Figure 18.3** *Continued*

Tax expense$_t$ ($\geq 0$) = ($r$) Net income before taxes$_t$
Net income$_t$ = Net income before taxes$_t$ − Tax expense$_t$

*Input Variables (Dollars)*

Sales$_{t-1, t-2, t-3}$
Loan$_t$
Loan repayment$_t$
Fixed expense$_t$
Depreciation$_t$
Selling price per unit
Variable cost per unit

**Input Parameters**

Accounts receivable collection patterns
a—Percent received within current period
b—Percent received with one-period lag
c—Percent received with two-period lag
$a + b + c < 1$
Lag in accounts payable cash flow
m—Percent paid from previous period
n—Percent paid from current period
$m + n = 1$
$r$ = Tax rate
$i$ = Interest rate
$x$ = Ratio of variable selling/administrative expense to sales

*Initial Values (Dollars)*
Plant
Common stock
Cash$_{t-1}$
Sales$_{t-1, t-2}$
Inventory$_{t-1}$
Retained earnings$_{t-1}$
Bank loan$_{t-1}$
Variable selling/administrative expenses$_{t-1}$
Accounts payable$_{t-1}$

*Assumptions*: time interval equals one month; accounts payable paid in full in next period; no lag between inventory purchase and receipt of goods; and no dividends paid.

financial statements and financial ratios. These are the basic tools for budgeting and profit planning. The financial model is a technique for risk analysis and "what-if" experiments. The model is also needed for day-to-day operational and tactical decisions for immediate planning problems.

In recent years, spreadsheet software and computer-based financial modeling software have been developed and utilized for budgeting and planning in an effort to speed up the budgeting process and allow budget planners and nonfinancial managers to investigate the effects of changes in budget assumptions and scenarios.

Chapter *19*

# SOFTWARE PACKAGES:
## *Computer-based Models and Spreadsheet Software*

Budgeting, financial forecasting and planning can utilize a microcomputer with a powerful spreadsheet program, templates, or add-ins. In addition, more and more companies are developing computer-based models for planning and budgeting, with powerful, yet easy-to-use, modeling languages such as Comshare's *Interactive Financial Planning System* (to be discussed later).

The models not only help build a budget for profit planning but answer a variety of "what-if" scenarios. The resulting calculations provide a basis for choice among alternatives under conditions of uncertainty.

In this chapter, we will illustrate how to use the more popular ones, such as *Lotus*® *1-2-3*, IFPS, and SIMPLAN.

## USE OF A SPREADSHEET PROGRAM FOR FINANCIAL MODELING AND BUDGETING

Spreadsheet programs such as *Lotus*® *1-2-3* and a stand-alone package such as *Up Your Cash Flow* can be used to develop a financial model. For illustrative purposes, we will present some examples of projecting an income statement.

## PROJECTING AN INCOME STATEMENT

We will show how to develop a projected contribution income statement (in Case 1) and a projected traditional income statement (in Case 2) for two hypothetical firms:

### Case 1

Sales for 1st month = $60,000
Cost of sales = 42% of sales, all variable
Operating expenses = $10,000 fixed plus 5% of sales
Taxes = 46% of net income
Sales increase by 5% each month

1. Based on this information, we will create a spreadsheet for the contribution income statement for the next 12 months and in total. This is shown in Figure 19.1.
2. We will do the same as above, assuming that sales increase by 10% and operating expenses = $10,000 plus 10% of sales. This is an example of what-if analysis. This is shown in Figure 19.2.

### Case 2

Delta Gamma Company wishes to prepare a three-year projection of net income, using the following information:

1. The 1994 base year amounts are:

| | |
|---|---:|
| Sales revenues | $4,500,000 |
| Cost of sales | 2,900,000 |
| Selling and Administrative expenses | 800,000 |
| Net income before taxes | 800,000 |

2. Use the following assumptions:

Sales revenues increase by 6% in 1995, 7% in 1996, and 8% in 1997.
Cost of sales increase by 5% each year.
Selling and administrative expenses increase only 1% in 1995 and will remain at the 1995 level thereafter.
The income tax rate = 46%

Figure 19.1

| | 1 | 2 | 3 | 4 | 5 | 6 | 7 | 8 | 9 | 10 | 11 | 12 | TOTAL |
|---|---|---|---|---|---|---|---|---|---|---|---|---|---|
| Sales | $60,000 | $63,000 | $66,150 | $69,458 | $72,930 | $76,577 | $80,406 | $84,426 | $88,647 | $93,080 | $97,734 | $102,620 | $955,028 |
| Less: VC | | | | | | | | | | | | | |
| Cost of sales | $25,200 | $26,460 | $27,783 | $29,172 | $30,631 | $32,162 | $33,770 | $35,459 | $37,232 | $39,093 | $41,048 | $43,101 | $401,112 |
| Operating ex. | $3,000 | $3,150 | $3,308 | $3,473 | $3,647 | $3,829 | $4,020 | $4,221 | $4,432 | $4,654 | $4,887 | $5,131 | $47,751 |
| CM | $31,800 | $36,540 | $38,367 | $40,285 | $42,300 | $44,415 | $46,635 | $48,967 | $51,415 | $53,986 | $56,686 | $59,520 | $550,916 |
| Less: FC | | | | | | | | | | | | | |
| Op. expenses | $10,000 | $10,000 | $10,000 | $10,000 | $10,000 | $10,000 | $10,000 | $10,000 | $10,000 | $10,000 | $10,000 | $10,000 | $120,000 |
| Net income | $21,800 | $26,540 | $28,367 | $30,285 | $32,300 | $34,415 | $36,635 | $38,967 | $41,415 | $43,986 | $46,686 | $49,520 | $430,916 |
| Less: tax | $10,028 | $12,208 | $13,049 | $13,931 | $14,858 | $15,831 | $16,852 | $17,925 | $19,051 | $20,234 | $21,475 | $22,779 | $198,221 |
| NI after tax | $11,772 | $14,332 | $15,318 | $16,354 | $17,442 | $18,584 | $19,783 | $21,042 | $22,364 | $23,753 | $25,210 | $26,741 | $232,695 |

Figure 19.2

| | 1 | 2 | 3 | 4 | 5 | 6 | 7 | 8 | 9 | 10 | 11 | 12 |
|---|---|---|---|---|---|---|---|---|---|---|---|---|
| Sales | $60,000 | $66,000 | $72,600 | $79,860 | $87,846 | $96,631 | $106,294 | $116,923 | $128,615 | $141,477 | $155,625 | $171,187 |
| Less: VC | | | | | | | | | | | | |
| Cost of sales | $25,200 | $27,720 | $30,492 | $33,541 | $36,895 | $40,585 | $44,643 | $49,108 | $54,018 | $59,420 | $65,362 | $71,899 |
| Operating ex. | $6,000 | $6,600 | $7,260 | $7,986 | $8,785 | $9,663 | $10,629 | $11,692 | $12,862 | $14,148 | $15,562 | $17,119 |
| CM | $28,800 | $38,280 | $42,108 | $46,319 | $50,951 | $56,046 | $61,650 | $67,815 | $74,597 | $82,057 | $90,262 | $99,288 |
| Less: FC | | | | | | | | | | | | |
| Op. expenses | $10,000 | $10,000 | $10,000 | $10,000 | $10,000 | $10,000 | $10,000 | $10,000 | $10,000 | $10,000 | $10,000 | $10,000 |
| Net income | $18,800 | $28,280 | $32,108 | $36,319 | $40,951 | $46,046 | $51,650 | $57,815 | $64,597 | $72,057 | $80,262 | $89,288 |
| Less: tax | $8,648 | $13,009 | $14,770 | $16,707 | $18,837 | $21,181 | $23,759 | $26,595 | $29,715 | $33,146 | $36,921 | $41,073 |
| NI after tax | $10,152 | $15,271 | $17,338 | $19,612 | $22,113 | $24,865 | $27,891 | $31,220 | $34,882 | $38,911 | $43,342 | $48,216 |

**Figure 19.3**
DELTA GAMMA COMPANY
THREE-YEAR INCOME PROJECTIONS (1994-1997)

|                    | 1994        | 1995        | 1996        | 1997        |
|--------------------|-------------|-------------|-------------|-------------|
| Sales              | $4,500,000  | $4,770,000  | $5,103,900  | $5,512,212  |
| Cost of sales      | $2,900,000  | $3,045,000  | $3,197,250  | $3,357,113  |
| Gross profit       | $1,600,000  | $1,725,000  | $1,906,650  | $2,155,100  |
| Selling & adm. exp.| $ 800,000   | $ 808,000   | $ 816,080   | $ 824,241   |
| Earnings before tax| $ 800,000   | $ 917,000   | $1,090,570  | $1,330,859  |
| Tax                | $ 368,000   | $ 421,820   | $ 501,662   | $ 612,195   |
| Earnings after tax | $ 432,000   | $ 495,180   | $ 588,908   | $ 718,664   |

We will develop a spreadsheet for the income statement for the next three years. This is shown in Figure 19.3.

### Case 3

We will make specific assumptions as shown in Figure 19.4 and develop a budget using *Up Your Cash Flow*, shown in Figure 19.5.

## BUDGETING SOFTWARE PACKAGES

Remember that financial models are essentially used to generate pro forma financial statements and financial ratios. These are the basic tools for budgeting and profit planning. Also, the financial model is a technique for risk analysis and "what-if" experiments. The financial model is also needed for day-to-day operational and tactical decisions for immediate planning problems. For these purposes, the use of computers is essential.

In recent years, spreadsheet software and computer-based financial modeling software have been developed and utilized for budgeting and planning in an effort to speed up the budgeting process and allow nonfinancial managers to investigate the effect of changes in budget assumptions and scenarios. They are all English-like languages.

**Figure 19.4**
BUDGET ASSUMPTIONS

| Category | Assumptions |
|---|---|
| Sales: | *alternative 1 from book up you cash flow* |
| Cost of goods sold: | *use 45% of sales* |
| Advertising: | *5% of sales* |
| Automobile: | *company has 4 autos @ 1500 ea. 4 x 1500 = 6000 + 12 = 500 per month* |
| Bad debts: | *maintain @ 2% of sales — I hope!* |
| Business promotion: | *Prev year was $65,000. 10% increase equals $71,500 + 12* |
| Collection costs: | *use 1000 per month* |
| Continuing education: | *$1000 per month* |
| Depreciation: | *$84,000 for year — use 7000 per month* |
| Donations: | *$10,000 for year = + 12* |
| Insurance—general: | *agent said $24,000; use 2000 per month* |
| Insurance—group: | *15 employees @ 1500 ea = 22500 + 12 = monthly #.* |
| Insurance—life: | *600 per month* |
| Interest: | *expect to borrow 250m @ 15% = 37,500 + 12 = 3125 per month + other borrowings* |
| Office Supplies: | *2% of sales — and keep it there please!* |
| Rent: | *4000 per month* |
| Repairs and maintenance: | *use 400 per month* |
| Salaries: | *schedule the payroll per month* |
| Taxes and license: | *Prior years was 1.5% of sales use same this year.* |
| Taxes, payroll: | *20% of monthly payroll* |
| Telephone—utilities: | *$29000 last year. Use 33000 + 12. Travel — use $1000 per month* |

Among the well-known system packages are:

1. IFPS (Interactive Financial Planning System)
2. SIMPLAN
3. EXPRESS
4. *Encore Plus*, Ferox Microsystems (Alexandria, Virginia),
5. *Venture*
6. *MicroFCS*, Pilot Executive Software (Boston, Massachusetts),

More budgeting programs are reviewed in the Appendix.

Figure 19.5
## COMPANY BUDGET FOR PERIOD JANUARY TO DECEMBER

| | Jan. | Feb. | Mar. | Apr. | May | Jun. | Jul. | Aug. | Sep. | Oct. | Nov. | Dec. | Total |
|---|---|---|---|---|---|---|---|---|---|---|---|---|---|
| Sales | $129,030 | $129,030 | $129,030 | $129,030 | $192,610 | $192,610 | $162,690 | $129,030 | $192,610 | $129,030 | $162,690 | $192,610 | $1,870,000 |
| Cost of Sales @ 45% | 58,063 | 58,063 | 58,063 | 58,063 | 86,675 | 86,675 | 73,211 | 58,063 | 86,675 | 58,063 | 73,211 | 86,675 | 841,500 |
| Gross profit | 70,967 | 70,967 | 70,967 | 70,967 | 105,935 | 105,935 | 89,479 | 70,967 | 105,935 | 70,967 | 89,479 | 105,935 | 1,028,500 |
| Advertising @ 5% | 6,450 | 6,450 | 6,450 | 6,450 | 9,600 | 9,600 | 8,100 | 6,450 | 9,600 | 6,450 | 8,100 | 10,050 | 93,750 |
| Automobile | 500 | 500 | 500 | 500 | 500 | 500 | 500 | 500 | 500 | 500 | 500 | 500 | 6,000 |
| Bad debts @ 2% | 2,580 | 2,580 | 2,580 | 2,580 | 3,840 | 3,840 | 3,240 | 2,580 | 3,840 | 2,580 | 3,240 | 3,920 | 37,400 |
| Business promotions | 5,958 | 5,958 | 5,958 | 5,958 | 5,958 | 5,958 | 5,958 | 5,958 | 5,958 | 5,958 | 5,958 | 5,962 | 71,500 |
| Collection costs | 1,000 | 1,000 | 1,000 | 1,000 | 1,000 | 1,000 | 1,000 | 1,000 | 1,000 | 1,000 | 1,000 | 1,000 | 12,000 |
| Continuing education | 1,000 | 1,000 | 1,000 | 1,000 | 1,000 | 1,000 | 1,000 | 1,000 | 1,000 | 1,000 | 1,000 | 1,000 | 12,000 |
| Depreciation | 7,000 | 7,000 | 7,000 | 7,000 | 7,000 | 7,000 | 7,000 | 7,000 | 7,000 | 7,000 | 7,000 | 7,000 | 84,000 |
| Donations | 833 | 833 | 833 | 833 | 833 | 833 | 833 | 833 | 833 | 833 | 833 | 837 | 10,000 |
| Dues & subscriptions | 833 | 833 | 833 | 833 | 833 | 833 | 833 | 833 | 833 | 833 | 833 | 837 | 10,000 |
| Insurance—general | 2,000 | 2,000 | 2,000 | 2,000 | 2,000 | 2,000 | 2,000 | 2,000 | 2,000 | 2,000 | 2,000 | 2,000 | 24,000 |
| Insurance—group | 1,875 | 1,875 | 1,875 | 1,875 | 1,875 | 1,875 | 1,875 | 1,875 | 1,875 | 1,875 | 1,875 | 1,875 | 22,500 |
| Insurance—life | 600 | 600 | 600 | 600 | 600 | 600 | 600 | 600 | 600 | 600 | 600 | 600 | 7,200 |
| Interest | 3,125 | 3,125 | 3,125 | 3,125 | 4,375 | 4,375 | 4,375 | 4,450 | 4,450 | 4,450 | 4,450 | 4,450 | 47,875 |
| Legal & accounting | 1,000 | 1,000 | 1,000 | 1,000 | 1,000 | 1,000 | 1,000 | 1,000 | 1,000 | 1,000 | 1,000 | 1,000 | 12,000 |
| Office supplies @ 2% | 2,580 | 2,580 | 2,580 | 2,580 | 3,840 | 3,840 | 3,240 | 2,580 | 3,840 | 2,580 | 3,240 | 3,920 | 37,400 |
| Rent | 4,000 | 4,000 | 4,000 | 4,000 | 4,000 | 4,000 | 4,000 | 4,000 | 4,000 | 4,000 | 4,000 | 4,000 | 48,000 |
| Repairs | 400 | 400 | 400 | 400 | 400 | 400 | 400 | 400 | 400 | 400 | 400 | 400 | 4,800 |
| Salaries | 21,000 | 21,000 | 21,000 | 21,000 | 21,000 | 21,000 | 24,833 | 24,833 | 24,833 | 24,833 | 24,833 | 24,835 | 275,000 |
| Taxes & license @ 1.5% | 1,935 | 1,935 | 1,935 | 1,935 | 2,880 | 2,880 | 2,430 | 1,935 | 2,880 | 1,935 | 2,430 | 2,890 | 28,000 |
| Taxes, payroll | 4,200 | 4,200 | 4,200 | 4,200 | 4,200 | 4,200 | 4,966 | 4,966 | 4,966 | 4,966 | 4,966 | 4,970 | 55,000 |
| Telephone—utilities | 2,750 | 2,750 | 2,750 | 2,750 | 2,750 | 2,750 | 2,750 | 2,750 | 2,750 | 2,750 | 2,750 | 2,750 | 33,000 |
| Travel | 1,000 | 1,000 | 1,000 | 1,000 | 1,000 | 1,000 | 1,000 | 1,000 | 1,000 | 1,000 | 1,000 | 1,000 | 12,000 |
| Profit | $(1,652) | $(1,652) | $(1,652) | $(1,652) | $25,451 | $25,451 | $7,546 | $(7,576) | $20,777 | $(7,576) | $7,471 | $20,139 | $85,075 |

We will discuss the more popular, IFPS and SIMPLAN, with illustrations. Then we will cover EXPRESS and Encore Plus very briefly.

### IFPS (INTERACTIVE FINANCIAL PLANNING SYSTEM)

IFPS is a multipurpose, interactive financial modeling system, often called a *decision support system (DSS)*, which supports and facilitates the building, solving, and asking of what-if questions of financial models.

The output from an IFPS model is in the format of a spreadsheet, that is a matrix or table, in which:

- The rows represent user-specified variables such as market share, sales, growth in sales, unit price, gross margin, variable cost, contribution margin, fixed cost, net income, net present value, internal rate of return, and earnings per share.
- The column designates a sequence of user-specified time periods such as month, quarter, year, total, percentages, or divisions.
- The entries in the body of the table display the values taken by the model variable over time or by segments of the firm such as divisions, product lines, sales territories, and departments.

IFPS offers the following key features:

- Like other special purpose modeling languages, IFPS provides an English-like modeling language. Therefore, without an extensive knowledge of computer programming, the manager can build budgeting models of his own and use them for what-if scenarios and managerial decisions.
- IFPS has a collection of built-in financial functions that perform calculations such as net present value (NPV), internal rate of return (IRR), loan amortization schedules, and depreciation alternatives.
- IFPS also has a collection of built-in mathematical and statistical functions such as linear regression, linear interpolation, polynomial autocorrelation, and moving average functions.
- IFPS supports use of leading and/or lagged variables which are commonly used in financial modeling. For example, cash collections lag behind credit sales of prior periods.
- IFPS also supports deterministic and probabilistic modeling. It of-

fers a variety of functions for sampling from probability distributions such as uniform, normal, bivariate normal, and user-described empirical distributions.

- IFPS is nonprocedural in nature. This means that the relationships, logic, and data used to calculate the various values in the output do not have to be arranged in any particular top-to-bottom order in an IFPS model. IFPS automatically detects and solves a system of two or more linear or nonlinear equations.

- IFPS has extensive editing capabilities that include adding statements to and deleting statements from a model, making changes in existing statements, and making copies of parts or all of a model.

- IFPS supports sensitivity analysis by providing the following solution options:

  (a) WHAT-IF

  IFPS lets you specify one or more changes in the relationships, logic, data, and/or parameter values in the existing model and recalculates the model to show the impact of these changes on the performance measures.

  (b) GOAL-SEEKING

  In the GOAL-SEEKING mode, IFPS can determine what change would have to take place in the value of a specified variable in a particular time period to achieve a specified value for another variable. For example, the marketing manager can ask the system to answer the question "What would the unit sales price have to be for the new product to achieve a target return on investment of 20%?"

  (c) SENSITIVITY

  This particular command is employed to determine the effect of a specified variable on one or more other variables. The SENSITIVITY command is similar to the WHAT-IF command but it provides a convenient, model-produced tabular summary for each new alternative value of the specified variable.

  (d) ANALYZE

  The ANALYZE command examines in detail those variables

and their values that have contributed to the value of a specified variable.

(e) IMPACT

The IMPACT command is used to determine the effect on a specified variable of a series of percentage changes in one or more variables.

(f) IFPS/OPTIMUM

The IFPS/OPTIMUM routine is employed to answer questions of "What is the best?" type rather than "What-if."

(g) Other features of IFPS include:
- routine graphic output
- interactive color graphics
- data files that contain both data and relationships
- a consolidation capability that lets the nonfinancial manager produce composite reports from two or more models.
- Extraction of data from existing non-IFPS data files and placing them in IFPS-compatible data files.
- Operating on all major computer mainframes and microcomputers.

In the following section, we present, step by step, how to build a model using IFPS. (The following example was adapted from Comshare, *IFPS Fundamental Seminar Book*, 1987, pp. 6–20, with permission).

## Example 1

This example illustrates how to use IFPS.

The MCL Corporation is considering diversifying and wishes to evaluate the profitability of the new venture over the next two years. A quarterly profit picture is desired. Marketing research has provided the following information: (1) The total market for the product will be 7,000 units at the start of production and will grow at the rate of 1 percent per quarter; (2) MCL's initial share of the market is 11 percent, and this is expected to grow at the rate of one-half percent per quarter if intense marketing efforts are maintained; (3) the selling price is expected to be $2.50 per unit the first year and $2.65 the following year; (4) the standard cost system has produced the following estimates: (a) selling expenses, $.233 per unit; (b) labor cost $.61 per unit; and (c) raw materials, $.42 per unit; (5) general and administrative expenses are estimated to be $450 in the first quarter with a quarterly growth rate of 1 percent; and (6) setup costs for the line are $3,500.

First log in to your computer and access IFPS.

1. *Establishing the Model*

INTERACTIVE FINANCIAL PLANNING SYSTEM

ENTER NAME OF FILE CONTAINING MODELS AND REPORTS

?PROFIT

FILE PROFIT NOT FOUND-NEW FILE WILL BE CREATED

READY FOR EXECUTIVE COMMAND

? MODEL EXAMPLE

BEGIN ENTERING NEW MODEL

? AUTO 10, 5

10? (Model is entered as shown in 19.6)

3. *Displaying the Model*

*Once the model is complete, the solution can be displayed by using a sequence of commands like those that follow. A brief discussion of each command follows the illustration.*

180? SOLVE

MODEL NEWPROD VERSION OF 12/20/93 16:38—11 COLUMNS 17

VARIABLES

ENTER SOLVE OPTIONS

? COLUMNS 1994,5-8.1995,GROWTH

? WIDTH 72, 16, 8

? ALL

*ALL instructs IFPS to print the values of all variables as shown in Exhibit*

Figure 19.7 presents the IFPS output.
Figure 19.8 illustrates "what-if" analysis.

Figure 19.6
ENTERING THE MODEL


```
10 COLUMNS 1-8, 1994, 1995, GROWTH
15 *EXAMPLE OF IFPS
20 *
25 **
30 PERIODS 4
35 * SALES DATA AND PROJECTIONS
40 PRICE = 2.5 FOR 4, 2.65
45 MARKET SHARE = .11, PREVIOUS MARKET SHARE + .005
50 TOTAL MARKET = 7000, PREVIOUS TOTAL MARKET*1.01
55 SALES VOLUME = L45*L50
60 * PREVIOUS CALCULATIONS
65 SALES REVENUE = SALES VOLUME*PRICE
70 NET INCOME = SALES REVENUE – TOTAL EXPENSES
75 * COSTS
80 UNIT SELLING COST = .233
85 UNIT LABOR COST = .61
90 UNIT MATERIAL COST = .42
95 UNIT COST = SUM(UNIT SELLING COST THRU UNIT MATERIAL COST)
100
65 SALES REVENUE = SALES VOLUME*PRICE
70 NET INCOME = SALES REVENUE – TOTAL EXPENSES
75 * COSTS
80 UNIT SELLING COST = .233
85 UNIT LABOR COST = .61
90 UNIT MATERIAL COST = .42
95 UNIT COST = SUM(UNIT SELLING COST THRU UNIT MATERIAL COST)
100 VARIABLE COST = UNIT COST*SALES VOLUME
105 ADMIN EXPENSES = 450, PREVIOUS ADMIN EXPENSES*1.01
110 TOTAL EXPENSES = VARIABLE COST + ADMIN EXPENSES
115 *PERFORMANCE MEASURES
120 INITIAL INVESTMENT = 3500.0
125 DISCOUNT RATE = .12
130 PRESENT VALUE = NPVC(NET INCOME, DISCOUNT RATE, INITIAL
    INVESTMENT)
140 RATE OF RETURN = IRR(NET INCOME, INITIAL INVESTMENT)
145 *
150 COLUMN 1989 FOR L55,L65,L70,L100,L105, L110,L120 = '
155    SUM(C1 THRU C4)
160 COLUMN 1990 FOR L55,L65,L70,L100,L105, L110,L120 = '
165    SUM(C5 THRU C8)
170 COLUMN GROWTH FOR L55,L65,L70,L100,L105,L110,L120 =
175    100*(C10-C9)/C9
END OF MODEL
?
```

Figure 19.7
IFPS OUTPUT

| Example of IFPS | 1994 | 5 | 6 | 7 | 8 | 1995 | Growth |
|---|---|---|---|---|---|---|---|
| *Sales data and projections | | | | | | | |
| Price | | 2.650 | 2.650 | 2.650 | 2.650 | | |
| Market share | | .1300 | .1350 | .1400 | .1450 | | |
| Total market | | 7284 | 7357 | 7431 | 7505 | | |
| Sales volume | 3341 | 946.9 | 993.2 | 1040 | 1088 | 4069 | 21.76 |
| Previous calculations | | | | | | | |
| Sales revenue | 8354 | 2509 | 2632 | 2757 | 2884 | 10782 | 29.07 |
| Net income | 2306 | 845.1 | 904.6 | 965.2 | 1027 | 3742 | 62.25 |
| Costs | | | | | | | |
| Unit selling cost | | .2330 | .2330 | .2330 | .2330 | | |
| Unit labor cost | | .6100 | .6100 | .6100 | .6100 | | |
| Unit material cost | | .4200 | .4200 | .4200 | .4200 | | |
| Unit cost | | 1.263 | 1.263 | 1.263 | 1.263 | | |
| Variable cost | 4220 | 1196 | 1254 | 1314 | 1374 | 5139 | 21.76 |
| Admin. expenses | 1827 | 468.3 | 473.0 | 477.7 | 482.5 | 1901 | 4.060 |
| Total expenses | 6047 | 1664 | 1727 | 1792 | 1857 | 7040 | 16.41 |
| Performance measures | | | | | | | |
| Initial investment | 3500 | 0 | 0 | 0 | 0 | 0 | −100 |
| Discount rate | | .1200 | .1200 | .1200 | .1200 | | |
| Present value | | −623.5 | 139.7 | 931.3 | 1750 | | |
| Rate of return | | | .1676 | .3988 | .5812 | | |

Figure 19.9 presents goal seeking analysis.

### 4. "What-if" Analysis

Instead of merely solving a model, as it is, the WHAT IF command can be used to determine the effect of changes in the definitions of variables in the model. The examples that follow show how these questions can be answered:

| Case | Question |
|---|---|
| 1 | What if the total market size starts out at 6,000 units instead of 7,000, but grows by 5 percent per quarter, instead of 1 percent? |
| 2 | What if the selling price is $2.70 in the second year instead of $2.65 (and total market follows the original assumptions)? |
| 3 | What if, in addition to the price being $2.70 in 1994; unit material cost is three cents higher than expected in both years? |

### Figure 19.8
### WHAT-IF ANALYSIS OUTPUT

? WHAT IF
WHAT IF CASE 1
ENTER STATEMENTS
? TOTAL MARKET = 6000, PREVIOUS TOTAL MARKET * 1.05
? SOLVE
ENTER SOLVE OPTIONS
? NET INCOME, PRESENT WORTH, RATE OF RETURN
***** WHAT IF CASE 1 *****
1 WHAT IF STATEMENT PROCESSED

|  | 1994 | 5 | 6 | 7 | 8 | 1995 | GROWTH |
|---|---|---|---|---|---|---|---|
| NET INCOME | 1941 | 846.7 | 960.9 | 1084 | 1215 | 4107 | 111.5 |
| PRESENT WORTH |  | −966.3 | −155.6 | 733.1 | 1702 |  |  |
| RATE OF RETURN |  |  | .0703 | .3240 | .5318 |  |  |

ENTER SOLVE OPTIONS
? WHAT IF
WHAT IF CASE 2
ENTER STATEMENTS
? PRICE = 2.5 FOR 4, 2.70
? SOLVE
ENTER SOLVE OPTIONS
? L70, L130, L140
***** WHAT IF CASE 2 *****
1 WHAT IF STATEMENT PROCESSED

|  | 1994 | 5 | 6 | 7 | 8 | 1995 | GROWTH |
|---|---|---|---|---|---|---|---|
| NET INCOME | 2306 | 892.5 | 954.3 | 1017 | 1081 | 3945 | 71.07 |
| PRESENT WORTH |  | −582.4 | 222.7 | 1057 | 1919 |  |  |
| RATE OF RETURN |  |  | .1952 | .4333 | .6198 |  |  |

ENTER SOLVE OPTIONS
? WHAT IF CONTINUE
WHAT IF CASE 3
ENTER STATEMENTS
? UNIT MATERIAL COST = UNIT MATERIAL COST + .03
? SOLVE
ENTER SOLVE OPTIONS
? UNIT MATERIAL COST THRU VARIABLE COST
***** WHAT IF CASE 3 *****
2 WHAT IF STATEMENTS PROCESSED

|  | 1994 | 5 | 6 | 7 | 8 | 1995 | GROWTH |
|---|---|---|---|---|---|---|---|
| UNIT MATERIAL CO |  | .4500 | .4500 | .4500 | .4500 |  |  |
| UNIT COST |  | 1.293 | 1.293 | 1.293 | 1.293 |  |  |
| VARIABLE COST | 4320 | 1224 | 1284 | 1345 | 1407 | 5261 | 21.76 |

### Figure 19.9
### GOAL SEEKING OUTPUT

ENTER SOLVE OPTIONS
? BASE MODEL
? GOAL SEEKING
GOAL SEEKING CASE 1
ENTER NAME OF VARIABLE TO BE ADJUSTED TO ACHIEVE
PERFORMANCE
? MARKET SHARE
ENTER COMPUTATIONAL STATEMENT FOR PERFORMANCE
? NET INCOME = 700, PREVIOUS NET INCOME * 1.03
***** GOAL SEEKING CASE 1 *****

|  | 1994 | 5 | 6 | 7 | 8 | 1995 | GROWTH |
|---|---|---|---|---|---|---|---|
| MARKET SHARE |  | .1243 | .1259 | .1274 | .1291 |  |  |

ENTER SOLVE OPTIONS
? NET INCOME, PRESENT WORTH, RATE OF RETURN

|  | 1994 | 5 | 6 | 7 | 8 | 1995 | GROWTH |
|---|---|---|---|---|---|---|---|
| NET INCOME | 2929 | 787.9 | 811.5 | 835.8 | 860.9 | 3296 | 12.55 |
| PRESENT WORTH |  | −89.41 | 595.2 | 1281 | 1967 |  |  |
| RATE OF RETURN |  | .0822 | .3446 | .5494 | .7073 |  |  |

ENTER SOLVE OPTIONS
? GOAL SEEKING
GOAL SEEKING CASE 2
ENTER NAME OF VARIABLE TO BE ADJUSTED TO ACHIEVE
PERFORMANCE
? INITIAL INVESTMENT(1)
ENTER COMPUTATIONAL STATEMENT FOR PERFORMANCE
? RATE OF RETURN(8) = 25%
***** GOAL SEEKING CASE 2 *****

|  | 1994 | 5 | 6 | 7 | 8 | 1995 | GROWTH |
|---|---|---|---|---|---|---|---|
| INITIAL INVESTMENT | 4595 | 0 | 0 | 0 | 0 | 0 | −100 |

ENTER SOLVE OPTIONS
? RATE OF RETURN

|  | 1994 | 5 | 6 | 7 | 8 | 1995 | GROWTH |
|---|---|---|---|---|---|---|---|
| RATE OF RETURN |  |  |  | .0835 | .2500 |  |  |

ENTER SOLVE OPTIONS
?

Note that Cases 1 and 2 are independent, while Case 3 builds on the changes made in Case 2. To handle both kinds of situations, two different WHAT IF commands are available:

WHAT IF            Enables the user to modify temporarily as many individual model statements as desired to determine the effect on the solution. Each WHAT IF erases the assumptions made by the previous one.

WHAT IF CONTINUE  Since each WHAT IF normally starts from the base case, this command makes possible, successive, cumulative, WHAT IF statements.

In the printout shown in Exhibit, the user has asked to see only selected variables. In Case 1, individual variable names, separated by commas, are used. In Case 2, model line numbers have been used instead. Case 3 illustrates the use of THRU to print an inclusive list of variables.

The SOLVE OPTIONS entered earlier to specify columns and page layout remain in effect through the modeling session.

### Summary of "What-if" Analysis

Case 1 If the total market size starts out at 6,000 units and grows by 5 percent per quarter, then net income will go up by 111.5 percent.

Case 2 If the selling price is $2.70 in the second year, then the net income will go up by 71.07 percent.

Case 3 If, in addition to price being $2.70 in 1994, unit material cost is three cents higher than expected in both years, then the variable cost will go up by 21.76 percent.

### 5. "Goal-Seeking" Analysis

The GOAL SEEKING command allows the user to work backward. That is, the user tells IFPS what assumption can be adjusted and what objective is to be sought. IFPS then solves the model repetitively until it finds the value that yields the desired objective. To illustrate the use of this command, consider the following two situations:

| Case | Question |
| --- | --- |
| 1 | Market share estimates could be less than originally expected. How low could it be and still provide first quarter net income of $700 and 3 percent more in each subsequent quarter? |
| 2 | The required initial investment might be larger than originally expected. How much larger could it be and still permit a 25 percent return over the eight-quarter horizon? |

The first question is really asking what market share would have to be in each column to achieve a certain net income in the same column. The second question asks what investment has to be in column 1 to produce a certain rate of return in column 8.

As shown in the example in Exhibit 19.9, the second question is handled by enclosing the column number in parentheses after the variable name. The variable is then said to be "subscripted".

The command BASE MODEL is issued before GOAL SEEKING. Without this command, modifications made by the last WHAT IF command would still be in effect.

### Summary of "Goal-Seeking" Analysis

Case 1  The market share could be as low as .1243 in the first quarter and still provide first quarter net income of $700 and 3 percent more in each subsequent quarter.

Case 2  The initial investment would have to be $4,595 in order to permit a 25 percent return over the eight-quarter horizon.

Prospective users of IFPS are encouraged to refer to the following sources:

- Comshare, IFPS Cases and Models, Austin, TX, 1979.
- Comshare, IFPS Tutorial, Austin, TX, 1980.
- Comshare, IFPS User's Manual, Austin, TX, 1984.
- Comshare, IFPS/Personal User's Manual, Austin, TX 1984.
- Comshare, IFPS University Seminar, Austin, TX, 1984.
- Comshare, Comprehensive Fundamentals of IFPS, Austin, TX, 1984.
- Comshare, Papers Available from the Comshare University Support Programs, Austin, TX, 1986.

## SIMPLAN: A PLANNING AND MODELING SYSTEM

SIMPLAN is more than a financial modeling package. In fact, it is an integrated, multipurpose planning, budgeting, and modeling system. A diagram of SIMPLAN's mode organization is provided in Figure 19.10.

As can be seen from Figure 19.10, in addition to general financial modeling function, the system has the capability to perform sales forecasting and time series analysis, as well as econometric modeling. Sophisticated users can really take advantage of the package. For forecasting sales, inter-

**Figure 19.10**
SIMPLAN MODE ORGANIZATION

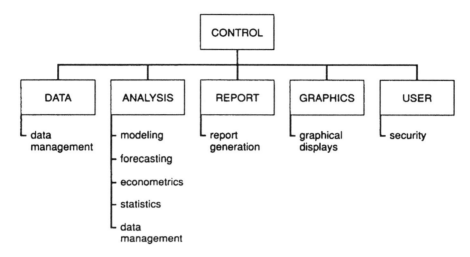

Corporate Planning and Modeling with SIMPLAN *by R. Britton Mayo and Social Systems, Inc, 1979. Courtesy of Addison-Wesley Publishing Company (Boston, Massachusetts).*

est rates, material supplies, factor input prices, and other key variables, SIMPLAN offers a variety of time series forecasting models. These include time trends, exponential smoothing, and adaptive forecasting. Forecasts developed by any of these methods may be incorporated directly into SIM-PLAN models and reports.

As for econometric modeling capability, SIMPLAN offers models for sales, market share and industry which can, with SIMPLAN, be specified, estimated, validated, simulated, and linked directly to division financial and production models or corporate financial models.

SIMPLAN can be used to estimate single-equation and simultaneous-equation linear and nonlinear models to simulate the effects of alternative marketing strategies and economic conditions on market share and industry demand. Direct access from SIMPLAN to all series of the National Business and Economic Research (NBER) macroeconomic database is available on several time-sharing networks.

With SIMPLAN, 16 major functions are integrated into a single planning and modeling system. These functions include:

- Database creation
- Database manipulation
- Consolidation
- Model specification
- Model changes
- Report formulation
- Report changes
- Statistical analysis

- Forecasting
- Econometrics
- Model solution
- Validation
- Policy simulation
- Report generation
- Security
- Graphical display

SIMPLAN contains a number of commands to facilitate logical operations.

EXAMPLE:

If the cash balances (CASH) fall below some minimum level (MBAL), the company's line of credit may be automatically increased by the amount of cash shortfall.

The SIMPLAN commands to accomplish this task would be:

$$IF\ CASH<MBAL$$
$$DEBT=DEBT(-1)+MBAL-CASH$$
$$CASH=MBAL$$

SIMPLAN utilizes a set of logical comparison operations, as well as a IF and GO TO command.

For a complete instruction about the system, refer to R. Britton Mayo and Social Systems, Inc., *Corporate Planning and Modeling with SIMPLAN*, Addison-Wesley Publishing Company, 1979.

### Example 2

The model we develop using SIMPLAN is designed to calculate the current asset portion of a typical balance sheet. First, Figure 19.11 shows a list of data records or variables. Figure 19.12 presents a sample model on SIMPLAN. The definitional equations, behavioral equations, and decision rules (using, for example, IF ELSE statements) constructed here are pretty much self-explanatory.

**Figure 19.11**
DATA RECORDS AND VARIABLES

| Name | Abbreviation | Units |
|---|---|---|
| Accounts receivable collected | GROWTHRATE | 000 units |
| Accounts payable | AP | $000 |
| Accounts receivable (net) | AR | $000 |
| Cash | CASH | $000 |
| Cost of goods sold | COGS | $000 |
| Accounts receivable collected | COLLECTION | $000 |
| Total current assets | CURASSETS | $000 |
| Dollar value of sales | DOLLARSALE | $000 |
| Fixed costs | FIXEDCOST | $000 |
| Sales growth rate | GROWTHRATE | % |
| Cost of labor | LABOR | $/unit |
| Raw material cost | MATCOST | $/unit |
| Raw material inventory | MATERIALS | 000 lbs. |
| Current value of inventory | MATVALUE | $000 |
| Reduction of accounts payable | PAYMENTS | $000 |
| Selling price | PRICE | $/unit |
| Production volume units | PRODUCTION | 000 |
| Additions to inventory | PURCHASES | 000 lbs. |
| Inventory reorder point | REORDER | 000 lbs. |
| Sales units | SALES | 000 |
| Production cost per unit | UNITCOST | $/unit |
| Variable costs | VARCOST | $000 |
| Production payroll | WAGES | $000 |

The first simulation for the period 1994–97 is given in Figure 19.13. To provide the reader with an idea of policy simulation, let us suppose that we want to determine the effects of an increase in the sales growth rate from 7% to 8.5%. Basically, all we need to do is replace statement 3 with

3 GROWTHRATE=8.5

With this new policy assumption, Figure 19.14 shows the simulated results.

We note that total current assets grow at an annual rate of 13.44% as

**Figure 19.12**
THE COMPLETE SIMPLAN MODEL

```
  3    GROWTHRATE = 7
  5    PRICE = 1.2
 10    MATCOST = .6
 15    REORDER = 3000
 20    LABOR = .285
 30    UNITCOST = LABOR+MATCOST
 40    PRODUCTION = SALES(−1)
 50    MATERIALS = MATERIALS(−1)-PRODUCTION
 60    WAGES = LABOR*PRODUCTION
 70    SALES = SALES(−1)*(1 + GROWTHRATE/100)
 80    FIXEDCOST = 50
 90    VARCOST = UNITCOST*SALES
100    COGS = FIXEDCOST + VARCOST
110    DOLLARSALE = SALES*PRICE
120    IF MATERIALS<REORDER
130    PURCHASES = REORDER + 2*PRODUCTION-MATERIALS
140    MATERIALS = MATERIALS + PURCHASES
145    ELSE
146    PURCHASES = 0
150    END
160    COLLECTION = 3/4*AR(−1)
170    AR = AR(−1) − COLLECTION + DOLLARSALE
180    PAYMENTS = .6*AP(−1)
190    AP = AP(−1) − PAYMENTS + (PURCHASES*MATCOST)
200    CASH = CASH(−1) + COLLECTION-PAYMENTS − WAGES
210    MATVALUE = MATERIALS*MATCOST
220    CURASSETS = CASH + AR + MATVALUE
```

opposed to 12.61%. The result indicates that a change in the assumed growth rate does not produce as large a change in the company's assets. In this case, a 1.5% increase in the growth rate causes cash and accounts receivable to rise by .67% and 1.4%, respectively. Thus, the company's financial position in terms of liquidity and working capital appears to be relatively inelastic with respect to the assumed growth rate in sales.

## EXPRESS

EXPRESS, which was developed by Management Decision Systems, provides the standard set of financial planning and analysis features, including the generation of pro forma financial statements, budgeting, analysis,

Figure 19.13
THE INITIAL **SIMPLAN** RESULT

### Policy Assumptions

|                                      | 1994  | 1995  | 1996  | 1997  | Average |
| ------------------------------------ | ----- | ----- | ----- | ----- | ------- |
| Sales growth rate (%)                | 7.00  | 7.00  | 7.00  | 7.00  | 7.00    |
| Selling price ($/unit)               | 1.20  | 1.20  | 1.20  | 1.20  | 1.20    |
| Raw material price ($/unit)          | 0.60  | 0.60  | 0.60  | 0.60  | 0.60    |
| Cost of labor ($/unit)               | 0.28  | 0.28  | 0.28  | 0.28  | 0.28    |
| Inventory reorder point (000 lbs.)   | 3,000 | 3,000 | 3,000 | 3,000 | 3,000   |

### Results (all in $000 unless otherwise noted)

|                                        | 1994    | 1995    | 1996    | 1997    | Percent Growth |
| -------------------------------------- | ------- | ------- | ------- | ------- | -------------- |
| Cash                                   | 1,432   | 1,997   | 1,860   | 2,346   | 17.88          |
| Accounts receivable (net)              | 1,527   | 1,481   | 1,546   | 1,645   | 2.51           |
| Current value of inventory             | 1,920   | 2,827   | 2,278   | 2,976   | 15.73          |
| Total current assets                   | 4,879   | 6,306   | 5,684   | 6,967   | 12.61          |
| Sales (000 units)                      | 856     | 916     | 980     | 1,049   | 7.00           |
| Variable costs                         | 758     | 811     | 867     | 928     | 7.00           |
| Fixed costs                            | 50      | 50      | 50      | 50      |                |
| Cost of goods sold                     | 808     | 861     | 917     | 978     | 6.59           |
| Dollar value of sales                  | 1,027   | 1,099   | 1,176   | 1,258   | 7.00           |
| Accounts receivablecollected           | (1,500) | (1,145) | (1,111) | (1,160) | (8.22)         |
| Accounts receivable (net)              | 1,527   | 1,481   | 1,546   | 1,645   | 2.51           |
| Reduction of accounts payable          | 840     | 336     | 987     | 395     | (22.25)        |
| Accounts payable                       | 560     | 1,645   | 658     | 1,550   | 40.39          |
| Production payroll                     | 228     | 244     | 261     | 279     | 7.00           |
| Production cost per unit ($/unit)      | 0.885   | 0.885   | 0.885   | 0.885   |                |
| Production volume (000 units)          | (800)   | (856)   | (916)   | (980)   | 7.00           |
| Additions to inventory (000 lbs.)      |         | 2,368   |         | 2,144   |                |
| Raw material inventory (000 lbs.)      | 3,200   | 4,712   | 3,796   | 4,960   | 15.73          |

**Figure 19.14**
**The Simulated Result with Policy Assumption**

## Policy Assumptions

|                                      | 1994  | 1995  | 1996  | 1997  | Average |
|--------------------------------------|-------|-------|-------|-------|---------|
| Sales growth rate (%)                | 8.50  | 8.50  | 8.50  | 8.50  | 8.50    |
| Selling price ($/unit)               | 1.20  | 1.20  | 1.20  | 1.20  | 1.20    |
| Raw material price ($/unit)          | 0.60  | 0.60  | 0.60  | 0.60  | 0.60    |
| Cost of labor ($/unit)               | 0.28  | 0.28  | 0.28  | 0.28  | 0.28    |
| Inventory reorder point (000 lbs.)   | 3,000 | 3,000 | 3,000 | 3,000 | 3,000   |

## Results (all in $000 unless otherwise noted)

|                                       | 1994    | 1995    | 1996    | 1997    | Percent Growth |
|---------------------------------------|---------|---------|---------|---------|----------------|
| Cash                                  | 1,432   | 2,005   | 1,873   | 2,386   | 18.55          |
| Accounts receivable (net)             | 1,542   | 1,516   | 1,605   | 1,732   | 3.95           |
| Current value of inventory            | 1,920   | 2,842   | 2,277   | 3,026   | 16.38          |
| Total current assets                  | 4,894   | 6,362   | 5,755   | 7,144   | 13.44          |
| Sales (000 units)                     | 868     | 942     | 1,022   | 1,109   | 8.50           |
| Variable costs                        | 768     | 833     | 904     | 981     | 8.50           |
| Fixed costs                           | 50      | 50      | 50      | 50      |                |
| Cost of goods sold                    | 818     | 883     | 954     | 1,031   | 8.02           |
| Dollar value of sales                 | 1,042   | 1,130   | 1,226   | 1,330   | 8.50           |
| Accounts receivable collected         | (1,500) | (1,156) | (1,137) | (1,204) | (7.07)         |
| Accounts receivable (net)             | 1,542   | 1,516   | 1,605   | 1,732   | 3.95           |
| Reduction of accounts payable         | 840     | 336     | 1,000   | 400     | (21.91)        |
| Accounts payable                      | 560     | 1,666   | 667     | 1,629   | 42.76          |
| Production payroll                    | 228     | 247     | 268     | 291     | 8.50           |
| Production cost per unit ($/unit)     | 0.885   | 0.885   | 0.885   | 0.885   |                |
| Production volume (000 units)         | (800)   | (868)   | (942)   | (1,022) | 8.50           |
| Additions to inventory (000 lbs.)     |         | 2,404   |         | 2,271   |                |
| Raw material inventory (000 lbs.)     | 3,200   | 4,736   | 3,794   | 5,044   | 16.38          |

projections, target analysis, and consolidations. One of the special modeling features of the system is risk analysis (including Monte Carlo simulation).

EXPRESS contains a variety of analytical and statistical features. Besides the standard mathematical capabilities, the system has the following automatic built-in calculations: sorting, percent difference, lags and leads, maximum/minimum of a set of numbers, year-to-date, and rounding.

The statistical features include a number of time series analysis and forecasting routines such as exponential smoothing, linear extrapolation, deseasonalization, multiple regression, cluster analysis, and factor analysis.

EXPRESS contains the report generator and display features for the system. All the display capabilities are integrated with the system's data management, analysis, and modeling routine. The system has full graphic display capabilities.

## ENCORE PLUS

This package was developed by Ferox Microsystems. The analytical functions are similar to IFPS, but Encore has more model building capability. For example, it is stronger in its risk analysis than IFPS and even includes a Monte Carlo Simulator. Since Encore Plus is more powerful at the application development level than, say, IFPS, it requires a higher level of programming ability.

## CHECKLIST

There are a number of software packages for divisional, departmental, and corporate modeling. Companies just entering the modeling arena must keep in mind that the differences between the software packages available in the market can be substantial. A comparison should be made by examining the software in light of the planning system, the information system, and the modeling activities.

The companies should also consider making effective use of in-house computer hardware, micro, mini, or mainframe computers, and data bases. An effective modeling system does not necessarily imply an outside time-sharing system or an external economic data base. Effective networking is highly recommended.

Figure 19.15 is a checklist for factors to consider in the evaluation of modeling software.

**Figure 19.15**

*Factors to Consider in the Evaluation of Modeling Software*

- Main application area
  —Corporate modeling
  —Financial modeling
  —Marketing modeling
  —Production modeling
- Type of system
  —Fixed structure
  —Flexible, modular structure
- Mode of operation
  —Batch
  —Real time
  —In-house
  —Service bureau
- Costs of system
  —Purchasing, leasing
  —Consulting, training
  —Storage
  —Operation
- Type of language
  —Free format-fixed format
  —Compiler-interpreter
  —Restrictions
  —English-like or symbolic text
- Flexibility of input and output
  —Choice and number of formats
  —Sequence
  —Graphics and histograms
- Type of data base
  —File and data set structure
  —Internal, external data base
  —Connection and hierarchies of
   data bases and files
- Basic time intervals
  —Maximum number
  —Specific periods
  —Interval transformations
- Maximum size of model
  —Statements
  —Number and size of arrays,
   matrices and tables, and files
   and number of data

- Arithmetic
  —Operators
  —Column arithmetic
  —Line arithmetic
  —Table arithmetic
  —Built-in functions
- Systems logic
  —Linear sequential
  —Logical branching
- Hardware requirements
  —Main storage
  —External storage
  —Input-output facilities
- Software requirements
  —Compilers and source languages
  —Interfaces
  —File organization, data access
   methods
  —Index calculations
  —IF, GOTO
  —DO loop, END
  —Forward, backward iterations
  —Labels
  —Subroutines
  —Table access methods
- Handling of nonnumeric data
  —Character string operations
  —List and tree processing
  —Set statements
- Macroinstructions
  —Practitioner methods; e.g.,
   interpolation and extra-
   polation; financial indicators
  —Short-term forecasting
  —Trend forecasting
  —Econometric methods
  —Specification and verification
   testing
  —Random numbers and
   stochastic simulation

**Figure 19.15**

*Factors to Consider in the Evaluation of Modeling Software*

—Matrix algebra and linear
   programming
—Nonlinear solution and methods
—Sensitivity analysis
—Experimental designs
—Graph analysis
• Security system
—Physical security of data base,
   model and CSPS
—Authorization codes and pass-
words for data base, files, models
   privacy
• Documentation and support
—User and system manuals
—Debugging and error tracing
—Menu programs, prompting,
   and "help" explanations
—Computer-aided instruction
—Consulting support

## CONCLUSION

In recent years, computer-based models and spreadsheet software have been utilized for budgeting in an effort to speed up the process and allow budget analysts to investigate the effects of changes in budget assumptions.

Financial models comprise a functional branch of a general corporate planning model. They are essentially used to generate pro forma financial statements and financial ratios. These are the basic tools for budgeting and profit planning.

The financial model is a technique for risk analysis and "what-if" experiments. The model is also needed for day-to-day operational and tactical decisions for immediate planning problems.

# Chapter 20

# CAPITAL BUDGETING:
## *Selecting the Optimum Long-term Investment*

Capital budgeting relates to planning for the best selection and financing of long-term investment proposals. Capital budgeting decisions are not equally essential to all companies. The relative importance of this essential function varies with company size, the nature of the industry, and the growth rate of the firm. As a business expands, problems regarding long-range investment proposals become more important. Strategic capital budgeting decisions can turn the tide for a company.

The types of scarce resources that may be committed to a project include cash, time of key personnel, machine hours, and floor space in a factory. When estimating costs for a proposed project, the allocation of the company's scarce resources must be converted in terms of money.

The two broad categories of capital budgeting decisions are *screening decisions* and *preference decisions*. Screening decisions relate to whether a proposed project satisfies some present acceptance standard. For instance, your company may have a policy of accepting cost reduction projects only if they provide a return of, say, 15 percent.

Preference decisions apply to selecting from *competing* courses of action. For example, your company may be looking at four different manufacturing machines to replace an existing one. The selection of the best machine is referred to as a preference decision.

The basic types of investment decisions involve selections between proposed projects and replacement decisions. Selection requires judgments concerning future events of which you have no direct knowledge. You have to consider timing and risk. Your task is to minimize your chances of being wrong. To help you deal with uncertainty, you may use the risk-return tradeoff method. Discounted cash flow methods are more realistic than methods not taking into account the time value of money in appraising investments. Consideration of the time value of money becomes more essential in inflationary periods.

Planning for capital expenditures requires you to determine the optimal proposal, the number of dollars to be spent, and the amount of time required for completion. An appraisal is needed of current programs, evaluating new proposals, and coordinating interrelated proposals within the company. In planning a project, consideration should be given to time, cost, and quality, which all interreact. For control, a comparison should be made between budgeted cost and time compared to actual cost and time.

Capital budgeting decisions must conform to your cash position, financing strategy, and growth rate. Will the project provide a return exceeding the long-range expected return of the business? Projects must be tied into the company's long-range planning, taking into account corporate strengths and weaknesses. The objectives of the business and the degree to which they depend on economic variables (e.g., interest rate, inflation), production (e.g., technological changes), and market factors must be established. Also, the capital budget may have to be adjusted after considering financial, economic, and political concerns. But consideration should be given to "sunk" and "fixed" costs that are difficult to revise once the initial decision is made.

**Recommendation:** Use cost-benefit analysis. Is there excessive effort for the proposal? Can it be performed internally or must it be done externally (e.g., make or buy)? Is there a more efficient means and less costly way of accomplishing the end result? Further, problem areas must be identified. An example is when long-term borrowed funds are used to finance a project where sufficient cash inflows will not be able to meet debt at maturity.

**Suggestion:** Measure cash flows of a project, using different possible assumed variations (e.g., change in selling price of a new product). By modifying the assumptions and appraising the results you can see the sensitivity of cash flows to applicable variables. An advantage is the appraisal of risk in proposals based on varying assumptions. An increase in risk should result in a higher return rate.

*Taxes* have to be considered in making capital budgeting decisions because a project that looks good on a before-tax basis may not be acceptable on an after-tax basis. Taxes have an effect on the amount and timing of cash flows.

*"What-if" questions* are often the most crucial and difficult with regard to the capital expenditure budget and informed estimates are needed for the major assumptions. Spreadsheets can be used to analyze the cash flow implications of acquiring fixed assets.

Once an investment proposal is approved, there has to be an implementation of controls over expenditures and a reporting system regarding the project's status. Expenditures should be traced to the project and controls in place, assuring the expenditures are in conformity with the approved investment proposal. Continuous monitoring will show how well the project is doing, relative to the original plan.

## FACTORS TO CONSIDER IN DETERMINING CAPITAL EXPENDITURES

- Rate of return
- Budget ceiling
- Probability of success
- Competition
- Tax rate
- Dollar amounts
- Time value of money
- Risk
- Liquidity
- Long-term business strategy
- Forecasting errors

## TYPES OF CAPITAL BUDGETING DECISIONS TO BE MADE

- Cost reduction program
- Undertaking an advertising campaign

- Replacement of assets
- Obtaining new facilities or expanding existing ones
- Merger analysis
- New and existing product evaluation
- No profit investments (e.g., health and safety)

**Exhibit 20.1**
**PROJECT APPLICATION**

| DEPARTMENT NAME | | | | APPLICATION NO. | |
|---|---|---|---|---|---|
| DEPARTMENT CODE _____ | | | | OFFENSIVE ☐ | |
| FUNCTION CODE _____ | | | | DEFENSIVE ☐ | |
| PROJECT TITLE | | | | | |
| DESCRIPTION/OBJECTIVES | | | | | |

**EXPENDITURE AMOUNTS**

| FISCAL YEAR | 1st Qtr. | 2nd Qtr. | 3rd Qtr. | 4th Qtr. | TOTAL |
|---|---|---|---|---|---|
| 19 | | | | | |
| 19 | | | | | |
| 19 | | | | | |
| 19 | | | | | |
| 19 | | | | | |
| TOTAL | | | | | |

| DATE | SUBMITTED BY |
|---|---|
| COMMENTS | |

_____
For The Division

Exhibit 20.1 shows a typical project application form, while Exhibit 20.2 presents an advice of project change. In Exhibit 20.3, we see an appropriation request.

This chapter discusses the various capital budgeting methods, including accounting rate of return, payback, discounted payback, net present value, profitability index, and internal rate of return. Consideration is given to contingent proposals, capital rationing, and nondiscretionary projects. The incorporation of risk into the analysis is also considered.

**Exhibit 20.2**
**ADVICE ON PROJECT CHANGE**

| DEPARTMENT NAME | | DATE | |
|---|---|---|---|
| DEPARTMENT CODE | | APPROPRIATION REQUEST NO. | |
| PROJECT TITLE | | | |
| EXPENDITURE AMOUNTS | | | |
| | ORIGINAL AUTHORIZED | LATEST ESTIMATE | INCREASE (DECREASE) |
| CAPITAL | | | |
| EXPENSE | | | |
| TOTAL | | | |

AMOUNT SPENT TO DATE $ _____ AMOUNT COMMITTED TO DATE $ _____

**WHY IS THIS NEW AMOUNT BEING REQUESTED?**



_____        _____
PROJECT SPONSOR                DEPARTMENT/AREA SUPERVISOR

| PROJECT TO BE CONTINUED ☐ | |
| REVISED REQUEST REQUIRED ☐ | |
| SEE COMMENT ON REVERSE | FINAL APPROVER _____ |
| SIDE ☐ | DATE _____ |

Exhibit 20.3
APPROPRIATION REQUEST

| ORIG. DEPT. NAME | DEPT. CODE | APPROPRIATION NO. |
|---|---|---|
| BUDGET CAPITALIZED ☐ EXPENSED ☐ | PROJECT APPLIC. NO. | |
| ACCOUNTING CODE | PROJECT APPL. TOT. EXP. $ | APPROPRIATION TOTAL $ |
| DESCRIPTION | | |
| PURPOSE | | |
| CURRENT FACILITIES | | |
| PROPOSED FACILITIES | | |
| COST JUSTIFICATION (SAVINGS/BENEFITS) | | |

| PROPOSED EXPENDITURES | | APPROVALS | | DATE |
|---|---|---|---|---|
| Equipment Cost | _____ | Originator | _____ | ___ |
| Material Cost | _____ | | _____ | ___ |
| Installation Costs: | _____ | | _____ | ___ |
| External Services | _____ | Dept/Area Suprv. | _____ | ___ |
| Internal Services | _____ | V. President | _____ | ___ |
| Miscellaneous Costs | _____ | Controller | _____ | ___ |
| Freight | _____ | Division Head | _____ | ___ |
| Taxes | _____ | C.E.O. | _____ | ___ |
| Total | _____ | Bd. of Dir. | _____ | ___ |

Net present value, internal rate of return, and profitability index are equally effective in selecting economically sound, independent investment proposals. But the payback method is inadequate since it does not consider the time value of money. For mutually exclusive projects, net present value, internal rate of return, and profitability index methods are not always able to rank projects in the same order. It is possible to come up with different rankings under each method. Risk should be taken into account in the capital budgeting process, using probabilities, simulation, and decision trees.

## ACCOUNTING (SIMPLE) RATE OF RETURN

*Accounting rate of return (ARR)* measures profitability from the conventional accounting standpoint by comparing the required investment (sometimes average investment) to future annual earnings.

**Rule of Thumb:** Select the proposal with the highest ARR.

### Example 1

| | |
|---|---|
| Initial investment | $8,000 |
| Life | 15 years |
| Cash inflows per year | $1,300 |

$$\text{Depreciation} = \frac{\text{Cost} - \text{Salvage value}}{\text{Life}} = \frac{\$8,000 - 0}{15} = \$533$$

$$\text{ARR} = \frac{\text{Cash inflows per year} - \text{Depreciation}}{\text{Initial investment}}$$

$$\frac{\$1,300 - \$533}{\$8,000} = \frac{\$767}{\$8,000} = 9.6\%$$

*If you use average investment, ARR is*

$$\text{ARR} = \frac{\$767}{\$8,000/2} = \frac{\$767}{\$4,000} = 19.2\%$$

**Note:** When average investment is used, rather than the initial investment, accounting rate of return is doubled.

### ADVANTAGES OF ARR

- Easy to comprehend and calculate
- Considers profitability
- Numbers relate to financial statement presentation
- Considers full useful life

### DISADVANTAGES OF ARR

- Ignores time value of money
- Uses income data rather than cash flow data

**Note:** In an automated environment, the cost of the investment would include engineering, software development, and implementation.

## PAYBACK PERIOD

Payback is the number of years it takes to recover your initial investment. Payback assists in evaluating a project's risk and liquidity, faster rate of return, and earlier recoupment of funds. A benefit of payback is that it permits companies that have a cash problem to evaluate the turnover of scarce resources in order to recover, earlier, those funds invested. In addition, there is likely to be less possibility of loss from changes in economic conditions, obsolescence, and other unavoidable risks when the commitment is short term.

Supporters of the payback period point to its use where preliminary screening is more essential than precise figures, in situations where a poor credit position is a major factor, and when investment funds are exceptionally scarce. Some believe that payback should be used in unstable, uncertain industries subject to rapid technological change because the future is so unpredictable that there is no point in guessing what cash flows will be more than two years from now.

As reported in the July/August 1988 issue of *Financial Executive*, a majority of executives want payback in three years or less.

A company may establish a limit on the payback period beyond which an investment will not be made. Another business may use payback to choose one of several investments, selecting the one with the shortest payback period.

### ADVANTAGES OF PAYBACK

- Easy to use and understand
- Effectively handles investment risk
- Good approach when a weak cash-and-credit position influences the selection of a proposal
- Can be used as a supplement to other more sophisticated techniques, since it does indicate risk

## DISADVANTAGES OF PAYBACK

- Ignores the time value of money
- Does not consider cash flows received after the payback period
- Does not measure profitability
- Does not indicate how long the maximum payback period should be
- Penalizes projects that result in small cash flows in their early years and heavy cash flows in their later years

**Warning:** Do not select a proposal simply because the payback method indicates acceptance. You still have to use the discounting methods such as present value and internal rate of return.

### Example 2

You are considering a new product. It will initially cost $250,000. Expected cash inflows are $80,000 for the next five years. You want your money back in four years.

$$\text{Payback period} = \frac{\text{Initial investment}}{\text{Annual cash inflow}} = \frac{\$250,000}{\$80,000} = 3.125$$

Because the payback period (3.125) is less than the cutoff payback period (4), you should accept the proposal.

### Example 3

You invest $40,000 and receive the following cash inflows:

Year 1    $15,000
Year 2     20,000
Year 3     28,000

$$\text{Payback period} = \frac{\$40,000}{\underset{\text{Year 1}}{} \quad \underset{\text{Year 2}}{} \quad \underset{\text{Year 3}}{}} = 2.18 \text{ years}$$

$$\underbrace{\$15,000 + \$20,000}_{\$35,000} + \frac{\$5,000}{\$28,000}$$

$$2 \text{ years} \quad + \quad .18$$

If there are unequal cash inflows each year, to determine the payback period just add up the annual cash inflows to come up with the amount of the cash outlay. The answer is how long it takes to recover your investment.

**Note:** As reported in the November 1987 issue of *Management Accounting*, published by the National Association of Accountants, it was found that the majority of manufacturers use an unadjusted payback period of between two and four years when appraising advanced manufacturing equipment.

## PAYBACK RECIPROCAL

Payback reciprocal is the reciprocal of the payback time. This often gives a quick, accurate estimate of the *internal rate of return (IRR)* on an investment when the project life is more than twice the payback period and the cash inflows are uniform every period.

### Example 4

ABC Company is contemplating three projects, each of which would require an initial investment of $10,000, and each of which is expected to generate a cash inflow of $2,000 per year. The payback period is five years ($10,000/$2,000) and the payback reciprocal is 1/5, or 20 percent. The table of the present value of an annuity of $1 shows that the factor of 5.00 applies to the following useful lives and internal rates of return:

| Useful Life | IRR |
|-------------|-----|
| 10 years | 15% |
| 15 | 18 |
| 20 | 19 |

It can be observed that the payback reciprocal is 20 percent as compared with the IRR of 18 percent when the life is 15 years, and 20 percent as compared with the IRR of 19 percent when the life is 20 years. This shows that the payback reciprocal gives a reasonable approximation of the IRR if the useful life of the project is at least twice the payback period.

## DISCOUNTED PAYBACK PERIOD

Before looking at discounted cash flow methods, it should be pointed out that there is less reliability with discounted cash flow analysis where there is future uncertainty, the environment is changing, and cash flows themselves are hard to predict.

You can take into account the time value of money by using the discounted payback method. The payback period will be longer using the discounted method because money is worth less over time.

**How To Do It:** *Discounted payback* is computed by adding the present value of each year's cash inflows until they equal the investment.

### Example 5

Assume the same facts as in Example 3 and a cost of capital of 10 percent.

$$\text{Discounted payback} = \frac{\text{Initial cash outlay}}{\text{Discounted annual cash inflows}}$$

$$\$40,000$$

| Year 1 | | Year 2 | | Year 3 |
|---|---|---|---|---|
| $15,000 | + | $20,000 | + | $28,000 |
| × .9091 | | × .8264 | | × .7513 |
| $13,637 | + | $16,528 | + | $21,036 |

$$\$30,165 + \underline{\$\ 9,835}$$
$$\$21,036$$

$$2 \text{ years} + \quad .47 \quad = 2.47 \text{ years}$$

## NET PRESENT VALUE

The present value method compares the present value of future cash flows expected from an investment project to the initial cash outlay for the investment. Net cash flows are the difference between forecasted cash inflow received because of the investment with the expected cash outflow of the investment. You should use as a discount rate the minimum rate of return earned by the company on its money. As reported in the November 1987 issue of *Management Accounting* (p. 29), 36 percent of manufacturers used discount rates of between 13 percent and 17 percent and more than 30 percent used discount rates of over 19 percent.

A company should use as the discount rate its cost of capital.

**Rule of Thumb:** Considering inflation and the cost of debt, the anticipated return should be about 10-13 percent.

**Note:** The net present value method discounts all cash flows at the cost of capital, thus implicitly assuming that these cash flows can be reinvested at this rate.

An advantage of net present value is that it considers the time value of money. A disadvantage is the subjectivity in determining expected annual cash inflows and expected period of benefit.

**Recommendation:** If a proposal is supposed to provide a return, invest in it only if it provides a positive net present value. If two proposals are mutually exclusive (acceptance of one precludes the acceptance of another), accept the proposal with the highest present value.

**Note:** In an advanced automated environment, the terminal value requires managers to forecast technological, economic, operational, strategic, and market developments over the investment's life so that a reasonable estimate of potential value may be made.

**Caution:** Using the return rate earned by the company as the discount rate may be misleading in certain cases. It may be a good idea to look at the return rate investors earn on similar projects. If the minimum rates selected are based on the company's return on average projects, an internal company decision will occur that helps to increase the corporate return. Yet if the company is earning a very high rate of return, you will take a lot of good projects and also leave some good ones. What if the project left would really enhance value?

If the corporate return rate is below what investors can earn elsewhere, you delude yourself in believing it's an attractive investment. The project may involve below-normal profitability, lower per share value, and result in lower creditor and investor ratings of the firm.

The net present value method typically provides more reliable signals than other methods. By employing net present value and using best estimates of reinvestment rates, you can select the most advantageous project.

## Example 6

You are considering replacing Executive 1 with Executive 2. Executive 2 requires a payment upon contract signing of $200,000. He will receive an annual salary of $330,000. Executive 1's current annual salary is $140,000. Executive 2 is superior in talent, you expect there will be an increase in annual cash flows from operations (ignoring salary) of $350,000 for each of the next ten years. The cost of capital is 12 percent.

As indicated in the following calculations, since there is a positive net present value, Executive 1 should be replaced with Executive 2.

| Year | Explanation | Amount | × | Factor | = | Present Value |
|------|-------------|--------|---|--------|---|---------------|
| 0 | Contract signing bonus | $−200,000 | × | 1 | | $−200,000 |
| 1-10 | Increased salary ($300,000 − $140,000) | −160,000 | × | 5.6502[a] | | −904,032 |
| 1-10 | Increase in annual cash flow from operations | +350,000 | × | 5.6502[a] | | 1,977,570 |
| | Net present value | | | | | $  873,538 |

[a]Present value of an ordinary annuity factor for 10 years and an interest rate of 12 percent.

## Example 7

You own a business for which you have received a $1,000,000 offer. If you do not sell, you will remain in business for eight years and will invest another $50,000 in your firm. If you stay, you will sell your business in the eighth year for $60,000.

You expect yearly sales to increase by 50 percent from its present level of $500,000. Direct material is proportional to sales. Direct labor is proportional to sales, but will increase by 30 percent for all labor. Variable overhead varies with sales and annual fixed overhead will total $70,000, including depreciation. Straight-line depreciation will increase from $7,000 to $10,000. At the end of eight years, all fixed assets will be fully depreciated. Selling and administrative expenses are assumed to remain constant. The cost of capital is 14 percent.

Your current year's income statement is

| Sales | | $500,000 |
|---|---|---|
| Less: Cost of Sales | | |
| Direct material | $100,000 | |
| Direct labor | 120,000 | |
| Variable overhead | 50,000 | |
| Fixed overhead | 65,000 | 335,000 |
| Gross margin | | $165,000 |
| Less: Selling and administrative expenses[a] | | 40,000 |
| Net income | | $125,000 |

[a]Includes your salary of $20,000.

Your forecasted income statement for each of the next eight years follows.

| Sales $500,000 × 1.5 | | $750,000 |
|---|---|---|
| Less: Cost of sales | | |
| Direct material $100,000 × 1.5 | $150,000 | |
| Direct labor $120,000 × 1.5 × 1.3 | 234,000 | |
| Variable overhead $50,000 × 1.5 | 75,000 | |
| Fixed overhead | 70,000 | 529,000 |
| Gross margin | | $221,000 |
| Less: Selling and administrative expenses | | $ 40,000 |
| Net income | | $181,000 |

Your annual cash flow from operations is

| Net income | $181,000 |
|---|---|
| Add: Depreciation | 10,000 |
| Salary | 20,000 |
| Annual cash flow from operations | $211,000 |

A comparison of your alternatives follows:

| Sell business | +$1,000,000 |
|---|---|

Stay in business

| Year | Explanation | Amount | × | Factor | = | Present Value |
|---|---|---|---|---|---|---|
| 0 | Investment in assets | $− 50,000 | × | 1 | | $− 50,000 |
| 1-8 | Annual cash inflow | +211,000 | × | 4.6389 | | +978,808 |
| 8 | Sales price of business | + 60,000 | × | 0.3506 | | + 21,036 |
| | Net present value | | | | | $+949,844 |

Since the net present value is higher to sell the business ($1,000,000) than staying in business ($949,844), you should sell now.

## Example 8

You are considering replacing an old machine with a new one. The old machine has a book value of $800,000 and a remaining life of ten years. The expected salvage value of the old machine is $50,000, but if you sold it now, you would obtain $700,000. The new machine costs $2,000,000 and has a salvage value of $250,000. The new machine will result in annual savings of $400,000. The tax rate is 50 percent, and the cost of capital is 14 percent. Use straight-line depreciation. You have to determine whether to replace the machine.

The net increase in annual cash flow is

|  | Net Income | Cash Flow |
|---|---|---|
| Annual savings | $400,000 | $400,000 |
| Less: Incremental depreciation |  |  |
| New machine $\dfrac{\$2,000,000-\$250,000}{10} = \$175,000$ |  |  |
| Old machine $\dfrac{\$800,000-\$50,000}{10} = \$75,000$ |  |  |
| Incremental depreciation | 100,000 |  |
| Income before tax | $300,000 |  |
| Tax, 50% | 150,000 | 150,000 |
| Income after tax | $150,000 |  |
| Net cash inflow |  | $250,000 |

The net present value follows:

| Year | Explanation | Amount | × | Factor | Present Value |
|---|---|---|---|---|---|
| 0 | Cost of new machine | $−2,000,000 | × | 1.000 | $−2,000,000 |
| 0 | Sale of old machine | 700,000 | × | 1.000 | 700,000 |
| 1 | Investment tax credit | 200,000 | × | .877 | 175,400 |
| 1 | Tax benefit from loss on sale of old machine | 50,000 | × | .877 | 43,850 |
| 1-10 | Yearly increase in cash flows | 250,000 | × | 5.216 | 1,304,000 |
| 10 | Incremental salvage value | 200,000 | × | .270 | 54,000 |
|  |  |  |  |  | $ 102,100 |

The replacement of the old machine with a new machine should be made because of the resulting positive net present value.

Deciding whether to lease or purchase involves comparing the leasing and purchasing alternatives.

### Example 9

You have decided to acquire an asset costing $100,000, with a life of five years and no salvage value. The asset can be purchased with a loan or it can be leased. If leased, the lessor wants a 12 percent return. Lease payments are made in advance at the end of the year prior to each of the 10 years. The tax rate is 50 percent and the cost of capital is 8 percent.

$$\text{Annual lease payment} = \frac{\$100,000}{1+3.3073} = \frac{\$100,000}{4.3073}$$

$$= \$23,216 \text{ (rounded)}$$

| Year | Lease Payment | Tax Savings | After-Tax Cash Outflow | Factor | Present Value |
|------|---------------|-------------|------------------------|--------|---------------|
| 0    | $23,216       |             | $23,216                | 1.0000 | $23,216       |
| 1-4  | 23,216        | $11,608[a]  | 11,608                 | 3.3121 | 38,447        |
| 5    |               | 11,608      | (11,608)               | .6806  | (7,900)       |
|      |               |             |                        |        | $53,763       |

[a]23,216 · 50% = $11,608.

If you buy the asset, you will take out a 10 percent loan. Straight-line depreciation is used with no salvage value.

$$\text{Depreciation} = \frac{\$100,000}{5} = \$20,000$$

$$\text{Annual loan payment} = \frac{\$100,000}{3.7906} = \$26,381$$

The loan amortization schedule follows:

| Year | Loan Payment | Beginning-of-Year Principal | Interest[a] | Principal[b] | End-of-Year Principal |
|------|--------------|------------------------------|-------------|---------------|------------------------|
| 1 | $26,381 | $100,000 | $10,000 | $16,381 | $83,619 |
| 2 | 26,381 | 83,619 | 8,362 | 18,019 | 65,600 |
| 3 | 26,381 | 65,600 | 6,560 | 19,821 | 45,779 |
| 4 | 26,381 | 45,779 | 4,578 | 21,803 | 23,976 |
| 5 | 26,381 | 23,976[c] | 2,398 | 23,983[c] | |

[a]10% × Beginning-of-year principal.
[b]Loan payment − interest.
[c]Slight difference due to rounding.

The computation of the present value of borrowing follows

| | (1) | (2) | (3) | (4) | (5) | (6) | (7) | (8) |
|---|-----|-----|-----|-----|-----|-----|-----|-----|
| | | | | | | | PV | PV of |
| | Loan | | Depre- | Total | Tax | Cash | Factor | Cash |
| Year | Payment | Interest | ciation | Deduction | Savings | Outflow | at 8% | Outflow |
| 1 | $26,381 | $10,000 | $20,000 | $30,000 | $15,000 | $11,381 | .9259 | $10,538 |
| 2 | 26,381 | 8,362 | 20,000 | 28,362 | 14,181 | 12,200 | .8573 | 10,459 |
| 3 | 26,381 | 6,560 | 20,000 | 26,560 | 13,280 | 13,101 | .7938 | 10,400 |
| 4 | 26,381 | 4,578 | 20,000 | 24,578 | 12,289 | 14,092 | .7350 | 10,358 |
| 5 | 26,381 | 2,398 | 20,000 | 22,398 | 11,199 | 15,182 | .6806 | 10,333 |
| | | | | | | | | $52,088 |

(4) = (2) + (3)
(5) = (4) × 50%
(6) = (1) − (5)
(8) = (6) × (7)

The present value of borrowing ($52,088) is less than the present value of leasing ($53,763). Thus, the asset should be bought.

## PROFITABILITY INDEX

The *profitability (ranking) index*, also called excess present value index, cost-benefit ratio, is a net instead of an aggregate index and is employed to differentiate the initial cash investment from later cash inflows. If you have budget constraints, proposals of different dollar magnitude can be ranked on a comparative basis. Use the index as a means of ranking projects in descending order of attractiveness.

$$\text{Profitability index} = \frac{\text{Present value of cash inflows}}{\text{Present value of cash outflows}}$$

**Rule of Thumb:** Accept a proposal with a profitability index equal to or greater than 1.

**Caution:** A higher profitability index does not always coincide with the project with the highest net present value.

**Key Point:** The internal rate of return and the net present value approaches may give conflicting signals, when competing projects have unequal times. The profitability index gives the correct decision, however, and is superior under these circumstances.

Capital rationing takes place when a business is not able to invest in projects having a net present value greater than or equal to zero. Typically, the firm establishes an upper limit to its capital budget based on budgetary constraints.

**Note:** With capital rationing, the project with the highest ranking index, rather than net present value, should be selected for investment.

Figure 20.1 shows the capital rationing decision process.

### Example 10

You have the following information regarding two proposals:

|                                | Proposal A | Proposal B |
| ------------------------------ | ---------- | ---------- |
| Initial investment             | $100,000   | $10,000    |
| Present value of cash inflows  | 500,000    | 90,000     |

The net present value of proposal A is $400,000 and that of proposal B is $80,000. Based on net present value, proposal A is better. However, this is very misleading when a budget constraint exists. In this case, proposal B's profitability index of 9 far surpasses proposal A's index of 5. Thus, profitability index should be used in evaluating proposals when budget constraints exist. The net result is that proposal B should be selected over proposal A.

**Figure 20.1**
FLOWCHART OF VARIABLES IN A CORPORATE MODEL

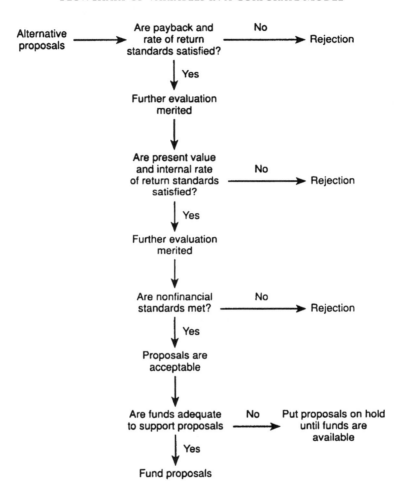

## Example 11

| Projects | Investment | Present Value | Profitability Index | Ranking |
|----------|-----------|---------------|---------------------|---------|
| A | $70,000 | $112,000 | 1.6 | 1 |
| B | $100,000 | 145,000 | 1.45 | 2 |
| C | 110,000 | 126,500 | 1.15 | 5 |
| D | 60,000 | 79,000 | 1.32 | 3 |
| E | 40,000 | 38,000 | .95 | 6 |
| F | 80,000 | 95,000 | 1.19 | 4 |

The budget constraint is $250,000. You should select projects A, B, and D as indicated by the following calculations.

| Project | Investment | Present Value |
|---------|-----------|---------------|
| A | $70,000 | $112,000 |
| B | 100,000 | 145,000 |
| D | 60,000 | 79,000 |
|   | $230,000 | $336,000 |

*where*

Net present value = $336,000 − $230,000 = $106,000

Unfortunately, the profitability index method has some limitations. One of the more serious is that it breaks down whenever more than one resource is rationed.

A more general approach to solving capital rationing problems is the use of *mathematical* (or zero-one) programming. Here the objective is to select the mix of projects that maximizes the net present value subject to a budget constraint.

## Example 12

Using the data given in Example 11, we can set up the problem as a mathematical programming one. First, we label project A as $X_1$, B as $X_2$, and so on; the problem can be stated as follows:

$$\text{Maximize NPV} = \$42,000X_1 + \$45,000X_2 + \$16,500X_3 + \$19,000X_4 - \$2,000X_5 + \$15,000X_6$$

subject to

$$\$70{,}000X_1 + \$100{,}000X_2 + \$110{,}000X_3 + \$60{,}000X_4 + \$40{,}000X_5$$
$$+ \$80{,}000X_6 \leqq \$250{,}000$$

$$X_i = 0, 1, (i = 1, 2, \ldots 6)$$

Using the mathematical program solution routine, the solution to this problem is

$$X_1 = 1, X_2 = 1, X_4 = 1$$

and the net present value is \$106,000. Thus, projects A, B, and D should be accepted.

### CONTINGENT PROPOSALS

A contingent proposal is one that requires acceptance of another related one. Hence, the proposals must be looked at together. You compute a profitability index for the group.

### Example 13

| Proposal | Present Value of Cash Outflow | Present Value of Cash Inflow |
|---|---|---|
| A | \$160,000 | \$210,000 |
| B | 60,000 | 40,000 |
| Total | \$220,000 | \$250,000 |

$$\text{Profitability Index} = \frac{\$250{,}000}{\$220{,}000} = 1.14$$

## INTERNAL RATE OF RETURN (TIME-ADJUSTED RATE OF RETURN)

The internal rate of return (IRR) is the return earned on a given proposal. It is the discount rate equating the net present value of cash inflows to the net present value of cash outflows to zero. The internal rate of return assumes cash inflows are reinvested at the internal rate.

This method involves trial-and-error computations. However, the use of a computer or programmable calculator simplifies the internal rate-of-return process.

The internal rate of return can be compared with the required rate of return (cutoff or hurdle rate).

**Rule of Thumb:** If the internal rate of return equals or exceeds the required rate, the project is accepted. The required rate of return is typically a company's cost of capital, sometimes adjusted for risk.

## ADVANTAGES OF IRR

- Considers the time value of money
- More realistic and accurate than the accounting rate of return method

## DISADVANTAGES OF IRR

- Difficult and time consuming to compute, particularly when there are uneven cash flows
- Does not consider the varying size of investment in competing projects and their respective dollar profitabilities
- When there are multiple reversals in the cash flow stream, the project could yield more than one IRR.

To solve for internal rate of return where unequal cash inflows exist, you can use the trial-and-error method while working through the present value tables.

## GUIDELINES

1. Compute net present value at the cost of capital, denoted here as $r_1$.
2. See if net present value is positive or negative.
3. If net present value is positive, use a higher rate ($r_2$) than $r_1$. If net present value is negative, use a lower rate ($r_2$) than $r_1$. The exact internal rate of return at which net present value equals zero is somewhere between the two rates.
4. Compute net present value using $r_2$.
5. Perform interpolation for exact rate.

## Example 14

A project costing $100,000 is expected to produce the following cash inflows:

| Year | |
|---|---|
| 1 | $50,000 |
| 2 | 30,000 |
| 3 | 20,000 |
| 4 | 40,000 |

Using trial and error, you can calculate the internal rate as follows:

| Year | 10% | Present Value | 16% | Present Value | 18% | Present Value |
|---|---|---|---|---|---|---|
| 1 | .909 | $45,450 | .862 | $43,100 | .847 | $ 42,350 |
| 2 | .826 | 24,780 | .743 | 22,290 | .718 | 21,540 |
| 3 | .751 | 15,020 | .641 | 12,820 | .609 | 12,180 |
| 4 | .683 | 27,320 | .552 | 22,080 | .516 | 20,640 |
| | | $+112,570 | | $+100,290 | | $+ 96,710 |
| Investment | | −100,000 | | −100,000 | | −100,000 |
| Net present value | | $−12,570 | | $ +290 | | $ −3,290 |

The internal rate of return on the project is a little more than 16 percent, because at that rate the net present value of the investment is approximately zero.

If the return on the investment is expected to be in one lump sum after a period of two years, you can use the Present Value of $1 table to find the internal rate.

## Example 15

You are considering two mutually exclusive investment proposals. The cost of capital is 10 percent. Expected cash flows are as follows:

| Project | Investment | Year 1 | Year 6 |
|---|---|---|---|
| A | $10,000 | $12,000 | |
| B | 10,000 | | $20,000 |

Internal rates of return are

$$\text{Project A: } = \frac{\$10,000}{\$12,000} = .8333$$

Looking across one year on the table, .8333 corresponds to an internal rate of 20 percent.

$$\text{Project B: } = \frac{\$10,000}{\$20,000} = .5000$$

Looking across six years on the table, .5000 corresponds to an internal rate of 12 percent. Project A should be selected because it has a higher internal rate of return than project B.

If the cash inflows each year are equal, the internal rate of return is computed first by determining a factor (which happens to be the same as the payback period) and then looking up the rate of return on the Present Value of an Annuity of $1 table.

### Example 16

You invest $100,000 in a proposal that will produce annual cash inflows of $15,000 a year for the next 20 years.

$$\text{Factor } = \frac{\$100,000}{\$15,000} = 6.6667$$

Refer to the Present Value of an Annuity of $1 table. Looking across 20 years, we find that the factor closest to 6.6667 is 6.6231 in the 14 percent column. Therefore the internal rate is about 14 percent.

### Example 17

| | |
|---|---|
| Initial investment | $12,950 |
| Estimated life | 10 years |
| Annual cash inflows | $3,000 |
| Cost of capital | 12% |

The internal rate of return calculation follows, including interpolation to get the exact rate.

$$\text{PV of annuity factor} = \frac{\$12,950}{\$3,000} = 4.317$$

The value 4.317 is somewhere between 18 percent and 20 percent in the 10-year line of the Present Value of annuity table. Using interpolation you get

|  | Present Value of Annuity Factor | |
|---|---|---|
| 18% | 4.494 | 4.494 |
| IRR | | 4.317 |
| 20% | 4.192 | |
| Difference | .302 | .177 |

Therefore,

$$\text{IRR} = 18\% + \frac{.177}{.302}(20\% - 18\%)$$

$$= 18\% + .586(2\%) = 18\% - 1.17\% = 19.17\%$$

Because the internal rate of return (19.17 percent) exceeds the cost of capital (12 percent), the project should be accepted.

## NONDISCRETIONARY PROJECTS

Some investments are made because of necessity rather than profitability (e.g., pollution control equipment, safety equipment). Here you will have solely a negative cash flow. Hence, your discretionary projects must earn a return rate in excess of the cost of capital to make up for the losses on nondiscretionary projects.

### Example 18

A company's cost of capital is 14 percent and $30 million of capital projects, 25 percent of which are nondiscretionary projects. It thus has to earn $4.2 million per year (14% × $30 million). The $22.5 million of discretionary projects ($30 million − 25%) must earn 18.7 percent ($4.2 million/$22.5 million) rather than 14 percent to achieve the overall corporate earnings goal of $4.2 million.

## COMPARISON OF METHODS

In general, the discounting cash flow methods (net present value, internal rate of return, and profitability index) come to the same conclusions for competing proposals. But these methods can give different rankings to mutually exclusive proposals in certain cases. Any one of the following conditions can cause contradictory rankings:

- Project lives of different duration.
- A higher cost for one project relative to another.
- The trend in cash flow of one project that is the reverse of that of another.

One of the following characteristics of the company may also produce conflicting rankings:

- Future investment opportunities are expected to be different than at present and the investor knows whether they will be better or worse.
- There is capital rationing, a maximum level of funding for capital investments.

The major cause for different rankings of alternative projects under present value and internal rate of return methods relates to the varying assumptions regarding the reinvestment rate employed for discounting cash flows. The net present value method assumes cash flows are reinvested at the cost of capital rate. The internal rate of return method assumes cash flows are reinvested at the internal rate.

**Key Point:** The net present value method typically provides a correct ranking because the cost of capital is a more realistic reinvestment rate.

**Recommendation:** Which method is best for a business really depends on which reinvestment rate is nearest the rate the business can earn on future cash flows from a project.

**Note:** The board of directors usually reviews the company's required rate of return each year and may increase or decrease it, depending on the company's current rate of return and cost of capital.

The minimum rate of return required for a proposal may be waived in a situation where the proposal has significant future benefit (research and development), applies to a necessity program (safety requirement), and has qualitative benefit (product quality).

### Example 19

Assume the following:

| Project | Cash Flows | | | | | |
|---------|------|------|---|---|---|---|
|         | 0 | 1 | 2 | 3 | 4 | 5 |
| A | $(100) | $120 | | | | |
| B | (100) | | | | | $201.14 |

Computing Internal Rate of Return and Net Present Value at 10 percent gives the different rankings as follows:

|   | Internal Rate of Return | Net Present Value |
|---|-------------------------|-------------------|
| A | 20%[a] | 9.09 |
| B | 15% | 24.90 |

[a]From present value of $1 table, the IRR for a factor of .8333 $\left(\dfrac{\$100}{\$120}\right)$ is 20 percent.

The general rule is to go by Net Present Value ranking. Thus, project B would be chosen over project A.

## CAPITAL BUDGETING PROCESS

*Questions that should be asked in the capital budgeting process are:*

- How is risk incorporated into the analysis?
- Is risk versus return considered in choosing projects?
- Prior to making a final decision, are all the results of the capital budgeting techniques considered and integrated?
- In looking at a proposal, are both dollars and time considered?
- Is the proposal consistent with long-term goals?
- Does each project have a cost-benefit analysis?

- Do you know which are your most profitable proposals and products? How much business is in each?
- Are there projects of an unusual nature?
- Do you periodically track the performance of current programs in terms of original expectations?
- In the capital budgeting process, are qualitative factors also considered, such as marketing, production, and economic and political variables?
- Has the proposal been considered incorporating the company's financial health?
- What is the quality of the project?
- Given the current environment, are your capital investments adequate?
- Are you risk prone or risk averse?
- Is the discounted payback method being used?
- How are probable cash flows computed?
- How do you come up with the expected life?

To look at the entire picture of the capital budgeting process, a comprehensive example is provided.

### Example 20

You are deciding whether to buy a business. The initial cash outlay is $35,000. You will receive annual net cash inflows (excluding depreciation) of $5,000 per year for 10 years. The cost of capital is 10 percent. The tax rate is 50 percent. Should you buy this business?

The annual cash inflow follows:

**Years 1-10**

|                            | Net Income | Cash Flow |
|----------------------------|:----------:|:---------:|
| Annual cash savings        | $5,000     | $+5,000   |
| Depreciation ($35,000/10)  | 3,500      |           |
| Income before tax          | $1,500     |           |
| Tax, 50%                   | 750        | − 750     |
| Net income                 | $ 750      |           |
| Net cash flow              |            | $+4,250   |

Average rate of return on investment:

$$\frac{\text{Net income}}{\text{Average investment}} = \frac{\$750}{\$35,000/2} = \frac{\$750}{\$17,500} = 4\%$$

Payback period:

$$\frac{\text{Initial investment}}{\text{Annual net cash inflow}} = \frac{\$35,000}{\$4,250} = 8.2 \text{ years}$$

Net present value:

| Year | Explanation | Amount | | Factor | Present Value |
|------|-------------|--------|---|--------|---------------|
| 0 | Initial investment | $-35,000 | × | 1 | $-35,000 |
| 1-10 | Annual net cash inflow | + 4,250 | × | 6.1446 | 26,095 |
| | Net present value | | | | $- 8,905 |

Profitability index:

$$\frac{\text{Present value of cash inflow}}{\text{Present value of cash outflow}} = \frac{\$26,095}{\$35,000} = .74$$

Internal rate of return:

$$\text{Factor} = \frac{\text{Initial outlay}}{\text{Annual cash inflow}} = \frac{\$35,000}{\$4,250} = 8.2$$

Referring to the Present Value of Annuity table, look for the intersection of 10 years and a factor of 8.2. Looking up the column, we find 4 percent, which is the internal rate.

**Conclusion**: The business should not be bought for the following reasons:

1. An average rate of return of 4 percent is low.
2. The payback period is long.
3. The net present value is negative.
4. The internal rate of return at 4 percent is less than the cost of capital at 10 percent.

## CAPITAL BUDGETING AND INFLATION

The accuracy of capital budgeting decisions depends on the accuracy of the data regarding cash inflows and outflows. For example, failure to incorporate price-level changes due to inflation in capital budgeting situations can result in errors in the prediction of cash flows and thus in incorrect decisions.

Typically, the nonfinancial manager has two options in dealing with a capital budgeting situation with inflation.

(1) Restate the cash flows in nominal terms and discount them at a nominal *cost of capital (minimum required rate of return)*.

(2) Restate both the cash flows and cost of capital in *constant* terms and discount the constant cash flows at a constant cost of capital.

The two methods are basically equivalent.

### Example 21

A company has the following projected cash flows estimated in real terms:

| | Real Cash Flows (000s) | | | |
|---|---|---|---|---|
| Period | 0 | 1 | 2 | 3 |
| | −100 | 35 | 50 | 30 |

The nominal cost of capital is 15 percent. Assume that inflation is projected at 10 percent a year. Then the first cash flow for year 1, which is $35,000 in current dollars, will be $35,000 \times 1.10 = \$38,500$ in year 1 dollars. Similarly the cash flow for year 2 will be $50,000 \times (1.10)^2 = \$60,500$ in year 2 dollars, and so on. By discounting these nominal cash flows at the 15 percent nominal cost of capital, you come up with the following net present value:

| Period | Cash Flows | Present Value Factor | Present Values |
|---|---|---|---|
| 0 | −100 | 1.000 | −100 |
| 1 | 38.5 | .870 | 33.50 |
| 2 | 60.5 | .756 | 45.74 |
| 3 | 39.9 | .658 | 26.25 |
| | | Net present value = | 5.49 or $5,490 |

Instead of converting the cash flow forecasts into nominal terms, we could convert the cost of capital into real terms by using the following formula:

$$\text{Real cost of capital} = \frac{1 + \text{nominal cost of capital}}{1 + \text{inflation rate}} - 1$$

In the example, this gives

$$\text{Real cost of capital} = \frac{(1 + .15)}{(1 + .10)}$$

$$= \frac{1.15}{1.10} = 0.045 \text{ of } 4.5 \text{ percent}$$

We will obtain the same answer except for rounding errors ($5,490 versus $5,580).

| Period | Cash Flows | Present Value Factor $1(1 + .045)^n$ | Present Values |
|--------|-----------|----------------------------------|----------------|
| 0 | −100 | 1.000 | −100 |
| 1 | 35 | $\frac{1}{(1+.045)^2}$ = .957 | 33.50 |
| 2 | 50 | $\frac{1}{(1+.045)}$ = .916 | 45.80 |
| 3 | 30 | $\frac{1}{(1+.045)^3}$ = .876 | 26.28 |

Net present value = 5.58 or $5,580

## POSTAUDIT PROJECT REVIEW

The postaudit (postcompletion) project review is a second aspect of reviewing the performance of the project. A comparison is made of the actual cash flow from operations of the project with the estimated cash flow used to justify the project.

There are reasons why the postaudit project review is helpful. First, managers who propose projects will be more careful before recommending a project. Second, it will identify managers who are repeatedly optimistic or pessimistic regarding cash flow estimates. How reliable are the proposals submitted and approved? (Perhaps additional investments can be made that result in even greater returns.) Top management will be better able to appraise the bias that may be expected when a certain manager proposes a project.

The postaudit review also gives an opportunity to:

- Reinforce successful projects
- Strengthen or salvage problem projects
- Stop unsuccessful projects before excessive losses occur
- Enhance the overall quality of future investment proposals

In conducting a postaudit, the same technique should be employed that was used in the initial approval process, to maintain consistency in evaluation. For example, if a project was approved using present value analysis, the identical procedures should be implemented in the post-audit review.

According to the management-by-exception principle, the managers responsible for the original estimates should be asked to furnish a complete explanation of any significant differences between estimates and actual results.

**Recommendation:** For control reasons, project performance appraisal should not be conducted by the group that proposed the project. Internal auditors should be given this responsibility. A review report should be issued. Typically, only projects above a specified dollar amount require post-audit, periodic evaluation, or both.

## CAPITAL BUDGETING AND NONPROFIT ORGANIZATIONS

With regard to nonprofit institutions, the only real problem in using capital budgeting is the selection of an appropriate discount rate. Some nonprofit entities employ the interest rate on special bond issues (e.g., building a school) as the discount rate. Others employ the interest rate that could be earned by putting money in an endowment fund instead of spending it on capital improvements. Discount rates arbitrarily established by governing boards, are also used.

**Caution:** Guard against using an excessively low discount rate. This may result in accepting projects that will not be profitable. To guard against this problem, the Office of Management and Budget promulgates a discount rate of at least 10 percent on all projects to be considered by federal government units (Office of Management and Budget Circular No. A-94, March 1972).

**Recommendation:** In the case of nonprofit units such as schools and hospitals, the discount rate should be the average rate of return on private sector investments. The average discount rate will provide more meaningful results than using a specific interest rate on a special bond issue or the interest return on an endowment fund.

## RISK AND UNCERTAINTY

Risk analysis is important in making capital investment decisions because of the significant amount of capital involved and the long-term nature of the investments being considered. The higher the risk associated with a proposed project, the greater the return rate that must be earned on the project to compensate for that risk.

You must consider the interrelation of risk among all investments. By properly diversifying, you can obtain the best combination of expected net present value and risk.

**Note:** Do not automatically reject a high-risk project. For example, a new product with much risk may be accepted if there is a chance of a major breakthrough in the market. The business may be able to afford a few unsuccessful new products if one is developed for extraordinary return.

Probabilities can be assigned to expected cash flows based on risk. The probabilities are multiplied by the monetary values to derive the expected monetary value of the investment. A probability distribution function can be generated by computer.

**Rule of Thumb:** The tighter the probability distribution of expected future returns, the lower is the risk associated with a project.

Several methods to incorporate risk into capital budgeting are

- Risk-adjusted discount rate
- Standard deviation and coefficient of variation
- Certainty equivalent

- Semivariance
- Simulation
- Sensitivity analysis
- Decision (probability) trees

Other means of adjusting for uncertainty include

- Decreasing the expected life of an investment
- Use of pessimistic estimates of cash flow
- Comparison of the results of optimistic, pessimistic, and best-guess estimates of cash flows

## RISK-ADJUSTED DISCOUNT RATE

Risk can be included in capital budgeting by computing probable cash flows on the basis of probabilities and assigning a discount rate based on the riskiness of alternative proposals.

Using this approach, an investment's value is determined by discounting the expected cash flow at a rate allowing for the time value of money and for the risk associated with the cash flow. The cost of capital (discount rate) is adjusted for a project's risk. A profitable investment is indicated by a positive net present value. Using the method, you judge the risk class of the proposed capital investment and the risk-adjusted discount rate appropriate for that class.

**Suggestion:** If doubtful of your results, check them by estimating the cost of capital of other companies specializing in the type of investment under consideration.

### Example 22

You are evaluating whether to accept proposal A or B. Each proposal mandates an initial cash outlay of $12,000 and has a three-year life. Annual net cash flows, as well as expected probabilities, are as follows.

*Proposal A:*

| Expected Annual Cash Inflow | Probability |
|---|---|
| $5,800 | .4 |
| 6,400 | .5 |
| 7,000 | .1 |

*Proposal B:*

| Expected Annual Cash Inflow | Probability |
|:---:|:---:|
| $3,400 | .3 |
| 8,000 | .5 |
| 11,000 | .2 |

The inflation rate and interest rate are estimated at 10 percent. Proposal A has a lower risk since its cash flows show greater stability than those of proposal B. Since proposal A has less risk, it is assigned a discount rate of 8 percent, while proposal B is assigned a 10 percent discount rate because of the greater risk.

*Proposal A:*

| Cash Flow | Probability | Probable Cash Flow |
|:---|:---:|:---:|
| $5,800 | .4 | $2,320 |
| 6,400 | .5 | 3,200 |
| 7,000 | .1 | 700 |
| Expected annual cash inflow | | $6,220 |

*Proposal B:*

| Cash Flow | Probability | Probable Cash Flow |
|:---|:---:|:---:|
| $ 3,400 | .3 | $1,020 |
| 8,000 | .5 | 4,000 |
| 11,000 | .2 | 2,200 |
| Expected annual cash inflow | | $7,220 |

*Proposal A:*

| Year | Explanation | Amount | | Factor | Present Value |
|:---:|:---|:---:|:---:|:---:|:---:|
| 0 | Initial investment | $−12,000 | × | 1 | $−12,000 |
| 1-3 | Annual cash flow | +6,220 | × | 2.5771[a] | +16,030 |
| | Net present value | | | | $+4,030 |

*Proposal B:*

| Year | Explanation | Amount | | Factor | Present Value |
|------|-------------|--------|---|--------|---------------|
| 0 | Initial investment | $-12,000 | × | 1 | $-12,000 |
| 1-3 | Annual cash flow | +7,220 | × | 2.4869[b] | -17,955 |
| | Net present value | | | | $+5,995 |

[a]Using an 8 percent discount rate.
[b]Using a 10 percent discount rate.

Even though project B has more risk, it has a higher risk-adjusted net present value. Project B should thus be selected.

### STANDARD DEVIATION AND COEFFICIENT OF VARIATION

Risk is a measure of dispersion around a probability distribution. It is the variability of cash flow around the expected value. Risk can be measured in either absolute or relative terms. First, the expected value, $\overline{A}$ is

$$\overline{A} = \sum_{i=1}^{n} A_i p_i$$

where
$A_i$ = the value of the $i$th possible outcome
$p_i$ = the probability that the $i$th outcome will take place
$n$ = the number of possible outcomes

Then, the absolute risk is determined by the standard deviation

$$\sigma = \sqrt{\sum_{i=1}^{n} (A_i - A)^2 \ p_i}$$

The relative risk is expressed by the coefficient of variation:

$$\frac{\sigma}{\overline{A}}$$

## Example 23

You are considering investing in one of two projects. Depending on the state of the economy, the projects would provide the following cash inflows in each of the next five years:

| Economic Condition | Probability | Proposal A | Proposal B |
|---|---|---|---|
| Recession | .3 | $1,000 | $ 500 |
| Normal | .4 | 2,000 | 2,000 |
| Boom | .3 | 3,000 | 5,000 |

We now compute the expected value $(\overline{A})$, the standard deviation $\sigma$, and the coefficient of variation $(\sigma/\overline{A})$.

*Proposal A*:

| $A_i$ | $P_i$ | $A_i P_i$ | $(A_i - \overline{A})$ | $(A_i - \overline{A})^2$ |
|---|---|---|---|---|
| $1,000 | .3 | $ 300 | −$1,000 | $1,000,000 |
| 2,000 | .4 | 800 | 0 | 0 |
| 3,000 | .3 | 900 | 1,000 | 1,000,000 |
| | | $\overline{A} = \$2,000$ | | $\sigma^2 = \$2,000,000$ |

Because $\sigma^2 = \$2,000,000$, $\sigma = \$1,414$. Thus

$$\frac{\sigma}{\overline{A}} = \frac{\$1,414}{\$2,000} = .71$$

*Proposal B*:

| $A_i$ | $P_i$ | $A_i P_i$ | $(A_i - \overline{A})$ | $(A_i - \overline{A})^2$ |
|---|---|---|---|---|
| $500 | .3 | $ 150 | $−1,950 | $ 3,802,500 |
| 2,000 | .4 | 800 | − 450 | 202,500 |
| 5,000 | .3 | 1,500 | 2,550 | 6,502,500 |
| | | $\overline{A} = \$2,450$ | | $\sigma^2 = \$10,507,500$ |

Since, $\sigma^2 = \$10,507,500$, $\sigma = \$3,242$. Thus,

$$\frac{\sigma}{\overline{A}} = \frac{\$3,242}{\$2,450} = 1.32$$

Therefore, proposal A is relatively less risky than is proposal B, as measured by the coefficient of variation.

### CERTAINTY EQUIVALENT

The certainty equivalent approach relates to utility theory. You specify at what point the company is indifferent to the choice between a certain sum of dollars and the expected value of a risky sum. The certainty equivalent is multiplied by the original cash flow to obtain the equivalent certain cash flow. You then use normal capital budgeting. The risk-free rate of return is employed as the discount rate under the net present value method and as the cutoff rate under the internal rate of return method.

### Example 24

A company's cost of capital is 14 percent after taxes. Under consideration is a four-year project that will require an initial investment of $50,000. The following data also exists:

| Year | After-Tax Cash Flow | Certainty Equivalent Coefficient |
|------|---------------------|----------------------------------|
| 1    | $10,000             | .95                              |
| 2    | 15,000              | .80                              |
| 3    | 20,000              | .70                              |
| 4    | 25,000              | .60                              |

The risk-free rate of return is 5 percent.
Equivalent certain cash inflows are

| Year | After-Tax Cash Inflow | Certainty Equivalent Coefficient | Equivalent Certain Cash Inflow | Present Value Factor at 5% | Present Value |
|------|----------------------|----------------------------------|--------------------------------|----------------------------|---------------|
| 1    | $10,000              | .95                              | $ 9,500                        | .9524                      | $ 9,048       |
| 2    | 15,000               | .80                              | 12,000                         | .9070                      | 10,884        |
| 3    | 20,000               | .70                              | 14,000                         | .8638                      | 12,093        |
| 4    | 25,000               | .60                              | 15,000                         | .8227                      | 12,341        |
|      |                      |                                  |                                |                            | $44,366       |

Net Present Value:
| | |
|---|---|
| Initial investment | $-50,000 |
| Present value of cash inflows | +44,366 |
| Net present value | $- 5,634 |

Using trial and error, you arrive at an internal rate of 4 percent.

The proposal should be rejected because of the negative net present value and an internal rate (4 percent) less than the risk-free rate (5 percent).

## SEMIVARIANCE

Semivariance is the expected value of the squared negative deviations of the possible outcomes from an arbitrarily chosen point of reference. Semivariance appraises risks applicable to different distributions by referring to a fixed point designated by you. In computing semivariance, positive and negative deviations contribute differently to risk, whereas in computing variance, a positive and negative deviation of the same magnitude contributes equally to risk.

**Key Point:** Since there is an opportunity cost of tying up capital, the risk of an investment is measured principally by the prospect of failure to earn the return.

## SIMULATION

You obtain probability distributions for a number of variables (e.g., investment outlays or unit sales) when doing a simulation. Selecting these variables from the distributions at random results in an estimated net present value. Since a computer is used to generate many results using random numbers, project simulation is expensive.

## SENSITIVITY ANALYSIS

Forecasts of many calculated net present values and internal rates of return, under various alternatives, are compared to identify how sensitive net present value or internal rate of return is to changing conditions. You determine whether one or more than one variable significantly affects net present value, once that variable is changed. If net present value is materially changed, you are dealing with a much riskier asset than was originally forecast. Sensitivity analysis provides an immediate financial measure of possible errors in forecasts. It focuses on decisions that may be sensitive.

Sensitivity analysis can take various forms. For example, a financial manager may want to know how far annual sales can decline and still break even on the investment. Sensitivity analysis can also be used to test the sensitivity of a decision to estimates of selling price and per unit variable cost.

**Key Point:** Sensitivity analysis provides managers with an idea of the degree to which unfavorable occurrences like lower volumes, shorter useful lives, or higher costs are likely to affect the profitability of a project. It is employed due to the uncertainty of dealing with actual situations.

### DECISION TREES

A decision (probability) tree graphically shows the sequence of possible outcomes. The capital budgeting tree shows cash flows and net present value of the project under different possible circumstances.

### Advantages:

- Shows possible outcomes of the contemplated project
- Makes you more cognizant of adverse possibilities
- Depicts the conditional nature of later years' cash flows.

### Disadvantage:

- Many problems are too complex to allow for a year-by-year depiction. For example, a three-year project with three possible outcomes following each year has 27 paths.)

### Example 25

You want to introduce one of two products. The probabilities and present values of expected cash inflows are

| Product | Investment | Present Value of Cash Inflows | Probability |
|---------|------------|-------------------------------|-------------|
| A | $225,000 | | |
| | | $450,000 | .4 |
| | | 200,000 | .5 |
| | | −100,000 | .1 |
| B | 80,000 | | |
| | | 320,000 | .2 |
| | | 100,000 | .6 |
| | | −150,000 | .2 |

| | Initial Investment (1) | Probability (2) | PV of Cash Inflows (3) | PV of Cash Inflows (2) × (3) = (4) |
|---|---|---|---|---|
| Product A | $225,000 | .40 | $450,000 | $180,000 |
| | | .50 | 200,000 | 100,000 |
| | | .10 | −100,000 | −10,000 |
| | | | | $270,000 |
| *or* | | | | |
| Product B | | .20 | $320,000 | $64,000 |
| | | .60 | 100,000 | 60,000 |
| | $80,000 | .20 | −150,000 | −30,000 |
| | | | | $ 94,000 |

Net present value:

> Product A: $270,000 − $225,000 = $45,000
>
> Product B: $94,000 − $80,000 = $14,000

Product A should be selected.

### CORRELATION OF CASH FLOWS OVER TIME

When cash inflows are independent from period to period, it is fairly easy to measure the overall risk of an investment proposal. In some cases, however, especially with the introduction of a new product, the cash flows experienced in early years affect the size of the cash flows in later years. This is called the *time dependence of cash flows* and it has the effect of increasing the risk of the project over time.

### Example 26

Janday Corporation's after-tax cash inflows (ATCI) are time dependent, so that year 1 results ($ATCI_1$) affect the cash flows in year 2 ($ATCI_2$) as follows:

If $ATCI_1$ is $8,000 with a 40 percent probability, the distribution for $ATCI_2$ is

|  |  |
|---|---|
| 0.3 | $ 5,000 |
| 0.5 | 10,000 |
| 0.2 | 15,000 |

If ATCI$_1$ is $15,000 with a 50 percent probability, the distribution for ATCI$_2$ is

|      |          |
|------|----------|
| 0.3  | $10,000  |
| 0.6  | 20,000   |
| 0.1  | 30,000   |

If ATCI$_1$ is $20,000 with a 10 percent chance, the distribution for ATCI$_2$ is

|      |          |
|------|----------|
| 0.1  | $15,000  |
| 0.8  | 40,000   |
| 0.1  | 50,000   |

The project requires an initial investment of $20,000, and the risk-free rate of capital is 10 percent.

The company uses the expected net present value from decision tree analysis to determine whether the project should be accepted. The analysis is as follows:

| Time 0 | Time 1 | | Time 2 | NPV at 10% | Joint Probability | Expected NPV |
|--------|--------|----|--------|------------|-------------------|--------------|
| | | .3 | $ 5,000 | $−8,595[a] | .12[b] | $−1,031 |
| | $ 8,000 | .5 | 10,000 | −4,463 | .20 | −893 |
| | | .2 | 15,000 | −331 | .08 | −26 |
| | | .3 | $10,000 | $1,901 | .15 | 285 |
| $−20,000 | $15,000 | .6 | 20,000 | 10,165 | .30 | 3,050 |
| | | .1 | 30,000 | 18,429 | .05 | 921 |
| | | .1 | $15,000 | $10,576 | .01 | 106 |
| | $20,000 | .8 | 40,000 | 21,238 | .08 | 2,499 |
| | | .1 | 50,000 | 39,502 | .01 | 395 |
| | | | | | 1.00 | $ 5,306 |

(paths from Time 0: .4, .5, .1)

[a]NPV = PV − I = $8,000 PVIF$_{10,1}$ + $5,000 PVIF$_{10,2}$ − $20,000
            = $8,000(.9091) + $5,000(.8264) − $20,000
            = $−8,595
[b]Joint probability of the first path = (.4)(.3) = .12

Since the NPV is positive ($5,306), Janday Corporation should accept the project.

## NORMAL DISTRIBUTION AND NPV ANALYSIS: STANDARDIZING THE DISPERSION

With the assumption of *independence* of cash flows over time, the expected NPV would be

$$NPV = PV - I$$

$$= \sum_{t=1}^{n} \frac{\overline{A}_t}{(1+r)^t} - I$$

The standard deviation of NPVs is

$$\sigma = \sqrt{\sum_{t=1}^{n} \frac{\sigma_t^2}{(1+r)^{2t}}}$$

The expected value $(\overline{A})$ and the standard deviation $\sigma$ give a considerable amount of information by which to assess the risk of an investment project. If the probability distribution is *normal*, some probability statement regarding the project's NPV can be made.

**Example:** The probability of a project's NPV providing an NPV of less than or greater than zero can be computed by standardizing the normal variate $x$ as follows:

$$z = \frac{x - NPV}{\sigma}$$

where
$\quad\quad\quad x$ = the outcome to be found
$\quad\quad NPV$ = the expected NPV
$\quad\quad\quad z$ = the standardized normal variate whose probability value can be found in Table 20.1

## Example 27

Assume an investment with the following data:

|                                 | Period 1 | Period 2 | Period 3 |
| ------------------------------- | -------- | -------- | -------- |
| Expected cash inflow $(\overline{A})$ | $5,000   | $4,000   | $3,000   |
| Standard deviation $(\sigma)$   | 1,140    | 1,140    | 1,140    |

**Table 20.1**
**NORMAL PROBABILITY DISTRIBUTION TABLE**

*Areas Under the Normal Curve*

| Z | 0 | 1 | 2 | 3 | 4 | 5 | 6 | 7 | 8 | 9 |
|---|---|---|---|---|---|---|---|---|---|---|
| .0 | .5000 | .5040 | .5080 | .5120 | .5160 | .5199 | .5239 | .5279 | .5319 | .5359 |
| .1 | .5398 | .5438 | .5478 | .5517 | .5557 | .5596 | .5636 | .5675 | .5714 | .5753 |
| .2 | .5793 | .5832 | .5871 | .5910 | .5948 | .5987 | .6026 | .6064 | .6103 | .6141 |
| .3 | .6179 | .6217 | .6255 | .6293 | .6331 | .6368 | .6406 | .6443 | .6480 | .6517 |
| .4 | .6554 | .6591 | .6628 | .6664 | .6700 | .6736 | .6772 | .6808 | .6844 | .6879 |
| .5 | .6915 | .6950 | .6985 | .7019 | .7054 | .7088 | .7123 | .7157 | .7190 | .7224 |
| .6 | .7257 | .7291 | .7324 | .7357 | .7389 | .7422 | .7454 | .7486 | .7517 | .7549 |
| .7 | .7580 | .7611 | .7642 | .7673 | .7703 | .7734 | .7764 | .7794 | .7823 | .7852 |
| .8 | .7881 | .7910 | .7939 | .7967 | .7995 | .8023 | .8051 | .8078 | .8106 | .8133 |
| .9 | .8159 | .8186 | .8212 | .8238 | .8264 | .8289 | .8315 | .8340 | .8365 | .8389 |
| 1.0 | .8413 | .8438 | .8461 | .8485 | .8508 | .8531 | .8554 | .8577 | .8599 | .8621 |
| 1.1 | .8643 | .8665 | .8686 | .8708 | .8729 | .8749 | .8770 | .8790 | .8810 | .8830 |
| 1.2 | .8849 | .8869 | .8888 | .8907 | .8925 | .8944 | .8962 | .8980 | .8997 | .9015 |
| 1.3 | .9032 | .9049 | .9066 | .9082 | .9099 | .9115 | .9131 | .9147 | .9162 | .9177 |
| 1.4 | .9192 | .9207 | .9222 | .9236 | .9251 | .9265 | .9278 | .9292 | .9306 | .9319 |
| 1.5 | .9332 | .9345 | .9357 | .9370 | .9382 | .9394 | .9406 | .9418 | .9430 | .9441 |
| 1.6 | .9452 | .9463 | .9474 | .9484 | .9495 | .9505 | .9515 | .9525 | .9535 | .9545 |
| 1.7 | .9554 | .9564 | .9573 | .9582 | .9591 | .9599 | .9608 | .9616 | .9625 | .9633 |
| 1.8 | .9641 | .9648 | .9656 | .9664 | .9671 | .9678 | .9686 | .9693 | .9700 | .9706 |
| 1.9 | .9713 | .9719 | .9726 | .9732 | .9738 | .9744 | .9750 | .9756 | .9762 | .9767 |
| 2.0 | .9772 | .9778 | .9783 | .9788 | .9793 | .9798 | .9803 | .9808 | .9812 | .9817 |
| 2.1 | .9821 | .9826 | .9830 | .9834 | .9838 | .9842 | .9846 | .9850 | .9854 | .9857 |
| 2.2 | .9861 | .9864 | .9868 | .9871 | .9874 | .9878 | .9881 | .9884 | .9887 | .9890 |
| 2.3 | .9893 | .9896 | .9898 | .9901 | .9904 | .9906 | .9909 | .9911 | .9913 | .9916 |
| 2.4 | .9918 | .9920 | .9922 | .9925 | .9927 | .9929 | .9931 | .9932 | .9934 | .9936 |
| 2.5 | .9938 | .9940 | .9941 | .9943 | .9945 | .9946 | .9948 | .9949 | .9951 | .9952 |
| 2.6 | .9953 | .9955 | .9956 | .9957 | .9959 | .9960 | .9961 | .9962 | .9963 | .9964 |
| 2.7 | .9965 | .9966 | .9967 | .9968 | .9969 | .9970 | .9971 | .9972 | .9973 | .9974 |
| 2.8 | .9974 | .9975 | .9976 | .9977 | .9977 | .9978 | .9979 | .9979 | .9980 | .9981 |
| 2.9 | .9981 | .9982 | .9982 | .9983 | .9984 | .9984 | .9985 | .9985 | .9986 | .9986 |
| 3. | .9987 | .9990 | .9993 | .9995 | .9997 | .9998 | .9998 | .9999 | .9999 | 1.0000 |

Assume that the firm's cost of capital is 8 percent and the initial investment is $9,000. Then the expected NPV is

$$
\begin{aligned}
\text{NPV} &= \text{PV} - I \\
&= \frac{\$5.000}{(1+.08)} + \frac{\$4.000}{(1+.08)^2} + \frac{\$3,000}{(1+.08)^3} - \$9,000 \\
&= \$5,000(\text{PVIF}_{8.1}) + \$4,000(\text{PVIF}_{8.2}) + \$3,000(\text{PVIF}_{8.3}) - \$9,000 \\
&= \$5,000(.9259) + \$4,000(.8573) + \$3,000(.7938) - \$9,000 \\
&= \$4,630 + \$3,429 + \$2,381 - \$9,000 = \$1,440
\end{aligned}
$$

The standard deviation about the expected NPV is

$$
\sigma = \sqrt{\sum_{t=1}^{n} \frac{\sigma_t^2}{(1+r)^{2t}}}
$$

$$
= \sqrt{\frac{\$1,140^2}{(1+.08)^2} + \frac{\$1,140^2}{(1+.08)^4} + \frac{\$1,140^2}{(1+.08)^6}}
$$

$$
= \sqrt{\$2,888,411} = \$1,670
$$

The probability that the NPV is less than zero is then

$$
z = \frac{x - \text{NPV}}{\sigma} = \frac{0 - \$1,440}{\$1,670} = -.862
$$

The area of normal distribution, that is, z standard deviations to the left or right of the mean, may be found in Table 20.1. A value of z equal to −.862 falls in the area between 0.1949 and 0.1922. Therefore, there is approximately a 19 percent chance that the project's NPV will be zero or less. Putting it another way, there is a 19 percent chance that the internal rate of return on the project will be less than the risk-free rate.

## CONCLUSION

Capital budgeting is the selection of the optimum, alternative, long-term, investment opportunity. It tells where to put corporate resources. It involves the calculation of how many years it takes to get your money back, the return earned on a proposal, and the net present value of cash flows to be derived.

# Chapter 21

# ZERO-BASED METHOD:
## *Priority Budgeting for Best Resource Allocation*

Zero-base budgeting (ZBB) can be used by nonfinancial managers to identify, plan, and control projects and programs. It enhances effectiveness and efficiency. There is a matching of service levels to available resources. Each manager must justify his budget request in detail, beginning with the zero balance. It can lower production, service, and operating costs.

ZBB is a *priority* form of budgeting, ranking activities such as products and services. It may be used by managers to review and analyze programs, proposals, activities, and functions to increase profitability, enhance efficiency, or lower costs. ZBB results in the optimum allocation of company resources. There exists an input-output relationship.

ZBB considers the objectives of the activity and how they are to be accomplished. The failure to fund an activity may result in adverse consequences that have to be taken into account. For example, the failure to produce a particular product may adversely effect the sales of related products in the company's overall product line.

Managers who benefit from using ZBB include production managers, purchase managers, marketing executives, general managers and other administrative staff, engineers, research managers, personnel managers, operations research staff, attorneys, and economists. For example, ZBB can be used by marketing managers to appraise competing alternative product lines, formulate an advertising strategy, evaluate salesperson performance, and establish and monitor marketing priorities. A cost/benefit analysis should be undertaken for each sales program in terms of staff, product, and territory. The objectives of each subunit (e.g., department, responsibility center) should be consistent with the overall goals of the company.

This chapter discusses the ZBB process, its effects, activity units, decision packages, ranking proposals, and project (program) budgets.

## THE ZERO-BASE BUDGETING PROCESS

ZBB begins with a zero balance and formulates objectives to be achieved. All activities are analyzed for the current year. The manager may decide to fund an existing project at the same level as last year after his review. However, it is most likely that funding will be increased or decreased, based on new information. It is also possible that an alternative way may be used for that project, based on current cost or time considerations.

The ZBB approach sets *minimum* funding amounts for each major activity (e.g., product, service). Amounts above the minimum level must be fully *justified* in order to be approved by upper management. Each program, product or service is looked at *each year* to determine its benefit. If an activity cannot be supported as having value, it is *not* funded. The manager is *not* concerned with the *past* but rather looks at the current and future viability. The manager, in effect, discards the dead wood. Programs with inefficiencies, waste, and anything that no longer makes financial sense are dropped.

The ZBB process involves:

- Developing assumptions
- Ranking proposals
- Appraising and controlling
- Preparing the budget
- Identifying and evaluating decision units

## ZERO-BASE BUDGETING EFFECTS

The manager must consider the negative effect, if any, of not accepting a proposed project. For example, if the production manager does not buy a certain type of machine, that will cause quality problems with the product.

## ACTIVITY UNITS

The manager should have control over the activities in his responsibility unit. He must be thoroughly familiar with how his department functions and what resources are needed for staff and money. Activities should be detailed to show work flow.

The *activity unit* is an important cost element of ZBB. It is the lowest unit within the company for which a budget is prepared. An activity unit may represent a function, program, organizational unit, or line item. A manager is typically accountable for the performance of a unit. Decision units include research and development, quality control, computer services, legal, engineering, production, marketing, and personnel.

There are alternative operating modes for activity units, including centralizing the activity, decentralizing the functions, integrating the operations, expanding or reducing activities, and eliminating the function.

Productivity and effectiveness measures should be utilized. The manager should consider financial information, work load, and established standards.

Measures of performance include:

- *Production control*—number of manufacturing trouble spots and poor productivity.
- *Quality control*—number of rejections and other deficiencies.
- *Regional marketing manager*—number of lost accounts and reasons therefore.

Control measures include:

- Quarterly output appraisal, using predetermined performance standards.
- Quarterly modifications to the budget, based on current information.

- Comparing actual cost and time to budgeted cost and time for variance determination.

Decision units should be compared within the company, particularly those that are comparable in size (e.g., number of workers, total assets, and revenue).

Priority should be given to activities that must conform to legal requirements, industry practice, or other constraints.

## DECISION PACKAGES

The first major step in ZBB is the development of decision packages for existing and new programs. The decision package contains a description of the project, specific measures, and employee responsibilities. The package includes the manager's recommended way of producing a product or rendering a service in terms of cost and time. Alternative ways of performing the activity are also specified. For example, improving the quality will increase the cost. Further, reducing the time may also increase the cost because of overtime pay.

A decision package contains the following information:

- Description of the activity and reasons to carry it out.
- Statement of objectives and benefits to be derived.
- The plan to achieve the program.
- The priorities established.
- Cost and time estimates along with evaluation.
- Alternative methods of achieving the activity stated in cost and time.
- Measures of output.
- Resources needed, including physical and personnel support from other responsibility centers.
- Legal, technical, and operational aspects.
- Risk considerations.

Decision packages must be carefully reviewed for possible deficiencies. The manager should assure himself that the packages are complete and independent. Further, decision packages should *not* cross functional and organizational lines. If information is missing or packages are lumped together, misleading conclusions may be drawn.

A decision package can be either *mutually exclusive* or *incremental*. The former are alternative options, meaning that the acceptance of one precludes the acceptance of another. Incremental packages involve additional effort levels. For example, one package may necessitate 3,000 labor hours per month while another may require 3,500 hours for that month.

Decision packages may cover either a short-term or long-term period. A matching of resources with objectives is necessary. Emphasis should be placed on higher return areas.

The format of decision packages should be standardized. Upper management has to approve the decision packages formulated by managers.

## RANKING PROPOSALS

In ranking proposals, upper management will rely heavily on the recommendations made by managers who have a keen knowledge of their decision units. Quantitative and qualitative factors must be considered. A cost/benefit analysis should be performed for each decision unit.

The ranking of decision packages goes in the order of decreasing benefit. The manager must identify those products or services that are the most crucial. The highest priority should be assigned to the *minimum* increment of service below which the unit cannot effectively operate.

Top management performs the final ranking after obtaining initial recommendations of managers within the company's divisions, departments, and cost centers. If a manager's recommendations are rejected, he should be notified why.

A dollar cutoff must be established for programs depending on budgetary constraints. For example, an 80% cutoff may be set, so if the programs total $1,000,000, only $800,000 is in available funds. The manager should also rank nonfunded packages, in the event that additional funds become available at a later date.

A low priority item may later become a high priority one because of changed circumstances. For example, the political climate may change due to a new legislature, governor, mayor, or president. Priorities may change during the year, so adjustments may be necessary.

There are different ranking techniques that may be used, such as single standard, voting, and major category. Single standard is best for similar packages. All packages are evaluated based on only one feature, such as revenue, earnings, return on investment, net present value, amount saved, and cost/benefit ratio. This approach is not suitable for dissimilar packages because it may not incorporate an essential aspect such as health and safety.

Under the voting method, there is a voting committee. Each member appraises the decision packages. The packages are then discussed at the committee meeting. The ranking is based on a committee vote.

Under the major category approach, decision packages are classified into areas. Decision packages are then ranked by categories, with more important ones receiving greater emphasis. A category promising rapid growth may receive ten times the funding of a questionable category of high risk and limited earning potential.

Once fund allocation has been decided upon, detailed budgets are drawn up. These budgets are usually based on incremental activities incorporated on the ranking table.

### Example 1

A company prepares a decision package for each product department managers wish to produce. There are 150 decision packages for all existing and proposed products. An illustration for a decision package for product A to be manufactured in Department X is presented in Figure 21.1.

Each of the 150 products from different departments are submitted by managers to senior management, who will appraise them. There is a budget constraint, so some products will not be funded. The decision package for product A may be flatly rejected. If approved, the manager may be able

**Figure 21.1**
**PRODUCT A—DECISION PACKAGE**

| | Alternative A | $200,000 | 1 year |
| | Recommended Way | $250,000 | 6 months |
| | Alternative B | $350,000 | 2 months |

to produce it either as recommended or in one of the alternative paths. The alternative may be chosen because it involves lower cost or a faster completion date. By specifying alternatives, innovation and better methods may result.

## PROJECT (PROGRAM) BUDGETS

A program may be by division, department, or segment within the department. A program budget is the estimated cost of conducting an activity or function. Program activities include products or services, research and development, capital assets and facilities, maintenance, marketing, training, engineering, and government contracts. A program budget provides functions for a specific activity such as quality control and marketing research.

After a goal is identified, the program and steps to achieve that goal are specified. There is an evaluation of alternatives to ascertain the most productive and least costly manner to achieve program objectives. Resources must be allocated to programs and projects.

A project should be segregated into major activities or tasks, which should then be subdivided into specific subactivities. Program budgeting examines the tasks needed to complete a program, the manpower required, and the time period for each activity.

Program budgeting includes planning, programming, and budgeting. It accumulates data and reviews the detailed plans. It contains a mix of resources, including staff, equipment, raw materials, and capital to achieve the desired objective within a reasonable time period. Alternatives are appraised. There is a downward progression of the decision-making process. There is an emphasis on output goals of products and services rather than input goals. The budgeting is future-oriented, examining the effect of current decisions on future results.

Program budgets are used for programs or projects of a one-time, long-term nature involving large cash outlays. Any potential problems should be anticipated. Responsibility should be assigned for particular activities. Adjustments to the plan may be required.

A cost/benefit analysis should be undertaken for programs. There should be a ranking of programs in priority order. Program interrelationships must be identified.

**Exhibit 21.1**
**WORK-AUTHORIZATION FORM**

Project:

Work-package number:

Issue date:

Revision date and number

|  | Cost | Center |
|---|---|---|
| Material |  |  |

|  | Hours | Cost | Center |
|---|---|---|---|
| Labor |  |  |  |

There should be a tracing of costs to individual projects, products, services, or individuals. This may be accomplished by assigning project numbers and having staff enter code numbers into the computer when supplies are requisitioned, expenses incurred, and salary payments made.

Work packages have to be approved by segment managers. An illustrative work-authorization form appears in Exhibit 21.1.

A time sheet is prepared for project activities. Estimated and actual times are compared to see if deadlines are being met. There should be a time schedule for each stage of the project. This schedule should cover the phases of planning, programming, and budgeting. Activities should be timed and scheduled, using the program evaluation and review technique (PERT). Work should be inspected at key points.

## CONCLUSION

A cost/benefit analysis must be undertaken to see if the benefits to be derived from ZBB are worth the costs to be incurred. Because of the costs and time required, ZBB should be conducted over a span of years (e.g., three years) instead of one year. An annual evaluation is not cost-effective.

ZBB is a continual process because decision packages must be revised for unexpected events.

# Chapter 22

# MANAGERS' PERFORMANCE:
## *Evaluation on the Division Level*

Divisional reports should describe performance and indicate whether objectives are being accomplished.

A segment is a part or activity of an organization from which a manager derives cost or revenue data. Examples of segments are sales territories, individual stores, service centers, manufacturing plants, sales departments, product lines, geographic areas, and types of customers.

Analysis of segmental performance assists in determining the success or failure of the divisional manager and his division. Performance reports should include industry and competitor comparisons. They should also match cycles of major business lines, activities, and geographic areas.

Performance measures consider the contribution of the division to profit and quantity as well as whether the division meets the overall goals of the company. It is difficult to compare profit of different segments, especially when they are of different sizes or provide different kinds of products or services. Measures of divisional performance for a particular segment should be compared to previous periods, other segments, and predetermined standards.

Profit planning by segments applies to selecting from alternative uses of company resources to accomplish a target profit figure. Profit planning by segments requires that the profitability of each segment be measured to see the overall profitability of all feasible combinations or alternatives.

## APPRAISING MANAGER PERFORMANCE

In appraising manager performance, you must determine which factors were under the manager's control (e.g., advertising budget) and which factors were not (e.g., economic conditions). Comparison should be made of one division in the company to other divisions as well as of a division in the company to a similar division in a competing company. Appraisal should also be made of the risk and earning potential of a division. Graphic presentation shows comparisons of an historical, current, or prognostic nature.

### IMPORTANCE OF MEASURING PERFORMANCE OF DIVISIONAL MANAGER

- Assists in formulating management incentives and controlling operations to meet corporate goals
- Directs upper management attention to where it would be most productive
- Determines whom to reward for good performance
- Determines who is not doing well so corrective action may be taken
- Provides job satisfaction, since the manager receives feedback

In decentralization, profit responsibility is assigned to subunits. The lower the level where decisions are made, the greater is the decentralization. It is most effective in organizations where cost and profit measurements are necessary and is most successful in organizations where subunits are totally autonomous. Decentralization is in different forms, including functional, geographical, and profit.

### ADVANTAGES OF DECENTRALIZATION

- Top management has more time for strategic planning
- Decisions are made by managers with the most knowledge of local conditions

- There is greater managerial input in decision-making
- Managers have more control over results, resulting in better motivation

### DISADVANTAGES OF DECENTRALIZATION

- Managers become narrow-sighted and look solely at the division rather than at the company as a whole
- Duplication of services can result
- There is an increased cost in obtaining additional information

For comparison purposes, replacement cost instead of historical cost should be employed. It furnishes a relative basis of comparison since it represents the comparable necessary investment at the end of a reporting period. Evaluating replacement cost assists in comparing asset valuation to current productivity. If replacement cost cannot be determined, valuation can be based on the present value of future net cash flows.

The major method of analyzing divisional performance is by responsibility center which consists of revenue center, cost center, profit center, and investment center.

## RESPONSIBILITY CENTER

A responsibility center is a segment of a company in which controls are used to appraise the manager's performance. These controls include costs, revenues, and investment funds and a center may be responsible for all three or one.

*Responsibility accounting* is the system for collecting and reporting revenue and cost information by responsibility centers. It operates on the premise that managers should be held responsible for their performances, those of their subordinates, and all activities within their centers. It is both a planning and control technique. Responsibility accounting, also called *profitability accounting* and *activity accounting*, has the following advantages:

- It facilitates delegation of decision making.
- It helps management promote the concept of management by objective, in which managers agree on a set of goals. The manager's

performance is then evaluated based on his attainment of these goals.

- It permits effective use of the concept of *management by exception*.

Figure 22.1 shows responsibility centers within an organization. Figure 22.2 presents an organization chart. Exhibit 22.1 depicts responsibility accounting at various levels.

Responsibility centers can be found in both centralized and decentralized organizations. A profit center is often associated with a decentralized organization and a cost center with a centralized one. However, this is not always the case.

There are lines of responsibility. Shell, for example, is organized primarily by business functions: exploitation, refining, and marketing. General Mills is organized by product lines.

**Figure 22.1**
**RESPONSIBILITY CENTERS WITHIN A COMPANY**

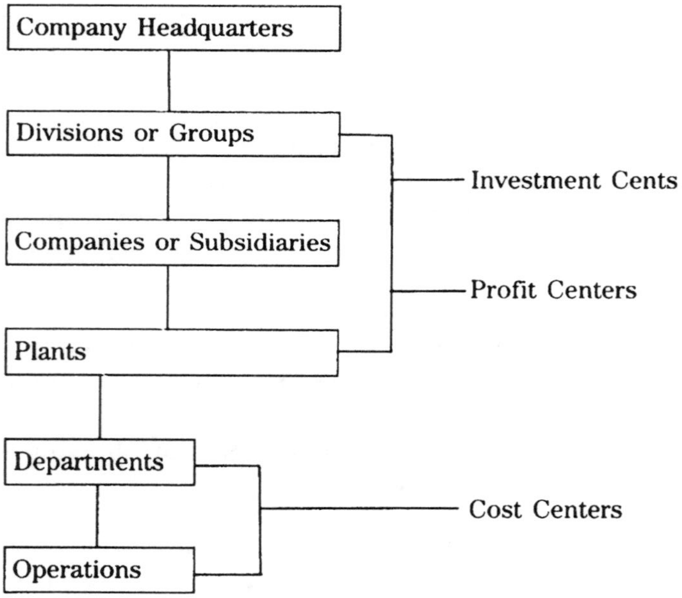

Figure 22.2
ORGANIZATION CHART OF A COMPANY

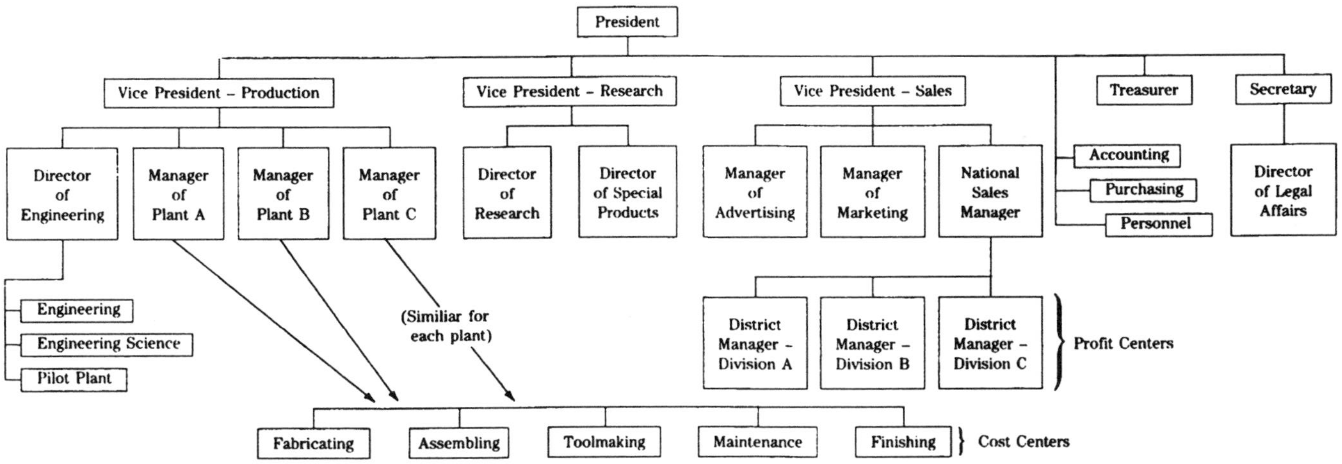

Exhibit 22.1

# PAUL BURGERS
## RESPONSIBILITY ACCOUNTING AT VARIOUS LEVELS
### (IN THOUSANDS)

| Northern California District Manager Monthly Responsibility Report | Budget | | Variance: Favorable (Unfavorable) | |
|---|---|---|---|---|
| Operating income of branches and district manager office expense: | *This Month* | *Year to Date* | *This Month* | *Year to Date* |
| District manager office expense | −145 | −605 | −8 | −20 |
| Berkeley branch | 475 | 1728 | −3 | −11 |
| Palo Alto branch | 500 | 1800 | 19 | 90 |
| Oakland Branch | 310 | 1220 | 31 | 110 |
| Others | 600 | 2560 | 47 | 130 |
| Operating income | 1740 | 6703 | 86 | 299 |

| Berkeley Branch Manager Monthly Responsibility Report | Budget | | Variance: Favorable (Unfavorable) | |
|---|---|---|---|---|
| Operating income of stores and branch manager office expense: | *This Month* | *Year to Date* | *This Month* | *Year to Date* |
| Branch manager office expense | −20 | −306 | −5 | 4 |
| Store X | 48 | 148 | −1 | −5 |
| Store Y | 64 | 226 | 9 | 9 |
| Store Z | 38 | 160 | 4 | 10 |
| Others | 345 | 1500 | −10 | −29 |
| Operating income | 475 | 1728 | −3 | −11 |

| Store Y Manager Monthly Responsibility Report | Budget | | Variance: Favorable (Unfavorable) | |
|---|---|---|---|---|
| Sales and Expenses: | *This Month* | *Year to Date* | *This Month* | *Year to Date* |
| Sales | 170 | 690 | 8 | 12 |
| Food expense | 40 | 198 | 5 | 14 |
| Supplies | 15 | 62 | −3 | −2 |
| Payroll | 24 | 98 | −4 | −5 |
| Repairs & Maintenance | 5 | 21 | 1 | −2 |
| General | 12 | 45 | — | −2 |
| Depreciation | 10 | 40 | = | = |
| Total expenses | 106 | 464 | −1 | 3 |
| Operating income | 64 | 226 | 9 | 9 |

## REVENUE CENTER

A revenue center is responsible for obtaining a target level of sales revenue. An example is a district sales office. The performance report for a revenue center should contain the budgeted and actual sales for the center by product, including evaluation. Usually, the manager of the center is responsible for marketing a product line. But a revenue center typically has a few costs (e.g., salaries, rent). Hence, a revenue center is responsible mostly for revenues and only incidentally for some costs, typically not product costs.

A revenue center approach is most suitable to a sales manager. He is responsible for sales volume, selling price, and total sales. If actual sales exceed budgeted sales, the sales manager is doing something right.

Sales analysis may involve prior sales performance, looking at sales trends over the years, and comparing actual sales to budgeted sales.

In a service business, some performance measures include billable time, average billing rate, and cost per hour of employee time.

Accountability for departmental sales revenue assumes the manager has authority to determine product sales prices.

## COST CENTER

A cost center is typically the smallest segment of activity or responsibility area for which costs are accumulated. This approach is usually employed by departments rather than divisions. A cost center has no control over sales or marketing activities. Departmental profit is difficult to derive because of problems in allocating revenue and costs.

A cost center is a department whose head has responsibility and accountability for costs incurred and for the quantity and quality of products or services. For example, the personnel manager is accountable for costs incurred and the quality of services rendered. The production manager compares expected and actual costs and quantities as a measure of productivity.

Examples of cost centers are a maintenance department and fabricating department in a manufacturing company.

Though a cost center may be relatively small, it can also be very large, such as an administrative area of an entire factory. Some cost centers may consist of a number of smaller cost centers.

A cost center is basically responsible for direct operational costs and meeting production budgets and quotas. Authority and responsibility must be under the control of the department head, usually a foreman.

In the cost center approach, you compare budgeted cost to actual cost. Variances are investigated, necessary corrective action is taken, and efficiencies are accorded recognition. This topic is covered in detail in Chapter 8.

The cost center approach is useful when a manager has control over his costs at a specified operating level. Use this approach when problems arise in relating financial measures to output.

Cost center evaluation is most suitable for accounting and financial reporting, legal, computer services, marketing, personnel, and public relations.

Provision should exist for chargebacks, where appropriate. For example, if a quality control department made an error in its evaluation of product quality, leading to acceptance by the purchasing department, the quality control department should be charged with the increased costs to improve the purchased goods.

The cost center approach may be appropriate for nonprofit and governmental units where budgetary appropriations are assigned. A manager's performance depends on his ability to achieve output levels, given budgetary constraints.

When looking at a manager's performance, relevant costs are those incremental costs over which he has control. Incremental costs are those expenditures that would not exist if the center were abandoned. Allocated common costs (e.g., general administration) should not be included in appraising manager performance. Such costs should, however, be allocated in determining the profit figure for the entire division. Cost allocation must conform to goal congruence and autonomy and should be applied consistently among divisions.

Cost center evaluation will not be worthwhile unless reliable budget figures exist. If a division's situation significantly changes, an adjustment to the initial budget is necessary. In such a case, actual cost should be compared with the initial budget figure (original goal) and the revised budget. Flexible budgets should be prepared that allow examination of costs incurred at different levels of capacity. For example, figures can be budgeted for expected capacity, optimistic capacity, and pessimistic capacity.

When a transfer occurs between cost centers, the transfer price should be based on actual cost, standard cost, or controllable cost. Transfer price is the price charged between divisions for a product or service. Using actual cost may pass cost inefficiencies onto the next division. There is no incentive for the transferer to control costs. Using standard cost corrects the problem of transferring cost inefficiencies. It should be noted that standard cost includes allocated fixed cost, which might be subjective.

A good transfer price is a controllable cost. Charge the cost center with actual controllable cost and credit it with standard controllable cost for the assembled product or service to other divisions.

In evaluating administrative functions, prepare performance reports that examine such dollar indicators as executive salaries and service department costs. The reports should also look at nondollar measures such as number of files handled, phone calls taken, and invoices processed.

In appraising a cost center, look at the ratio of indirect to direct personnel. This ratio reveals the division manpower planning and control.

Manpower needs are based on the individual unit's variable activities and needs. There should be a proper relationship between indirect and direct labor so that services generate maximum profitability. A high ratio of indirect labor may mean the division is top-heavy in administrative and clerical staff.

### Example 1

The indirect personnel to direct personnel ratio averaged about 45% each month over a six-month period. This is favorable because management has maintained a fairly consistent relationship between direct and indirect personnel.

In order to appraise the effectiveness of employee staff in generating divisional revenue, the following ratios may be computed:

* Sales to direct manpower
* Sales to total number of employees
* Sales to total dollar salaries of employees

Higher ratios are desirable because they indicate favorable employee performance in generating sales. For example, an increasing trend in revenue per employee indicates greater productivity. A decline in the ratios may be due to lower sales because of external factors beyond the control of the division manager.

Cost reduction measures may be implemented *without* having a negative long-term effect on the company. Such measures may improve short-term profitability. Short-term cost cutting measures may include:

- Marketing
  1. Paying salespeople on a commission basis instead of a fixed salary
  2. Using distributors rather than direct selling

- Manufacturing
  1. Hiring per diem laborers rather than subcontracting the work
  2. Buying raw materials outside rather than producing them. When the quantity of the product required is relatively low, it is typically better to buy from the outside. Once production exceeds a specified level, the company can increase profitability by doing its own manufacturing
  3. Using parts rather than subassemblies as raw materials

## PROFIT CENTER

A profit center is a responsibility unit that measures the performance of a division, product line, or geographic area. Net income and contribution margin can be computed for a center, which typically does not have significant amounts of invested capital. The profit center approach enhances decentralization and provides units for decision-making purposes.

Use it for a self-contained division—with its own manufacturing and distribution facilities—when there are a limited number of interdivision transfers. The profit reported by the division is basically independent of other divisions' operating activities. Divisional earnings should not be increased by any action reducing overall corporate profitability.

A profit center should also be used when divisional managers have decision-making authority for quantity and mix of goods or services manufactured. With a profit center, net income is determined as if the division were a separate economic entity and the manager is more cognizant of outside market considerations. Profit may be expressed as net income, contribution margin, gross profit, controllable profit, and incremental profit. Examples of profit centers are an auto repair center in a department store and an appliance department in a retail store.

In some instances, profit centers are formed when the product or service is used solely within the company. For example, the computer department may bill each of the firm's administrative and operating units for computing services.

It is not essential that fixed costs be allocated, so contribution margin may be a good indicator of divisional performance. If each division meets its target contribution margin, excess contribution margin will be adequate to cover general corporate expenses.

A contribution margin income statement can evaluate divisional and managerial performance. It also aids in computing selling price, the price to accept for an order given, an idle capacity situation, output levels, maximization of resource uses, and break-even analysis.

The contribution margin income statement is illustrated in Figure 22.3.

**Figure 22.3**
CONTRIBUTION MARGIN INCOME STATEMENT FOR
DIVISIONAL PERFORMANCE EVALUATION

Sales

Less variable production cost of sales

Manufacturing contribution margin

Less variable selling and administrative expenses

Contribution margin

Less controllable fixed costs (i.e., salesperson salaries)

Controllable contribution margin by manager (measures performance of the segment manager)

Less uncontrollable fixed costs (i.e., depreciation, property taxes, insurance)

Segment contribution margin (measures performance of the division)

Less unallocated costs to divisions (excessively difficult to allocate objectively or illogical to allocate, such as the president's salary, corporate research)

Income before taxes (measures performance of the company in its entirety)

Controllable costs are under the division manager's control. They are the incremental costs of operating a division. In effect, they are costs that could have been avoided by the company if the division was closed. Noncontrollable costs are common to a group of divisions that are rationally allocated to them.

A difficulty with the profit center idea is that profit is calculated after subtracting noncontrollable costs or costs not directly related to divisional activity that have been arbitrarily allocated. The ensuing profit figure may be erroneous. However, cost allocation is required, since divisions must incorporate nondivisional costs that have to be met before the company will show a profit.

It is important to recognize that while an uncontrollable income statement item is included in appraising the performance of a profit center, it should *not* be used in evaluating the performance of the manager. An example is the effect of a casualty loss.

A profit center manager should be responsible for not only profit and loss items attributable directly to the division, but also costs incurred outside of the center (e.g., headquarters, other divisions) for which the center will be billed directly. The manager should also be responsible for an expense equal to the company's interest rate times controllable working capital. This charge will take into account tradeoffs between working capital levels and profits. For example, increased inventory balances will mean fewer losses from stock-outs. The manager is the only person who comprehends these tradeoffs. (For a greater discussion of this topic, see John Dearden, "Measuring Profit Center Managers," *Harvard Business Review*, September-October 1987, pp. 84-88.)

Advantages of the profit center approach are that it creates competition in a decentralized company, provides goal congruence between a division and the company, and aids performance evaluation. A drawback is that profits can be "messaged", since expenses may be shifted among periods. Examples of discretionary costs, where management has wide latitude, are research and repairs. Also, not considered are the total assets employed in the division to obtain the profit.

### Example 2

You can sell a product at its intermediate point in Division A for $170 or its final point in Division B at $260. The outlay cost in Division A is $120, while the outlay cost in Division B is $110. Unlimited product demand exists for both the intermediate product and the final product. Capacity is interchangeable. Division performance follows:

|  | Division A | Division B |
| --- | --- | --- |
| Selling Price | $170 | $260 |
| Outlay Cost—A | (120) | (120) |
| Outlay Cost—B |  | (110) |
| Profit | $ 50 | $ 30 |

Sell at the intermediate point because of the higher profit.

Other measures in appraising nonprofit divisional performance are:

- Ratios between cost elements and assets to appraise effectiveness and efficiency

- Productivity measures, including input-output relationships. An example is labor hours in a production run. We have to consider the input in terms of time and money and the resulting output in terms of quantity and quality. Does the maintenance of equipment ensure future growth? Another example is the utilization rate of facilities.

- Personnel development (e.g., number of promotions, turnover)

- Market measures (e.g., market share, product leadership, growth rate, customer service)

- Product leadership indicators (e.g., patented products, innovative technology, product quality, safety record)

- Human resource relationships (e.g., employee turnover rate, customer relations, including on-time deliveries)

- Social responsibility measures (e.g., consumer medals)

A profit center manager is *not* doing his job if he milks operations for a profit now but fails to provide for future profit growth. Examples are cutting back on R&D, advertising, sales promotion, and repairs and maintenance. If these costs are reduced, the current year's division profit will be higher but the long-term results will be disastrous. Long-term profitability can be assured by introducing new products, improving marketing channels and contacts, employee training, expanding plant facilities, and computerization.

## TRANSFER PRICING

A transfer price has to be formulated so that a realistic profit figure can be determined for each division. This price is the one credited to the selling division and charged to the buying division for internal transfer of an assembled product or service.

In establishing a transfer price, the following should be noted:

- It should promote the goals of the company and harmonize divisional goals with organizational goals.
- It should be equitable to all parties involved.
- It should preserve autonomy, so the selling and buying division managers operate their divisions as decentralized entities.
- There should be minimization of duplication and paperwork.
- It should provide flexibility.
- It should be quick in responding to changing business conditions in various countries.
- It should act as an incentive to keep costs under control.
- It should be developed in such a way as to minimize the conflict between buying and selling divisions.
- It should put profits where you want them. For example, put higher profits in low tax areas and lower profits in high tax areas. It should minimize tariffs in international dealings. Also, put profits where they can best be used, such as constructing a new building.
- It should satisfy legal requirements.
- There should be cooperation across divisional and country lines.
- There should exist internal and external reliability.

The best transfer price is the negotiated market value of the assembled product or service, since it is a fair price and treats each profit center as a separate economic entity. It equals the outside service fee or selling price for the item (a quoted price for a product or service is only comparable if the credit terms, grade, quality, delivery, and auxiliary conditions are precisely the same) less internal cost savings that result from dealing within the organization (e.g., advertising sales commission, delivery charges, bookkeeping costs for customers' ledgers, credit and collection costs, and bad debts).

In many cases, if the buying center were an outside customer, the selling center would provide a volume discount. So a similar discount should be offered as an element of the transfer price. The market value of services performed is based on the going rate for a specific job (e.g., equipment tuneup) and/or the standard hourly rate (e.g., the hourly rate for a plumber). Market price may be determined from price catalogues, obtaining outside bids, and examining published data on completed market transactions. However, an outside supplier may intentionally quote a low price to obtain the business, with the thought of increasing the price at a later date.

If two divisions cannot agree on the transfer price, it will be settled by arbitration at a higher level. A temporarily low transfer price (due to oversupply of the item) or high transfer price (due to a strike's causing a supply shortage), should not be employed.

A negotiated transfer price works best when outside markets for the intermediate product exist, all parties have access to market information, and one is permitted to deal externally if a negotiated settlement is impossible. If one of these conditions is violated, the negotiated price may break down and cause inefficiencies.

If the outside market price is not ascertainable (e.g., new product, absence of replacement market, or too costly to be used for transfer pricing), budgeted cost plus profit markup should be used, because this transfer price approximates market value and will spot divisional inefficiencies. Budgeted cost includes the factory cost and any administrative costs applicable to production, such as cost accounting, production planning, industrial engineering, and research and development.

Direct material, direct labor, and variable factory overhead are based on standard rates for the budget period. Fixed factory overhead and administrative expenses are unitized at either forecast or normal volume. It is preferred to use normal volume because it levels out the intracompany prices over the years.

Profit markup should take into account the particular characteristics of the division rather than the overall corporate profit margin. Profit is often calculated on a percentage return on capital which is budgeted to be used at the budgeted or normal volume used for unitizing fixed costs. This percentage is established by company policy. It may be the average expected return for the manufacturing unit, purchasing unit, or company. When budgeted cost plus profit is used as the transfer price, a provision typically exists to adjust for changes in raw material prices and wage rates.

There is an incentive for the selling division to control its costs because it will not be credited for an amount in excess of budgeted cost plus a markup. Thus, if the selling division's inefficiencies result in actual costs being excessive, it will have to absorb the decline in profit to the extent that actual cost exceeds budgeted cost. Profit markup should be as realistic as possible, given the nature of the division and its product.

Even though actual cost plus profit markup is used by some, it has the drawback of passing on cost inefficiencies. In fact, the selling division is encouraged to be cost-inefficient, since the higher its actual cost, the higher its selling price will be. Some companies employ actual cost as the transfer price because of ease of use, but the problem is that no profit is shown by the selling division and cost inefficiencies are passed on.

Further, the cost-based method treats the divisions as cost centers rather than profit or investment centers. Therefore, measures such as return on investment and residual income cannot be used for evaluation purposes.

The variable-cost-based transfer price has an advantage over the full cost method because, in the short run, it may tend to ensure the best utilization of the company's overall resources. The reason is that fixed costs do not change over a short period. Any use of facilities, without incurrence of additional fixed costs, will increase the company's overall profits. In the case where division managers are responsible for costs in their divisions, the cost price approach to transfer pricing is often used.

A transfer price based on cost may be appropriate when there are minimal services provided by one department to another.

A company may have more than one department providing a product or service that is identical or very similar. It may be cost beneficial to centralize that product or service into one department. But more than one department does provide an identical or very similar service, a cost basis transfer price may be used, since the receiving department will select the services of the department providing the highest quality. Thus, the providing department has an incentive to do a good job.

A company may use a below-cost transfer price to favor a division newly spun off by the parent. This may provide the new firm with a better competitive position, allowing it to get started in an industry other than that of the parent and compete effectively with established industry leaders.

Incremental cost is another transfer pricing possibility, incremental costs are the variable costs of making and shipping goods and any costs directly and exclusively traceable to the product. This cost is quite good for use with the company as a whole, but does little for measuring divisional performance. The incremental cost approach assumes the selling division has sufficient capacity to satisfy internal company demands as well as demands of outside customers.

Another way of setting the transfer price is dual pricing. It occurs when the buying division is charged with variable cost ($1) and the selling division is credited with absorption cost and markup ($1.50 plus 60%). Under dual pricing, there is a motivational effect, since each division's performance is enhanced by the transfer. However, profit for the company as a whole will be less than the sum of the divisions' profits.

A last possibility is allocating profit among divisions based on input by departments (e.g., time spent, costs incurred).

### Example 3

Division A manufactures an assembled product that can be sold to outsiders or transferred to Division B. Relevant information for the period follows.

| Division A | Units |
|---|---|
| Production | 1,500 |
| Transferred to Division B | 1,200 |
| Sold Outside | 300 |
| Selling Price | $25 |
| Unit Cost | $5 |

The units transferred to Division B were processed further at a cost of $7. They were sold outside at $45. Transfers are at market value.

Division profit is

| | Division A | Division B | Company |
|---|---|---|---|
| Sales | $ 7,500 | $54,000 | $61,500 |
| Transfer Price | 30,000 | | |
| | $37,500 | $54,000 | $61,500 |
| Product Cost | $ 7,500 | $ 8,400 | $15,900 |
| Transfer Price | | 30,000 | |
| | $ 7,500 | $38,400 | $15,900 |
| Profit | $30,000 | $15,600 | $45,600 |

### Example 4

Zeno Corporation manufactures radios. It has two production divisions (assembly and finishing) and one service division (maintenance). The assembly division both sells assembled radios to other companies and transfers them for further processing to the finishing division. The transfer price used is market value. Relevant data follow.

*Assembly Division*

Outside sales: 1,000 assembled radios at $30 (included in the price is selling commission fees of $1 per unit and freight costs of $2 per unit). Transferred to finishing division: 10,000 assembled radios.

| | |
|---|---|
| Direct costs | $80,000 |
| Indirect costs | $45,000 |

*Finishing Division*

Outside sales: 10,000 finished radios at $55

| | |
|---|---|
| Direct costs | $90,000 |
| Indirect costs | $30,000 |

*Maintenance Division*

| | |
|---|---|
| Direct costs (direct labor, parts) | $80,000 |
| Indirect costs | $25,000 |

9,000 hours rendered for servicing to Assembly Division
12,000 hours rendered for servicing to Finishing Division
Standard hourly rate: $8

A schedule of the gross profit of the separate divisions and the gross profit of Zeno Corporation is shown in Table 22.1.

### Example 5

An assembly division wants to charge a finishing division $80 per unit for an internal transfer of 800 units. The variable cost per unit is $50. Total fixed cost in the assembly division is $200,000. Current production is 10,000 units. Idle capacity exists. The finishing division can purchase the item outside for $73 per unit.

The maximum transfer price should be $73, which is the cost to buy it from outside. The finishing division should not have to pay a price greater than the outside market price.

**Table 22.1**
**GROSS PROFIT, ZENO CORPORATION**

|  | **Assembly** | **Finishing** | **Maintenance** | **Transfers** | **Zeno** |
|---|---|---|---|---|---|
| Revenue |  |  |  |  |  |
| Sales | $ 30,000 | $550,000 |  |  | $580,000 |
| Transfers | 270,000 |  |  | $270,000 |  |
|  |  |  | $ 72,000 | 72,000 |  |
|  |  |  | 96,000 | 96,000 |  |
| Total | $300,000 | $550,000 | $168,000 | $438,000 | $580,000 |
| Costs |  |  |  |  |  |
| Direct | $ 80,000 | $ 90,000 | $ 80,000 |  | $250,000 |
| Indirect | 45,000 | 30,000 | 25,000 |  | 100,000 |
| Transfers: |  |  |  |  |  |
| —Maintenance | 72,000 | 96,000 |  | $168,000 |  |
| —Assembly |  | 270,000 |  | 270,000 |  |
| Total Costs | $197,000 | $486,000 | $105,000 | $438,000 | $350,000 |
| Gross Profit | $103,000 | $ 64,000 | $ 63,000 | — | $230,000 |

Assembly revenue
Sales $30 × 1000
Transfer price $27 × 10,000

Whether the buying division should be permitted to buy the item outside or be forced to buy inside depends on what is best for overall corporate profitability. Typically, the buying division is required to purchase inside at the maximum transfer price ($73), since the selling division still has to meet its fixed cost when idle capacity exists. The impact on corporate profitability of having the buying division go outside is determined as follows:

| | | |
|---|---|---|
| Savings to assembly division (Units × Variable cost per unit): | | |
| | 800 × $50 | $40,000 |
| Cost to finishing division (units × outside selling price): | | |
| | 800 × $73 | 58,400 |
| Stay Inside | | $18,400 |

The buying division will be asked to purchase inside the company, because if it went outside, corporate profitability would decline by $18,400.

## INVESTMENT CENTER

An investment center is a responsibility center that has control over revenue, cost, and investment funds. It is a profit center whose performance is evaluated on the basis of the return earned on invested capital. Corporate headquarters and product line divisions in a large decentralized organization are examples of investment centers. They are widely used in highly diversified companies.

A divisional investment is the amount placed in that division, under division management control. Two major performance indicators are return on investment (ROI) and residual income. We should use available total assets in these measures to take into account all assets in the division, whether used or not. By including nonproductive assets in the base, the manager is motivated either to retain or sell them. Assets assigned to a division include direct assets in the division and allocated corporate assets. Assets are reflected at book value. Include facilities being constructed in the investment base, if the division is committing the funds for the new asset.

You should distinguish between controllable and noncontrollable investment. While the former is helpful in appraising a manager's performance, the latter is used to evaluate the entire division. Controllable investment depends on the degree of a division's autonomy. Thus, an investment center manager accepts responsibility for both the center's assets and its controllable income.

In obtaining divisional investment, there has to be an allocation of general corporate assets to that division. These allocated assets are not considered part of controllable investment. Assets should be allocated to divisions on the basis of measures (e.g., area occupied).

The allocated investment should be part of the division's investment base, but not as an element of controllable investment. Do not allocate general corporate assets attributable to the company as a whole (e.g., security investments). Do not allocate an asset if it requires excessive subjectivity.

The optimal way to assign cash to a division is to agree upon a cash level that meets the minimum needs of the division. If cash is held in excess of this level, there should be an interest income credit using current interest rates. Because the division typically earns a higher return rate on investment than the prevailing interest rate, it will voluntarily return excess cash to the company. This policy maximizes the overall corporate return. Accounts receivable should be assigned to divisions based on sales.

Finished goods should be included in the asset base. The division manager has control over it because he determines the production level on the basis of expected sales. Excessive finished goods inventory is partly due to a division's inadequate planning.

Use the opportunity cost of funds tied up in inventory that could be invested elsewhere for a return in determining divisional profit. Plant and equipment should be allocated on the basis of square footage.

The valuation of assets can be based on book value, gross cost, consumer price index (CPI) adjusted cost, replacement cost, or sales value. Typically, historical cost measures are employed in practice because of availability and consistency with balance sheet valuation.

Using book value for asset valuation will artificially increase divisional return on investment as assets become older, since the denominator using book value becomes lower over time. Gross cost corrects for this decline in value, but it still does not consider inflationary cost increases. However, an advantage of using gross book value to value assets is that it is not affected by changes in expansion rates.

CPI adjusted value takes into account changing price levels.

Replacement cost is ideal because it truly reflects the current prices of assets. Alternative ways exist to determine replacement cost (e.g., present value of future cash flows, specific price index of item, and current market value). Inventory accounted for using LIFO should be adjusted to the FIFO basis or the replacement value, so that inventory is stated at current prices.

Current liabilities should be subtracted in determining the asset base because division financing policy depends on the decision of upper management.

## RETURN ON INVESTMENT

Net income determination for return on investment (ROI) purposes requires that divisional earnings measurements:

- Should not be tied to operational efficiency and quality of managerial decisions of other segments.
- Should include all items over which the divisional manager has control.
- Should not be increased because of any action that negatively affects current or future profits.

ROI is a superior indicator when the investment employed is outside of the manager's determination. But if a manager can significantly determine the capital employed, the return rate is a weakened tool.

$$\text{ROI} = \frac{\text{Net income}}{\text{Available total assets}}$$

Alternative measures are

$$\frac{\text{Operating profit}}{\text{Available total assets}}$$

$$\frac{\text{Controllable operating profit}}{\text{Controllable net investment}}$$
$$\text{(Controllable assets} - \text{Controllable liabilities)}$$

With respect to the last measure, depreciation is a controllable cost since changes in the asset base are controllable by the division manager. Excluded from controllable investment is equipment the manager wants to sell but is unable to because the company is trying to get an alternative use by another division or central headquarters. Transfer this asset from the division's controllable investment base. Also, controllable fixed assets allocated to divisions (e.g., research facilities, general administrative offices) should be excluded from controllable investment.

Assets have to be allocated to divisions on some rational basis. Actual cash at each location is known. Home office cash is typically allocated to plants based on sales or cost of sales. Usually, accounts receivable are segregated by division or plant but, if not, they may be allocated based on sales. Inventories and fixed assets are generally identified (e.g., account coding) to a specific plant or division. Other fixed assets (e.g., home/office building, equipment trucking, research facilities) may be allocated to plants and divisions based on services rendered. Building may be allocated based on physical space. Prepaid expenses, deferred charges, and other assets may be allocated based on sales or cost of sales.

Idle facilities should be included in the investment base when the inactivity of the assets is caused by a division not attaining the budgeted share of the actual market or results from insufficient maintenance.

ROI for each division enables management to appraise divisions from the view of efficient utilization of resources allocated to each division. Divisional management effectiveness is assessed and related to salary and/or bonuses. To work effectively, managers should have control over operations and resources.

### ADVANTAGES OF ROI

- Focuses on maximizing a ratio instead of improving absolute profits
- Highlights unprofitable divisions
- Can be used as a base against which to evaluate divisions within the company and to compare the division to a comparable division in a competing company
- Assigns profit responsibility
- Aids in appraising divisional manager performance
- When a division maximizes its ROI, the company similarly maximizes its ROI
- Places emphasis on high-return items
- Represents a cumulative audit or appraisal of all capital expenditures incurred during a division's existence
- Serves as a guideline to the division manager in analyzing discounted cash flow internal rates of return for proposed capital expenditures
- Broadest possible measure of financial performance. Because divisions are often geographically disbursed internationally, division managers are given broad authority in using division assets and acquiring and selling assets
- Helps make the goals of the division manager coincide with those of corporate management

### DISADVANTAGES OF ROI

- Focuses on maximizing a ratio instead of improving absolute profits
- Alternative profitability measures could be used in the numerator besides net income (e.g., gross profit, contribution margin, segment margin)
- Different assets in the division must earn the same return rate regardless of the assets' riskiness

- To boost profits, needed expenditures may not be incurred (e.g., repairs, research). Here, look at the ratio over time of discretionary costs to sales
- A division may not want to acquire fixed assets because it will lower its ROI
- A labor-intensive division generally has a higher ROI than a capital-intensive one
- ROI is a static indicator and does not show future flows
- A lack of goal congruence may exist between the company and a division. For instance, if a company's ROI is 12%, a division's ROI is 18%, and a project's ROI is 16%, the division manager will not accept the project because it will lower his ROI, even though the project is best for the entire company
- It ignores risk
- ROI emphasizes short-run performance instead of long-term profitability. To protect the current ROI, a manager is motivated to reject other profitable investment opportunities
- ROI may not be completely controllable by the division manager because of the existence of committed costs. The inability to control ROI may be a problem in distinguishing between the manager's performance and the performance of the division as an investment
- If the projected ROI at the beginning of the year is set unrealistically high, it could result in discouragement of investment center incentive

A manager should not be criticized for a disappointing ROI if he does not have significant influence over the factors making up the ROI.

### Example 6

You are concerned about your company's current return on investment. Your company's income statement for year 19X1 follows.

| | |
|---|---:|
| Sales (100,000 units (@$10) | $1,000,000 |
| Cost of Sales | 300,000 |
| Gross Margin | $ 700,000 |
| Selling and General Expenses | 200,000 |
| Income Before Taxes | $ 500,000 |
| Taxes (40%) | 200,000 |
| Net Income | $ 300,000 |

On December 31, total assets available consist of current assets of $300,000 and fixed assets of $500,000.

You forecast that sales for 19X2 will be 120,000 units at $11 per unit. The cost per unit is estimated at $5. Fixed selling and general expenses are forecast at $60,000 and variable selling and general expenses are anticipated to be $1.50 per unit. Depreciation for the year is expected to be $30,000.

Forecasted earnings for 19X2 are calculated as follows:

| | | | |
|---|---|---|---|
| Sales (120,000 (@$11) | | | $1,320,000 |
| Cost of Sales 120,000 (@$5) | | | 600,000 |
| Gross Margin | | | $ 720,000 |
| Selling and General Expenses: | | | |
| Fixed | | $ 60,000 | |
| Variable (120,000 (@$1.50) | | 180,000 | |
| Total | | | 240,000 |
| Income Before Tax | | | 480,000 |
| Tax (40%) | | | 192,000 |
| Net Income | | | $ 288,000 |

The investment expected at December 31, 19X2 is:

| | | | |
|---|---|---|---|
| Ratio of current assets to sales in 19X1: | | | |
| $300,000/$1,000,000 | | | 30% |
| Expected current assets at December 31, 19X2: | | | |
| 30% × $1,320,000 | | | $396,000 |
| Expected fixed assets at December 31, 19X2: | | | |
| Book value on January 1 | $500,000 | | |
| Less: Depreciation for 19X2 | 30,000 | 170,000 | |
| Total Investment | | $866,000 | |

$$ROI = \frac{\$288.000}{\$866,000} = 33.3\%$$

## RESIDUAL INCOME

The optimal measure of divisional performance is residual income, which equals divisional net income less minimum return times average available total assets.

### Example 7

Divisional earnings are $250,000, average available total assets are $2,000,000, and the cost of capital is 9%.

Residual income equals
   Divisional net income                                          $250,000
   Less minimum return × Average available total assets
      9% × $2,000,000                                 $180,000
   Residual income                                          $ 70,000

The minimum rate of return is based upon the company's overall cost of capital adjusted for divisional risk. The cost of capital should be periodically calculated and used because of shifts in the money rate over time.

Residual income may be projected by division, center, or specific program to assure that the company's rate of return on alternative investments is met or improved upon by each segment of the business.

By looking at residual income, we are assured that segments are not employing corporate credit for less return than could be obtained by owning marketable securities or through investment in a different business segment.

A target residual income may be formulated to act as the division manager's objective. The trend in residual income to total available assets should be examined in appraising divisional performance. (See Figure 22.4).

A division manager's performance should be appraised on the basis of controllable residual income. A manager should not be penalized for uncontrollable matters. To evaluate a division, we use net residual income after taxes. This is a key figure, because it aids in the decision to make new investments or withdrawals of funds in that division.

## ADVANTAGES OF RESIDUAL INCOME

- The same asset may be required to earn the same return rate throughout the company, regardless of the division where the asset is located
- Different return rates may be employed for different types of assets, depending on riskiness
- Different return rates may be assigned to different divisions, depending on the risk associated with those divisions
- Provides an economic income, taking into account the opportunity cost of tying up assets in the division
- Identifies operating problem areas

**Figure 22.4.**
RESIDUAL INCOME STATEMENT
FOR DIVISIONAL EVALUATION PURPOSES

| | | |
|---|---|---|
| Sales | $1,200,000 | |
| Transfers at market value to other divisions | 400,000 | |
| Total | | $1,600,000 |
| Less | | |
| Variable cost of goods sold and transferred | $800,000 | |
| Variable divisional expenses | 200,000 | |
| Total | | 1,000,000 |
| Variable income | | $600,000 |
| Less | | |
| Controllable divisional overhead | $200,000 | |
| Depreciation on controllable plant and equipment | 110,000 | |
| Property taxes and insurance on controllable fixed assets | 40,000 | |
| Total | | $350,000 |
| Controllable operating income | | $250,000 |
| Add | | |
| Nonoperating gains | $300,000 | |
| Nonoperating losses | 20,000 | |
| Net nonoperating gains | | 280,000 |
| Total | | $530,000 |
| Less interest on controllable investment | | 30,000 |
| Controllable residual income | | $500,000 |
| Less | | |
| Uncontrollable divisional overhead (e.g., central advertising) | $40,000 | |
| Incremental central expenses chargeable to the division | 10,000 | |
| Interest on noncontrollable investment | 50,000 | |
| Total | | 100,000 |
| Residual income before taxes | | $400,000 |
| Less income taxes (40%) | | 160,000 |
| Net residual income after taxes | | $240,000 |

- Precludes the difficulty that a division with a high ROI would not engage in a project with a lower ROI even though it exceeds the overall corporate ROI rate. This is because residual income maximizes dollars instead of a percentage. It motivates divisional managers to take into account all profitable investments. Unprofitable investments are not included

## DISADVANTAGES OF RESIDUAL INCOME

- Assignment of a minimum return involves estimating a risk level that is subjective
- It may be difficult to determine the valuation basis and means of allocating assets to divisions
- If book value is used in valuing assets, residual income will artificially increase over time, since the minimum return times total assets becomes lower as the assets become older
- It cannot be used to compare divisions of different sizes. Residual income tends to favor the larger divisions due to the large amount of dollars involved
- It does not furnish a direct decision criterion for capital expenditures which have to be based on incremental cash flows, rather than incremental profits
- Since it is a mixture of controllable and uncontrollable elements, there is no segregation

Computerized reports should be prepared at critical points for timely managerial action. Such instance may occur when a product's contribution margin percent is below target or when a product is behind the scheduled days to produce it.

Reports showing excessive age of inventory should be prepared so needed action may be taken, such as price reduction, package deals, or other promotions.

Nonfinancial managers must make key marketing and general business decisions. Examples are changes in sales mix, pricing, production, product expansion or contraction, territory evaluation, and customer analysis.

## CONCLUSION

It is essential to evaluate a segment's performance to identify problem areas. Factors that are controllable or not controllable by the division manager must be considered. The various means of evaluating performance include cost center, profit center, revenue center, and investment center. The calculations for each method, along with proper analysis, are vital in appraising operating efficiency. You should understand the advantages and disadvantages of each method as well as when each is most appropriate.

The manager should be familiar with the profit and loss statements by territory, commodity, method of sale, customer, and salesperson. The profit and loss figures will indicate areas of strength and weakness.

The establishment of a realistic transfer price is essential in order to properly evaluate divisional performance and to arrive at appropriate product costing and profitability.

# Chapter 23

# COST ACCUMULATION SYSTEM:
## *Essential for Managers*

A cost accumulation system is a product costing system. This process accumulates manufacturing costs, such as materials, labor and factory overhead, and assigns them to cost objectives, such as finished goods and work-in-process. Product costing is necessary not only for inventory valuation and income determination but also for establishing the unit sales price.

Nonfinancial managers must have a general understanding of cost accumulation, analysis, and reporting because they must be familiar with how costs associated with their responsibility units are determined. This chapter will discuss the essentials of the cost accumulation system that is used to measure the manufacturing costs of products. This is essentially a two-step process: (1) the measurement of costs that are applicable to manufacturing operations during a given accounting period and (2) the assignment of these costs to products.

There are two basic approaches to cost accounting and accumulation:

(1) Job order costing
(2) Process costing

Exhibit 23.1
DIFFERENCES BETWEEN JOB ORDER COSTING
AND PROCESS COSTING

|  | Job order costing | Process costing |
|---|---|---|
| 1. Cost unit | Job, order, or contract | Physical unit |
| 2. Costs are accumulated | By jobs | By departments |
| 3. Subsidiary record | Job cost sheet | Cost of production report |
| 4. Used by | Custom manufacturers | Processing industries |
| 5. Permits computation of | (a) A unit cost for inventory costing purposes<br><br>(b) A profit or loss each job | A unit cost to be used to compute the costs of goods completed and on work in process |

## JOB ORDER COSTING AND PROCESS COSTING COMPARED

The distinction between job order costing and process costing centers largely around how product costing is accomplished. Job order costing applies costs to specific jobs, which may consist of a single physical unit or a few like units.

Under process costing, data are accumulated by the production department (or cost center) and averaged over all of the production that occurred in the department. There is mass production of like units which are manufactured on a continuous basis through a series of uniform production steps known as *processes*.

Exhibit 23.1 summarizes the basic differences between these two methods.

## JOB ORDER COSTING

Job order costing is the cost accumulation system under which costs are accumulated by jobs, contracts, or orders. This method is appropriate when the products are manufactured in identifiable lots or batches or when the products are manufactured to customer specifications. Job order costing is widely used by custom manufacturers such as printing, aircraft, and construction companies. It may also be used by service businesses such as auto repair shops and professional services.

Job order costing keeps track of costs because direct material and direct labor are traced to a particular job. Costs not directly traceable—factory overhead—are applied to individual jobs, using a predetermined overhead (application) rate.

## JOB COST RECORDS

A *job cost sheet* is used to record various production costs for work-in-process inventory. A separate cost sheet is kept for each identifiable job, accumulating the direct materials, direct labor, and factory overhead assigned to that job as it moves through production. The form varies according to the needs of the company.

Exhibit 23.2 presents the basic records or source documents used for job costing.

These include:

1. The *job cost sheet*. This is the key document in the system. It summarizes all of the manufacturing costs—direct materials, direct labor, and applied factory overhead (to be discussed in detail later)—of producing a given job or batch of products. One sheet is maintained for each job and the file of job cost sheets for unfinished jobs is the subsidiary record for the Work in Process Inventory account. When the jobs are completed and transferred, the job order sheets are transferred to a completed jobs file and the number of units and their unit costs are recorded on inventory cards supporting the Finished Goods Inventory account.

2. The *materials requisition form*. This form shows the types, quantities and prices of each type of material issued for production.

3. The *work ticket*. It shows who worked on what job for how many hours and at what wage rate. This is also called *time ticket* and illustrated in Exhibit 23.2.

4. The *factory overhead cost sheet*. It summarizes the various factory overhead costs incurred.

## Exhibit 23.2
## BASIC RECORDS IN A JOB COST SYSTEM

**STORES CARD**

Material A

| Received | Issued | Balance |
|----------|--------|---------|
| PI | SR | |

**WORK TICKET**

Employee No. _____ Date _____ Job No. _____
Operation _____ Dept. No. _____
Stop _____ Rate _____
Start _____ Amount _____

WT

**JOB ORDER SHEET**

Job No.

| Direct Material | Direct Labor | Factory Overhead |
|-----------------|--------------|------------------|
| SR | WT | Applied by overhead rate |

| Summary | |
|---------|---|
| Direct Material | xx |
| Direct Labor | xx |
| Overhead | xx |
| Total | x xx |

**FINISHED GOODS CARD**

Product DG

| Received | Issued | Balance |
|----------|--------|---------|
| JCS | ST | |

PI = Purchase invoice
SR = Store requisition
WT = Work ticket
JCS = Job cost sheet
ST = Sales ticket
V = Voucher
GJ = General journal

**FACTORY OVERHEAD COST SHEET**

| Depreciation | Indirect Labor | Indirect Materials | Power | Payroll Taxes | Insurance | Others |
|--------------|----------------|--------------------|-------|---------------|-----------|--------|
| GJ | WT | SR | V | V | V | V |

5. The *memo for applied factory overhead*. This is a memorandum that shows how the factory overhead applied rate has been developed.

6. The *finished goods record*. This is a record maintained for each type of product manufactured and sold. Each record contains a running record of units and costs of products received, sold, and on hand.

### Example 1

Holden Works collects its cost data by the job order cost system. For Job 123, the following data are available:

| Direct Materials | Direct Labor |
|---|---|
| 7/14 Issued............$1,200 | Week of July 20........180 hrs. @$6.50 |
| 7/20 Issued........... 650 | Week of July 26........140 hrs. @7.25 |
| 7/25 Issued........... 350 | |
| $2,200 | |

Factory overhead is applied at the rate of $4.50 per direct labor hour.

We will compute (a) the cost of Job 123 and (b) the sales price of the job, assuming that it was contracted with a markup of 40% of cost.

(a) The cost of job is:

| | | |
|---|---|---|
| Direct material | | $2,200 |
| Direct labor: | | |
| 180 hrs. × $6.50 | $1,170 | |
| 140 hrs. × $7.25 | 1,015 | 2,185 |
| Factory overhead applied: | | |
| 320 hrs. × $4.50 | | 1,440 |
| Cost of Job 123 | | $5,825 |

(b) The sales price of the job is:

$5,825 + 40% ($5,825) = $5,825 + $2,330 = $8,155

## FACTORY OVERHEAD APPLICATION

Many items of factory overhead cost are incurred for the entire factory and for the entire accounting period and cannot be specifically identified with particular jobs. Furthermore, the amount of actual factory overhead costs incurred is not usually available until the end of the accounting period. But it is often critical to make cost data available for pricing purposes as each job is completed. Therefore, in order for job costs to be available on a timely basis, it is customary to apply factory overhead by using a *predetermined factory overhead rate*.

## PREDETERMINED FACTORY OVERHEAD RATE

Regardless of the cost accumulation system used (i.e., job order or process), factory overhead is applied to a job or process. The predetermined overhead rate is determined as follows:

$$\text{Predetermined overhead rate} = \frac{\text{Budgeted annual overhead}}{\text{Budgeted annual activity units}}$$
$$\text{(direct labor hours, machine hours, etc.)}$$

Budgeted activity units used in the denominator of the formula, more often called the *denominator activity* level, are measured in direct labor hours, machine hours, direct labor costs, production units, or any other representative surrogate of production activity.

### Example 2

A company uses a budgeted overhead rate in applying overhead to production orders on a labor-cost basis for Department A and on a machine-hour basis for Department B. At the beginning of the year, the company made the following predictions:

|                   | Department A | Department B |
|-------------------|:------------:|:------------:|
| Factory overhead  | $72,000      | $75,000      |
| Direct labor cost | 64,000       | 17,500       |
| Machine hours     | 500          | 10,000       |

The predetermined overhead rates for each department are:

Department A: $72,000/$64,000 = $1.125 per labor dollar or 112.5%
Department B: $75,000/10,000 = $7.50 per machine hour

During the month of January, the cost record for a job order, No. 105, that was processed through both departments, shows the following:

|                    | Department A | Department B |
|--------------------|:------------:|:------------:|
| Materials issued   | $30          | $45          |
| Direct labor cost  | 36           | 25           |
| Machine hours      | 6            | 15           |

The total applied overhead for job order No. 105 follows:

| | |
|---|---:|
| Department A: $36 × 1.125 | $ 40.50 |
| Department B: 15 × $7.50  | 112.50 |
| | $153.00 |

Assuming job order No. 105 consisted of 30 units of product, what is the total cost and unit cost of the job?

|                    | Department A | Department B |
|--------------------|:------------:|:------------:|
| Direct material    | $ 30.00      | $ 45.00      |
| Direct labor       | 36.00        | 25.00        |
| Applied overhead   | 40.50        | 112.50       |
| Total              | $106.50      | $182.50      |

Therefore, the total cost of the job is $106.50 + $182.50 = $289; the unit cost is $9.63 ($289/30 units).

## PROCESS COSTING

Process costing is a cost-accumulation system that aggregates manufacturing costs by departments or by production processes. Total manufacturing costs are accumulated by two major categories, direct materials and conversion costs (the sum of direct labor and factory overhead applied). Unit cost is determined by dividing the total costs charged to a cost center by the output of that cost center. In that sense, the unit costs are averages.

Process costing is appropriate for companies that produce a continuous mass of like units through a series of operations or processes. It is generally used in such industries as petroleum, chemicals, oil refinery, textiles, and food processing.

### STEPS IN PROCESS-COSTING CALCULATIONS

The five steps in accounting for process costs are:

(1) *Summarize the flow of physical units.* The first step of the accounting provides a summary of all units on which some work was done in the department during the period. *Input must equal output.* This step helps to detect lost units during the process. The basic relationship may be expressed in the following equation:

Beginning inventory + units started for the period
= units completed and transferred out + ending inventory

(2) *Compute output in terms of equivalent units.* In order to determine the unit costs of the product in a processing environment, it is important to measure the total amount of work done during an accounting period. A special problem arises in processing industries—the work partially completed at the end of the period. The partially completed units are measured on an equivalent whole-unit basis for process-costing purposes.

   Equivalent units are a measure of how many whole units of production are represented by the units completed plus the units partially completed. For example, 100 units that are 60% completed are the equivalent of 60 completed units.

(3) *Summarize the total costs to be accounted for by cost categories.* This step summarizes the total costs assigned to the department during the period.

(4) *Compute the unit costs per equivalent unit.* The unit costs per equivalent is computed as follows:

$$\text{Unit cost} = \frac{\text{Total costs incurred during the period}}{\text{Equivalent units of production during the period}}$$

(5) *Apply total costs to units completed and transferred out and to units in ending work-in-process.*

### COST-OF-PRODUCTION REPORT

The process-costing method uses what is called the cost-of-production report. It summarizes total and unit costs charged to a department and indicates the allocation of total costs between work-in-process inventory and the units completed and transferred to the next department or the finished goods inventory.

The cost-of-production report covers all five steps described above. It is a convenient compilation from which cost data may be presented to management.

## PROCESS-COST COMPUTATION: NO BEGINNING INVENTORY

The first illustration of unit-cost computations under a process system assumes for simplicity that there is no beginning work-in-process inventory. A company produces and sells a chemical product that is processed in two departments. In Department A the basic materials are crushed, powdered, and mixed. In Department B the product is tested, packaged, and labeled.

Assume the following for Production Department A for May. Materials are added when production is begun. Therefore, all finished units and all units in the ending work-in-process inventory will have received a full complement of materials.

Actual production costs:
    Direct materials used, 18,000 gallons costing $27,000.
    Direct labor and factory overhead, $25,000.
Actual production:
    Completed and transferred to Production Department B, 8,000
        gallons.
    Ending work-in-process, 10,000 gallons, 20% complete as to
        conversion.

(1) *Summarize the flow of physical units.*

To be accounted for:
    Added this period                              18,000 gallons

Accounted for as follows:
    Completed this period.......................................8,000 gallons
    In process, end of period..................................10,000
    Total.......................................................18,000 gallons

(2) *Compute output in terms of equivalent units*

|                                          | Materials (gal.) | Conversion Cost |
|------------------------------------------|------------------|-----------------|
| Units completed                          | 8,000            | 8,000           |
| Ending work-in-process (10,000 gallons)  |                  |                 |
| 100% of materials                        | 10,000           |                 |
| 20% of conversion cost                   |                  | 2,000           |
| Equivalent units produced                | 18,000           | 10,000          |

*Steps (3) through (5)*

**COST OF PRODUCTION**

|                          | Total Cost | Equivalent Production (gal.) | Unit Cost |
|--------------------------|-----------|------------------------------|-----------|
| Materials                | $27,000   | 18,000                       | $1.50     |
| Conversion cost          | 25,000    | 10,000                       | 2.50      |
| To be accounted for      | $52,000   |                              | $4.00     |
|                          |           |                              |           |
| Ending work-in-process:  |           |                              |           |
| Materials                | $15,000   | 10,000                       | $1.50     |
| Conversion cost          | 5,000     | 2,000                        | 2.50      |
| Total work-in-process    | $20,000   |                              |           |
| Completed and transferred| 32,000    | 8,000                        | 4.00      |
| Total accounted for      | $52,000   |                              |           |

## CONCLUSION

Unit costs are necessary for inventory valuation, income determination, and pricing. This chapter provided an introduction to the two basic cost accumulation systems: (1) job order costing and (2) process costing.

Job order costing attaches costs to specific jobs by means of cost sheets established for each job. Direct material and direct labor costs are traced to specific jobs. Factory overhead costs are applied by jobs, using a predetermined overhead rate.

Process costing makes no attempt to cost any specific lot in process. All costs, direct and indirect, are accumulated by departments for periods of time and an average cost for the period is computed.

Managers must have a general understanding of cost accumulation and reporting because they must be familiar with how costs associated with their responsibility units are determined.

*Appendix* **I**

# PRESENT AND FUTURE VALUE TABLES

## Table 1
### FUTURE VALUE OF $1

*Interest Rate*

| Number of Years | 1% | 2% | 3% | 4% | 5% | 6% | 7% | 8% | 9% | 10% | 12% | 14% | 15% | 16% | 18% | 20% | 24% | 28% | 32% | 36% |
|---|---|---|---|---|---|---|---|---|---|---|---|---|---|---|---|---|---|---|---|---|
| 1 | 1.0100 | 1.0200 | 1.0300 | 1.0400 | 1.0500 | 1.0600 | 1.0700 | 1.0800 | 1.0900 | 1.1000 | 1.1200 | 1.1400 | 1.1500 | 1.1600 | 1.1800 | 1.2000 | 1.2400 | 1.2800 | 1.3200 | 1.3600 |
| 2 | 1.0201 | 1.0404 | 1.0609 | 1.0816 | 1.1025 | 1.1236 | 1.1449 | 1.1664 | 1.1881 | 1.2100 | 1.2544 | 1.2996 | 1.3225 | 1.3456 | 1.3924 | 1.4400 | 1.5376 | 1.6384 | 1.7424 | 1.8496 |
| 3 | 1.0303 | 1.0612 | 1.0927 | 1.1249 | 1.1576 | 1.1910 | 1.2250 | 1.2597 | 1.2950 | 1.3310 | 1.4049 | 1.4815 | 1.5209 | 1.5609 | 1.6430 | 1.7280 | 1.9066 | 2.0972 | 2.3000 | 2.5155 |
| 4 | 1.0406 | 1.0824 | 1.1255 | 1.1699 | 1.2155 | 1.2625 | 1.3108 | 1.3605 | 1.4116 | 1.4641 | 1.5735 | 1.6890 | 1.7490 | 1.8106 | 1.9388 | 2.0736 | 2.3642 | 2.6844 | 3.0360 | 3.4210 |
| 5 | 1.0510 | 1.1041 | 1.1593 | 1.2167 | 1.2763 | 1.3382 | 1.4026 | 1.4693 | 1.5386 | 1.6105 | 1.7623 | 1.9254 | 2.0114 | 2.1003 | 2.2878 | 2.4883 | 2.9316 | 3.4360 | 4.0075 | 4.6526 |
| 6 | 1.0615 | 1.1262 | 1.1941 | 1.2653 | 1.3401 | 1.4185 | 1.5007 | 1.5869 | 1.6771 | 1.7716 | 1.9738 | 2.1950 | 2.3131 | 2.4364 | 2.6996 | 2.9860 | 3.6352 | 4.3980 | 5.2899 | 6.3275 |
| 7 | 1.0721 | 1.1487 | 1.2299 | 1.3159 | 1.4071 | 1.5036 | 1.6058 | 1.7138 | 1.8280 | 1.9487 | 2.2107 | 2.5023 | 2.6600 | 2.8262 | 3.1855 | 3.5832 | 4.5077 | 5.6295 | 6.9826 | 8.6054 |
| 8 | 1.0829 | 1.1717 | 1.2668 | 1.3686 | 1.4775 | 1.5938 | 1.7182 | 1.8509 | 1.9926 | 2.1436 | 2.4760 | 2.8526 | 3.0590 | 3.2784 | 3.7589 | 4.2998 | 5.5895 | 7.2058 | 9.2170 | 11.703 |
| 9 | 1.0937 | 1.1951 | 1.3048 | 1.4233 | 1.5513 | 1.6895 | 1.8385 | 1.9990 | 2.1719 | 2.3579 | 2.7731 | 3.2519 | 3.5179 | 3.8030 | 4.4355 | 5.1598 | 6.9310 | 9.2234 | 12.166 | 15.916 |
| 10 | 1.1046 | 1.2190 | 1.3439 | 1.4802 | 1.6289 | 1.7908 | 1.9672 | 2.1589 | 2.3674 | 2.5937 | 3.1058 | 3.7072 | 4.0456 | 4.4114 | 5.2338 | 6.1917 | 8.5944 | 11.805 | 16.059 | 21.646 |
| 11 | 1.1157 | 1.2434 | 1.3842 | 1.5395 | 1.7103 | 1.8983 | 2.1049 | 2.3316 | 2.5804 | 2.8531 | 3.4785 | 4.2262 | 4.6524 | 5.1173 | 6.1759 | 7.4301 | 10.657 | 15.111 | 21.198 | 29.439 |
| 12 | 1.1268 | 1.2682 | 1.4258 | 1.6010 | 1.7959 | 2.0122 | 2.2522 | 2.5182 | 2.8127 | 3.1384 | 3.8960 | 4.8179 | 5.3502 | 5.9360 | 7.2876 | 8.9161 | 13.214 | 19.342 | 27.982 | 40.037 |
| 13 | 1.1381 | 1.2936 | 1.4685 | 1.6651 | 1.8856 | 2.1329 | 2.4098 | 2.7196 | 3.0658 | 3.4523 | 4.3635 | 5.4924 | 6.1528 | 6.8858 | 8.5994 | 10.699 | 16.386 | 24.748 | 36.937 | 54.451 |
| 14 | 1.1495 | 1.3195 | 1.5126 | 1.7317 | 1.9799 | 2.2609 | 2.5785 | 2.9372 | 3.3417 | 3.7975 | 4.8871 | 6.2613 | 7.0757 | 7.9875 | 10.147 | 12.839 | 20.319 | 31.691 | 48.756 | 74.053 |
| 15 | 1.1610 | 1.3459 | 1.5580 | 1.8009 | 2.0789 | 2.3966 | 2.7590 | 3.1722 | 3.6425 | 4.1772 | 5.4736 | 7.1379 | 8.1371 | 9.2655 | 11.973 | 15.407 | 25.195 | 40.564 | 64.358 | 100.71 |
| 16 | 1.1726 | 1.3728 | 1.6047 | 1.8730 | 2.1829 | 2.5404 | 2.9522 | 3.4259 | 3.9703 | 4.5950 | 6.1304 | 8.1372 | 9.3576 | 10.748 | 14.129 | 18.488 | 31.242 | 51.923 | 84.953 | 136.96 |
| 17 | 1.1834 | 1.4002 | 1.6528 | 1.9479 | 2.2920 | 2.6928 | 3.1588 | 3.7000 | 4.3276 | 5.0545 | 6.8660 | 9.2765 | 10.761 | 12.467 | 16.672 | 22.186 | 38.740 | 66.461 | 112.13 | 186.27 |
| 18 | 1.1961 | 1.4282 | 1.7024 | 2.0258 | 2.4066 | 2.8543 | 3.3799 | 3.9960 | 4.7171 | 5.5599 | 7.6900 | 10.575 | 12.375 | 14.462 | 19.673 | 26.623 | 48.038 | 85.070 | 148.02 | 253.33 |
| 19 | 1.2081 | 1.4568 | 1.7535 | 2.1068 | 2.5270 | 3.0256 | 3.6165 | 4.3157 | 5.1417 | 6.1159 | 8.6129 | 12.055 | 14.231 | 16.776 | 23.214 | 31.948 | 59.567 | 108.89 | 195.39 | 344.53 |
| 20 | 1.2202 | 1.4859 | 1.8061 | 2.1911 | 2.6533 | 3.2071 | 3.8697 | 4.6610 | 5.6044 | 6.7275 | 9.6463 | 13.743 | 16.366 | 19.460 | 27.393 | 38.337 | 73.864 | 139.37 | 257.91 | 468.57 |
| 21 | 1.2324 | 1.5157 | 1.8603 | 2.2788 | 2.7860 | 3.3996 | 4.1406 | 5.0338 | 6.1088 | 7.4002 | 10.803 | 15.667 | 18.821 | 22.574 | 32.323 | 46.005 | 91.591 | 178.40 | 340.44 | 637.26 |
| 22 | 1.2447 | 1.5460 | 1.9161 | 2.3699 | 2.9253 | 3.6035 | 4.4304 | 5.4365 | 6.6586 | 8.1403 | 12.100 | 17.861 | 21.644 | 26.186 | 38.142 | 55.206 | 113.57 | 228.35 | 449.39 | 866.67 |
| 23 | 1.2572 | 1.5769 | 1.9736 | 2.4647 | 3.0715 | 3.8197 | 4.7405 | 5.8715 | 7.2579 | 8.9543 | 13.552 | 20.361 | 24.891 | 30.376 | 45.007 | 66.247 | 140.83 | 292.30 | 593.19 | 1178.6 |
| 24 | 1.2697 | 1.6084 | 2.0328 | 2.5633 | 3.2251 | 4.0489 | 5.0724 | 6.3412 | 7.9111 | 9.8497 | 15.178 | 23.212 | 29.625 | 35.236 | 53.108 | 79.496 | 174.63 | 394.14 | 783.02 | 1602.9 |
| 25 | 1.2824 | 1.6406 | 2.0938 | 2.6658 | 3.3864 | 4.2919 | 5.4274 | 6.8485 | 8.6231 | 10.834 | 17.000 | 26.461 | 32.918 | 40.874 | 62.668 | 95.396 | 216.54 | 478.90 | 1033.5 | 2180.0 |
| 26 | 1.2953 | 1.6734 | 2.1566 | 2.7725 | 3.5557 | 4.5497 | 5.8074 | 7.3964 | 9.3992 | 11.918 | 19.040 | 30.166 | 37.856 | 47.414 | 73.948 | 114.47 | 268.51 | 612.99 | 1364.3 | 2964.9 |
| 27 | 1.3082 | 1.7069 | 2.2213 | 2.8834 | 3.7335 | 4.8223 | 6.2139 | 7.9881 | 10.245 | 13.110 | 21.324 | 34.389 | 43.535 | 55.000 | 87.259 | 137.37 | 332.95 | 784.63 | 1800.9 | 4032.2 |
| 28 | 1.3213 | 1.7410 | 2.2879 | 2.99897 | 3.9201 | 5.1117 | 6.6488 | 8.6271 | 11.167 | 14.421 | 23.883 | 39.204 | 50.065 | 63.800 | 102.96 | 164.84 | 412.86 | 1004.3 | 2377.2 | 5483.8 |
| 29 | 1.3345 | 1.7758 | 2.3566 | 3.1187 | 4.1161 | 5.4184 | 7.1143 | 9.3173 | 12.172 | 15.863 | 26.749 | 44.693 | 57.575 | 74.008 | 121.50 | 197.81 | 511.95 | 1285.5 | 3137.9 | 7458.0 |
| 30 | 1.3478 | 1.8114 | 2.4273 | 3.2434 | 4.3219 | 5.7435 | 7.6123 | 10.062 | 13.267 | 17.449 | 29.959 | 50.950 | 66.211 | 85.849 | 143.37 | 237.37 | 634.81 | 1645.5 | 4142.0 | 10143. |
| 40 | 1.4889 | 2.2080 | 3.2620 | 4.8010 | 7.0400 | 10.285 | 14.974 | 21.724 | 31.409 | 45.259 | 93.050 | 188.88 | 267.86 | 378.72 | 750.37 | 1469.7 | 5455.9 | 19426. | 66520 | • |
| 50 | 1.6446 | 2.6916 | 4.3839 | 7.1067 | 11.467 | 18.420 | 29.457 | 46.901 | 74.357 | 117.39 | 289.00 | 700.23 | 1083.6 | 1670.7 | 3927.3 | 9100.4 | 46890. | • | • | • |
| 60 | 1.8167 | 3.2810 | 5.8916 | 10.519 | 18.679 | 32.987 | 57.946 | 101.25 | 176.03 | 304.48 | 897.59 | 2595.9 | 4383.9 | 7370.1 | 20555 | 56347 | • | • | • | • |

Table 2
FUTURE VALUE OF AN ANNUITY OF $1

Interest Rate

| Number of Years | 1% | 2% | 3% | 4% | 5% | 6% | 7% | 8% | 9% | 10% | 12% | 14% | 15% | 16% | 18% | 20% | 24% | 28% | 32% | 36% |
|---|---|---|---|---|---|---|---|---|---|---|---|---|---|---|---|---|---|---|---|---|
| 1 | 1.0000 | 1.0000 | 1.0000 | 1.0000 | 1.0000 | 1.0000 | 1.0000 | 1.0000 | 1.0000 | 1.0000 | 1.0000 | 1.0000 | 1.0000 | 1.0000 | 1.0000 | 1.0000 | 1.0000 | 1.0000 | 1.0000 | 1.0000 |
| 2 | 2.0100 | 2.0200 | 2.0300 | 2.0400 | 2.0500 | 2.0600 | 2.0700 | 2.0800 | 2.0900 | 2.1000 | 2.1200 | 2.1400 | 2.1500 | 2.1600 | 2.1800 | 2.2000 | 2.2400 | 2.2800 | 2.3200 | 2.3600 |
| 3 | 3.0301 | 3.0604 | 3.0909 | 3.1216 | 3.1525 | 3.1836 | 3.2149 | 3.2464 | 3.2781 | 3.3100 | 3.3744 | 3.4396 | 3.4725 | 3.5056 | 3.5724 | 3.6400 | 3.7776 | 3.9184 | 4.0624 | 4.2096 |
| 4 | 4.0604 | 4.1216 | 4.1836 | 4.2465 | 4.3101 | 4.3746 | 4.4399 | 4.5061 | 4.5731 | 4.6410 | 4.7793 | 4.9211 | 4.9934 | 5.0665 | 5.2154 | 5.3680 | 5.6842 | 6.0156 | 6.3624 | 6.7251 |
| 5 | 5.1010 | 5.2040 | 5.3091 | 5.4163 | 5.5256 | 5.6371 | 5.7507 | 5.8666 | 5.9847 | 6.1051 | 6.3528 | 6.6101 | 6.7424 | 6.8771 | 7.1542 | 7.4416 | 8.0484 | 8.6999 | 9.3983 | 10.146 |
| 6 | 6.1520 | 6.3081 | 6.4684 | 6.6330 | 6.8019 | 6.9753 | 7.1533 | 7.3359 | 7.5233 | 7.7156 | 8.1152 | 8.5355 | 8.7537 | 8.9775 | 9.4420 | 9.9299 | 10.980 | 12.135 | 13.405 | 14.798 |
| 7 | 7.2135 | 7.4343 | 7.6625 | 7.8983 | 8.1420 | 8.3938 | 8.6540 | 8.9228 | 9.2004 | 9.4872 | 10.089 | 10.730 | 11.066 | 11.413 | 12.141 | 12.915 | 14.615 | 16.533 | 18.695 | 21.126 |
| 8 | 8.2857 | 8.5830 | 8.8923 | 9.2142 | 9.5491 | 9.8975 | 10.259 | 10.636 | 11.028 | 11.435 | 12.299 | 13.232 | 13.726 | 14.240 | 15.327 | 16.499 | 19.122 | 22.163 | 25.678 | 29.731 |
| 9 | 9.3685 | 9.7546 | 10.159 | 10.582 | 11.026 | 11.491 | 11.978 | 12.487 | 13.021 | 13.579 | 14.775 | 16.085 | 16.785 | 17.518 | 19.085 | 20.798 | 24.712 | 29.369 | 34.895 | 41.435 |
| 10 | 10.462 | 10.949 | 11.463 | 12.006 | 12.577 | 13.180 | 13.816 | 14.486 | 15.192 | 15.937 | 17.548 | 19.337 | 20.303 | 21.321 | 23.521 | 25.958 | 31.643 | 38.592 | 47.061 | 57.351 |
| 11 | 11.566 | 12.168 | 12.807 | 13.486 | 14.206 | 14.971 | 15.783 | 16.645 | 17.560 | 18.531 | 20.654 | 23.044 | 24.349 | 25.732 | 28.755 | 32.150 | 40.237 | 50.398 | 63.121 | 78.998 |
| 12 | 12.682 | 13.412 | 14.192 | 15.025 | 15.917 | 16.869 | 17.888 | 18.977 | 20.140 | 21.384 | 24.133 | 27.270 | 29.001 | 30.850 | 34.931 | 39.580 | 50.894 | 65.510 | 84.320 | 108.43 |
| 13 | 13.809 | 14.680 | 15.617 | 16.626 | 17.713 | 18.882 | 20.140 | 21.495 | 22.953 | 24.522 | 28.029 | 32.088 | 34.351 | 36.786 | 42.218 | 48.496 | 64.109 | 84.852 | 112.30 | 148.47 |
| 14 | 14.947 | 15.973 | 17.086 | 18.291 | 19.598 | 21.015 | 22.550 | 24.214 | 26.019 | 27.975 | 32.392 | 37.581 | 40.504 | 43.672 | 50.818 | 59.195 | 80.496 | 109.61 | 149.23 | 202.92 |
| 15 | 16.096 | 17.293 | 18.598 | 20.023 | 21.578 | 23.276 | 25.129 | 27.152 | 29.360 | 31.772 | 37.279 | 43.842 | 47.580 | 51.659 | 60.965 | 72.035 | 100.81 | 141.30 | 197.99 | 276.97 |
| 16 | 17.257 | 18.639 | 20.156 | 21.824 | 23.657 | 25.672 | 27.888 | 30.324 | 33.003 | 35.949 | 42.753 | 50.980 | 55.717 | 60.925 | 72.939 | 87.442 | 126.01 | 181.86 | 262.35 | 377.69 |
| 17 | 18.430 | 20.012 | 21.761 | 23.697 | 25.840 | 28.212 | 30.840 | 33.750 | 36.973 | 40.544 | 48.883 | 59.117 | 65.075 | 71.673 | 87.068 | 105.93 | 157.25 | 233.79 | 347.30 | 514.66 |
| 18 | 19.614 | 21.412 | 23.414 | 25.645 | 28.132 | 30.905 | 33.99 | 37.450 | 41.301 | 45.599 | 55.749 | 68.394 | 75.836 | 84.140 | 103.74 | 128.11 | 195.99 | 300.25 | 459.44 | 700.93 |
| 19 | 20.810 | 22.840 | 25.116 | 27.671 | 30.539 | 33.760 | 37.379 | 41.446 | 46.018 | 51.159 | 63.439 | 78.969 | 88.211 | 98.603 | 123.41 | 154.74 | 244.03 | 385.32 | 607.47 | 954.27 |
| 20 | 22.019 | 24.297 | 26.870 | 29.778 | 33.066 | 36.785 | 40.995 | 45.762 | 51.160 | 57.275 | 72.052 | 91.024 | 102.44 | 115.37 | 146.62 | 186.68 | 303.60 | 494.21 | 802.86 | 1298.8 |
| 21 | 23.239 | 25.783 | 28.676 | 31.969 | 35.719 | 39.992 | 44.865 | 50.442 | 56.764 | 64.002 | 81.698 | 104.76 | 118.81 | 134.84 | 174.02 | 225.02 | 377.46 | 633.59 | 1060.7 | 1767.3 |
| 22 | 24.471 | 27.299 | 30.536 | 34.248 | 38.505 | 43.392 | 49.005 | 55.456 | 62.873 | 71.402 | 92.502 | 120.43 | 137.63 | 157.41 | 206.34 | 271.03 | 469.05 | 811.99 | 1401.2 | 2404.6 |
| 23 | 25.716 | 28.845 | 32.452 | 36.617 | 41.430 | 46.995 | 53.436 | 60.893 | 69.531 | 79.543 | 104.60 | 138.29 | 159.27 | 183.60 | 244.48 | 326.23 | 582.62 | 1040.3 | 1850.6 | 3271.3 |
| 24 | 26.973 | 30.421 | 34.426 | 39.082 | 44.502 | 50.815 | 58.176 | 66.764 | 76.789 | 88.497 | 118.15 | 158.65 | 184.16 | 213.97 | 289.49 | 392.48 | 723.46 | 1332.6 | 2443.8 | 4449.9 |
| 25 | 28.243 | 32.030 | 36.459 | 41.645 | 47.727 | 54.864 | 63.249 | 73.105 | 84.700 | 98.347 | 133.33 | 181.87 | 212.79 | 249.21 | 342.60 | 471.98 | 898.09 | 1706.8 | 3226.8 | 6052.9 |
| 26 | 29.525 | 33.670 | 38.553 | 44.311 | 51.113 | 59.156 | 68.676 | 79.954 | 93.323 | 109.18 | 150.33 | 208.33 | 245.71 | 290.08 | 405.27 | 567.37 | 1114.6 | 2185.7 | 4260.4 | 8233.0 |
| 27 | 30.820 | 35.344 | 40.709 | 47.084 | 54.669 | 63.705 | 74.483 | 87.350 | 102.72 | 121.09 | 169.37 | 238.49 | 283.56 | 337.50 | 479.22 | 681.85 | 1383.1 | 2798.7 | 5624.7 | 11197.9 |
| 28 | 32.129 | 37.051 | 42.930 | 49.967 | 58.402 | 68.528 | 80.697 | 95.338 | 112.96 | 134.20 | 190.69 | 272.88 | 327.10 | 392.50 | 566.48 | 819.22 | 1716.0 | 3583.3 | 7425.6 | 15230.2 |
| 29 | 33.450 | 38.792 | 45.218 | 52.966 | 62.322 | 73.689 | 87.346 | 103.96 | 124.13 | 148.63 | 214.58 | 312.09 | 377.16 | 456.30 | 669.44 | 984.06 | 2128.9 | 4587.6 | 9802.9 | 20714.1 |
| 30 | 34.784 | 40.568 | 47.576 | 56.084 | 66.438 | 79.058 | 94.460 | 113.28 | 136.30 | 164.49 | 241.33 | 356.78 | 434.74 | 530.31 | 790.94 | 1181.8 | 2640.9 | 5873.2 | 12940 | 28172.2 |
| 40 | 48.886 | 60.402 | 75.401 | 95.025 | 120.79 | 154.76 | 199.63 | 259.05 | 337.88 | 442.59 | 767.09 | 1342.0 | 1779.0 | 2360.7 | 4163.2 | 7343.8 | 22728 | 63977 | • | • |
| 50 | 64.463 | 84.579 | 112.79 | 152.66 | 209.34 | 290.33 | 406.52 | 573.76 | 815.08 | 1163.9 | 2400.0 | 4994.5 | 7217.7 | 10435 | 21813 | 45497 | • | • | • | • |
| 60 | 81.669 | 114.05 | 163.05 | 237.90 | 353.58 | 533.12 | 813.52 | 1253.2 | 1944.7 | 3034.8 | 7471.6 | 18535 | 29219 | 46057 | • | • | • | • | • | • |

# Table 3
## PRESENT VALUE OF $1

*Interest Rate*

| Number of Years | 1% | 2% | 3% | 4% | 5% | 6% | 7% | 8% | 9% | 10% | 12% | 14% | 15% | 16% | 18% | 20% | 24% | 28% | 32% | 36% |
|---|---|---|---|---|---|---|---|---|---|---|---|---|---|---|---|---|---|---|---|---|
| 1 | 0.9901 | 0.9804 | 0.9709 | 0.9615 | 0.9524 | 0.9434 | 0.9346 | 0.9259 | 0.9174 | 0.9091 | 0.8929 | 0.8772 | 0.8696 | 0.8621 | 0.8475 | 0.8333 | 0.8065 | 0.7813 | 0.7576 | 0.7353 |
| 2 | 0.9803 | 0.9612 | 0.9426 | 0.9246 | 0.9070 | 0.8900 | 0.8734 | 0.8573 | 0.8417 | 0.8264 | 0.7972 | 0.7695 | 0.7561 | 0.7432 | 0.7182 | 0.6944 | 0.6504 | 0.6104 | 0.5739 | 0.5407 |
| 3 | 0.9706 | 0.9423 | 0.9151 | 0.8890 | 0.8638 | 0.8396 | 0.8163 | 0.7938 | 0.7722 | 0.7513 | 0.7118 | 0.6750 | 0.6575 | 0.6407 | 0.6086 | 0.5787 | 0.5245 | 0.4768 | 0.4348 | 0.3975 |
| 4 | 0.9610 | 0.9238 | 0.8885 | 0.8548 | 0.8227 | 0.7921 | 0.7629 | 0.7350 | 0.7084 | 0.6830 | 0.6355 | 0.5921 | 0.5718 | 0.5523 | 0.5158 | 0.4823 | 0.4230 | 0.3725 | 0.3294 | 0.2923 |
| 5 | 0.9515 | 0.9057 | 0.8626 | 0.8219 | 0.7835 | 0.7473 | 0.7130 | 0.6806 | 0.6499 | 0.6209 | 0.5674 | 0.5194 | 0.4972 | 0.4761 | 0.4371 | 0.4019 | 0.3411 | 0.2910 | 0.2495 | 0.2149 |
| 6 | 0.9420 | 0.8880 | 0.8375 | 0.7903 | 0.7462 | 0.7050 | 0.6663 | 0.6302 | 0.5963 | 0.5645 | 0.5066 | 0.4556 | 0.4323 | 0.4104 | 0.3704 | 0.3349 | 0.2751 | 0.2274 | 0.1890 | 0.1580 |
| 7 | 0.9327 | 0.8706 | 0.8131 | 0.7599 | 0.7107 | 0.6651 | 0.6227 | 0.5835 | 0.5470 | 0.5132 | 0.4523 | 0.3996 | 0.3759 | 0.3538 | 0.3139 | 0.2791 | 0.2218 | 0.1776 | 0.1432 | 0.1162 |
| 8 | 0.9235 | 0.8535 | 0.7894 | 0.7307 | 0.6768 | 0.6274 | 0.5820 | 0.5403 | 0.5019 | 0.4665 | 0.4039 | 0.3506 | 0.3269 | 0.3050 | 0.2660 | 0.2326 | 0.1789 | 0.1388 | 0.1085 | 0.0854 |
| 9 | 0.9143 | 0.8368 | 0.7664 | 0.7026 | 0.6446 | 0.5919 | 0.5439 | 0.5002 | 0.4604 | 0.4241 | 0.3606 | 0.3075 | 0.2843 | 0.2630 | 0.2255 | 0.1938 | 0.1443 | 0.1084 | 0.0822 | 0.0628 |
| 10 | 0.9053 | 0.8203 | 0.7441 | 0.6756 | 0.6139 | 0.5584 | 0.5083 | 0.4632 | 0.4224 | 0.3855 | 0.3220 | 0.2697 | 0.2472 | 0.2267 | 0.1911 | 0.1615 | 0.1164 | 0.0847 | 0.0623 | 0.0462 |
| 11 | 0.8963 | 0.8043 | 0.7224 | 0.6496 | 0.5847 | 0.5268 | 0.4751 | 0.4289 | 0.3875 | 0.3505 | 0.2875 | 0.2366 | 0.2149 | 0.1954 | 0.1619 | 0.1346 | 0.0938 | 0.0662 | 0.0472 | 0.0340 |
| 12 | 0.8874 | 0.7885 | 0.7014 | 0.6246 | 0.5568 | 0.4970 | 0.4440 | 0.3971 | 0.3555 | 0.3186 | 0.2567 | 0.2076 | 0.1869 | 0.1685 | 0.1372 | 0.1122 | 0.0757 | 0.0517 | 0.0357 | 0.0250 |
| 13 | 0.8787 | 0.7730 | 0.6810 | 0.6006 | 0.5303 | 0.4688 | 0.4150 | 0.3677 | 0.3262 | 0.2897 | 0.2292 | 0.1821 | 0.1625 | 0.1452 | 0.1163 | 0.0935 | 0.0610 | 0.0404 | 0.0271 | 0.0184 |
| 14 | 0.8700 | 0.7579 | 0.6611 | 0.5775 | 0.5051 | 0.4423 | 0.3878 | 0.3405 | 0.2992 | 0.2633 | 0.2046 | 0.1597 | 0.1413 | 0.1252 | 0.0985 | 0.0779 | 0.0492 | 0.0316 | 0.0205 | 0.0135 |
| 15 | 0.8613 | 0.7430 | 0.6419 | 0.5553 | 0.4810 | 0.4173 | 0.3624 | 0.3152 | 0.2745 | 0.2394 | 0.1827 | 0.1401 | 0.1229 | 0.1079 | 0.0835 | 0.0649 | 0.0397 | 0.0247 | 0.0155 | 0.0099 |
| 16 | 0.8528 | 0.7284 | 0.6232 | 0.5339 | 0.4581 | 0.3936 | 0.3387 | 0.2919 | 0.2519 | 0.2176 | 0.1631 | 0.1229 | 0.1069 | 0.0930 | 0.0708 | 0.0541 | 0.0320 | 0.0193 | 0.0118 | 0.0073 |
| 17 | 0.8444 | 0.7142 | 0.6050 | 0.5134 | 0.4363 | 0.3714 | 0.3166 | 0.2703 | 0.2311 | 0.1978 | 0.1456 | 0.1078 | 0.0929 | 0.0802 | 0.0600 | 0.0451 | 0.0258 | 0.0150 | 0.0089 | 0.0054 |
| 18 | 0.8360 | 0.7002 | 0.5874 | 0.4936 | 0.4155 | 0.3503 | 0.2959 | 0.2502 | 0.2120 | 0.1799 | 0.1300 | 0.0946 | 0.0808 | 0.0691 | 0.0508 | 0.0376 | 0.0208 | 0.0118 | 0.0068 | 0.0038 |
| 19 | 0.8277 | 0.6864 | 0.5703 | 0.4746 | 0.3957 | 0.3305 | 0.2765 | 0.2317 | 0.1945 | 0.1635 | 0.1161 | 0.0829 | 0.0703 | 0.0596 | 0.0431 | 0.0313 | 0.0168 | 0.0092 | 0.0051 | 0.0029 |
| 20 | 0.8195 | 0.6730 | 0.5537 | 0.4564 | 0.3769 | 0.3118 | 0.2584 | 0.2145 | 0.1784 | 0.1486 | 0.1037 | 0.0728 | 0.0611 | 0.0514 | 0.0365 | 0.0261 | 0.0135 | 0.0072 | 0.0039 | 0.0021 |
| 25 | 0.7798 | 0.6095 | 0.4776 | 0.3751 | 0.2953 | 0.2330 | 0.1842 | 0.1460 | 0.1160 | 0.0923 | 0.0588 | 0.0378 | 0.0304 | 0.0245 | 0.0160 | 0.0105 | 0.0046 | 0.0021 | 0.0010 | 0.0005 |
| 30 | 0.7419 | 0.5521 | 0.4120 | 0.3083 | 0.2314 | 0.1741 | 0.1314 | 0.0994 | 0.0754 | 0.0573 | 0.0334 | 0.0196 | 0.0151 | 0.0116 | 0.0070 | 0.0042 | 0.0016 | 0.0006 | 0.0002 | 0.0001 |
| 40 | 0.6717 | 0.4529 | 0.3066 | 0.2083 | 0.1420 | 0.0972 | 0.0668 | 0.0460 | 0.0318 | 0.0221 | 0.0107 | 0.0053 | 0.0037 | 0.0026 | 0.0013 | 0.0007 | 0.0002 | 0.0001 | | |
| 50 | 0.6080 | 0.3715 | 0.2281 | 0.1407 | 0.0872 | 0.0543 | 0.0339 | 0.0213 | 0.0132 | 0.0085 | 0.0035 | 0.0014 | 0.0009 | 0.0006 | 0.0003 | 0.0001 | • | • | • | • |
| 60 | 0.5504 | 0.3048 | 0.1697 | 0.0951 | 0.0535 | 0.0303 | 0.0173 | 0.0099 | 0.0057 | 0.0033 | 0.0011 | 0.0004 | 0.0002 | 0.0001 | • | • | • | • | • | • |

## Table 4
### PRESENT VALUE OF AN ANNUITY OF $1

*Interest Rate*

| Number of Years | 1% | 2% | 3% | 4% | 5% | 6% | 7% | 8% | 9% | 10% | 12% | 14% | 15% | 16% | 18% | 20% | 24% | 28% | 32% |
|---|---|---|---|---|---|---|---|---|---|---|---|---|---|---|---|---|---|---|---|
| 1 | 0.9901 | 0.9804 | 0.9709 | 0.9615 | 0.9524 | 0.9434 | 0.9346 | 0.9259 | 0.9174 | 0.9091 | 0.8929 | 0.8772 | 0.8696 | 0.8621 | 0.8475 | 0.8333 | 0.8065 | 0.7813 | 0.7576 |
| 2 | 1.9704 | 1.9415 | 1.9135 | 1.8861 | 1.8594 | 1.8334 | 1.8080 | 1.7833 | 1.7591 | 1.7355 | 1.6901 | 1.6467 | 1.6257 | 1.6052 | 1.5656 | 1.5278 | 1.4568 | 1.3916 | 1.3315 |
| 3 | 2.9410 | 2.8839 | 2.8286 | 2.7751 | 2.7232 | 2.6730 | 2.6243 | 2.5771 | 2.5313 | 2.4869 | 2.4018 | 2.3216 | 2.2832 | 2.2459 | 2.1743 | 2.1065 | 1.9813 | 1.8684 | 1.7663 |
| 4 | 3.9020 | 3.8077 | 3.7171 | 3.6299 | 3.5460 | 3.4651 | 3.3872 | 3.3121 | 3.2397 | 3.1699 | 3.0373 | 2.9137 | 2.8550 | 2.7982 | 2.6901 | 2.5887 | 2.4043 | 2.2410 | 2.0957 |
| 5 | 4.8534 | 4.7135 | 4.5797 | 4.4518 | 4.3295 | 4.2124 | 4.1002 | 3.9927 | 3.8897 | 3.7908 | 3.6048 | 3.4331 | 3.3522 | 3.2743 | 3.1272 | 2.9906 | 2.7454 | 2.5320 | 2.3452 |
| 6 | 5.7955 | 5.6014 | 5.4172 | 5.2421 | 5.0757 | 4.9173 | 4.7665 | 4.6229 | 4.4859 | 4.3553 | 4.1114 | 3.8887 | 3.7845 | 3.6847 | 3.4976 | 3.3255 | 3.0205 | 2.7594 | 2.5342 |
| 7 | 6.7282 | 6.4720 | 6.2303 | 6.0021 | 5.7864 | 5.5824 | 5.3893 | 5.2064 | 5.0330 | 4.8684 | 4.5638 | 4.2883 | 4.1604 | 4.0386 | 3.8115 | 3.6046 | 3.2423 | 2.9370 | 2.6775 |
| 8 | 7.6517 | 7.3255 | 7.0197 | 6.7327 | 6.4632 | 6.2098 | 5.9713 | 5.7466 | 5.5348 | 5.3349 | 4.9676 | 4.6389 | 4.4873 | 4.3436 | 4.0776 | 3.8372 | 3.4212 | 3.0758 | 2.7860 |
| 9 | 8.5660 | 8.1622 | 7.7861 | 7.4353 | 7.1078 | 6.8017 | 6.5152 | 6.2469 | 5.9952 | 5.7590 | 5.3282 | 4.9464 | 4.7716 | 4.6065 | 4.3030 | 4.1925 | 3.5655 | 3.1842 | 2.8681 |
| 10 | 9.4713 | 8.9826 | 8.5302 | 8.1109 | 7.7217 | 7.3601 | 7.0236 | 6.7101 | 6.4177 | 6.1446 | 5.6502 | 5.2161 | 5.0188 | 4.8332 | 4.4941 | 4.3271 | 3.6819 | 3.2689 | 2.9304 |
| 11 | 10.3676 | 9.7858 | 9.2526 | 8.7605 | 8.3064 | 7.8869 | 7.4987 | 7.1390 | 6.8052 | 6.4951 | 5.9377 | 5.4527 | 5.2337 | 5.1971 | 4.6560 | 4.4392 | 3.7757 | 3.3351 | 2.9776 |
| 12 | 11.2551 | 10.5753 | 9.9540 | 9.3851 | 8.8633 | 8.3838 | 7.9427 | 7.5361 | 7.1607 | 6.8137 | 6.1944 | 5.6603 | 5.4206 | 5.3423 | 4.7932 | 4.5327 | 3.8514 | 3.3868 | 3.0133 |
| 13 | 12.1337 | 11.3484 | 10.6350 | 9.9856 | 9.3936 | 8.8527 | 8.3577 | 7.9038 | 7.4889 | 7.1034 | 6.4235 | 5.8424 | 5.5831 | 5.4675 | 4.9095 | 4.6106 | 3.9124 | 3.4272 | 3.0404 |
| 14 | 13.0037 | 12.1062 | 11.2961 | 10.5631 | 9.8986 | 9.2950 | 8.7455 | 8.2442 | 7.7862 | 7.3667 | 6.6282 | 6.0021 | 5.7245 | 5.5755 | 5.0081 | 4.6755 | 3.9616 | 3.4587 | 3.0609 |
| 15 | 13.8651 | 12.8493 | 11.9379 | 11.1184 | 10.3797 | 9.7122 | 9.1079 | 8.5595 | 8.0607 | 7.6061 | 6.8109 | 6.1422 | 5.8474 | 5.6685 | 5.0916 | 4.7296 | 4.0013 | 3.4834 | 3.0764 |
| 16 | 14.7179 | 13.5777 | 12.5611 | 11.6523 | 10.8378 | 10.1059 | 9.4466 | 8.8514 | 8.3126 | 7.8237 | 6.9740 | 6.2651 | 5.9542 | 5.7487 | 5.1724 | 4.7746 | 4.0333 | 3.5026 | 3.0882 |
| 17 | 15.5623 | 14.2919 | 13.1661 | 12.1657 | 11.2741 | 10.4773 | 9.7632 | 9.1216 | 8.5436 | 8.0216 | 7.1196 | 6.3729 | 6.0472 | 5.8178 | 5.2223 | 4.8122 | 4.0591 | 3.5177 | 3.0971 |
| 18 | 16.3983 | 14.9920 | 13.7535 | 12.6593 | 11.6896 | 10.8276 | 10.0591 | 9.3719 | 8.7556 | 8.2014 | 7.2497 | 6.4674 | 6.1280 | 5.8775 | 5.2732 | 4.8435 | 4.0799 | 3.5294 | 3.1039 |
| 19 | 17.2260 | 15.6785 | 14.3238 | 13.1339 | 12.0853 | 11.1581 | 10.3356 | 9.6036 | 8.9501 | 8.3649 | 7.3658 | 6.5504 | 6.1982 | 5.9288 | 5.3162 | 4.8696 | 4.0967 | 3.5386 | 3.1090 |
| 20 | 18.0456 | 16.3514 | 14.8775 | 13.5903 | 12.4622 | 11.4699 | 10.5940 | 9.8181 | 9.1285 | 8.5136 | 7.4694 | 6.6231 | 6.2593 | 6.0971 | 5.3527 | 4.9476 | 4.1103 | 3.5458 | 3.1129 |
| 25 | 22.0232 | 19.5235 | 17.4131 | 15.6221 | 14.0939 | 12.7834 | 11.6536 | 10.6748 | 9.8226 | 9.0770 | 7.8431 | 6.8729 | 6.4641 | 6.1772 | 5.4669 | 4.9789 | 4.1474 | 3.5640 | 3.1220 |
| 30 | 25.8077 | 22.3965 | 19.6004 | 17.2920 | 15.3725 | 13.7648 | 12.4090 | 11.2578 | 10.2737 | 9.4269 | 8.0552 | 7.0072 | 6.5660 | 6.2335 | 5.5168 | 4.9966 | 4.1601 | 3.5693 | 3.1242 |
| 40 | 32.8347 | 27.3555 | 23.1148 | 19.7928 | 17.1591 | 15.0463 | 13.3317 | 11.9246 | 10.7574 | 9.7791 | 8.2438 | 7.1050 | 6.6418 | 6.2463 | 5.5482 | 4.9995 | 4.1659 | 3.5712 | 3.1250 |
| 50 | 39.1961 | 31.4236 | 25.7298 | 21.4822 | 18.2559 | 15.7619 | 13.8007 | 12.2335 | 10.9617 | 9.9148 | 8.3045 | 7.1327 | 6.6605 | 6.2492 | 5.5541 | 4.9999 | 4.1666 | 3.5714 | 3.1250 |
| 60 | 44.9550 | 34.7609 | 27.8656 | 22.6235 | 18.9293 | 16.1614 | 14.0392 | 12.3766 | 11.0480 | 9.9672 | 8.3240 | 7.1401 | 6.6651 | 6.2492 | 5.5553 | 4.9999 | 4.1667 | 3.5714 | 3.1250 |

# STATISTICAL TABLES

**Table 5**
*t-DISTRIBUTION TABLE*

**Values of t**

| d.f. | t0.100 | t0.050 | t0.025 | t0.010 | t0.005 | d.f. |
|------|--------|--------|--------|--------|--------|------|
| 1 | 3.078 | 6.314 | 12.706 | 31.821 | 63.657 | 1 |
| 2 | 1.886 | 2.920 | 4.303 | 6.965 | 9.925 | 2 |
| 3 | 1.638 | 2.353 | 3.182 | 4.541 | 5.841 | 3 |
| 4 | 1.533 | 2.132 | 2.776 | 3.747 | 4.604 | 4 |
| 5 | 1.476 | 2.015 | 2.571 | 3.365 | 4.032 | 5 |
| 6 | 1.440 | 1.943 | 2.447 | 3.143 | 3.707 | 6 |
| 7 | 1.415 | 1.895 | 2.365 | 2.998 | 3.499 | 7 |
| 8 | 1.397 | 1.860 | 2.306 | 2.896 | 3.355 | 8 |
| 9 | 1.383 | 1.833 | 2.262 | 2.821 | 3.250 | 9 |
| 10 | 1.372 | 1.812 | 2.228 | 2.764 | 3.169 | 10 |
| 11 | 1.363 | 1.796 | 2.201 | 2.718 | 3.106 | 11 |
| 12 | 1.356 | 1.782 | 2.179 | 2.681 | 3.055 | 12 |
| 13 | 1.350 | 1.771 | 2.160 | 2.650 | 3.012 | 13 |
| 14 | 1.345 | 1.761 | 2.145 | 2.624 | 2.977 | 14 |
| 15 | 1.341 | 1.753 | 2.131 | 2.602 | 2.947 | 15 |
| 16 | 1.337 | 1.746 | 2.120 | 2.583 | 2.921 | 16 |
| 17 | 1.333 | 1.740 | 2.110 | 2.567 | 2.898 | 17 |
| 18 | 1.330 | 1.734 | 2.101 | 2.552 | 2.878 | 18 |
| 19 | 1.328 | 1.729 | 2.093 | 2.539 | 2.861 | 19 |
| 20 | 1.325 | 1.725 | 2.086 | 2.528 | 2.845 | 20 |
| 21 | 1.323 | 1.721 | 2.080 | 2.518 | 2.831 | 21 |
| 22 | 1.321 | 1.717 | 2.074 | 2.508 | 2.819 | 22 |
| 23 | 1.319 | 1.714 | 2.069 | 2.500 | 2.807 | 23 |
| 24 | 1.318 | 1.711 | 2.064 | 2.492 | 2.797 | 24 |
| 25 | 1.316 | 1.708 | 2.060 | 2.485 | 2.787 | 25 |
| 26 | 1.315 | 1.706 | 2.056 | 2.479 | 2.779 | 26 |
| 27 | 1.314 | 1.703 | 2.052 | 2.473 | 2.771 | 27 |
| 28 | 1.313 | 1.701 | 2.048 | 2.467 | 2.763 | 28 |
| 29 | 1.311 | 1.699 | 2.045 | 2.462 | 2.756 | 29 |
| Inf. | 1.282 | 1.645 | 1.960 | 2.326 | 2.576 | Inf. |

The *t*-value describes the sampling distribution of a deviation from a population value divided by the standard error.

Degrees of freedom (d.f.) are in the first column. The probabilities indicated as subvalues of *t* in the heading refer to the sum of a one-tailed area under the curve that lies outside the point *t*.

For example, in the distribution of the means of samples of size $n = 10$, d.f. $= n - 2 = 8$; then 0.025 of the area under the curve falls in one tail outside the interval $t \pm 2.306$.

# LIST OF POPULAR BUDGETING SOFTWARE

In addition to specialized budgeting and financial modeling software discussed in Chapter 19, the variety of computer software designed specifically for budgeting includes *stand-alone* packages, *templates*, and spreadsheet *add-ins*.

### 1. Budget Express

Budget Express "understands" the structure of financial worksheets and concepts such as months, quarters, years, totals, and subtotals, speeding up budget and forecast preparation. The program creates column headers for months, automatically totals columns and rows, and calculates quarterly and yearly summaries. And for sophisticated "what if" analyses, just specify your goal and Budget Express displays your current and target values as you make changes.
(Add-in)

### 2. ProPlans

ProPlans creates your financial plan automatically and accurately— and slices months from your annual planning and reporting process. You

413

simply enter your forecast data and assumptions into easy-to-follow, comprehensive data-entry screens, and ProPlans automatically creates the detailed financials you need to run your business for the next year—your income statement, balance sheet, cash flow statements, receipts and disbursements cash flow statements, and ratio reports.
(Template)

### 3. Profit Planner

Profit Planner provides titles and amounts for revenues, cost of sales, expenses, assets, liabilities, and equity in a ready-to-use 1-2-3 template. Financial tables are automatically generated on screen. It presents results in 13 table formats, including a pro forma earnings statement, balance sheet, and cash flow. Profit Planner even compares your earnings statement, balance sheet, and ratios against industry averages, so you're not working in a vacuum.
(Template)

### 4. Up Your Cash Flow

The program generates cash flow and profit & loss forecasts, detailed sales by product/product line and payroll by employee forecasts, monthly balance sheets, bar graphs, ratio and break-even analyses & more.
(Stand-alone)

### 5. Cash Collector

This program assists you in reviewing and aging receivables. You always know who owes what. Nothing falls through the cracks. When collection action is required, simply click through menu-driven screens to automatically generate letters and other professionally written collection documents (all included) that are proven to pull in the payments.
(Stand-alone)

### 6. Cash Flow Analysis

This software provides projections of cash inflow and cash outflow. You enter data into eight categories: sales, cost of sales, general and administrative expense, long-term debt, other cash receipts, inventory build-up/reduction, capital expenditures (acquisition of long-term assets such as store furniture), and income tax. The program allows changes in assump-

tions and scenarios and provides a complete array of reports.
(Stand-alone)

### 7. Quicken

This program is a fast, easy to use, inexpensive accounting and budgeting program that can help you manage your small business. You record bills as postdated transactions when they arrive and the program's *Billminder* feature automatically reminds you when bills are due. Then, you can print checks for due bills with a few keystrokes. Similarly, you can record invoices and track aged receivables. Together, these features help you to maximize cash on hand.
(Stand-alone)

### 8. Inventory Analyst

Inventory Analyst tells precisely how much inventory to order and when to order it. Choose from four carefully explained ordering methods: economic order quantity (EOQ), fixed order quantity, fixed months requirements, and level load by work days. And Inventory Analysts ensures that you'll always have enough stock to get you through your ordering period.

Load up to 48 months of inventory history and Inventory Analyst makes the forecast based on time series, exponential smoothing, or moving averages. It explains which method is best for you. Inventory Analyst will adjust your forecast for seasonality, too.
(Template)

### 9. CapPLANS

CapPLANS evaluates profitability based on Net Present Value (NPV), Internal Rate of Return (IRR), and payout period. Choose among five depreciation methods, including Modified Accelerated Cost Recovery System (MACRS). Run up to four sensitivity analyses. And project profitability over a 15-year horizon.

In addition to a complete report of your analysis, CapPLANS generates a concise executive summary—great for expediting approval. Add ready-made graphs to illustrate profitability clearly, at a glance.
(Template)

### 10. Project Evaluation Toolkit

It calculates the dollar value of your project based on six valuation methods, including discounted cash flow and impact on the corporate balance sheet. Assess intangibles such as impact on corporate strategy, investors, or labor relations. And use scenario planning to show the effects of changing start dates, sales forecasts, and other critical variables.
(Template)

### 11. @Risk

How will a new competitor affect your market share? @RISK calculates the likelihood of changes and events that affect your bottom line. First, use @Risk's familiar @ functions to define the risk in your worksheet. Then, let @Risk run thousands of what-if tests using one of two proven statistical sampling techniques—Monte Carlo or Latin Hypercube. You get a clear, colorful graph that tells you the likelihood of every possible bottom-line value. At a glance you'll know if your risk is acceptable or if you need to make a contingency plan.
(Add-in)

### 12. CFO Spreadsheet Applications

These ready-to-use spreadsheet templates offer easy ways to make many financial decisions. They are divided into four modules: cash management, tax strategies, capital budgeting, and advanced topics.
(Template)

# GLOSSARY OF BUDGETING TERMS

ADMINISTRATIVE BUDGET a formal and comprehensive financial plan through which management may control day-to-day business affairs and activities.

ALLOTMENT part of an appropriation which may be encumbered or expended during an allotment period, which is usually less than one fiscal year. Bimonthly and quarterly allotment periods are most common.

ANALYSIS OF VARIANCES analysis and investigation of causes for variances between standard costs and actual costs. It is also called variance analysis. A variance is considered favorable if actual costs are less than standard costs. It is unfavorable if actual costs exceed standard costs.

ANNUAL BUDGET a budget prepared for a calendar or fiscal year. *See also* Long Range Budget.

BALANCED BUDGET a budget in which total expenditures equal total revenue. An entity has a budget surplus if expenditures are less than tax revenues. It has a budget deficit if expenditures are greater than tax revenues.

BREAK-EVEN ANALYSIS analysis that determines the break-even sales, which is the level of sales where total costs equal total revenue. See Contribution Margin Analysis.

BREAK-EVEN CHART the chart where sales revenue, variable costs, and fixed costs are plotted on the vertical axis while volume, x, is plotted on the horizontal axis. The break-even point is the point where the total sales revenue line intersects the total cost line.

PV CHART *See* Profit-Volume Chart.

BREAK-EVEN SALES the sales which results in there being no profit or loss, also called break-even point. It is the sales volume, in units or in dollars, where total sales revenue equals total costs. Thus, zero profit results. *See also* Break-Even Analysis.

BUDGET a quantitative plan of activities and programs expressed in terms of the assets, equities, revenues, and expenses which will be involved in carrying out the plans, or in other quantitative terms such as units of product or service. The budget expresses the organizational goals in terms of specific financial and operating objectives. *See also* Master Budget.

BUDGET CONTROL budgetary actions carried out according to a budget plan. Through the use of a budget as a standard, an organization ensures that managers are implementing its plans and objectives and their activities are appraised by comparing their actual performance against budgeted performance. Budgets are used as a basis for rewarding or punishing them, or perhaps for modifying future budgets and plans.

BUDGET VARIANCE 1. any difference between a budgeted figure and an actual figure. 2. flexible budget variance. This is the difference between actual factory overhead costs and standard (flexible budget) costs, multiplied by the standard units of activity allowed for actual production. The budget variance is used in the two-way analysis of factory overhead. It includes the fixed and variable spending variances and the variable overhead efficiency variance which are used in the three-way analysis.

BUDGETING FUND annual budgets of estimated revenues and expenditures prepared for most governmental funds. The approved budgets of such funds are recorded in budgetary accounts in the accounting system to provide control over revenues and expenditures.

BUDGETING MODELS mathematical models that generate a profit planning budget. The models help planners and budget analysts answer a variety of what-if questions. The resultant calculations provide a basis for choice among alternatives under conditions of uncertainty.

CAPITAL BUDGET  a budget or plan of proposed acquisitions and re-placements of long-term assets and their financing. A capital budget is de-veloped by using a variety of capital budgeting techniques, such as the payback method, the net present value (NPV) method, or the internal rate of return (IRR) method. *See also* Capital Budgeting.

CAPITAL BUDGETING  the process of making long-term planning deci-sions for capital investments. There are typically two types of investment decisions: (1) Selecting new facilities or expanding existing facilities. Ex-amples include investments in long-term assets such as property, plant, and equipment, and resource commitments in the form of new product development, market research, refunding of long-term debt, and introduc-tion of a computer. (2) Replacing existing facilities with new facilities. Ex-amples include replacing a manual bookkeeping system with a computer-ized system and replacing an inefficient lathe with one that is numerically controlled.

CAPITAL EXPENDITURE BUDGET  a budget plan prepared for individ-ual capital expenditure projects. The time span depends upon the project. Capital expenditures to be budgeted include replacement, acquisition, or construction of plants and major equipment. *See also* Capital Budgeting.

CAPITAL RATIONING  the problem of selecting the mix of acceptable pro-jects that provides the highest overall net present value (NPV), where a company has a limit on the budget for capital spending. The profitability index is used widely in ranking projects competing for limited funds.

CASH BUDGET  a budget for cash planning and control, presenting ex-pected cash inflow and outflow for a designated time period. The cash budget helps management keep cash balances in reasonable relationship to its needs. It aids in avoiding idle cash and possible cash shortages.

CASH FLOW FORECASTING  forecasts of cash flow, including cash col-lections from customers, investment income, and cash disbursements.

CAUSAL FORECASTING MODEL  a forecasting model which relates the variable to be forecast to a number of other variables that can be observed.

COEFFICIENT OF DETERMINATION  a statistical measure of how good the estimated regression equation is, designated as $R^2$ (read as R-squared).

Simply put, it is a measure of "goodness of fit" in the regression. Therefore, the higher the R-squared, the more confidence we can have in our equation.

COMPREHENSIVE BUDGET *See* Master Budget.

CONTINUOUS BUDGET an annual budget which continues to the earliest one month or period and adds the most recent one month or period, so that a twelve-month or other periodic forecast is always available.

CONTRIBUTION MARGIN (CM) the difference between sales and the variable costs of the product or service, also called marginal income. It is the amount of money available to cover fixed costs and generate profits.

CONTRIBUTION MARGIN ANALYSIS Also, called *cost–volume–profit (CVP) analysis* that deals with how profits and costs change with a change in volume. More specifically, it looks at the effects on profits of changes in such factors as variable costs, fixed costs, selling prices, volume, and mix of products sold. By studying the relationships of costs, sales and net income, management is better able to cope with many planning decisions.

CONTRIBUTION (MARGIN) INCOME STATEMENT an income statement that organizes the cost by behavior. It shows the relationship of variable costs and fixed costs, regardless of the functions with which a given cost item is associated.

CONTRIBUTION MARGIN (CM) RATIO the contribution margin (CM) as a percentage of sales.

CONTRIBUTION MARGIN (CM) VARIANCE the difference between actual contribution margin per unit and the budgeted contribution margin per unit, multiplied by the actual number of units sold. If the actual CM is greater than the budgeted CM per unit, a variance is favorable. Otherwise, it is unfavorable. CM variance = (actual CM per unit − budgeted CM per unit) × actual sales

CONTROL CONCEPT a concept that ensures that actions are carried out or implemented according to a plan or goal.

CORPORATE PLANNING MODEL an integrated business planning model in which marketing and production models are linked to the financial model. Corporate planning models are the basic tools for risk analysis and what-if experiments.

CORRELATION   the degree of relationship between business and economic variables such as cost and volume. Correlation analysis evaluates cause/effect relationships. It looks consistently at how the value of one variable changes when the value of the other is changed. A prediction can be made based on the relationship uncovered. An example is the effect of advertising on sales. A degree of correlation is measured statistically by the coefficient of determination (R-squared).

CORRELATION COEFFICIENT   (r) a measure of the degree of correlation between the two variables. The range of values it takes is between $-1$ and $+1$. A negative value of r indicates an inverse relationship. A positive value of r indicates a direct relationship. A zero value of r indicates that the two variables are independent of each other. The closer r is to $+1$ and $-1$, the stronger the relationship between the two variables.

COST BEHAVIOR PATTERNS   the way a cost will react or respond to changes in the level of activity. Costs may be viewed as variable, fixed, or mixed (semivariable). A mixed cost is one that contains both variable and fixed elements. For planning, control, and decision purposes, mixed costs need to be separated into their variable and fixed components, using such methods as the high-low method and the least-squares method. An application of the variable-fixed breakdown is a break-even and contribution margin analysis.

COST-BENEFIT ANALYSIS   an analysis to determine whether the favorable results of an alternative are sufficient to justify the cost of taking that alternative. This analysis is widely used in connection with capital expenditure projects.

COST CONTROL   the steps taken by management to assure that the cost objectives set down in the planning stage are attained and to assure that all segments of the organization function in a manner consistent with its policies. For effective cost control, most organizations use standard cost systems, in which the actual costs are compared to standard costs for performance evaluation and the deviations are investigated for remedial actions. Cost control is also concerned with feedback that might change any or all of the future plans, the production method, or both.

COST EFFECTIVE   the most cost effective program would be the one whose cost-benefit ratio is the lowest among various programs competing for a given amount of funds. *See also* Cost–Benefit Analysis.

COST–VOLUME FORMULA  a cost function in the form of

Y = a + bX

where Y = the semivariable (or mixed) costs to be broken up
     X = any given measure of activity such as volume and labor hours
     a = the fixed cost component
     b = the variable rate per unit of X

The formula is used for cost prediction and flexible budgeting purposes.

COST-VOLUME-PROFIT ANALYSIS  *See* Contribution Margin Analysis

DECISION SUPPORT SYSTEM (DSS)  a branch of the broadly defined Management Information System (MIS). It is an information system that provides answers to problems and that integrates the decision-maker into the system as a component. The system utilizes such quantitative techniques as regression and financial planning modeling. DSS software furnishes support to the accountant in the decision-making process.

DELPHI METHOD  a qualitative forecasting method that seeks to use the judgment of experts systematically in arriving at a forecast of what future events will be or when they may occur. It brings together a group of experts who have access to each other's opinions in an environment where no majority opinion is disclosed.

DEPENDENT VARIABLE  a variable whose value depends upon the values of other variables and constants in some relationship. For example, in the relationship Y = f(X), Y is the dependent variable. Market price of stock is a dependent variable influenced by various independent variables, such as earnings per share, debt-equity ratio, and beta. *See also* Independent Variable.

DIRECT LABOR BUDGET  a schedule for expected labor cost. Expected labor cost is dependent upon expected production volume (production budget). Labor requirements are based on production volume multiplied by direct labor hours per unit. Direct labor hours needed for production are then multiplied by direct labor cost per hour to derive budgeted direct labor costs.

DIRECT MATERIALS BUDGET  a budget that shows how much material will be required for production and how much material must be bought to meet this production requirement. The purchase depends on both expected usage of materials and inventory levels.

DISCOUNTED CASH FLOW (DCF) TECHNIQUES methods of selecting and ranking investment proposals, such as the net present value (NPV) and internal rate of return (IRR) methods where time value of money is taken into account.

DSS *See* Decision Support System.

EFFICIENCY VARIANCE difference between inputs (materials and labor) that were actually used and inputs that should have been used (i.e., standard quantity of inputs allowed for actual production), multiplied by the standard price per unit. *See also* Material Quantity Variance and Labor Efficiency Variance.

EXPONENTIAL SMOOTHING a forecasting technique that uses a weighted moving average of past data as the basis for a forecast. The procedure gives heaviest weight to more recent information and smaller weights to observations in the more distant past. The method is effective when there is random demand and no seasonal fluctuations in the data. The method is a popular technique for short-run forecasting.

FACTORY OVERHEAD BUDGET a schedule of all expected manufacturing costs except for direct material and direct labor. Factory overhead items include indirect material, indirect labor, factory rent, and factory insurance. Factory overhead may be variable, fixed, or a combination of both.

FAVORABLE VARIANCE the excess of standard (or budgeted) costs over actual costs. *See also* Standard Cost System and Variance.

FINANCIAL BUDGET a budget that embraces the impacts of the financial decisions of the firm. It is a plan including a budgeted balance sheet, which shows the effects of planned operations and capital investments on assets, liabilities, and equities. It also includes a cash budget, which forecasts the flow of cash and other funds in the business.

FINANCIAL MODEL a functional branch of a general corporate planning model. It is essentially used to generate pro forma financial statements and financial ratios. A financial model is a mathematical model describing the interrelationships among financial variables of the firm. It is the basic tool for budgeting and budget planning. Also, it is used for risk analysis and what-if experiments. Many financial models today use special modeling languages such as *Interactive Financial Planning System (IFPS)* or spreadsheet programs such as *Lotus 1-2-3*. *See also* Corporate Planning Model.

FINANCIAL PROJECTION  an essential element of planning that is the basis for budgeting activities and estimating future financing needs of a firm. Financial projections (forecasts) begin with forecasting sales and their related expenses.

FIXED BUDGET  *See* Static Budget.

FIXED OVERHEAD VARIANCE  the difference between actual fixed overhead incurred and fixed overhead applied to production.

FLASH REPORT  a report that provides the highlights of key information promptly to the responsible nonfinancial manager. An example is an exception report, such as performance reports, that highlight favorable or unfavorable variances. A flash report allows managers to take a corrective action for an unfavorable variance.

FLEXIBLE (VARIABLE) BUDGET  a budget based on different levels of activity. It is an extremely useful tool for comparing the actual cost incurred to the cost allowable for the activity level achieved. It is dynamic in nature rather than static.

FLEXIBLE BUDGET FORMULA  *See* Cost–Volume Formula.

FLEXIBLE BUDGET VARIANCE  *See* Budget Variance.

FLEXIBLE BUDGETING  *See* Flexible Budget.

FORECAST  1. a projection or an estimate of future sales, revenue, earnings, or costs. *See also* Sales Forecasting. 2. a projection of future financial position and operating results of an organization. *See also* Financial Projection.

GOODNESS-OF-FIT  a degree to which a model fits the observed data. In a regression analysis, the goodness-of-fit is measured by the coefficient of determination (R-squared).

INDEPENDENT VARIABLE  a variable which may take on any value in a relationship. For example, in a relationship $Y = f(X)$, X is the independent variable. Independent variables that influence sales are advertising and price. *See also* Dependent Variable.

INTERNAL RATE OF RETURN (IRR)  the rate earned on a proposal. It is the rate of interest that equates the initial investment (I) with the present value (PV) of future cash inflows. That is, at IRR, I = PV, or NPV (net present value) = 0.

INVESTMENT CENTER a responsibility center within an organization that has control over revenue, cost and investment funds. It is a profit center whose performance is evaluated on the basis of the return earned on invested capital.

JUDGMENTAL (QUALITATIVE) FORECAST a forecasting method that brings together, in an organized way, personal judgments about the process being analyzed.

LABOR EFFICIENCY VARIANCE the difference between the amount of labor time that should have been used and the labor that was actually used, multiplied by the standard rate.

LABOR RATE (PRICE) VARIANCE any deviation from standard in the average hourly rate paid to workers, multiplied by the hours worked.

LABOR VARIANCE the difference between the actual costs of direct labor and the standard costs of direct labor. Labor variance is divided into labor rate variance and labor efficiency variance.

LEAST SQUARES METHOD a statistical technique for fitting a straight line through a set of points in such a way that the sum of the squared distances from the data points to the line is minimized.

LINEAR REGRESSION a regression that deals with a straight line relationship between variables. It is in the form of $Y = a + bX$, whereas nonlinear regression involves curvilinear relationships, such as exponential and quadratic functions. *See also* Regression Analysis.

LONG RANGE BUDGET projections that cover more than one fiscal year. It is also called strategic budgeting. The five-year budget plan is the most commonly used. *See also* Annual Budget.

MANAGEMENT BY EXCEPTION a management concept or policy by which management devotes its time to investigating only those situations in which actual results differ significantly from planned results. The idea is that management should spend its valuable time concentrating on the more important items (such as the shaping of the company's future strategic course).

MANAGEMENT BY OBJECTIVE (MBO) a system of performance appraisal having the following characteristics: (1) It is a formal system in that each manager is required to take certain prescribed actions and to complete certain written documents, and (2) The manager and subordinates discuss the subordinate's job description, agree to short-term performance targets, discuss the progress made towards meeting these targets, and periodically evaluate the performance and provide the feedback.

MANAGEMENT CONTROL SYSTEM  a system under which managers assure that resources are obtained and used effectively and efficiently in the accomplishment of the organization's goals.

MANAGEMENT INFORMATION SYSTEM (MIS)  a computer-based or manual system which transforms data into information useful in the support of decision making.

MASTER (COMPREHENSIVE) BUDGET  a plan of activities expressed in monetary terms of the assets, equities, revenues, and costs which will be involved in carrying out the plans. Simply put, a master budget is a set of projected or planned financial statements.

MATERIAL REQUIREMENT PLANNING (MRP) a computer-based information system designed to handle ordering and scheduling of dependent-demand inventories, such as raw materials, component parts, and subassemblies, which will be used in the production of a finished product.

MATERIALS PRICE VARIANCE  the difference between what is paid for a given quantity of materials and what should have been paid, multiplied by actual quantity of materials used.

MATERIALS PURCHASE PRICE VARIANCE  *See* Materials Price Variance.

MATERIALS QUANTITY (USAGE) VARIANCE  the difference between the actual quantity of materials used in production and the standard quantity of materials allowed for actual production, multiplied by the standard price per unit.

MATERIALS VARIANCE  the difference between the actual costs of materials and the standard costs of materials. Material variance is divided into materials price variance and materials quantity variance.

MEAN SQUARED ERROR (MSE)  a measure of accuracy computed by squaring the individual error for each item in a data set and then finding the average or mean value of the sum of those squares. The mean squared error gives greater weight to large errors than to small errors because the errors are squared before being summed.

MODELING LANGUAGES usually, English-like programming languages that are used to solve a specific task and generate various reports based on the solution and analysis. For example, financial planning modeling languages, such as *Integrated Financial Planning System (IFPS)*, are computer software packages that help planners develop a financial model in English terms, do not require any computer programming knowledge, perform various analyses such as "what-if" analysis, and further generate pro forma financial reports.

MOVING AVERAGE for a time series, an average that is updated as new information is received. With the moving average, the manager employs the most recent observations to calculate an average, which is used as the forecast for the next period.

MULTIPLE REGRESSION a statistical procedure that attempts to assess the relationship between the dependent variable and two or more independent variables. For example, sales of Coca Cola are a function of various factors, such as price, advertising, taste, and the prices of its major competitors. For forecasting purposes, a multiple regression equation falls into the category of a casual forecasting model. *See also* Regression Analysis.

NAIVE FORECAST forecasts obtained with a minimal amount of effort and data manipulation and based solely on the most recent information available. One such naive method would be to use the most recent datum available as the future forecast.

NET PRESENT VALUE (NPV) the difference between the present value (PV) of cash inflows generated by the project and the amount of the initial investment (I).

NET PRESENT VALUE METHOD a method widely used for evaluating investment projects. Under the net present value method, the present value (PV) of all cash inflows from the project is compared to the initial investment (I).

OPERATIONAL (OPERATING) BUDGET a budget that embraces the impacts of operating decisions. It contains forecasts of sales, net income, the cost of goods sold, selling and administrative expenses, and other expenses.

PAYBACK PERIOD the length of time required to recover the initial amount of a capital investment.

PLANNING the selection of short- and long-term objectives and the drawing up of tactical and strategic plans to achieve those objectives. After deciding on a set of strategies to be followed, the organization needs more specific plans, such as locations, methods of financing, and hours of operation. As these plans are made, they will be communicated throughout the organization. When implemented, the plans will serve to coordinate the efforts of all parts of the organization toward the company's objectives.

PRO FORMA BALANCE SHEET a Budgeted Balance Sheet.

PRO FORMA INCOME STATEMENT a Budgeted Income Statement.

PRODUCT MIX *See* Sales Mix.

PRODUCTION BUDGET a schedule for expected units to be produced. It sets forth the units expected to be manufactured to satisfy budgeted sales and inventory requirements. Expected production volume is determined by adding desired ending inventory to planned sales and then subtracting beginning inventory.

PROFIT CENTER the unit in an organization that is responsible for revenues earned and costs incurred. The manager of a profit center has control over revenues and costs, as well as attempts to maximize profit.

PROFIT PLANNING a process of developing a profit plan which outlines the planned sales revenues and expenses and the net income or loss for a time period. Profit planning requires preparation of a master budget and various analyses for risk and "what-if" scenarios. Tools for profit planning include the cost–volume–profit (CVP) analysis and budgeting.

PROFIT VARIANCE a difference between actual profit and budgeted profit. Profit, whether it is gross profit in absorption costing or contribution margin in direct costing, is affected by sales price, sales volume, and costs.

PROFIT–VOLUME CHART a chart that determines how profits vary with changes in volume. Profits are plotted on the vertical axis while units of output are shown on the horizontal axis.

PROFITABILITY INDEX the ratio of the total present value (PV) of future cash inflows to the initial investment (I).

PROJECTED (BUDGETED) BALANCE SHEET a schedule for expected assets, liabilities, and stockholders' equity. It projects a company's financial position at the end of the budgeting year. A budgeted balance sheet discloses unfavorable financial conditions that management may want to avoid, serves as a final check on the mathematical accuracy of all other budgets and highlights future resources and obligations.

PROJECTED (BUDGETED) INCOME STATEMENT a summary of various component projections of revenues and expenses for the budget period. It indicates the expected net income for the period.

QUANTITATIVE FORECASTING a technique that can be applied when information about the past is available, if that information can be quantified and if the pattern included in past information can be assumed to continue into the future.

R-SQUARED *See* Coefficient of Determination.

REGRESSION ANALYSIS a statistical procedure for estimating mathematically the average relationship between the dependent variable (sales, for example) and one or more independent variables (price and advertising, for example).

REGRESSION COEFFICIENTS when a dependent measure Y is regressed against a set of independent measures $X_1$ through $X_k$, the manager wishes to estimate the values of the unknown coefficients by least squares procedures. For example, in a linear regression equation $Y = a + bX$, a and b are regression coefficients. Specifically, a is called y-intercept or constant, while b is called a slope.

The properties of these regression coefficients can be used to understand the importance of each independent variable (as it relates to Y) and the interrelatedness among the independent variables (as they relate to Y).

REGRESSION EQUATION (MODEL) a forecasting model which relates the dependent variable (factory overhead, for example) to one or more independent variables (direct labor hours and machine hours, for example).

RESIDUAL a synonym for error. It is calculated by subtracting the forecast value from the actual value to give a residual or error value for each forecast period.

RESPONSIBILITY ACCOUNTING the collection, summarization, and reporting of financial information about various decision centers (responsibility centers) throughout an organization.

RESPONSIBILITY CENTER  a unit in the organization which has control over costs, revenues, or investment funds. Responsibility centers are classified as cost centers, revenue centers, profit centers, and investment centers.

RISK ANALYSIS  the process of measuring and analyzing the risks associated with financial and investment decisions. Risk refers to the variability of expected returns (earnings or cash flows).

SALES BUDGET  an operating plan for a period expressed in terms of sales volume and selling prices for each class of product or service. Preparation of a sales budget is the starting point in budgeting, since sales volume influences nearly all other items.

SALES FORECASTING  a projection or prediction of future sales. It is the foundation for the quantification of the entire business plan and a master budget. Sales forecasts serve as a basis for capacity planning, budgeting, production and inventory planning, manpower planning, and purchasing planning.

SALES MIX  the relative proportions of the product sold.

SALES PRICE VARIANCE  the difference between actual selling price per unit and the budgeted selling price per unit, multiplied by the actual number of units sold.

SALES VOLUME VARIANCE  the difference between the actual number of units sold and the budgeted number, multiplied by the budgeted selling price per unit. It is also called sales quantity variance.

SIMPLE REGRESSION  a regression analysis which involves one independent variable. For example, the demand for automobiles is a function of its price only. *See also* Multiple Regression and Regression Analysis.

SIMULATION  an attempt to represent a real life system via a model to determine how a change in one or more variables affects the rest of the system. It is also called "what-if" analysis. *See also* Financial Model and Simulation Model.

SIMULATION MODEL  "what-if" model that attempts to simulate the effects of alternative management policies and assumptions about the firm's external environment. It is basically a tool for management's laboratory.

SLOPE  the steepness and direction of the line. More specifically, the slope is the change in Y for every unit change in X.

STANDARD a quantitative expression of a performance objective, such as standard hours of labor allowed for actual production or a standard purchase price of materials per unit. Sometimes the terms standard and budget are used interchangeably.

STANDARD COST SYSTEM a system by which production activities are recorded at standard costs and variances from actual costs are isolated.

STANDARD COSTS production or operating costs that are carefully predetermined. A standard cost is a target cost that should be attained.

STANDARD ERROR OF THE ESTIMATE The standard deviation of the regression. The statistic can be used to gain some idea of the accuracy of our predictions.

STANDARD ERROR OF THE REGRESSION COEFFICIENT a measure of the amount of sampling error in a regression coefficient.

STANDARD HOURS ALLOWED the standard time that should have been used to manufacture actual units of output during a period. It is obtained by multiplying actual units of production by the standard labor time.

STANDARD LABOR RATE the standard rate for direct labor that includes not only base wages earned but also an allowance for fringe benefits and other labor-related costs.

STANDARD MATERIALS PRICE the standard price per unit for direct materials. It reflects the final, delivered cost of the materials, net of any discounts taken.

STANDARD QUANTITY ALLOWED the standard amount of materials that should have been used to manufacture units of output during a period. It is obtained by multiplying actual units of production by the standard material quantity per unit.

STATIC (FIXED) BUDGET a budget based on one level of activity (e.g., one particular volume of sales or production).

STRATEGIC PLANNING the implementation of an organization's objectives. Strategic planning decisions will have long-term impacts on the organization while operational decisions are day-to-day in nature.

t-TEST in regression analysis, a test of the statistical significance of a regression coefficient. It involves basically two steps:

(1) Compute the t-value of the regression coefficient as follows: t-value = coefficient/standard error of the coefficient.

(2) Compare the value with the t table value. High t-values enhance confidence in the value of the coefficient as a predictor. Low values (as a rule of thumb, under 2.0) are indications of low reliability of the coefficient as a predictor. *See also* t-Value.

t-VALUE  a measure of the statistical significance of an independent variable b in explaining the dependent variable Y. It is determined by dividing the estimated regression coefficient b by its standard error.

TEMPLATE  A worksheet or computer program that includes the relevant formulas for a particular application but not the data. It is a blank worksheet that we save and fill in with the data as needed for a future forecasting and budgeting application.

TIME SERIES  a chronologically arranged sequence of values of a particular variable.

VARIABLE OVERHEAD EFFICIENCY VARIANCE  the difference in actual and budgeted variable overhead costs that are incurred due to inefficient use of indirect materials and indirect labor.

VARIABLE OVERHEAD SPENDING VARIANCE  the difference in actual and budgeted variable overhead costs that result from price changes in indirect materials and indirect labor and insufficient control of costs of specific overhead items.

VARIANCE  the difference of revenues, costs, and profit from the planned amounts. One of the most important phases of responsibility accounting is establishing standards in costs, revenues, and profit and establishing performance by comparing actual amounts with the standard amounts. The differences (variances) are calculated for each responsibility center, analyzed, and unfavorable variances are investigated for possible remedial action.

"WHAT-IF" ANALYSIS  *See* Simulation.

ZERO-BASE BUDGETING (ZBB)  a planning and budgeting tool that uses cost/benefit analysis of projects and functions to improve resource allocation in an organization. Traditional budgeting tends to concentrate on the incremental change from the previous year. It assumes that the previous year's activities and programs are essential and must be continued. Under zero-base budgeting, however, cost and benefit estimates are built up from scratch, from the zero level, and must be justified.

# INDEX

**ADDENDUM TO *BUDGETING BASICS AND BEYOND***

**by Jae Shim and Joel Siegel**

**IF YOU ARE USING LOTUS 1-2-3/WINDOWS**

You must change the page setup in order for the printout of the **USER'S GUIDE** to fit on the entire width of the page.

To do this: once the **GUIDE** has been put on the screen, hit escape to clear the macro. Then use the mouse to go to the top of the screen. Pull down <u>File</u>. Then <u>Page Setup</u>. Then go to the <u>Size</u> window and, putting the mouse on the arrow, change the size from <u>Actual Size</u> to <u>Fit Columns to Page</u>. Press the <u>OK</u> button. Press <Control M> to bring up the macro to print and run the macro by selecting the <u>Print Introduction</u> prompt.

This should print out the **USER'S GUIDE**.